WAYNE SHUMAKER

Professor of English
University of California
Berkeley

AN
APPROACH
TO POETRY

Prentice-Hall, Inc.   Englewood Cliffs, N.J.

Prentice-Hall Introduction to Literature Series

MAYNARD MACK, EDITOR

© 1965 by Prentice-Hall, Inc., Englewood Cliffs, N.J.

All rights reserved. No part of this book may be reproduced in any form, by mimeograph or any other means, without permission in writing from the publishers.

Library of Congress Catalog Card No.: 65-10149

PRINTED IN THE UNITED STATES OF AMERICA [04385-C]

PRENTICE-HALL INTERNATIONAL, INC., *London*
PRENTICE-HALL OF AUSTRALIA, PTY., LTD., *Sydney*
PRENTICE-HALL OF CANADA, LTD., *Toronto*
PRENTICE-HALL OF INDIA (PRIVATE) LTD., *New Delhi*
PRENTICE-HALL OF JAPAN, INC., *Tokyo*
PRENTICE-HALL DE MEXICO, S.A., *Mexico City*

ACKNOWLEDGMENTS FOR MATERIAL IN COPYRIGHT

On this and pages iii, iv, and v, which constitute an extension of this copyright page, acknowledgment is gratefully made to those publishers, agents, and individuals who have permitted the use of copyrighted materials.

AUDEN
    "The Unknown Citizen" and "Musée des Beaux Arts," from *Another Time,* copyright 1940 by W. H. Auden; "The Climbers" and "Who's Who," copyright 1945 by W. H. Auden; "O where are you going?" from *Poems,* copyright 1934, renewed 1961, by W. H. Auden. Reprinted from *The Collected Poetry of W. H. Auden,* by permission of Random House, Inc., and Faber and Faber Ltd., Publishers.

BARKER
"To My Mother," by George Granville Barker. From *Collected Poems, 1930-1955*. © 1957 by George Granville Barker. Reprinted by permission of Faber and Faber, Ltd. and Oscar Williams.

BETJEMAN
"St. Savior's, Aberdeen Park, Highbury, London, N." (excerpt), by John Betjeman. From *Collected Poems*. Published in the United States by Houghton Mifflin Company. Reprinted by permission of John Murray (Publishers) Ltd.

CUMMINGS
"In Just—" (excerpt), by E. E. Cummings. From *Poems, 1923-1954*. Reprinted by permission of Harcourt, Brace & World, Inc.

DICKINSON
"I like a look of agony," "A bird came down the walk," "The wind tapped like a tired man," "I started early, took my dog," "I like to see it lap the miles," "Because I could not stop for Death," "I stepped from plank to plank," "A narrow fellow in the grass," and "The bustle in a house," by Emily Dickinson, have all been printed as originally published on the dates indicated with the texts. However, the annotations of Professor Thomas H. Johnson given in the notes to the above poems and the Johnson versions of "The Soul's distinct connection" and "Tell all the Truth, but tell it slant" are reprinted by permission of Harvard University Press and the Trustees of Amherst College from Thomas H. Johnson, ed., *The Poems of Emily Dickinson* (Cambridge, Mass.: The Belknap Press of Harvard University Press. Copyright 1951, 1955 by the President and Fellows of Harvard College). "After great pain a formal feeling comes" and "The Soul's distinct connection" are also reprinted by permission of Little, Brown and Company from Thomas H. Johnson, ed., *The Complete Poems of Emily Dickinson* (Copyright 1929, © 1957 by Mary L. Hampson).

ELIOT
"The Love Song of J. Alfred Prufrock," "Gerontion," "Journey of the Magi," and excerpts from *The Waste Land* and "The Hollow Men," by T. S. Eliot. From *Collected Poems, 1909-1962*. Copyright 1936 by Harcourt, Brace & World, Inc.; © 1963, 1964 by T. S. Eliot. Reprinted by permission of Harcourt, Brace & World, Inc. and Faber and Faber, Ltd.

FEARING
"Art Review" (excerpt), by Kenneth Fearing. From *Afternoon of a Pawnbroker and Other Poems*. Reprinted by permission of Harcourt, Brace & World, Inc.

FROST
"The Tuft of Flowers," "Fire and Ice," "Stopping by Woods on a Snowy Evening," "Acquainted with the Night," "Desert Places," by Robert Frost. From *Complete Poems of Robert Frost*. Copyright 1923, 1928, 1934 by Holt, Rinehart and Winston, Inc. Copyright 1936 by Robert Frost. Copyright renewed 1951, © 1956, 1962 by Robert Frost. Copyright renewed © 1964 by Lesley Frost Ballantine. Reprinted by permission of Holt, Rinehart and Winston, Inc.

GRAVES
"Flying Crooked," by Robert Graves. From *Collected Poems*. © 1955, 1959 by Cassell & Company, Ltd. Reprinted by permission of A. P. Watt & Son.

34689

ACKNOWLEDGMENTS FOR MATERIAL NOT IN COPYRIGHT

BEDDOES

Death's Jest-Book (excerpt): "Song, Old Adam, the carrion crow," by Thomas Lovell Beddoes. Adapted from H. W. Donner, ed., *Plays and Poems of Thomas Lovell Beddoes*. Reprinted with the permission of Routledge & Kegan Paul, Ltd.

BLAKE

"Introduction to *Songs of Innocence*," "The Lamb," "The Echoing Green," "The Tiger," "Ah, sunflower," by William Blake. Adapted from Geoffrey Keynes, ed., *Poetry and Prose of William Blake*. Reprinted with the permission of The Nonesuch Press, Ltd.

BROWNE

"Venus by Adonis' side," "On the Death of Marie, Countess of Pembroke." Adapted from Gordon Goodwin, ed., *The Poems of William Browne of Tavistock*. London, 1894.

BROWNING

"Porphyria's Lover," "My Last Duchess," "The Bishop Orders His Tomb," "De Gustibus—," "Meeting at Night," "Parting at Morning." Adapted from Horace E. Scudder, ed., *The Complete Poetic and Dramatic Works of Robert Browning*, Houghton Mifflin Company, 1895.

BURNS

"To a Mouse" and "Ye flowery banks o' bonie Doon," by Robert Burns. Adapted from William Wallace, ed., *Poetical Works of Robert Burns*. Reprinted with the permission of W. and R. Chambers, Ltd.

BYRON

"When we two parted," *English Bards and Scotch Reviewers:* Lines 235-64, 1053-70, *Don Juan:* Canto II, Stanzas 199-201, and Canto I, Stanza 2, 11. 1-3, by George Noel Gordon, Lord Byron. Adapted from Oxford Standard Authors, *The Poetical Works of Lord Byron*. Reprinted with the permission of Oxford University Press.

CAMPION

"When to her lute Corinna sings," "Rose-cheeked Laura, come," "There is a garden in her face," by Thomas Campion. Adapted from Percival Vivian, ed., *Campion's Works*. Reprinted with the permission of The Clarendon Press.

CAREW

"An Elegy Upon the Death of the Dean of Paul's, Dr. John Donne" and "Ingrateful Beauty Threatened," by Thomas Carew. Adapted from Rhodes Dunlap, ed., *The Poems of Thomas Carew, with His Masque Coelum Brittannicum*. Reprinted with the permission of The Clarendon Press.

COLERIDGE

"The Eolian Harp," "Kubla Khan," "Zapolya (excerpt): Song," by Samuel Taylor Coleridge. Adapted from Ernest Hartley Coleridge, ed., *The Poems of Samuel Taylor Coleridge*. Reprinted with the permission of The Clarendon Press.

COWLEY

"Anacreontics: Drinking" and "The Wish," by Abraham Cowley. Adapted from A. R. Waller, ed., *Abraham Cowley: Poems, Miscellanies, Etc.* Reprinted with the permission of Cambridge University Press.

COWPER

The Task: "Book I, The Sofa," lines 1-88, by William Cowper; also a note by Cowper. Adapted from H. S. Milford, ed., *The Complete Poetical Works of William Cowper*. Reprinted with the permission of Oxford University Press.

CRABBE

The Village, lines 1-54. Adapted from *The Village: A Poem in Two Books*, London, 1783.

CRASHAW

"The Flaming Heart: Upon the Book and Picture of the Seraphical Saint Teresa" and an excerpt from "The Weeper," by Richard Crashaw. Adapted from L. C. Martin, ed., *The Poems, English, Latin, and Greek, of Richard Crashaw*. Reprinted with the permission of The Clarendon Press.

DANIEL

Delia (excerpt): "Sonnets I, III, IX," by Samuel Daniel. Adapted from Arthur Colby Sprague, ed., *Samuel Daniel: Poems and a Defence of Ryme*. Reprinted with the permission of Harvard University Press.

DENHAM

From *Cooper's Hill*, lines 161-92. Adapted from the London, 1709, edition.

DONNE

"Love's Alchemy," "To the Countess of Bedford" (excerpt), "The Canonization," "The Flea," "A Valediction: Forbidding Mourning," "The Ecstasy," "Satire III," *Holy Sonnets:* "VII, X, XI, XIV, XVII," "Hymn to God My God, in My Sickness," "Love's Alchemy," by John Donne. Adapted from Sir Herbert Grierson, ed., *The Poems of John Donne*. Reprinted with the permission of The Clarendon Press.

DRAYTON

"Idea, In Sixty-Three Sonnets" (excerpts), by Michael Drayton. Adapted from J. William Hebel, ed., *The Works of Michael Drayton*. Reprinted with the permission of The Clarendon Press.

DRYDEN

"Mac Flecknoe," "To the Memory of Mr. Oldham," and excerpts from "Roundelay," "Absalom and Achitophel," and "The Secular Masque," by John Dryden. Adapted from James Kinsley, ed., *The Poems of John Dryden*. Reprinted with the permission of The Clarendon Press.

GAY

"The Toilette: A Town Eclogue," by John Gay. Adapted from G. C. Faber, ed., *The Poetical Works of John Gay*. Reprinted with the permission of The Clarendon Press.

GOLDSMITH

From *The Deserted Village*, lines 137-218. Adapted from Peter Cunningham, ed., *The Works of Oliver Goldsmith*, G. P. Putnam's Sons, 1908.

GRAY

"Ode on the Death of a Favorite Cat" (excerpt) and "Elegy Written in a Country Churchyard," by Thomas Gray. Adapted from Austin Lane Poole, ed., *The Poems of Gray and Collins*. Reprinted with the permission of Oxford University Press.

HERBERT

"Humility," "Peace," "Artillery," "The Pulley," "The Elixir," by George Herbert. Adapted from F. E. Hutchinson, ed., *The Works of George Herbert*. Reprinted with the permission of The Clarendon Press.

In Memoriam Felicem

F.H.S.　　*E.S.S.*

PREFACE

This book contains an anthology of excellent poems, well distributed over four centuries and well diversified as to type, for reading in an introductory course at the college or university. It also contains an expository "Introduction to Poetry," aimed at helping students read the poems effectively. Together with the exercises, the chapters of the Introduction can be assigned successively in the early weeks of the course; or, without the exercises, they can be assigned along with poems and not given class time. The anthology, however, is in the main quite separate from the Introduction, so that the teacher will not be constrained steadily to follow a path already laid out for him.

The stimulus to the preparation of the volume was dissatisfaction with poetry texts hitherto available. On one hand, excellent anthologies are available—possibly better as anthologies, because they include a larger body of poetry than the one which forms the major part of the present text. The teacher who adopts one of these must, however, present in lecture form whatever he wants his students to learn about the techniques of reading. In my own classes I have frequently found it necessary to stop discussing poems in order to comment at length on the nature and function of symbols, to describe the principles of meter, or to show by illustrations how often interpretation fails because the student has neglected to hunt for an unknown word or to identify an allusion. Because the occasions for the lectures were often unexpected, the organization was less tight and the illustrations were less apt than if my remarks had been prepared in advance. When I anticipated the necessity of an expository excursus these faults were minimized, but class time was expended which I would have preferred to devote to the close reading of individual poems. On the other hand, texts are readily available which offer far too much help. The teacher who uses them is usually forced to take up topics and poems in a prescribed order and to put emphasis upon some narrowly limited aspect; he is told what questions to ask; he finds readings forced upon him which he must either accept passively or fight against. In a word, he discovers that he is teaching someone else's course instead of his own.

The present volume is meant to avoid both extremes. Like the anthology, it presents poems in simple chronological order, without differentiation as to genre, subject, or technique, so that the instructor may take them up in whatever order he pleases. Like the guided texts, it offers a series of chapters on how to read poems; but it does so in such a way as to provide either an orderly series of introductory assignments which move from simpler to more complex difficulties or a body of reference materials which the students can be asked to master alone as occasions arise. Briefly, the Introduction is meant to be helpful without being dictatorial: to do what the guided text does, but without imposing upon the instructor a rigidly predetermined program. Even in the Appendix, where a day-by-day schedule for a semester has been laid out for any instructor who may want it, no effort has been made to offer detailed interpretations of individual poems.

The advice given about reading is intended not to be crotchety, although, inevitably, few teachers will find it to be exactly what they themselves would have written. If a critical bias is present, it is that the effective reading of poetry does not depend on mental processes wholly different from those which are used in nonaesthetic activities: and this in spite of the fact that poetry is a special mode of discourse. Even if the good reader of poetry has an unusual quickness and depth of perception (so that he is not disconcerted by the equation of a girl with a rose or the comparison of jealousy to a fever), he does not transcend ordinary intelligence in some mystical way, but uses simultaneously more parts of his mind than are needed for the reading of expository prose.

Some instructors may wish to assign the chapters in such a way as to begin with the more peculiarly poetic aspects of poetry instead of with those that are shared with prose. If so, the following order is recommended:

Chapter I, Why Study Poetry?
Chapter VI, Images
Chapter VII, Figurative Language
Chapter VIII, Symbols
Chapter II, Words
Chapter III, Syntax
Chapter IV, The Prose Paraphrase
Chapter V, Allusions
Chapter IX, Ambiguity and Ambivalence
Chapter X, Tone
Chapter XI, The Implied Speaker
Chapter XII, Prosody
Chapter XIII, Form
Chapter XIV, The Historical Background

Chapter XV, The Evaluation of Poetry, may be assigned last or not at all. When studied in this sequence, the chapters will compose an introduction of a more familiar type. The author has been convinced by experiment, however, that undergraduates who are indifferent or hostile to poetry can be interested most quickly by a demonstration that poems are not wholly unlike prose. Once their defenses are down, poetic characteristics which are more properly aesthetic can be shown them; but they are alienated quickly by a too early emphasis on precisely those traits which are responsible for their discomfort. In any event, by the time the Introduction has been finished, the student will not only have been alerted to common difficulties but will also possess a basic vocabulary which will help him to talk about poems with something less than the usual undergraduate vagueness. In consequence, the teacher will find that the sources of differing interpretations can be pinned down more quickly to particular phrases or even to individual words.

The Anthology, which is large enough to provide more than enough reading for a semester, is also meant not to be crotchety. The time span, from 1550 to 1950, is as great as can be coped with by students who have had no special linguistic training, and the coverage of the four centuries, if not equal, is more than usually well balanced. Within each of the major periods, an effort has been made both to include "best" poems and to avoid stressing any particular genre or technique (for example, the metaphysical lyric). The result, I hope, is an exceptionally attractive and teachable body of texts.

One special feature is an unusually broad range of subject matter and techniques. If the aim had been to represent poets instead of poetry, a sizable excerpt from Pope's *Dunciad* would have been appropriate. The inclusion of Dryden's *Mac Flecknoe,* which is much the same type of poem (though short enough to be included in its entirety), permitted instead the choice of Canto I of Pope's *Essay on Criticism.* Similarly, "Mary the Cook-Maid's Letter to Dr. Sheridan" by Swift was preferred to one of his less kindly satires because selections by other authors were adequately bitter. What seemed most important was a full representation of poetic possibilities, not a survey of the most characteristic achievements of individual poets. Yet the major poets are sufficiently emphasized to evoke a recognition that certain names are especially noteworthy. An important advantage of a wide range is the possibility that students who are not attracted by one kind of poetry will be captured by another. A historical survey of major figures can more appropriately be undertaken in a course intended for English majors than in one aimed at awakening an initial interest in poetry.

In difficulty, as well as in scope, the poems vary widely: from Donne's third satire, Milton's "Lycidas," Crashaw's "The Flaming Heart," Eliot's "Gerontion," and Yeats' "Among School Children," on the hard side, to Rochester's "The Maimed Debauchee" and Hood's "Faithless Nelly Gray," on the easy; from works soaked in allusion, like Browning's "The Bishop Orders His Tomb," to more immediately accessible lyrics, like Sackville's "Corydon beneath a willow." The inclusion of the readily understandable as well as the densely packed will allow the frequent assignment of poems which need not be worked over in class: a necessity, if the discussions are not to lag far behind the assignments.

The treatment of long poems has been determined by practical considerations. Spenser's *Faerie Queene,* which cannot be well represented by less than a whole book, has been omitted; but his "Prothalamion," chosen instead of the better-known "Epithalamion," will invite a few comments about Spenser's fondness for allegory. Further, it is more teachable than the "Epithalamion"—always an important consideration—because the marriage of "two swans of goodly hue" to "two gentle knights" raises an interesting aesthetic problem. In contrast, bits of Milton's *Paradise Lost,* Pope's *Rape of the Lock,* Goldsmith's *The Deserted Village,* and a number of other long poems have been included, not only to indicate the importance of long poems in literary history but also in the hope of intriguing a few students into reading more on their own initiative.

In the main, the Anthology is of British poetry. There simply was not room to do American poetry justice. Beginning with Whitman, however, American poets have been admitted on an equal basis with British. Even in so brief a collection, I did not want to imply that good English poetry can be written only across the sea.

The texts have been normalized, according to American usage, in spelling, capitalization, and punctuation; but I have tended to change less in proportion as the poems were more recent, and I have not changed twentieth-century poems at all. The scholarly reader, of course, likes to have before him exactly what the author wrote, and perhaps also a record of successive revisions; or, failing that, to work with editions which the poets themselves have seen through the press. Even juniors and seniors should, I think, be required to read our older poets as they were read by contemporaries. However, the situation of the beginner is quite different, and I have tried to hold his needs steadily in mind. He is perhaps himself an indifferent speller, and he is unlikely to appreciate the values of the older rhetorical punctuation. But not all poets are themselves good editors. Emily Dickinson, for instance, by using the dash almost exclusively, was unable to differentiate among several useful varieties of pauses, and therefore is not well served by religious adherence to her manuscripts. In other respects I have tried to work scrupulously, and I have preserved not only the words of the best texts but also the contractions, where these were indicated.

The problem of dating has been troublesome. Most anthologies date only the births and deaths of the poets; I have also wanted to date the poems. This has been done by giving the date of first publication for each poem (usually, though not invariably, in book form), because it was then, and not when the pieces were first written, that they entered into the public corpus of English poetry. The text, however, is normally that of the latest revised edition. Songs from plays are dated in the years when the plays are believed to have been first performed. Groups of sonnets published together are dated only once, at the end of the last sonnet. The order in which the poems are printed is the probable order of composition, which often is not identical with the order of publication.

In the course of my work I have incurred obligations to many of my colleagues at the University of California. I wish to express my gratitude especially to Robert Bloom, Jackson Burgess, Seymour Chatman, Martin Halpern, Brendan O Hehir, Thomas Parkinson, Norman Rabkin, Ralph Rader, Sheldon Sacks, and John Traugott, all of whom have helped me either with advice or with the explication of textual cruxes. Criticism of a first draft of the Introduction by Maynard Mack resulted in notable improvement; and my editor, Barry Anthony Jedrick, has been admirably patient and more than usually skillful in resolving difficulties. My greatest debt, however, is to the small army of editors and scholars whose discoveries, over several generations, have permitted the explanation of poetic difficulties in the notes.

WAYNE SHUMAKER

CONTENTS

Part One

AN INTRODUCTION TO POETRY

Part Two

AN ANTHOLOGY OF POEMS

Part One

AN INTRODUCTION TO POETRY

I

WHY STUDY POETRY

Unless he has already developed literary interests, a student who is about to undertake the study of poetry in college may wonder why the subject enjoys such academic repute. At home he may never have heard poems discussed, and the enthusiasm of one or two of his high school teachers for poetry may have appeared to him eccentric and faintly unmanly. In college, however, he soon discovers that large numbers of students are majoring in English literature, and he may overhear snatches of conversation which imply that poetry can be exciting. Now, either by choice or because he has been required to do so, he has enrolled in a course in which he himself must confront poems seriously. He may wonder what causes many educated people to value

3

poetry so highly. Is regard for it, possibly, nothing more than a cultural superstition? The question is reasonable and deserves an honest answer.

Unfortunately, full answers are impossible to give. One reason is that poetry has an enormously wide range and serves a variety of interests. Another is that problems which involve cultural values sometimes have less to do with concrete objects, which can be measured and weighed, than with the superiority of certain mental states to others; and such states are notoriously hard to describe. Still a third is that every question about value becomes more deeply implicated in philosophical doubts the further it is pursued. Chapter XV, "The Evaluation of Poetry," explains why this is so. The most that can be attempted in the present chapter is to show that poems, although they may appear to be needlessly indirect and complicated, manage to *say things* which cannot be said equally well in any other way. Poetry is, in fact, a special mode of discourse, and insensitivity to the mode limits and narrows our consciousness. Learning to read poetry with comprehension is nothing less than a process of discovering additional dimensions in reality. If this thesis can be proved—or, since "proof" is next to impossible, rendered antecedently plausible—the student may be willing to let poems demonstrate their value to him directly.

Let us begin with two short poems by Robert Browning which are at once relatively simple and obviously different from expository prose (the kind of writing assigned in most nonliterary courses).

MEETING AT NIGHT

The gray sea and the long black land;
And the yellow half-moon large and low;
And the startled little waves that leap
In fiery ringlets from their sleep,
As I gain the cove with pushing prow,
And quench its speed i' the slushy sand.

Then a mile of warm sea-scented beach;
Three fields to cross till a farm appears;
A tap at the pane, the quick sharp scratch
And blue spurt of a lighted match,
And a voice less loud, through its joys and fears,
Than the two hearts beating, each to each!

PARTING AT MORNING

Round the cape of a sudden came the sea,
And the sun looked over the mountain's rim:
And straight was a path of gold for him,
And the need of a world of men for me.

The poems are not "great," but run-of-the-mill; hence they will serve as fair samples. The words are familiar; there are no allusions which require explanations in footnotes; and the language is not obviously figurative. The meaning is apparently clear. A young man keeps an assignation with his sweetheart and in the morning returns where he came from. Nevertheless, the total effect is quite different from that of a prose summary of the event. Do the poems differ from prose in the way poetry has been said typically to differ—by being richer, by recognizing dimensions of reality that would have been ignored in the prose equivalent? Let us undertake a brief examination to see.

For one thing, the lyrics deal largely with perceptions. They do not reason from premises to a conclusion or state a thesis which is supported by evidence or by argument. They are not, in a narrow sense of the word, *logical*. In the first poem we are given glimpses of a gray sea, a long black shoreline, a large yellow half-moon, and so on, until we infer (we are never told) that the lovers have met and are embracing ecstatically. In the sequel, three more lines of sensory description culminate in the statement of a felt need, which is not, however, explained. The usual signs of rational explanation are lacking: the clauses are not interrelated by such analytic expressions as "Therefore," "On the other hand," "A second illustration is," and "Thus we see. . . ." The speaker's mind does not attempt to dominate the experience rationally, but rather to perceive it vividly and to feel it intensely.

Such an effort is common in poetry and such other arts as painting and sculpture but is rarely found elsewhere. In general, our schooling has encouraged us to think but not to see or to feel. When we were taught in history class that before the French Revolution the peasants were cruelly oppressed, we were expected to understand that the oppression was a motive for social change, but we were not expected to feel along our nerves what "oppression" meant experientially to the persons who suffered it. We have not been trained in *living* situations, but only in thinking them. If our feelings and sense organs have preserved some organic vitality, the reason is that we have maintained an awareness not explicitly sanctioned by our teachers. Yet, in fact, most of our knowledge of the world has come to us through our senses. We *perceive* the character of our acquaintances rather than reason it out; what we know about trees and mountains and sidewalks and weather and store-fronts we have learned far more through sight and touch and smell than through scientific study. If poetry does nothing but preserve our senses from atrophy, its service is inestimably important.

In "Meeting at Night," the speaker's movement toward the farmhouse in which his sweetheart awaits him is presented to us not in abstract summary but as a series of visual flashes. The sea across which he rows is predominantly *gray;* besides the grayness, he is impressed chiefly by the long black shoreline and the large yellow half-moon on the horizon. When he comes into shallow water, he notices also the little waves, bright in the moonlight, which are thrown up by his oars; and in a moment the boat's speed is halted abruptly by moist sand. As he walks for a mile along the beach he feels warmth and notices the smell of the sea. The three fields he hardly notices, for his eagerness increases as he nears the end of his journey; he counts them off merely as obstacles to be passed. Once at the farmhouse, the essential elements in the situation are his tap at the windowpane and the blue spurt which answers it. Whether he entered the farmhouse or his sweetheart came out to him we must guess; for him, nothing intervenes between the signal and the embrace, when the murmur of her voice seems to him less loud than the pounding of their hearts.

It will be observed that the description is *economical.* More is omitted than is stated. By concentrating on dominant impressions, Browning has suggested an impatience which at once sharpens salient details and suppresses trivial ones. One obvious meaning of the description is that the speaker was in a hurry. Although the walk along the beach and across the fields must have taken at least fifteen minutes, he has been nearly oblivious to his surroundings while it lasted. Indeed, his sensory awareness decreases steadily, until at the end only those sights and sounds are meaningful to him which indicate the fulfillment of his expectation. Such a concentration of the mind implies that he is being driven by his passion. We are thus shown, rather than told (as a psychology textbook might tell us), that an erotic urge, as it approaches satisfaction, can deflect attention from everything but its object.

Besides these details, the lyric contains others which are even more distinctively poetic. In life we often feel a similarity between objects or situations which to the analytic reason seem utterly different. The basis is often a *structural* likeness: the relationship of parts in one resembles that in the other. John Milton's *Paradise Regained* offers a clear illustration. Satan, who has been tempting Christ in the wilderness, has often been repulsed but will not be discouraged. Milton compares him to flies which refuse to be driven away from a wine press and to waves which beat against a rock. ("Must," in the second line, means "grape juice.")

> . . . as a swarm of flies in vintage time,
> About the wine press where sweet must is poured,
> Beat off, returns as oft with humming sound,
> Or surging waves against a solid rock,
> Though all to shivers dashed, the assault renew,
> Vain batt'ry, and in froth or bubbles end;
> So Satan, whom repulse upon repulse
> Met ever, and to shameful silence brought,
> Yet gives not o'er though desperate of success,
> And his vain importunity pursues.
>
> (IV, 15–24)

What is common to Satan, the flies, and the waves is persistency; though beaten off repeatedly, they all continue to attack. Such structural perceptions, although usually excluded from expository prose, are freely admitted to poetry; and they are not humanly negligible, for they are a part of our living experience. The race's tendency to perceive structural similarities in objects apparently quite different is attested by a thousand linguistic forms—for example, "After *simmering* for a while, he began to *storm* at her." The first of Browning's poems contains two examples, one easily recognizable, the other so submerged that it may be overlooked.

The easier example is that of the waves. The water's quiescence before it is disturbed is sensed to have an analogical resemblance to sleep, and its startled movements suggest waking. The "fiery ringlets" produced by the dipping oars may—or may not—imply anger. Actually, of course, the brightness is caused by the moon; but since people who are awakened suddenly are often irritable, entertainment of the deception can do us no harm. Our intelligence is no more vitiated than if we allow ourselves to speak of a "cheerful fire." Moreover, what is important at this point is not so much the objective truth about the waves as the way in which the rower perceives them. Under the influence of excitement, he allows himself to attribute emotions to inanimate nature, as the race did in its infancy and we ourselves did as children. The tendency of an agitated mind to project feelings upon its surroundings tells us something interesting about the mind, if not about the surroundings. A poet can be more faithful to the phenomena of living consciousness than a writer of expository prose, whose interest is usually in something more inclusive than an individual psyche and whose problem is to conceptualize his data.

The second example is not only difficult to explain but also rather shocking. The reader of poetry should prepare himself for shock, because poets, like other creative artists, remain close to instinctual drives which most of us try to repress or sublimate. It is a serious misconception to believe that poetry is basically prettified speech, that poems are typically about harmless things like flowers and skylarks and moonbeams, which are described elegantly but without much real point, so that poetry can be enjoyed by sentimental old ladies but not by intellectually adventurous young men and women. On the contrary, poems are often dangerous—as might be expected if we did not dissociate our conception of poetry from our image of the poet as a ragged and hot-eyed nonconformist. Plato would have banished poets from his ideal commonwealth. In Browning's poem, the surprise lies in a vivid, if concealed, sexual symbolism.

No reader can fail to observe that the lover in the first poem is keeping a tryst, and nearly all will have understood that he has remained with his sweetheart until dawn. Doing what? The shock is not so much in the answer to this question as in the means by which the answer is communicated. Let us reconsider the following two lines:

> . . . I gain the cove with pushing prow,
> And quench its speed i' the slushy sand.

When we first read the lines, we do not yet know the speaker's destination. On a subsequent reading, we may realize suddenly that the lines signalize a felt likeness between driving a boat ashore in a cove and sexual consummation. A motor image which fills the lover's mind has eroticized his perception of a stage in his journey.

Was Browning consciously aware of what he was doing? Although the question is interesting enough to provoke one of the animated debates in which lovers of literature often engage, the answer we give to it is not ultimately important to the interpretation. That the subconscious part of Browning's mind should have worked more meaningfully than he knew is not at all impossible. A psychologist can often find significance in images which are obscure to the originating mind—for instance, those of dreams. A fictive incident resembles a dream in having some of the qualities of vision; but it is imagined by an intelligence which, instead of being relaxed, is working under a creative tension that brings into play more parts of the mind than are normally active. As we read, our own minds can be stirred sympathetically. The relative coolness of aesthetic contemplation permits us, however, to subject the data of our consciousness—and the poet's—to leisurely analysis, and thus to perceive fitnesses which may have been sensed rather than reasoned out.

The interpretation given the two lines is corroborated by the second poem, which is a brief sequel to the first. Returning, the lover rows out of the cove to a position from which the open sea is visible beyond a cape. The sun has now replaced the moon on the horizon, giving the setting a different tone; and the contrast of "Parting" with "Meeting" in the titles also marks a change. The sunlight lies brightly across the water:

> And straight was a path of gold for him,
> And the need of a world of men for me.

Hitherto we have been offered nothing even distantly resembling a "message." In general, the habit of searching for messages in poetry is to be deprecated. "He prayeth best who loveth best/All things both great and small"; "It is better to have loved and lost/Than never to have loved at all"—such explicit moral assertions can be found in good poetry, but not often, and a determination to find them is a common source of misreadings. Also, the effort distracts attention from meanings which are more properly poetic. Yet the final line of the epilogue implies a judgment of sorts. Once the lover's physical urge has been satisfied, he is disenchanted with the affair and craves male companionship.

The reaction is not only psychologically sound but suggests a less than total commitment to love. The positive evaluation of the meeting implied by the lover's impatience is thus qualified by his sense of repletion once consummation has been achieved. We may, perhaps, infer that the poems ultimately criticize rather than praise fugitive sexual adventures. The poet himself, however, has made no explicit choice between the alternative evaluations. He has left the issues poised in doubtful balance, as they are often poised in life. Taken as a whole, the poems are rather an experience than a judgment.

Thus far we have observed several differences between Browning's poems and the treatment that might be accorded the same event in a prose essay. The poems deal richly with perceptions; they present the effects of strong feelings on the human awareness of external surroundings through the use of concrete images, instead of asserting them directly; they permit the cognizing (that is, the bringing to consciousness) of structural similarities in objects and situations which differ materially; and they imply—as life itself implies—double or multiple evaluations of complex experiences. All this is accomplished with extraordinary brevity, as appears from the fact that a commentary requires many times the space needed for the poems. A final, eminently practical observation must be added. It is more important than the others because it helps to establish the general truth that, as Konrad Fiedler has insisted, art raises into consciousness by its special techniques "certain things which are accessible to no other means of presentation," so that "without art, our picture of the world would be incomplete." *

What Browning or any other competent poet accomplishes can often be done *only* by writing poems. Poetry is the sole existing medium for the expression of certain kinds of perceptions, feelings, and even thoughts. Because cognition is limited by the availability of reflective patterns, the destruction of poetry would gradually lead to such a narrowing of our corporate human awareness that the psychic life of the race would be terribly impoverished.

That this is so can be suggested by an experiment. Let us imagine that the two poems we have been considering were written in prose instead of in verse. Their content would remain unchanged except in so far as rhythm and rhyme may contribute to it, but the possi-

---

* Konrad Fiedler, *Vom Wesen der Kunst* (Munich: R. Piper & Co. Verlag, 1942), pp. 69 and 51.

bility of such contribution has intentionally been ignored; it need not concern us. What kind of writing would the poems have become, and where might the prosaic equivalents be published?

The reply is that the prose would be of no recognizable kind and could not be published at all. No short literary form other than poetry exists which would admit the combination of ingredients we have discovered. At best, an incident of the kind Browning described might form part of a longer work—a short story, a novel, a technically adventurous autobiography, a small volume of odd, semipoetic effusions. It could not, however, stand alone. It could appear in no journal in any of the recognized departments—news articles, essays, short stories, book reviews, and so on—and it could not be printed separately. As a thing-in-itself it could not be disseminated, and consequently it would be unlikely to be written. The sole outlet for such brief confrontations of experience would have been destroyed. In time, perhaps, a new prose genre or type could be developed which would substitute for short poems; but there is no assurance that this would happen, and in the meantime the scope of literary subject matter would be severely constricted.

Would the loss be great? Indubitably, for the human mind can fasten pleasurably and usefully on small happenings and even on fleeting impressions. Poems are not, of course, always brief, nor do all of them have the specific characteristics we have noted in Browning's lyrics. Some kinds of poetic subject matter could be adapted to other literary forms—always with considerable change, and usually with loss, but without absolute destruction. Thus the rise of the novel in the last two centuries has been accompanied by the decline of epic, and straightforward didacticism in poetry began to decrease with the invention of the essay. Other kinds of poetry have no prosaic equivalents; among them are lyrics which, like Browning's, emphasize single aspects of complex situations or choose for exploration subjects too small, or perceptions too evanescent, to bear large-scale development without changing character. The sudden splash made when a frog leaps into a quiet pond; sorrow at the death of a small child; delight at the swaying of a silk skirt; sympathy for a mouse disturbed by the plow; awe at the beautiful strength of a tiger; regret at a parting; horror evoked by the sudden glimpse of a snake; the relation between a young girl's sorrow at the falling of autumn leaves and her dim sense of personal mortality—these and a thousand other subjects are not trivial, since entertainment of them enriches our psychic life, but they can often be presented best, or only, in poems. To develop them beyond the scope of a short lyric would destroy their distinctive qualities.

Learning to read poems like Browning's thus helps us to cognize aspects of the world and of ourselves which otherwise would remain, at best, no more than half-conscious—felt, perhaps, but not sharply focused, not held up to the intelligence for quick but piercing contemplation. And the same process goes on even more strikingly in longer poems, which, although they may treat subjects that could also be handled in prose, cut across the materials in different directions and reveal to us new dimensions of structure and significance. If our culture lacked poetry, it would be far duller than it is; and persons within our culture who are oblivious to poetry lead mental lives that are unnecessarily thin.

What has been said in the present chapter does not constitute proof of the value of poetry. At most, it may have persuaded the reader to suspend disbelief until he has tested the claims which have been made. We have generalized on the basis of two short poems, which of course are imperfectly typical, besides being more than usually simple. More complex poems would have required longer analysis. The student is invited, however, to begin the serious study of poetry in the hope that he may experience a kind of awakening.

Exercises

Examine the following brief poems to see (a) whether prose equivalents would be publishable as short stories, descriptive essays, character sketches, or any other traditional kind of writing, and (b) how the materials differ from those of expository prose.

1. Ben Jonson, "On My First Daughter" (p. 185).
2. William Blake, "The Tiger" (p. 296).
3. Emily Dickinson, "A narrow fellow in the grass" (p. 363).

II

WORDS

If the student has been persuaded by the foregoing chapter that poetry may be worth serious study, he will perhaps consent to entertain suggestions about how to read it effectively. The best approach will be to move in a series of orderly stages from the simpler principles to the more complex ones. Hitherto the emphasis has been on differences between poetry and prose; but there are also similarities, and with these we can most profitably begin.

On one level, poetry consists wholly of words, for it is only by putting words together that poems can be written. This fact is so obvious that everyone will agree theoretically on the necessity of looking up unknown words. How can the whole be understood if one is ig-

13

norant of the parts? Yet, in practice, inability to sense the meanings of words provides one of the most frequent hindrances to accurate comprehension.

The difficulty is easily recognized when the words are wholly unfamiliar. If the phrase *timor mortis conturbat me* (fear of death distresses me) appears as the refrain of an English poem, the reader who knows no Latin will realize that at this point he needs help. He will usually look for a footnote, and if one is not supplied he will put a question mark in the margin to remind him that he should ask his instructor for help. In the same way, a student who comes upon the phrase "ferne halwes, kowthe in sondry londes" in his early reading of Chaucer has immediate recourse to the glossary. Many lexical problems are not, however, recognized as lexical; when they are not, the tendency is either to invent a plausible interpretation or to assume that the meaning is unimportant.

John Milton's "Sonnet VII" furnishes an example. After lamenting his failure to accomplish anything noteworthy in his first twenty-three years, the poet writes as follows:

> Yet be it less or more, or soon or slow,
>   It shall be still in strictest measure even
>   To that same lot, however mean or high,
> Toward which time leads me, and the will of Heaven.
>   All is, if I have grace to use it so,
>   As ever, in my great Taskmaster's eye.

The excerpt does not sound puzzling. All the words are in common use, and the general sense, that the poet accepts his failure and intends to be satisfied with God's will, is unmistakable. Yet a conscientious reader—if he is not too tired or too rushed—is likely to feel dissatisfaction. What is the grammatical construction of the first three lines? The phrase "to that same lot" appears to have nothing to modify. It cannot modify the main verb ("It shall be . . . / To that same lot"); neither does it seem to fit in anywhere else. The grammar apparently has broken down. Poetry, however, like prose, ought to make sense; and the assumption should always be initially made that it does. The principle cannot be stated too early or too often.

Upon reflection, the reader may discover that the root of the problem lies in "even." Is it adverb or adjective? Upon a sudden impulse, he turns to "even" in a standard desk dictionary and finds that the second adjectival meaning is "on the same level; in the same plane or line; parallel; *even with the ground.*" * The passage now opens up: Milton is saying that his life will be "in strictest measure *level with,* or *proportioned to*" the lot which Heaven has appointed for him. The problem at first appeared to be syntactical only because it was wrongly focused.

The corpus of English poetry is thickly strewn with such difficulties. Words often have not one meaning, but several; words current in one period fall into disuse in another; meanings sometimes change drastically. The student will do well, accordingly, to form *at once* the habit of reading with a good dictionary constantly at his elbow. (How many readers understood "lexical" when they came upon it three paragraphs back? Of those who did not, how many looked it up?) The dictionary should be adequate to the needs of a college student: not a cheap paperback useful for helping poor spellers, but a large, solid, relatively expensive volume. Nothing less will suffice. Furthermore, the dictionary should be reasonably up-to-date—not printed in 1873 or 1912 or even 1938— and should have a deep historical orientation. Many technical terms which the student will need to look up for his non-English courses postdate the Second World War, and many literary texts use words in outmoded ways. Failure to own such a dictionary will force him to work under a severe handicap not only in this course, but in many of his college courses. Neither should he be satisfied merely to have access to the dictionary—in a nearby library, down a hallway, three feet away on a roommate's desk. It should be *his,* on *his* desk, constantly at hand; and he should consult it regularly, as a matter of habit, whenever he is preparing a reading assignment. It is likely to prove his single most valuable tool.

The usefulness of the dictionary will be especially evident in the reading of poetry, drama, and fiction. Let us suppose that Shakespeare's "Sonnet XCIV" has been assigned.

> They that have power to hurt and will do none;
> That do not do the thing they most do show;
> Who, moving others, are themselves as stone,
> Unmovèd, cold, and to temptation slow:
> They rightly do inherit Heaven's graces,
> And husband nature's riches from expense . . .

* All definitions quoted in the present text, unless otherwise annotated, are from *The American College Dictionary* (Copyright 1947, © 1964 by Random House, Inc., and reprinted by permission), but there are other good dictionaries about which your instructor can tell you.

"Husband nature's riches"? If the preceding example has struck home, the student who is puzzled by the phrase will turn immediately to "husband" in his dictionary. He will find some such explanation as *"v. t. [verb transitive]* 2. To manage, esp. with prudent economy; economize; *to husband one's resources."* The phrase is now clear, and the student is prepared to read on. If he remembers what he has discovered, he may later experience the pleasure of recognition when he comes upon a sentence in *Macbeth:* "There's husbandry in heaven;/ Their candles are all out" (II, i). Months and years of such reference produce a steadily sharpening sense of linguistic meanings; but the time will never come when the language is completely mastered. A university professor who has taught English for twenty-five years may frequently look up a dozen words in a day.

Sometimes, of course, the advisability of recourse to a dictionary is obvious. "The Peer now spreads the glitt'ring forfex wide/ To inclose the lock; now joins it, to divide" (Alexander Pope, *The Rape of the Lock,* III, 147–48): in the absence of a note—which should be provided—the good student may guess that "forfex" means "shears," but he will wish to check the meaning. In this instance, he may have to go to an unabridged dictionary. The poorer student, who is probably lacking in energy (it is one of the reasons he does badly), will be content to let the meaning slumber in fog or hope to learn it in class. Often, however, a certain perspicacity is needed to localize the source of obscurity. "Great Fletcher," writes John Dryden of a school for actors, "never treads in buskins here,/ Nor greater Jonson dares in socks appear" (*Mac Flecknoe,* 79–80). If the editor has not added a note, the dictionary will reveal that *buskin* is "the high shoe or cothurnus of ancient Greek and Roman tragic actors," and that *sock* is "a light shoe worn by ancient Greek and Roman comic actors, sometimes taken as a symbol of comedy." Evidently the poet is making a rather startling assertion about limitations in the actors' training. What can be taught them if not how to act in either of the two major dramatic forms? Additional flipping of pages in the dictionary will reveal a "Fletcher, John, 1579–1625," who wrote dramas (evidently tragedies), and a "Jonson, Ben, 1573?–1637," also a dramatist (who must have written comedies). Not every student, however, will have realized that "sock" may not have its present meaning and that proper names as well as common nouns are entered in good dictionaries (often in a biographical appendix). Three lines down the page the word "clinches" appears: "Pure clinches the suburbian muse affords." The C and D students will not be seriously troubled to fit the term into the context, or, if they do, will perhaps construct a vague image of ham actors embracing. The B and A students, recognizing a problem, will run down the list of dictionary meanings until they come to "12. *Obs.* [*Obsolete*] a pun." The dialogue on which the actors are trained is of a low order.

Obvious as all this may seem, no more immediately useful suggestion can be made to the college student of poetry—or almost any other subject—than that he buy a good dictionary and use it. Juniors and seniors as well as freshmen and sophomores—sometimes, alas, even graduate students—puzzle vainly over poems whose very titles include unfamiliar or misunderstood words. "Pediment," in Wallace Stevens' "The Pediment of Appearance," might be thought by a student who knows that the Latin root *ped-* means "foot" to be something to stand on; instead, it is "a low triangular gable, crowned with a projecting cornice. . . ." Young men, says the poet, hunt for a form which,

> By its form alone, by being right,
> By being high, is the stone
> For which they are looking.

Although the more sensitive readers would be jarred by having to look up at a foundation, many of them might fail to check the meaning of the key term; and some of the most ingenious might invent farfetched interpretations based on a simple misunderstanding.

Again, the whole tonality of a passage may be misconstrued because a modern meaning is substituted for an older one.

> The Sea of Faith
> Was once, too, at the full, and round earth's shore
> Lay like the folds of a bright girdle furled.

Thus Matthew Arnold in "Dover Beach," a familiar poem about religious disillusionment. The nineteenth-century girdle was "1. a belt, cord, sash, or the like, worn about the waist," or "2. any encircling band. . . ." If Arnold thought of particular girdles, his mind may have turned (for example) to the magical girdle of the Greek goddess Aphrodite. The grossly "modern" reader might picture instead—rumpled, with utilitarian appendages projecting—

"2. a lightweight undergarment which supports the abdominal region of the body." Let us hope that he would shudder.

The first lesson to be learned about the careful reading of poetry, then, is that the words of a good poem will be found, by consultation of an adequate dictionary, always, or almost always, to fit. The chief exceptions are in very recent poetry, which has sometimes, with dubious success, been aimed at transcending logic, and in older songs which include nonverbal refrains ("Hey nonny nonny," "Hey ding-a-ding-ding," and the like). As a general rule, the student may assume that the words of the poems which will be assigned in the present course, when examined, will fall together into sense, and that it is regularly his duty to *look up every word of whose meaning in the context he is unsure*. If the burden at first seems heavy, it will lessen with time, and the benefits in improved comprehension will be enormous. In the present text, the glosses at the bottoms of the pages will offer much assistance—more in proportion as the poetry makes heavy lexical demands. But it cannot be assumed that all the difficult or treacherous words have been annotated.

Exercises

1. Look up whatever words you must to make good sense of the following passage. The words most likely to give trouble are italicized.

> 'Tis a sad truth: the pulpit may her plain
> And sober Christian precepts still retain;
> Doctrines it may, and wholesome *uses,* frame,
> Grave *homilies,* and *lectures;* but the flame
> Of thy brave soul, that shot such heat and light
> As burnt our earth, and made our darkness bright,
> Committed holy *rapes* upon our will.

> (Thomas Carew, "An Elegy Upon the Death of
> the Dean of Paul's, Dr. John Donne," 11–17)

2. In each of the following passages, the italicized word has a sense different from what might be expected. Discover the word's meaning in the context.

> (a) You may as well spread out the unsunned heaps
> Of miser's treasure by an outlaw's den
> And tell me it is safe, as bid me hope
> Danger will *wink* on opportunity.

> (John Milton, "Comus," 397–400)

(b) Ridotta sips and dances, till she see
The doubling *lusters* dance as fast as she.

(Alexander Pope, "The First Satire of the
Second Book of Horace Imitated, 47–48)

(c) Lo where she comes along with *portly* pace,
Like Phoebe from her chamber of the East.

(Edmund Spenser, "Epithalamion," 148–49)

(d) Numb were the Beadsman's fingers, while he *told*
His rosary, and while his frosted breath,
Like pious incense from a censer old,
Seemed taking flight for heaven.

(John Keats, "The Eve of St. Agnes," 5–8)

(e) Deferential, glad to be of use,
Politic, cautious, and meticulous;
Full of high *sentence,* but a bit obtuse.

(T. S. Eliot, "The Love Song of
J. Alfred Prufrock," 115–17)

3. Prepare to explain all the doubtful words in the following excerpt.

Great red church of my parents, cruciform crossing they knew—
Over these same encaustics they and their parents trod
Bound through a red-brick transept for a once familiar pew
Where the organ set them singing and the sermon let them nod,
And up this colored brickwork the same long shadows grew
As these in the stenciled chancel where I kneel in the Presence of God.

Wonder beyond Time's wonders, that Bread so white and small
Veiled in golden curtains, too mighty for men to see,
Is the Power which sends the shadows up this polychrome wall,
Is God who created the present, the chain-smoking millions and me;
Beyond the throb of the engines is the throbbing heart of all—
Christ, at this Highbury altar, I offer myself to Thee.

(John Betjeman, "St. Savior's, Aberdeen
Park, Highbury, London, N.," 25–36)

III

SYNTAX

It should have already become clear that the unit within which word meanings fit together is the sentence. Sentences, in turn, blend into larger units—paragraphs, stanzas, and so forth; but we must next consider opportunities for misunderstanding which arise within the sentence even though the words are correctly grasped. Many errors of interpretation are caused by the misconstruing of syntax (the grammatical relations of the parts of the sentence to the whole). The student is warned that parts of the following discussion will require close attention. Grammar cannot be discussed without the help of a rather precise analytic terminology.

A foreign language can again be used for illustration. To a student who knows Latin words but is bad at

Latin grammar, the sentence *Leonem edit Maria* might appear to mean "The lion ate Mary." Actually, it was Mary who did the eating. The grammatical signals are in fact very clear, for *-em* indicates the accusative (or objective) case, and *-a* is one ending for a subject. Modern English contains fewer case-endings than Latin and relies more heavily on word order (which is sometimes modified by poets). Nevertheless, misconstruing of the syntax can usually be avoided by an alert reader.

Consider the following stanza from Thomas Gray's "Elegy Written in a Country Churchyard" (33–36):

> The boast of heraldry, the pomp of power,
>   And all that beauty, all that wealth e'er gave,
> Awaits alike the inevitable hour:
>   The paths of glory lead but to the grave.

Untrained readers often take "hour" to be the direct object of "awaits": the boast of heraldry, the pomp of power, and so on, terminate in death. The reading is not altogether illogical, and it does not damage the poem seriously. Yet it is almost certainly incorrect.

The reasons for suspecting it are chiefly two. First, "awaits," as a singular verb, demands a singular subject; and "boast . . . , pomp . . . , and all" is not singular. Confronted with this objection, the reader may urge that the syntax breaks after "e'er gave," and that the poet abandons the grammatical pattern with which he began. If nothing better can be found, the reading, although forced, will have to be accepted; but it ought not to be accepted quickly, especially if the sense is not satisfactory—and it is not. (This is the second reason for being skeptical.) Do "The boast of heraldry, the pomp of power," and so on, "wait for" death, "look for or expect" it; are they "in store for" it, "ready for" it; do they "lie in wait for" it, "wait as in expectation" of it? None of the dictionary definitions of the verb quite fits this context. We may intelligently doubt that noblemen, men in important political position, beautiful women, or wealthy people remind themselves frequently that they will die. If the poet can be acquitted of making an absurd claim, we have a responsibility to defend him. In principle, we ought not to assume that poets are less wise or clever than we are. And the grammar makes acquittal easy. "The inevitable hour" can be taken as subject and the series of introductory items as direct objects. As in the Latin example, the normal English order of subject and object has been inverted.

Reluctance to demand syntactical correctness of poetry often derives from a belief that poets must frequently violate grammatical rules because they write in an odd way. True, their syntax is sometimes rather free, and we shall see that on occasion they compress thoughts in such a way as to require the supplying of omitted words. Only in rare cases, however, do they transcend ordinary grammatical principles. Even if they tried, they would find it difficult to do so, because the syntactical patterns they have heard and used from childhood have become forms of their linguistic awareness.

Let anyone who doubts what has just been said try the experiment of making a nonsense-utterance. We shall make the attempt here. With the aim of producing a free and grammatically irresponsible statement I produce, let us say, the following: "He phostipated the smickleburker in the hoosyganny." Have I transcended ordinary grammar? There is an unmistakable subject, "He," in the nominative case; a verb of unknown meaning, "phostipated," in the past tense; a direct object, "smickleburker"; and a prepositional phrase, "in the hoosyganny," which obviously modifies the predicate. Without in the least meaning to do so, I have modeled my syntax on that of a sentence like "He struck his tormentor in the teeth." Although we have not space to examine them, the nonsense-words, too, derive from my ordinary speech-habits; they are all readily pronounceable by an American or Englishman, and they contain elements of *phos*phorus, cons*tipated,* ham*burger* (with a slight change), *hoose*gow, and *granny.*

Clearly, my inventiveness has not been very great. And I am unable, I confess, to put together any utterance at all which contains only recognizable words but does not at least strongly suggest a syntactical pattern, either of English or of some other language with which I am acquainted. Poets no doubt are more gifted—but not much more. Like other people, they rarely stray far beyond the limits of syntactical convention. The difference is rather that as specialists in language they know more conventions. In the whole body of English poetry, probably not more than one sentence in several hundred will be found to be ungrammatical otherwise than because a few words have been omitted or the utterance has been left unfinished.

We may look at additional examples. Here is one in which words have to be supplied mentally by the reader. Thomas Hood, in "The Bridge of Sighs" (27–28), writes of a prostitute who has drowned herself:

> Still, for all slips of hers,
> One of Eve's family.

We recognize immediately that in spite of her faults "she is" one of Eve's family.

In a poem by Emily Dickinson, "The soul selects her own society" (1–8), compression goes further:

> The soul selects her own society,
> Then shuts the door;
> On her divine majority
> Obtrude no more.
>
> Unmoved, she notes the chariot's pausing
> At her low gate;
> Umoved, an emperor is kneeling
> Upon her mat.

"Obtrude" in the fourth line is plural and cannot take "soul" as its subject. At first reading the impression may arise that the form is that of a command: "Don't bother me!" Nowhere else, however, does the poet show irritation or address an unspecified audience directly. The dominant mood is strongly declarative. The verb can be construed as indicative instead of imperative if "No more" is understood to mean "No more people," "No more suitors for friendship." Once the poet has closed her door on the circle of chosen friends, nobody else is allowed to break into the group.

In the second stanza, we wonder why the emperor who has come in a chariot to sue for acceptance is "unmoved." The poet, secure among her friends, ought to be unmoved, not the emperor, who presumably feels hope. Accordingly, we carry over into the seventh line two words from the fifth: "Unmoved, *she notes* [that] an emperor is kneeling upon her mat." By this time it should have appeared that "majority" cannot mean "the greater number or part." We search for another possibility in the dictionary and find "the state or time of being of full legal age: *to attain one's majority.*" Evidently the sense is that a person who is mature enough to make his own decisions may prefer as friends people who lack importance or high social station.

In the above example, the commentary on syntax included redefinition of a word. Frequently word meanings and grammar must be comprehended simultaneously because neither can be separated from the other. We have distinguished lexical difficulties from syntactical for the sake of expository clarity, not because understanding necessarily has two successive stages. It may come in a single flash, as a passage from John Donne's "The Good-Morrow" (1–5) will show. This time the seventeenth-century spellings and punctuation must be retained in order to preserve a structural ambiguity.

> I wonder by my troth, what thou, and I
> Did, till we lov'd? were we not wean'd till then?
> But suck'd on countrey pleasures, childishly?
> Or snorted we in the seaven sleepers den?
> T'was so; But this, all pleasures fancies bee.

"Suck'd" suggests the suckling of a child; "snorted" is an older equivalent of "snored"; the seven sleepers' den was a cave in which, according to legend, seven Christian men slept for two centuries. The phrase in question at the moment, however, is "But this, all pleasures fancies bee." It may be understood for years as meaning "Yet this is our fancy, our ideal image, of all pleasures." * Then one day the words may suddenly tumble about before the eyes to make a new configuration, as hollows can all at once turn into swellings in a picture. Now we see that "But," instead of being a conjunction meaning "yet," is a preposition meaning "except": "All pleasures except this one are mere fancies." And this reading is so obviously correct that the other more complicated one is rejected forever.

Failure to grasp the syntax of a passage sometimes results in ludicrous misinterpretations. In Milton's *Paradise Lost* (II, 18–24), Satan, sitting on a throne in Hell, addresses the other devils:

> Me though just right and the fixed laws of Heav'n
> Did first create your leader, next, free choice,
> With what besides, in counsel or in fight,
> Hath been achieved of merit, yet this loss,
> Thus far at least recovered, hath much more
> Established in a safe, unenvied throne,
> Yielded with full consent.

---

* Actually, this reading is impossible because "bee" is a plural form. The student, however, may have no intimate acquaintance with Elizabethan grammar.

The phrase to be considered is "though just right." Classroom interrogation has revealed that many college students take "just" to be an adverb modifying the adjective "right": "although I am just right (for the position). . . ." But this produces nonsense. What can be done with "and" (a syntactical question), and how can "though" be explained (a question about meaning)? If we normalize the word order, the clause would come out like this: "And the fixed laws of Heaven did create me—though just right [for the job] —your leader." "And," however, clearly joins "just right' and "fixed laws," which therefore must be in parallel structure. "Though just right," again, jars with the context. The fixed laws of Heaven surely did not create Satan king of the devils *in spite of* the fact that he was the ideal choice. Resurveying the passage, we arrive at the alternative, and correct, interpretation: "Although legal right and the fixed laws of Heaven first created me your leader. . . ." "Right" is noun, not adjective, and "just" is adjective, not adverb.

To good students, as well as to inexperienced teachers, the possibility of such absurd misunderstandings may come as a shock. They had better adjust themselves to reality. Few readers—and certainly neither the typical university instructor nor the writer of this introduction—are totally immune to wild errors. Yet we can all take pains to be ridiculous as seldom as possible.

Exercises

1. Study the syntax of the phrase "hath/ Charmed magic casements" in the following excerpt, and prepare to defend what seems to you to be the correct interpretation.

> Thou wast not born for death, immortal bird!
>   No hungry generations tread thee down.
> The voice I hear this passing night was heard
>   In ancient days by emperor and clown:
> Perhaps the self-same song that found a path
>   Through the sad heart of Ruth, when, sick for home,
>   She stood in tears amid the alien corn;
>   The same that ofttimes *hath*
>   *Charmed magic casements,* opening on the foam
>   Of perilous seas, in faery lands forlorn.
>
>   (John Keats, "Ode to a Nightingale," 61–70)

"Ruth" is the Biblical Ruth, who after the death of her husband accompanied her mother-in-law, Naomi, from Moab to Bethlehem and there followed the reapers of a landowner named Boaz, picking up barley ("corn") which the reapers had missed. What, however, is to be done with the underlined phrase? Is "hath charmed" a verb in the perfect tense, or is "hath" the verb and "charmed" a participial adjective modifying "casements"?

Consider the alternative suggestions thoughtfully; if neither is satisfactory, search for another. Do not conclude hastily that the phrase is meaningless or "only poetry," and do not irresponsibly invent meanings for "to charm" which are not justified by the dictionary. The stanza has been much admired by critics who presumably knew, or thought they knew, what it meant.

2. The following little poem by Robert Herrick, "Upon Julia's Clothes," raises a problem which has a syntactical aspect because it relates to grammatical signals. Read the poem two or three times, and then, when you think you have understood it, read it again in accordance with the instructions given beneath it.

> Whenas in silks my Julia goes,
> Then, then (methinks) how sweetly flows
> That liquefaction of her clothes.
>
> Next, when I cast mine eyes and see
> That brave vibration each way free,
> O how that glittering taketh me!

Now read the poem again, putting a very heavy stress on the following words. (You may indicate the stress by underlining.) "Then, then" in line 2, "Next" in line 4, "free" in line 5 and "that" in line 6. Does the meaning change?

Do grammatical signals—for example, the sharply pointed contrasting of "Then, then" with "Next"—suffice to establish the correctness of the second reading?

IV

THE

PROSE

PARAPHRASE

Explication of a poem or part of a poem by rearranging the syntactical elements and substituting synonyms or equivalent phrases for difficult words or groups of words results in a *prose paraphrase*. No other means of illuminating poetic obscurities is so effective or so economical of time as a good paraphrase. To be sure, the paraphrase is not the same thing as the poem, and an ability to write it does not guarantee an appreciation of total meaning; also, to paraphrase an eloquent passage is usually to degrade and coarsen it. No other exercise, however, forces students to reveal their misapprehensions so nakedly, and the teacher has no equally efficient technique for correcting false readings.

How the procedure works will be illustrated by a

series of examples, given in the order of increasing complexity. The poetic excerpts will be followed immediately by the paraphrases in parentheses.

> you must serve
> For each of the five pictures we require;
> It saves a model.

(Browning, "Andrea del Sarto," 23–25)

("You must pose for each of the five pictures we need. Doing so will save the expense of a model.")

> I meet and dole
> Unequal laws unto a savage race,
> That hoard, and sleep, and feed, and know not me.

(Tennyson, "Ulysses," 3–5)

("I interpret and administer unsuitable laws to a rude people who accumulate possessions, and sleep, and stuff themselves, and don't understand my character.")

> It were a vain endeavor,
> Though I should gaze forever
> On that green light that lingers in the west:
> I may not hope from outward forms to win
> The passion and the life whose fountains are within.

(Coleridge, "Dejection: An Ode," 42–46)

("It would be useless for me to gaze forever on the green light which lingers in the west after sunset. I can't hope to acquire from the observation of nature a vitality which must come from my own inner resources.")

> When statutes glean the refuse of the sword,
> How much more safe the vassal than the lord.

(Johnson, *The Vanity of Human Wishes*, 31–32)

("When laws against the defeated party complete the destruction begun by war, the dependent is safer than his master.")

> 'Twas a child, that so did thrive
> In grace, and feature,
> As Heaven and nature seemed to strive
> Which owned the creature.

(Jonson, "Epitaph on S. P.," 5–8)

("It was a child who throve so, in God's favor and in physical beauty, that Heaven and the world seemed to compete for possession of him.")

> To Pales, or Pomona, thus adorned,
> Likest she seemed, Pomona when she fled
> Vertumnus, or to Ceres in her prime,
> Yet virgin of Proserpina from Jove.
>
> (Milton, *Paradise Lost,* IX, 393–96)

("Thus adorned, she resembled most nearly Pales, the goddess of flocks, or Pomona, the goddess of orchards—Pomona at the time, especially, when she fled from Vertumnus, the god of seasonal change; or Ceres, the goddess of agriculture, before she had with Jove the union from which Proserpina was to be born.")

> Go, soar with Plato to th' empyreal sphere,
> To the first good, first perfect, and first fair;
> Or tread the mazy round his follow'rs trod,
> And quitting sense call imitating God.
>
> (Pope, *An Essay on Man,* II, 23–26)

("Like Plato, contemplate the highest goodness, perfection, and beauty, which have their seat in the heavens; or walk round in confused circles with his followers, who called a retreat from sensory pleasures an imitation of God.")

Earlier chapters have contained numerous paraphrases like these, and later chapters will contain more. Indeed, without the help of paraphrases the discussion of poetic meanings would hardly be possible. Sometimes making a paraphrase requires the interpretation of a metaphor, as in the following example:

> And the hapless soldier's sigh
> Runs in blood down palace walls.
>
> (Blake, "London," 11–12)

("The misery of the soldier wounded or slain in battle is the responsibility of the government which started the war.") Here the boundary between paraphrase and other explications becomes thin.

A final complex illustration will indicate in greater detail how paraphrases are constructed, sometimes at the expense of much effort. The student is urged not to be satisfied with anything less than full comprehension of what follows. The passage to be considered is not only intrinsically difficult but also is presented without the footnotes which would normally be provided in a text. (If the course is successful in making the student understand and enjoy poetry, not all his future reading will be in annotated editions.) Few passages require so much work; but he should be mentally prepared and spiritually willing at every moment to undertake the same *kind* of analysis. If he is not, his poetic awareness may remain permanently at a childish level, and he will be forced to defend his gropings by arguing that poetry means anything anybody wants it to mean—an obvious untruth.

In Act II, Scene i, of Shakespeare's *Hamlet*, Polonius speaks the following passage to a servant whom he is instructing to spy on his son, Laertes, in Paris. The fact that the passage occurs in a play does not make it inappropriate for the present exercise.

> Marry, sir, here's my drift,
> And I believe it is a fetch of warrant.
> You laying these slight sullies on my son,
> As 'twere a thing a little soiled i' the working,
> Mark you,
> Your party in converse, him you would sound,
> Having ever seen in the prenominate crimes
> The youth you breathe of guilty, be assured
> He closes with you in this consequence:
> "Good sir," or so, or "Friend," or "Gentleman"—
> According to the phrase or the addition
> Of man or country—

The sentence is left uncompleted because Polonius, who prides himself on the artfulness of his speech, wishes for a sign that he has been understood up to this point. He has reason to be unsure. Nevertheless, the passage can be understood, as a whole and in all its parts, if the student is willing to work on it with something less than the concentration he knows must be brought to the solution of a problem in calculus. Good poetry deserves nothing less.

The first step is to confront the lexical difficulties. "Marry," in the first line, is *"interj. Archaic.* an exclamation of surprise, etc." "Drift" means "6. the course of anything; tendency; aim: *the drift of an argument."* "Here's my drift" is thus roughly equivalent to "This is my meaning." "Fetch," in line two, means "22. *Archaic.* a stroke; effort; *a fetch of the imagination.* "Warrant" can best be understood as "1. authorization, sanction, or justification." Although the limitations of a desk dictionary are apparent at this point, a clever student can perhaps guess that "a stroke of justification" means "a justifiable stroke (or, better, *trick*): "I think it is a justifiable stratagem." "Sully" is "5. a stain." "Mark" means "31. to give heed or attention to," hence "to observe." "Sound" fits best as "5. to seek to elicit the view or sentiments of (a person) by indirect inquiries. . . ." Evidently the servant is being told to accuse Laertes of indiscretions in order to elicit comments about his behavior. "Prenominate" is *"Archaic.* forementioned." "Breathe" is either "11. to give utterance to; whisper" or "12. to express; manifest." "Speak softly," or perhaps "speak with polite delicacy," will be adequately synonymous. "Closes with you in this consequence" is especially thorny. For "close," the dictionary gives "11. to grapple; engage in close encounter"; for "consequence" it yields "1. act or fact of following as an effect or result upon something antecedent" and "4. the conclusion of an argument or inference." A reader with a good language sense may perhaps decide finally that the phrase can be paraphrased as "carries on the dialogue by speaking as follows." Finally, "addition" is "5. *Obs. except Law.* a particularizing designation added to a person's name, as *Plaintiff* in *John Doe, Plaintiff."* Evidently it does not differ greatly from "title."

Having done so much, we go back and substitute the discovered meanings for the original words, making such small adjustments as seem to be necessary, and come out with something like this:

> Indeed, sir, here's my meaning—and I believe it is a justifiable stratagem (which I propose). You laying these slight stains on my son, as it were a thing a little soiled in the working, observe, your party in converse, him whose views you would elicit, having ever seen in the forementioned crimes the youth you speak of guilty (we drop "softly" or "with polite delicacy" as awkward and unnecessary), be assured he carries on the dialogue by speaking as follows: "Good sir," or so, or "Friend," or "Gentleman"—according to the phrase or title of man or country—

But this, although clearer, is still not satisfactory, partly because of syntactical problems. "You laying . . . observe" is grammatically obscure; so too is the construction of " 'Good sir' . . . according to the phrase or title of man or country—" More work seems to be necessary.

Actually, we are near the end of our toil. "You laying" (for the American "Your laying") clearly introduces a conclusion beginning with "Your party in converse." We may change the phrase to "As a result of your laying," or, more simply, "When you have laid."

Finally, making another guess, we decide that "According to the phrase or the title of man or country" must be equivalent to "according to whatever phrase or title the speaker or his countrymen ordinarily use." Also, we have an inspiration about "a thing a little soiled in the working." Accordingly we rephrase again, this time somewhat more freely:

> Indeed, sir, here's my meaning—and I believe the trick is justifiable. Once you have laid these slight aspersions on my son, as if he had been a little stained by experience—like a piece of clay dirtied by the potter, or a piece of cloth soiled by the dressmaker—the person to whom you are speaking, if he has ever seen the youth committing any of the faults you have mentioned, will assuredly follow up your lead by saying, "Good sir," or "Friend," or "Gentleman," using whatever form of address is customary for him and his countrymen—

This makes both lexical and syntactical sense.

Not many passages require so much labor. This one is muddied by a pomposity characteristic of the speaker, who is always at least slightly comic. Neither should the impression be left that puzzling out meanings like a dog worrying a slipper is one of the chief activities connected with the study of poetry. For the most part, after he gains practice, the student will be able to sail through his reading fairly smoothly. Nevertheless, when he finds himself balked, a struggle somewhat like the one from which we have just emerged sometimes offers the only solution of the difficulty.

When the instructor calls for a paraphrase, the student should keep as much as possible to the general syntactical structure of the original, making only such changes as are necessary for the sake of clarifying grammatical relationships and explicating hard words. An impulse may be felt to change familiar words and retain unfamiliar ones. He should resist it. The opposite practice is the correct one. Also, he should not retain the line breaks of the original passage, but should write it out as continuous prose. Once he has mastered the discipline, he will find himself, perhaps for the first time, actually convinced that good poetry does not consist of vague jumbles of words upon which any kind of personally satisfying interpretation can be put. The path to this realization will not, perhaps, be easy, and sometimes the task may put a strain on intelligence and concentration. That will be because the mind is being stretched, given new strength and resilience.

It probably will not break under the strain.

Exercises

Since paraphrasing usually requires some knowledge of the context, the following exercises refer the student to poems in the anthology. Paraphrase all the passages indicated below, or whichever ones your instructor may select.

1. Sidney, "Having this day my horse, my hand, my lance" (9–12), p. 135.
2. Spenser, the October eclogue (40–42), p. 138.
3. Donne, "The Canonization" (31–34), p. 170.
4. Milton, from *Paradise Lost* (VIII, 83–88), p. 224.
5. Pope, *The Rape of the Lock* (105–08), p. 267.
6. Gray, "Elegy Written in a Country Churchyard" (97–100), p. 279.
7. Browning, "The Bishop Orders His Tomb" (17–19), p. 346.
8. Eliot, "Gerontion" (35–37 [to the period]), p. 404.

V

ALLUSIONS

Before moving on to a consideration of such more obviously aesthetic traits of poems as images, figurative language, and symbols, we must observe one other obstacle to the comprehension of literal meanings. Poets are fond of dropping hints which their readers are expected to pick up, and many of the hints take the form of allusions. If these are disregarded or misinterpreted, full understanding becomes impossible.

Examples appear everywhere. Robert Herrick begins "Corinna's Going a-Maying" as follows:

> Get up, get up for shame! The blooming morn
> Upon her wings presents the god unshorn.
>> See how Aurora throws her fair
>> Fresh-quilted colors through the air.

The references are to mythology. Aurora is "1. *Class. Myth.* dawn, often personified, by the Romans and others, as a goddess (Eos)." The fresh-quilted colors are those of sunrise. The "god" of line 2, however, because he is not named, will be recognized only by readers who have some previous acquaintance with classical myths as Phoebus, god of the sun, who is "unshorn" because his flaming rays suggest bright hair.

So often with allusions. The student who has access to a dictionary of classical—that is, Greek and Roman—mythology will find it useful; but even he will sometimes have to rely upon notes or upon his instructor.

> Are all th' Aonian springs
> Dried up? Lies Thespia waste?

"Aonian," in these lines from Ben Jonson's "An Ode: To Himself" (7–8) will be easily identified as the name of some springs which were sacred to the Muses, located at the foot of Mt. Helicon in Greece. "Thespia" will give more trouble. The dictionary defines "Thespian" as "2. pertaining to tragedy or to the dramatic art in general; tragic; dramatic." This is the usual meaning; but the adjective in Jonson's poem derives from Thespia, a town on Mt. Helicon—not from Thespis, the founder of Greek tragedy. Through no fault, the dictionary definition is misleading.

Fortunately, most allusions are easily run down. When T. S. Eliot, in "The Love Song of J. Alfred Prufrock" (13–14), writes, "In the room the women come and go/ Talking of Michelangelo," the rare student who does not at once recognize the Italian painter can quickly identify him by the dictionary. Evidently the conversation is about art—and probably superficial. The "Magi" of the same poet's "Journey of the Magi" are "1. the three 'wise men' who 'came from the east' to Jerusalem to do homage to the infant Jesus. Matt. 2:1–12." "Nineveh" and "Tyre," in Rudyard Kipling's "Recessional" (13–16), are described by the dictionary as important ancient cities, one of which is specifically said to be now in ruins:

> Far-called, our navies melt away;
> On dune and headland sinks the fire:
> Lo, all our pomp of yesterday
> Is one with Nineveh and Tyre!

The glory of England, like that of the two ancient cities, will fade. The allusions in the following stanza from Thomas Gray's "Ode on the Death of a Favorite Cat, Drowned in a Tub of Goldfishes" (31–36) can be partly looked up and partly guessed.

> Eight times emerging from the flood,
>   She mewed to every wat'ry god
>   Some speedy aid to send.
> No dolphin came, no Nereid stirred,
> Nor cruel Tom nor Susan heard:
>   A fav'rite has no friend!

A dolphin is a large aquatic mammal, thought of here as a possible source of help; a Nereid is ". . . a sea nymph." Tom and Susan—the former evidently unfriendly to the cat—are perhaps servants or children. Actually, we know from other evidence that they are servants. "Every wat'ry god" is every god who is connected with the ocean or rivers—for example, Neptune or Triton. The favorite is the favorite of a king or nobleman, envied by others who aspire to replace him. Some students will also remember the folk belief that a cat has nine lives and connect it with the fact that this cat emerged from the water eight times before drowning. Finally, one or two members of the class will recall that Arion, a Greek poet, was said to have been rescued from the sea by a dolphin. But the stanza can still be enjoyed, if only imperfectly, provided most of the hints are picked up.

So it goes typically, some of the allusions being readily identifiable, some not, and others relatively unimportant, although catching them enhances enjoyment. George Meredith's "Lucifer in Starlight" begins with a description of a strange prince who must be recognized if the sonnet is to have meaning:

> On a starred night Prince Lucifer uprose.
> Tired of his dark dominion, swung the fiend
> Above the rolling ball in cloud part screened,
> Where sinners hugged their specter of repose.

Identification is easy: Lucifer is "1. a proud rebellious angel, identified with Satan, who fell from heaven." Without this information the poem remains murky; with it the basic meanings emerge readily. But what is the "dark dominion"—Hell or the Earth? Satan can claim a sort of dominion over each. The answer to this question, unlike that to the other, does not touch the poem's heart. Still it is better that we answer it. Unfortunately, doing so is hard because whereas "dark" suits Hell better than Earth, Lucifer's swinging over the Earth ("the rolling ball") gives the impression that he has just left it.

Thomas Babington Macaulay's "The Battle of Naseby" begins very oddly indeed:

THE BATTLE OF NASEBY

By Obadiah Bind-their-kings-in-chains-and-their-nobles-with-links-of-iron, serjeant in Ireton's regiment

Oh! wherefore come ye forth, in triumph from the North,
With your hands, and your feet, and your raiment all red?

In the absence of a note, which should be furnished, the reader of these lines may be baffled. To be sure, Naseby appears in the dictionary as "a village in central England, in Northamptonshire: Royalist defeat, 1645." For the rest, the discovery must be made somehow that Ireton was a Parliamentary general in the English Civil War of 1642–46 and that Obadiah's grotesque name is a parody of such Puritan names as Praise–God–Barebone.

Recent poets (as well as older ones) sometimes put a very heavy burden on their readers' memories. T. S. Eliot's *The Waste Land,* a startling and much imitated poem first published in 1922, is a mosaic of hidden references. The following excerpt (187–97) contains at least three phrases varied from works which few readers are likely to recall in detail.

A rat crept softly through the vegetation
Dragging its slimy belly on the bank
While I was fishing in the full canal
On a winter evening round behind the gashouse
Musing upon the king my brother's wreck
And on the king my father's death before him.
White bodies naked on the low damp ground
And bones cast in a little low dry garret
Rattled by the rat's foot only, year to year.
But at my back from time to time I hear
The sound of horns and motors . . .

The basic image is drawn from a medieval cycle of stories about a fisher-king, which the reader is expected to know. Besides this, the passage reflects lines by earlier poets. "Musing upon the king my brother's wreck" echoes "Weeping again the King my father's wrack," in Shakespeare's *The Tempest* (I, ii). The last two lines quoted are ironically parallel to "But at my back I always hear/ Time's wingèd chariot hurrying near," in Andrew Marvell's "To His Coy Mistress" (20–21), and also to "When of the sudden, listening, you shall hear/ A noise of horns and hunting," in an obscure Renaissance poem by John Day, "The Parliament of Bees." Whether the game is worth the candle can be argued; and certainly lovers of poetry, however well read, cannot be expected to have freshly in mind whatever passages in Eliot's wide reading may have stuck in his memory. Nevertheless, an appreciative understanding of *The Waste Land* demands the spotting of many, if perhaps not all, such allusions.

Rarely, the student may decide that pinning down all the references is unnecessary.

> Vernon, the butcher Cumberland, Wolfe, Hawke,
> Prince Ferdinand, Granby, Burgoyne, Keppel, Howe,
> Evil and good, have had their tithe of talk.

Thus Lord Byron in Canto I, Stanza 2 of *Don Juan*. Wolfe and Burgoyne may be recognized as British generals, and Prince Ferdinand may be suspected to have a connection with Spain or some other Latin power. The reader can easily guess, however, that the names are of military and political figures, some admirable, some not.

Again, when Milton, in *Paradise Regained* (IV, 68–79), describes a geographical panorama laid out before Christ by Satan, the mere hurry of academic life may prevent the identification of all the localities (and therefore a full relishing of the grandeur depicted). Embassies are described coming to Rome

> on the Appian road,
> Or on the Aemilian, some from farthest south,
> Syene, and where the shadow both way falls,
> Meroe, Nilotic isle, and more to west
> The realm of Bocchus to the Blackmoor Sea;
> From the Asian kings and Parthian among these,
> From India and the golden Chersoness,
> And utmost Indian isle Taprobane,
> Dusk faces with white silken turbans wreathed;
> From Gallia, Gades, and the British West,
> Germans, and Scythians, and Sarmatians north
> Beyond Danubius to the Tauric pool.

Such a dense collocation of names offers special difficulty to both student and teacher. If adequate notes are not given, the student may be uncertain whether he is expected to look up all the items, and, if so, where he can find them. He is unlikely to think of looking in a dictionary of classical geography, and he probably is not sufficiently skilled in bibliography to discover the existence of such specialized reference works as Edward Le Comte's *A Milton Dictionary* or Robert Cawley's *Milton and the Literature of Travel.* The teacher, who is more likely to know where the place names can be located, may be so pressed by other duties—including incessant paper-grading—that he is unable to give the passage the detailed attention he knows it deserves.

In the present volume the problem has been minimized by the inclusion of copious notes. If the course is successful in its purpose, however, the student will not permanently limit his reading to this text. When he begins to read poetry on his own initiative, he may assume that the most exotic names *mean* as well as *sound* and that knowing what they mean is essential to full understanding and appreciation.

Exercises

Explain the allusions in the italicized passages below. As in the preceding discussion, "allusion" means ". . . an incidental mention of something, either directly or by implication." In the first exercise, the allusions are so indirectly implied as to constitute something like hints; in the second, the mention is explicit. Thereafter the allusions may be of either kind. Some can be identified by means of a dictionary; others must simply be guessed with the help of such general information or poetic sensitivity as the student may have. The range of possible allusions is so wide that no simple rule can be given for coping with them.

> (1) In yon deep bed of whisp'ring reeds
>   His *airy harp* shall now be laid,
> That he whose heart in sorrow bleeds
>   May love through life the soothing shade.
>
> Then maids and youths shall linger here;
>   And while its sounds at distance swell,
> Shall sadly seem in Pity's ear
>   To hear *the Woodland Pilgrim*'s knell.
>   (William Collins, "Ode on the Death
>   of Mr. Thomson," 5–12)
>
> (2)   Miss Danaë, when fair and young
>   (As *Horace* has divinely sung),

Could not be kept from Jove's embrace
By doors of steel and walls of brass.

(Matthew Prior, "An English
Padlock," 1–4)

(3) Keen as are the arrows
Of *that silver sphere,*
Whose intense lamp narrows
In the white dawn clear
Until we hardly see—we feel that it is there.

(Percy Bysshe Shelley, "To a Skylark," 63–67)

(4) *He* was the son of blackest *Acheron,*
Where many frozen souls do chatt'ring lie,
And ruled the burning waves of *Phlegethon,*
Where many more in flaming sulfur fry.

(Giles Fletcher, "Christ's Victory on Earth,"
stanza 22, 1–4)

(5) Where is *the land with milk and honey flowing,*
The promise of our God, our fancy's theme?
Here over shattered walls dank weeds are growing,
And blood and fire have run in mingled stream.

(John Keble, "First Sunday after Trinity," 1–4)

(6) Cupid and my Campaspe played
At cards for kisses; Cupid paid.
He stakes his quiver, bow, and arrows,
His mother's doves and team of sparrows,
Loses them too . . .

(John Lyly, from
Alexander and Campaspe, 1–5)

VI

IMAGES

In considering words, syntax, the prose paraphrase, and allusions, we have not differentiated poetry sharply from prose. We approach now the first of several poetic qualities which suggest the necessity of a specifically aesthetic training; for poetry, whatever else it may be, is also art.

By an "image" in poetry is meant, here and in much recent critical discussion (but not in all), "The representation in poetry of any sense experience." * In the present context, the word is not limited to such figurative turns of speech as metaphors and similes. If I say

---

* Cleanth Brooks and Robert Penn Warren, *Understanding Poetry* (New York: Holt, Rinehart & Winston, Inc., 1950), p. 687.

41

"The house is painted white," I have evoked, let us hope, an image of whiteness—if not on the retina, then in the parts of the brain which are stimulated by pictures on the retina. The image need not, of course, be visual. King Lear's speech about Cordelia, "Her voice was ever soft,/ Gentle, and low—an excellent thing in woman" (V, iii), contains an auditory image of sorts. So do such single words as "bang," "crash," "murmur," and "hiss," wherever used. Because hearing and sight are the principal means by which we observe objects and events at a proper aesthetic distance, the other senses are appealed to less frequently in poems. Nevertheless, touch, taste, smell, and the sense of movement are often stimulated. Gerard Manley Hopkins included a tactile image when he wrote at the beginning of a sonnet, "I wake and feel the fell ["the skin or hide of an animal; a pelt"] of dark, not day." Keats worked hard, although rather indirectly, on the sense of taste in a passage of "The Eve of St. Agnes" (265–67):

> Of candied apple, quince, and plum, and gourd;
> With jellies soother than the creamy curd,
> And lucent syrups, tinct with cinnamon.

Milton offered gentle stimulation to the sense of smell when he said that "off at sea northeast winds blow/ Sabean odors from the spicy shore/ Of Araby the Blest" (*Paradise Lost,* IV, 161–63). The cooperative reader of poetry responds gratefully to such hints by accepting every sensory stimulus offered him.

Not everyone has active sense organs, partly because formal education has always been predominantly conceptual. Only the rare student has had the good fortune to have his eyes and ears trained to acuteness—for example, by good instruction in painting and music. Neither are the opportunities afforded by literature for the sharpening of perceptions always capitalized on by teachers. In consequence, students often expose their sensory dullness by writing sentences like the following in their papers: "The candidate for mayor ran on a wide-open platform," or "Henry Adams was unable to digest all this new information that was suddenly thrown into his lap." The first of these sentences should evoke the image of a startled orator disappearing through a trapdoor, and the second should produce, after an astonished pause, a half-incredulous guffaw. Yet both are taken from actual student compositions. Born writers are usually incapable of such enormities. James Thurber has confessed a childhood habit of visualizing even such dead metaphors as "Your aunt is upstairs crying her heart out" and "He left town under a cloud." Not everyone is capable of developing his senses to the point where he will wince instinctively if he hears someone speak about "a liberal stance" or say "The decision triggered a snowballing chain of events." All of us, however, can improve our responses to literary images by practice.

The problem is in knowing exactly what and how much to sense. The following stanza from Tennyson's "Mariana" (1–8) is richly visual and should evoke a whole series of vivid pictures:

> With blackest moss the flower-pots
> Were thickly crusted, one and all,
> The rusted nails fell from the knots
> That held the pear to the gable-wall.
> The broken sheds looked sad and strange;
> Unlifted was the clinking latch;
> Weeded and worn the ancient thatch
> Upon the lonely moated grange.

The flower beds, nails, knots, pear tree, sheds, latch, and grange should be entertained not merely as ideas but also as objects. Together they indicate, through sensation rather than through thought, that the property is uncared for and falling into ruin.

Not all imagery is meant to be sensed so graphically or carries rewards for readers who visualize it sharply. Tact demands that a stanza by Richard Crashaw on St. Mary Magdalene ("The Weeper," 19–22) should be registered mainly as idea:

> Upwards thou dost weep.
> Heaven's bosom drinks the gentle stream.
> Where the milky rivers creep
> Thine floats above, and is the cream.

In praising the repentant tears shed by St. Mary, the poet says that they mount to heaven and float above the Milky Way. Such a figure of speech (sometimes called a "conceit") requires special treatment, but it may—as here—occasionally be criticized as denying the very image it appears to intend. The statement that "Heaven's bosom drinks the gentle stream" calls upon the reader not only to see the sky (or the heaven inhabited by God and the angels) as a maternal bosom but also to imagine it as absorbing, instead of emitting, streams of milk which ascend vertically. If the passage is admired, emphasis must be put upon its wit.

Other imagery falls between these two extremes. In the following passage by Walt Whitman ("Song of Myself," 48–50), the visual imagery is chiefly of colors:

> This grass is very dark to be from the white heads of
> old mothers,
> Darker than the colorless beards of old men,
> Dark to come from under the faint red roofs of mouths.

The green of the grass is sensed as dark in comparison with white hair, indeterminate beards, and the pink of a hard palate. The visualizing should probably go no farther. In the absence of additional details, the old mothers should not be endowed arbitrarily by the reader with complete bodies, starched aprons, wrinkled hands, and tender smiles; and the colorless beards and faint red roofs of mouths should be kept in such shallow focus that no image is created of their possessors. If the poet had wanted us to see more, he would have told us more.

Sometimes a choice must be made between possible sensory responses. "Hyacinth," in a line by Edgar Allan Poe ("To Helen," 7), disconcerts if it is allowed to suggest color: "Thy hyacinth hair, thy classic face." To be sure, a rather unusual hyacinth is reddish-orange, and Helen of Troy is traditionally supposed to have had blond hair. The typical hyacinth, however, was purple in antiquity and is purple now. The Greek word *hyakinthos* originally meant a blue stone, and the flower said to have sprung from the blood of the mythical Hyacinthus is described as very dark. Poe may have been thinking primarily of shape. The modern hyacinth strikingly resembles tightly curled hair, and the description of Odysseus' hair as hyacinthine in the *Odyssey* (xxiii, 158) is thought by scholars to refer to shape rather than to color.

Often objects, postures, and the like are mentioned so fleetingly that the image should remain vague. John Dryden, in "Roundelay" (1–4), writes of a lover found in dejection by his sweetheart:

> Chloe found Amyntas lying
> All in tears, upon the plain;
> Sighing to himself, and crying,
> "Wretched I, to love in vain!"

A perceptive reader understands easily that Amyntas is "lying" somewhere as he sighs and weeps. No specific posture should be imagined, however, since a dejected man can lie in a variety of positions; and the "plain," about which nothing more is said, can properly imply nothing more than horizontality. In Milton's *Samson Agonistes* (118–19), the manner in which a man lies is so clearly specified that we know an image was intended: "See how he lies at random, carelessly diffused,/ With languished head unpropped . . ." The limbs are relaxed (*diffused*, "poured out"), the attitude is one of resigned abandon, the head has sunk back. In general, poets can be relied on to provide the key to a correct reading. For the reader's imagination to outrun the provided data is usually a mistake.

What has been said may provoke objection on the ground that the aesthetic experience is richer when the poetic materials are voluntarily amplified. In "The Hollow Men" (5–10), T. S. Eliot describes the members of his own generation as lacking vital energy:

> Our dried voices, when
> We whisper together
> Are quiet and meaningless
> As wind in dry grass
> Or rats' feet over broken glass
> In our dry cellar.

When asked about the image in the last two lines of this excerpt, a typical student of poetry may say, "It makes me think of pain." If the instructor observes that the poet says nothing about pain, the reply may be that the rats must have cut their feet. This assumption, however, is unsupported by any textual evidence and may be an inaccurate prediction of what would actually happen in the circumstances. Forced back upon a different line of defense, the student may argue that the impressions aroused in him by poetry are inestimably precious. Is he not to have the enjoyment accessible by allowing his fancy to conjure up images not explicitly demanded by the text?

The problem is too complex to be fully resolved in a short discussion. At the moment, it can be said merely that the kind of reading for which the student has argued stimulates him rather to recall items of his own past experience than to have new experiences under the guidance of someone who may have sensed life more profoundly and differently. If, whenever I hear the word "farm," I am reminded of a particular farm which I knew as a child, I am forever prevented from enriching my image of farms. In the long run greater enjoyment, and also greater psychic enrichment, comes from a willingness to let poets do what they wish with my consciousness. The possibility of standing back from the poem to observe it critically once it has been sympathetically apprehended preserves us from any actual risk.

A final example may be developed in somewhat greater detail. The following passage is part of a speech made by the King in Shakespeare's *King Henry the Fourth, Part One* (I, i). It will be considered here not as drama but as poetry.

> Forthwith a power of English shall we levy,
> Whose arms were molded in their mother's womb
> To chase these pagans in those holy fields
> Over whose acres walked those blessèd feet
> Which fourteen hundred years ago were nailed
> For our advantage on the bitter cross.

The gist of the speech is that the King intends to lead a crusade of Englishmen to recapture the Holy Land from the infidels. Let us focus our attention on "feet" and observe what happens to them in the excerpt.

The feet appear first in connection with "holy fields" and "acres," over which we are told they "walked." In some contexts, the word "feet" is rather concept than object. If I say "He is old enough to stand on his own feet," nothing is gained by seeing the feet standing at the lower extremity of legs. Shakespeare, however, does something with the feet and therefore clearly intends that we watch them.

What we should sense is both picture and movement. The acres provide background, the walking provides movement, the feet are the objects in motion against the background. "Walked" is usually a colorless verb; here, by contrast with the immediately preceding "chase," it has special significance. The owner of the feet, Christ, moves in a way which suggests tranquillity, stateliness, confidence. Motor imagery contributes in an important way to the effectiveness of the description. Visual imagery, too, is present. The acres should be sensed chiefly as flatness, because no indication is given of color or texture. We cannot know whether the soil has recently been plowed, is covered with young grain, or is too sandy or rocky for cultivation. As for the feet, the motion is perhaps more meaningful than the appearance. At third or fourth reading, we may elect to picture them as sandaled, but more than this—together, possibly, with the hem of a flowing robe—is not only unmotivated but harmful. To visualize the whole body of Christ in accordance with some preconceived notion of His appearance would impose our Christ upon the poet's. In the final two lines of the excerpt, we see the feet being nailed to the upright of a wooden cross. Here they may certainly be pictured as bare; and the reaction should include the ghost of a shudder, a kind of slight involuntary shrinking, as the nails are felt to pierce the flesh.

So much, but no more, the poet has called for. Having responded in some such way as has been described, we may then experience a distinctively aesthetic thrill as we recognize how very skillfully the poet has used the feet to provide a transition from the notion of a war (English soldiers chasing pagans across *battle*fields) to the justification of the war (a desire to reclaim for Christian Europe the *holy* fields in which Christ preached and suffered.

The development of an ability to make accurate responses to the sensory content of poetry—to sense all that the poem requires, but no more—is of extreme importance to effective reading and needed to be dwelt on because it is so often slighted. Unfortunately, many people seem to be permanently insensitive to some kinds of imagery. One person may be unable to see much as he reads, another unable to hear much. (Auditory imagery, which often receives greater attention than visual imagery in class discussions, will be considered at length in Chapter XIII.) Both persons may read with admirable acuteness within the range of their special capabilities and yet remain unconscious of important values.

Ideally, of course, every reader should be responsive to every meaning actually in the poetry, whether sensory or conceptual. In practice, students will do all that can fairly be expected of them if they try honestly to work up to the limits of their native abilities. For those who can learn to sense poetry accurately as well as to conceptualize it accurately, the rewards are great.

Exercises

1. Describe in detail the vase which is the subject of Keats' "Ode on a Grecian Urn" (p. 324).

2. To what extent can Death be visualized in the excerpt (p. 357) from

Whitman's "When Lilacs Last in the Dooryard Bloomed"? Be careful not to incorporate into the image any details not expressed or clearly implied by the poem.

3. Describe in your own words, and in a more coherent order, the setting and events of Stevens' "The Emperor of Ice-Cream" (p. 388).

4. Do the towers, brass, ocean, shore, and state mentioned in Shakespeare's "Sonnet LXIV" (p. 163) exist in the poems as images or only as concepts? What, if anything, should the reader sense as he reads the poem?

VII

FIGURATIVE
LANGUAGE

The language of poetry is seldom literally exact. Unlike the language of expository prose, it may seem trivial or even nonsensical when interpreted to mean exactly what it asserts. The reader of poetry must therefore develop a special alertness to catch what is meant but not stated; he must also train himself to tolerate, and gradually to enjoy, conceptions and images which appear to violate ordinary logic. Some of these peculiarities derive from a tendency of poetic language to be *figurative*—to represent or express by means of objects or ideas which have an *analogical* equivalence to the intended meanings.

One illustration of how analogical language works is provided by William Butler Yeats' "The Rose Tree":

49

"O words are lightly spoken,"
Said Pearse to Connolly,
"Maybe a breath of politic words
Has withered our Rose Tree;
Or maybe but a wind that blows
Across the bitter sea."

"It needs to be but watered,"
James Connolly replied,
"To make the green come out again
And spread on every side,
And shake the blossom from the bud
To be the garden's pride."

"But where can we draw water,"
Said Pearse to Connolly,
"When all the wells are parched away?
O plain as plain can be
There's nothing but our own red blood
Can make a right Rose Tree."

If read as meaning no more than it says, this little lyric is worse than trivial. How could "a breath of politic words" wither a rose tree? Who can believe that two men—gardeners, presumably—would be willing, because water is not at hand, to restore a tree to health by feeding it with their blood?

Few students will fail to perceive that the rose tree "stands for" something besides itself, but not all will interpret the poem satisfactorily. Some may hope it will be interpreted for them in class; others will undertake what they think of as research—that is, they will look up the poet in a reference book, find essays written about him, and perhaps hunt for an annotated edition of his works. There are, of course, times when research is necessary; and a willingness to undertake it is creditable. In this poem, however, enough hints are present in the stanzas themselves to put the basic meaning beyond reasonable doubt. If the student wishes, he can corroborate the interpretation later by doing outside reading.

Two men named Pearse and Connolly are speaking about a withered rose tree. The "politic words" mentioned by Pearse should engage attention first. In what sense might it be true that such words can wither a tree? For "politic," the desk dictionary has "1. characterized by policy; sagacious or prudent. 2. shrewd; artful. 3. in keeping with policy; expedient, or judicious. 4. political (now chiefly in *body politic,* which see)." None of the first three senses quite fits, at least if accepted in isolation. The synonyms *sagacious, prudent, shrewd, artful, expedient,* and *judicious* have complimentary senses, whereas the meaning needed here is evidently pejorative (depreciative, disparaging). Trying the remaining definition, we perceive that politic words might be words about the body politic—political discussion, which, perhaps, has been timidly sagacious or an inappropriate substitute for something else.

Accepting this reading tentatively, we proceed to the next difficult phrase, "a wind that blows/ Across the bitter sea." In a political context, the expression might have to do with political influence across a body of water. The notion now strikes us that the conversation may have to do with a political struggle involving two nations or states. One, evidently the stronger, has in some way oppressed or mistreated the other. Because oppression implies rather close political relations, we hypothesize that Pearse and Connolly are citizens of a colony which is dissatisfied with the treatment accorded it by an overseas government. This hypothesis is now to be checked by observing whether it accommodates the poetic data in the two remaining stanzas.

The second stanza asserts that the rose tree is not dead but will revive if given water; that, indeed, it will become "the garden's pride," a peerless tree among trees. Continuing the political reading, we understand this to mean that the oppressed country, if given a chance, will flourish wonderfully. In the third and final stanza, we are told that no water is available and the tree must be nourished with blood—"our" blood, the blood of Pearse and Connolly and also, perhaps, their fellow citizens. Evidently the poet is recommending armed revolution. Fruitless political discussion with the mother country must be replaced by decisive action.

Everything now falls satisfactorily together, and we feel a reasonable confidence that the interpretation is at least possible. Checking through the poem once more, we are struck in a new way by the adjective "green" in the second stanza, possibly because the names Pearse and Connolly have already been subconsciously recognized as Irish. Ireland is the Emerald Isle; people of Irish ancestry celebrate St. Patrick's day by including something green in their dress; and we remember a song called "The Wearin' o' the Green," which also had something to do with oppression.

With this observation our reading is virtually complete. If we wish to check it, we can learn from the dictionary that Yeats (1865–1939) was an "Irish poet . . ."; and an annotated anthology which contains the poem or a history book of the relevant sort will reveal that Patrick Pearse and James Connolly were leaders of the Easter Rising of 1916. The poem implies that they lost their lives in the insurrection; the history book will tell us that they were captured and executed. Clearly in "The Rose Tree" Yeats has at once celebrated their memory and encouraged survivors to continue the struggle for freedom.

The student may feel that the example has been unfair, and that he ought not to be expected to interpret such a poem without help. He is partly right. Normally a text edition of the poem will at least identify the two speakers, and it may also contain a note on the uprising. After the passage of time, a literary work which was immediately clear to its original audience may become somewhat obscure, like a letter reread after the passage of years. Nevertheless, the example was chosen deliberately to suggest that students often stop short of reading as well as they could. Typically, they give up much too easily when an assigned poem is highly figurative, just as they give up when it contains unfamiliar words and allusions or the syntactical pattern is difficult.

Hardly any poem is devoid of figurative meanings, and many poems rely heavily on them. Here is a seventeenth-century example, a sonnet by George Herbert called "Redemption":

> Having been tenant long to a rich Lord,
>   Not thriving, I resolvèd to be bold
>   And make a suit unto him, to afford
> A new small-rented lease, and cancel th' old.
> In Heaven at his manor I him sought;
>   They told me there, that he was lately gone
>   About some land which he had dearly bought
> Long since on Earth, to take possessïon.
> I straight returned, and, knowing his great birth,
>   Sought him accordingly in great resorts:
>   In cities, theaters, gardens, parks, and courts.
> At length I heard a ragged noise and mirth
>   Of thieves and murderers; there I him espied,
>   Who straight, "Your suit is granted," said, and died.

The student should require no help to perceive that the rich lord is God, that the old lease represents an unsatisfactory relationship between the speaker and God, that the land which has been dearly bought is the earth, that the thieves and murderers have gathered to see Christ crucified, and that the granting of the petitioner's suit is the beginning of a new life under the dispensation initiated by Christ's redemption of mankind. The whole poem is an extended metaphor. To fail to catch the meaning (or *tenor*) of a metaphor as well as to sense the *vehicle* is to read on a superficial and unsatisfying level.

As must already have been apparent, the use of figures often reaches down into the poetic minutiae, but it is not necessary that every poem be read as a single elaborately developed analogy. Most poems should not. The usual tendency is for figurative language to be used in the details, and that is where most discussions assume it is located.

When William Blake writes "the stars threw down their spears" ("The Tiger," 17), we recognize "spears" as a *metaphor* of "rays." When Andrew Marvell exclaims, "Fair Quiet, have I found thee here,/ And Innocence, thy sister dear?" ("The Garden," 9–10), we know that the sisters are *personifications*. Robinson Jeffers *animizes* something not endowed with consciousness when he speaks of the sea's voice as fainting and ceasing ("All the Little Hoofprints," 1), or Ben Jonson when he says, "Tonight, grave sir, both my poor house and I/ Do equally desire your company" ("Inviting a Friend to Supper," 1–2). Robert Burns uses a *simile* in the phrase "Your locks were like the raven" ("John Anderson, My Jo," 3). "Tenderest," in William Mason's "thy pain/ The pitying Muse can well relate:/ Ah, let her, plaintive, pour the tenderest strain!" ("Ode to a Water Nymph," 16–18), is a *transferred epithet* because it attributes to the song a tenderness felt by the Muse—herself a personification. In *metonymy* something is alluded to by the name of something associated with it, as in a phrase of Shakespeare's quoted in the preceding chapter: "a power of English shall we levy." "Power" stands here for the army which will possess the power. *Synecdoche* is the naming of something by one of its parts, as when we call a farm laborer a "hand" or refer to a body of soldiers as "twenty rifles." Tennyson uses the figure when he calls a neighborhood girl a "daughter of our meadows" (*The Brook,* 69), where "meadows" stands for "part of the country." And there are many other figures of thought, as these are sometimes called to distinguish them from figures of speech, or *rhetorical* figures. (The latter have to do with the way an expression is turned syntactically: for example, *antithesis, chiasma, apostrophe, oxymoron,* which you can identify with help from your dictionary.) The essential thing, however, is that the beginning student of poetry recognize the obliquity of much poetic language and learn to feel at home with it. The memorizing of technical definitions can be left to more advanced courses.

What is surprising is that the obliquity causes no more trouble than it does. No one would be likely to read the following lines about Cupid (John Lyly, *Cupid and Campaspe,* 6–8) literally:

> The coral of his lip, the rose
> Growing on's cheek (but none knows how);
> With these, the crystal of his brow . . .

We understand without conscious thought that the lip is not made of real coral, that the rose is not an actual rose, that the forehead is not carved from a transparent mineral or finely cut glass. The reason is that figurative language is common in everyday speech as well as in poetry, although in poetry it tends to be more concentrated and to call more attention to itself. When we remark that Cecily wept *floods* of tears, or that Theodore is an *idiot,* or that Aunt Rhoda has a fine *nose* for scandal, we expect intended rather than expressed meanings to be recognized. Interpreted literally, much speech, as well as much poetry, is nonsense.

What marks the poetic use of figures is partly the greater attentiveness given to speech forms and partly a fondness for describing an analogy rather than the thing itself. When Emily Dickinson writes "It dropped so low in my regard/ I heard it hit the ground," she shows a poet's awareness of a metaphor hidden in a common expression. As for the tendency to analogize, a little poem called "Uphill" by Christina Rossetti marks rather accurately the dividing line between simplicity and mild difficulty:

> Does the road wind uphill all the way?
>   Yes, to the very end.
> Will the day's journey take the whole long day?
>   From morn to night, my friend.
>
> But is there for the night a resting-place?
>   A roof for when the slow dark hours begin.
> May not the darkness hide it from my face?
>   You cannot miss that inn.

Skilled readers will understand at once, and without any conscious weighing of alternative readings, that the journey is life, night is death, and the inn that cannot be missed is the grave. So much indirectness, however, everyone can become accustomed to.

What has been said in the present chapter does not contradict what was said earlier about not stretching meanings beyond the lexical and syntactical possibilities. No warrant has been given for wild or irresponsible readings. The student must learn early, however, that the appreciation of literal meanings is often only the beginning of interpretation.

Exercises

1. What words and phrases in the following brief excerpts are figurative? Remember that there is a figurative element in much ordinary speech —as when we mention the "leg" of a chair or speak of a "warm" color.

(a) Now twenty springs had clothed the Park with green,
Since Lydia knew the blossom of fifteen.
(John Gay, "The Toilette:
A Town Eclogue," 1–2)

(b) Tree-leaves labor up and down,
And through them the fainting light
Succumbs to the crawl of night.
(Thomas Hardy, "Nobody Comes," 1–3)

(c) For three years, out of key with his time,
He strove to resuscitate the dead art
Of poetry.
(Ezra Pound, *Ode pour L'Election
de son Sépulchre*, 1–3)

(d) Here I unclasp the book of my charged soul,
Where I have cast th' accounts of all my care;
Here have I summed my sighs, here I enroll
How they were spent for thee: look what they are.
(Samuel Daniel, *Delia*, "Sonnet I," 5–8)

2. Interpret the figurative structure of George Herbert's "Artillery" (p. 198). Specifically, what is meant by the title, and how is the basic metaphor worked out in detail?

VIII

SYMBOLS

By this time it will have become abundantly clear that in poetry objects often have some kind of representative value; they stand for something other than themselves. If the eye is intended to linger on them and to appreciate their sensory qualities, it is also meant to see through them to meanings which are not explicitly stated. This is to say that poetry tends to be rich in symbols, although by no means all figurative expressions are symbolic. A symbol is "1. something used or regarded as standing for or representing something else; a material object representing something immaterial; an emblem, token, or sign." Thus the Stars and Stripes are a symbol of the American union, and a seal bearing an open book and the word "Veritas" (Truth) is the symbol of a well-known university. (In literary usage, the dictionary definition is often somewhat extended.) Strictly, a *sign* differs from a *symbol* by having some kind of natural relationship to its meaning. Dark clouds are a sign that a storm may be coming; a particular kind of noise in an engine is a sign that one of the cylinders is not firing. A symbol, in contrast, does not so much precede or accompany the thing with which it is associated as have a metaphorical relation to it, as in medieval poetry a rose behind a garden wall often stands for an inaccessible sweetheart. In the present discussion, however, this technical distinction will not much concern us.

Many of the excerpts already quoted have contained symbols. In Yeats' "The Rose Tree," the tree is a symbol of Ireland. In Christina Rossetti's "Uphill," life is symbolized as a journey in which one must climb hills. In Kipling's "Recessional," Ninevah and Tyre are symbols of the ruin which may come upon a flourishing and powerful civilization. In Eliot's "The Hollow Men," and again in *The Waste Land,* rats scurrying over broken glass or creeping through vegetation symbolize cultural decay. The gradually disintegrating farm in Tennyson's "Mariana," however, is properly a *sign* of the spiritual desolation produced in the title character by her lover's infidelity.

The way symbols originate may be suggested, if not fully explained, by consideration of William Wordsworth's "Strange Fits of Passion I Have Known" (21–28). The poet has been riding through the moonlight toward the cottage of a girl named Lucy when the moon drops out of sight:

> My horse moved on; hoof after hoof
> He raised, and never stopped;
> When down behind the cottage roof,
> At once, the bright moon dropped.
>
> What fond and wayward thoughts will slide
> Into a lover's head!
> "O mercy!" to myself I cried,
> "If Lucy should be dead!"

The association of the symbol with its referent often results from structural similarity—as the rose behind the garden wall shares with a reluctant or prohibited sweetheart the situation of a desired object behind an obstacle. In Wordsworth's poem the basic point of contact is between the ideas of going down, setting, disappearing, and the idea of death; but more than this is involved. The moon is beautiful, as Lucy presumably is beautiful; the poet has fixed his eye on it, as he has centered his affection on Lucy; because it hung directly over the cottage toward which he was riding, he may have felt subconsciously that he was riding toward it as well as—or even, if an involuntary substitution was involved, instead of—riding toward the girl. In these circumstances the sinking of the moon almost (but not quite) "naturally" suggested the death of the girl. Yet the connection was by no means logical. The setting of the moon does not really cause human beings to die; indeed, the words "fond" (used here with at least a trace of its old meaning, "foolish") and "wayward" tell us that Lucy is still well. Wordsworth has caught in the poem an irrational but easily comprehended psychological movement of a kind avoided by most prose but often capitalized on by poetry.

Symbolism is most consistently present in *allegory* ("1. figurative treatment of one subject under the guise of another; a presentation of an abstract or spiritual meaning under concrete or material forms"). Edmund Spenser's *The Fairy Queen* is a classical example in English. In Book I, the Red Cross Knight (Holiness) sets out to kill a dragon (Sin) under the guidance of Una (Truth, or True Religion). On the way he meets an enchantress, Duessa (Deceit), who contrives to separate him temporarily from his guide; he is imprisoned by a giant named Orgoglio (the sin of Carnal Pride), has to recuperate in the House of Holiness, and finally, in the course of his fight with the dragon, is helped by the water of a magic well (Christian baptism) and the balm which oozes from a tree (Christ's blood, shed on the cross). And so on. In fact, in this work the allegorical meanings are multiple. Duessa represents not only deceit (doubleness) but also Roman Catholicism and Mary Queen of Scots, a dangerous rival of Queen Elizabeth's; and the other characters also have historical prototypes. Further, the symbolism extends both to the descriptive details and to the smaller events. The armor worn by the Knight is the armor of the Christian spoken of by St. Paul (Ephesians vi: 13–17), and the destruction of a forest hermitage by a lion represents the dissolution of the Catholic monasteries by King Henry VIII. Allegories were often written in the Middle Ages—Dante's *Divine Comedy* also has several layers of allegorical meaning—and John Bunyan's *The Pil-*

grim's Progress is a notable seventeenth-century example in English prose. As a result of nineteenth-century *realism,* allegory became unpopular for a time; but recently it has seemed to be coming back into vogue in the novel, which has replaced poetry as the major medium for long narratives. Allegorical symbols must of course be recognized if the central and basic meanings of such works are not to be missed.

In short poems the entire structure may be symbolic, as we found that of "The Rose Tree" to be. (*The Rose Tree* is not allegory, however, because in allegory a considerable part of the meaning is symbolized by actions.) In Matthew Arnold's "Philomela," a nightingale's song becomes a symbol of human suffering: "Eternal Passion! Eternal Pain!" In Percy Bysshe Shelley's well-known sonnet "Ozymandias," "two vast and trunkless legs of stone" which stand in a desert ironically contradict an inscription carved on the pedestal: "Look on my works, ye Mighty, and despair!" The ruin of the statue and the waste surrounding it thus symbolize the disappointment of prideful expectations of immortality. Samuel Taylor Coleridge's "The Rime of the Ancient Mariner" is in the borderland between symbolism and allegory, and perhaps for that reason has given rise to a variety of interpretations. Even clear symbols may confuse unpracticed readers; but the symbolic process is not ultimately mysterious, and everyone can develop at least an elementary competence in understanding it.

Elsewhere symbols may, and often do, appear in subsidiary parts of the poetic structure. In Eliot's "Journey of the Magi," "three trees on the low sky" (24) suggest the three crosses to be raised on Golgotha after the infant Jesus has reached manhood. At this point, however, the boundary between symbol and suggestion becomes vague. Gestures as well as objects may have symbolic value—for example, thumbing the nose, genuflecting—but what is one to say of a characteristic action? In Chaucer's "Summoner's Tale" (Fragment D, line 1775), the tendency of a begging friar to appropriate other people's property is indicated by his action upon entering a house: "And fro the bench he droof (drove) awey the cat." The action "stands for or represents" a trait of the friar's character; but is it therefore a symbol? Again, in "A Grammarian's Funeral" (129–32), Robert Browning celebrates the wholehearted devotion of a Renaissance scholar to his studies by saying that he puzzled out the meanings of three small Greek words. The accomplishment is perhaps best conceived of as illustrative rather than as symbolic. In contrast, John Donne's use of the phoenix, a fabulous bird, in The "Canonization" (23–24) is clearly symbolic:

> The phoenix riddle hath more wit
> By us; we two, being one, are it.

As the phoenix burns itself to death and rises newborn from its ashes, so the physical consummation of human love (often referred to in the seventeenth century, by a metonymy, as "dying") may give love new strength.

The limits of the term *symbol* are, however, of more concern to the professional critic than to the beginning student. For our purposes, it is enough to emphasize that events, objects, actions, and qualities often have a second (and sometimes a third and fourth) layer of meaning beyond the literal signification and that the reader must be constantly on the alert to discover the extended significance. It may be added still again, however, that the surface meaning too must be carefully attended to.

Exercises

1. In Hopkins' "Spring and Fall: To a Young Child" (p. 368), what does the falling of the leaves symbolize? What is the meaning of the last line, "It is Margaret you mourn for"? Is there a difference between the poet's understanding of the child's grief and her own? Do "Spring" and "Fall" in the title have symbolic values?

2. The "Emblem" of Francis Quarles (p. 201) interprets in detail symbolic values in the drawing which accompanies the poem. Prepare to discuss some of the more important meanings Quarles finds in the drawing.

IX

AMBIGUITY

AND

AMBIVALENCE

Since the publication of a book by the English critic William Empson called *Seven Types of Ambiguity*, persons deeply concerned with poetry have become more aware that words and phrases often permit alternate readings. Sometimes one reading accords best with the poem's total sense and therefore must be preferred. Again, more than one interpretation may fit, but the choice made between them affects the sense of the immediate context and perhaps of the whole poem. Occasionally the poet seems to have intended the phrase to be understood in two or more ways, so that different but meaningful interpretations must be entertained either simultaneously or successively. In the present discussion, doubtful readings will be called *ambiguous,* double readings *ambivalent,* three or more readings *multivalent.*

61

A fairly typical example of syntactical ambiguity is offered by Ben Jonson's familiar "Song: To Celia" (1–4):

> Drink to me, only, with thine eyes,
> And I will pledge with mine;
> Or leave a kiss but in the cup,
> And I'll not look for wine.

Does "only," which in early editions is set off with commas, belong with "Drink" ("Just drink to me"), with "to me" ("Drink to me only"—that is, to nobody else), or with "thine eyes" ("Drink to me merely with your eyes; you need not drink with your lips")? Nothing would be gained by trying to accept all three senses: "JUST drink ONLY TO ME, MERELY with your eyes." Moreover, Jonson was not, like certain contemporary poets of the "metaphysical" school, much given to an intentional complication of meanings. For these two reasons—though the first alone would be adequate—we test the possible readings one after another to see which does the poem the most good.

Reading the stanza aloud helps, for doing so suggests where the metrical stress falls. We try "DRINK to me only," "Drink to ME ONLY," and "Drink to me ONLY WITH thine eyes." Of these, the third is most strongly implied by the meter. Moreover, the sense of the third reading is clearly best. "Drink to me ONLY WITH THINE EYES,/And I will pledge with MINE": the poet's attention is focused on eyes, not on suspected rivals or on drinking; hence "only" fits best in the sense of "merely." Either of the other choices creates unnecessary difficulty; and the whole tone and movement of the poem are so simple that intricate readings are suspect.

In spite of its delusive transparency, the second stanza of the same poem contains a deeper ambiguity touching the relation not of syntactical elements but of two large structural units:

> I sent thee late a rosy wreath,
> Not so much honoring thee
> As giving it a hope that there
> It could not withered be.
> But thou thereon didst only breathe
> And sent'st it back to me;
> Since when it grows and smells, I swear,
> Not of itself, but thee.

Jonson appears now to be more interested in the wreath than in

Celia. Although she has rejected his gift, he feels satisfaction that its value has been enhanced by her breathing upon it. Yet his purpose in sending the wreath was clearly to further his suit. Does he mean that the wreath will now be an adequate substitute for her; that in spite of her scorn he has obtained, as it were, something from her which he can cherish; or that having achieved a limited success in this indirect way he will persevere in his courtship? *What* is said offers no difficulty, but we are puzzled as to why he said it and how the second stanza relates to the first. The first stanza implied a perfect understanding between lovers. The second accuses the lady of scorn, which, however, is shown to have the power of invigorating, of imparting vitality. The best interpretation is perhaps that as the lady's contempt failed to destroy the wreath, so it will not discourage the suitor. The suspicion remains, however, that this meaning is not so much in the poem as thought up by the reader to keep its halves from breaking apart.

Another passage which requires a choice between alternatives—this time in reading a single word—appears in Gerard Manley Hopkins' "The Windhover: To Christ Our Lord" (6–10). The poet has been watching the windhover (a kind of falcon) swooping and soaring high in the air and has been much impressed:

> My heart in hiding
> Stirred for a bird—the achieve of, the mastery of the thing!
> Brute beauty and valor and act, oh, air, pride, plume, here
> Buckle! AND the fire that breaks from thee then, a billion
> Times told lovelier, more dangerous, O my chevalier!

The word "Buckle!" has provoked a controversy which has not yet been resolved. Does it mean "join together" ("5. to fasten with a buckle or buckles") or "to yield" ("9. to bend, warp, or give way suddenly, as with heat or pressure")? In the one instance, the meaning is that the atmosphere, the bird's pride, and the skill of his feathered wings here come together in beautiful union or harmony. In the other, we are to understand that the atmosphere, the *poet's* pride, and the bird's wing, which bends under the pressure of air resistance, yield to the superiority of, give way before, the falcon's valorous spirit.

Such problems as these are more characteristic of poetry than of prose, because poetry tends to be especially packed with meaning and to lack careful explanatory transitions. Although not negligible, the importance of making a correct choice is less when the ambiguity appears somewhere other than at the work's center, as in the following passage from Alexander Pope's *An Essay on Man* (III, 27–30):

> Has God, thou fool! worked solely for thy good,
> Thy joy, thy pastime, thy attire, thy food?
> Who for thy table feeds the wanton fawn,
> For him as kindly spread the flowery lawn.

Does "kindly" have its usual modern sense, "kind-heartedly," "graciously," or does it preserve a common older meaning, "according to nature"? Has God spread the flowery lawn benevolently for the fawn to graze on, or has He done so because His plan for nature requires that provision be made for the fawn's food, as for man's? Readers who are unacquainted with the older meaning will of course take the first sense for granted, and no great harm will be done if they are mistaken. The opinions of scholars are likely to be divided. Possibly this is an instance of ambivalence rather than of ambiguity: God acts both benevolently and in accordance with a total plan for nature. The poem as a whole describes this very plan.

In a song from Shakespeare's *Cymbeline* (IV, ii), there can be no doubt that two levels of meaning must be appreciated simultaneously, or as nearly simultaneously as is possible.

> Fear no more the heat o' the sun,
> Nor the furious winter's rages;
> Thou thy worldly task hast done,
> Home art gone, and ta'en thy wages.
> Golden lads and girls all must,
> As chimney-sweepers, come to dust.

On the primary level, "worldly task" means "life in the world, with its duties to God and man"; "home" means "to Heaven or Hell"; and "ta'en thy wages" means "received reward or punishment." Recognition of the metaphor's tenor should not, however, lead to disregard of its vehicle. The image of a day-worker finishing his task, receiving his pay, and going home for the night does not fade from notice behind an awareness of the extended meaning.

In this sense, an element of ambivalence exists in every good metaphor. The literal and figurative senses are both apprehended, although one of the two usually dominates. In the last two lines of the quoted stanza, however, the ambivalence is visual as well as conceptual. "Golden lads and girls" are both *rich* and *blond* (or at least *clean*); "chimney-sweepers," besides being *dirty* as a result of their work, are to be thought of as poor and unfortunate. The phrase "come to dust" means both "get dirty by working in the chimneys" and "are buried" (or "die and decay"). None of the images can be ignored, for all are clearly present.

Ambivalences are often created by puns, which appear more frequently, even in serious poetry, than is always recognized. (The belief that a pun is the lowest form of wit does not much antedate the eighteenth century and gained currency only slowly.) In Robert Herrick's "Litany to the Holy Spirit" (13–16), there is perhaps a pun on "artless":

> When the artless doctor sees
> No one hope, but of his fees,
> And his skill runs on the lees:
> Sweet Spirit, comfort me!

The two possibly relevant meanings are "1. free from deceit, cunning, or craftiness . . ." and "3. lacking art, knowledge, or skill." The doctor may be both honest—that is, lacking in trickiness, not given to hiding his thoughts—and without art to effect a cure. In John Donne's "Hymn to God My God, in My Sickness" (9–10), "straits" undoubtedly means both "1. (*often pl. with sing. sense*) a narrow passage of water connecting two large bodies of water" and "2. (*often pl.*) a position of difficulty, distress, or need."

> This is my southwest discovery,
> *Per fretum febris,* by these straits to die.

Fretum is Latin for *straits; febris,* because it means both "fever" and "torment," itself contains a pun. Dying is a passage through both torment and fever. The southwest passage, moreover, is a route to the mercantile East, to earthly Utopias traditionally situated in the West, and to Paradise. The whole poem, indeed, is a network of elaborate puns and intricate metaphors; but Donne's seriousness is not in doubt. According to Donne's contemporary biographer, Izaak Walton, the "Hymn" was written during the poet's last illness and only eight days before his death.

With the last example we have already encountered *multivalence,* or a number of acceptable readings exceeding two. Rarely an especially complex passage may have as many as four meanings. Interpretations requiring the acceptance of more than four meanings may usually be regarded as suspect. The critic is more likely to be showing his cleverness than to be rendering meanings organically implicit within the passage.

On the whole, students will be well advised not to strain habitually for multiple interpretations. After Empson's book had had a rather delayed impact in the United States, some advanced students and a few professional critics developed a habit of combing through the largest dictionary available, the *Oxford English Dictionary*, in search of recondite meanings which could be made to fit. The result was sometimes the assigning of six or eight (or even ten or a dozen) quite improbable significations to expressions which syntactical signals or the gist of the whole poem revealed to have only one or two. The practice was encouraged by a belief, stimulated by a desire to make poetry seem important in an age of science, that poets were especially profound thinkers whose mental complexity enabled them to cram so much meaning into a short passage that less gifted people might be expected to spend several hours humbly consulting dictionaries in order to seize all that had been said. Normally, a sense of aesthetic wholeness, not a desire to demonstrate critical ingenuity, should guide the interpretation of difficult passages. Yet many poetic passages are undeniably, and brilliantly, ambivalent, some certainly, probably, or possibly multivalent, and many ambiguous. In interpreting such passages, the student should aim rather at making sense out of the poem than at demonstrating his own ingenuity. In the meaning of the term adopted here, an ambiguity is usually an aesthetic flaw, and double or triple readings are an aesthetic good only if they all fit not only the immediate passage but also the entire poem.

Exercises

The following poem by John Donne is especially rich in possible double meanings. Decide which of the alternative interpretations suggested in each footnote is to be preferred or whether both are acceptable.*

---

* Some of the words in the poem require explanation. "Chymic," in line 7, means "alchemist." "Elixir," in the same line, is "an alchemic preparation for transmuting base metals into gold, or for prolonging life." "Pot," in line 8, is either the alchemist's retort, used for distillation, or the vessel in which he cooks various ingredients together. "My man," in line 15, means "my manservant." The "spheres" mentioned in line 22 were the heavenly bodies, which, by revolving in their orbits, were thought to produce a divine music inaudible to sinful man.

LOVE'S ALCHEMY

Some that have deeper digged love's mine than I
Say,[1] where his centric happiness doth lie.
    I have loved, and got,[2] and told;
But should I love, get, tell,[3] till I were old
I should not find that hidden mystery.   5
      Oh, 'tis imposture all.
And as no chymic yet th' elixir got,
    But glorifies[4] his pregnant[5] pot
    If by the way to him befall
Some odoriferous thing, or medicinal,   10
    So lovers dream a rich and long delight,
    But get a winter-seeming[6] summer's night.

Our ease, our thrift,[7] our honor, and our day,
Shall we for this vain bubble's shadow pay?
    Ends love in this, that my man   15
Can be as happy as I can, if he can
Endure the short scorn[8] of a bridegroom's play?[9]
      That loving wretch that swears
'Tis not the bodies marry, but the minds,
    Which he in her angelic finds,   20
    Would swear as justly that he hears,
In that day's rude, hoarse minstrelsy, the spheres.
    Hope not for mind in women: at their best
Sweetness and wit, they are but mummy,[10] possessed.

---

1 "Some that . . ./ Say": (a) Some who . . . are able to explain; (b) Tell me, some of you who . . . ! 2 "got": (a) obtained; (b) begot children. 3 "tell": (a) report publicly; (b) count (as in bank *teller*). 4 "But glorifies": (a) but nevertheless praises; (b) without praising. 5 "pregnant": (a) round-bodied; (b) on the point of producing something. 6 "winter-seeming": (a) seeming long, like a winter night; (b) chilling, disagreeable. 7 "thrift": (a) thriving, worldly success; (b) economical management of funds. 8 "scorn": (a) contempt of the wedding guests; (b) disdainful treatment by the bride. 9 "play": (a) dramatic performance of a role; (b) amorous dalliance. 10 "mummy": (a) "medicinal preparation of the substance of mummies; hence, an unctuous liquid or gum used medicinally" (NED); (b) a lifeless and revolting body.

X

TONE

Just as a speech assigned to a fictive person in a play or novel not only conveys information but also tells us something about the speaker, so every poem implies an attitude toward its subject matter. If this is misunderstood, interpretation may err wildly.

The importance of correctly sensing *tone* ("14. a particular state or temper of the mind; spirit, character, or tenor") is not peculiar to literature. In ordinary conversation we are occasionally left wondering how a remark was intended. "What did she mean by saying I was an unusual dancer?" a young man may ask himself worriedly. That such perplexities do not arise more often is due partly to help offered by facial expression and in*ton*ation. The attitude implied by printed words must be interpreted without such assistance. In compensation, the words are more carefully chosen than in casual talk, and signals are usually included which the perceptive reader will notice.

Edwin Arlington Robinson's "Miniver Cheevy" offers a simple illustration. The subject is a twentieth-century man who wished he had lived during the Middle Ages:

> Miniver loved the days of old
> When swords were bright and steeds
> were prancing;
> The vision of a warrior bold
> Would set him dancing.

On the basis of this stanza only—the second, not the first—what literate person would think Miniver is to be presented as a hero? The rapid movement of the lines suggests fun rather than earnestness, and the image of the modern dreamer dancing when he conjures up the picture of a brave knight makes him appear slightly ridiculous. The yearning for a bygone era is mildly satirized; the mood of the poem cannot be nostalgic.

This guess is amply confirmed by other data in the poem. When we learn that Miniver "missed the mediaeval grace/ Of iron clothing," we realize without logical analysis that the imputation of grace to armor is absurd. And the last stanza is the opposite of respectful.

> Miniver Cheevy, born too late,
> Scratched his head and kept on thinking;
> Miniver coughed, and called it fate,
> And kept on drinking.

Heroes do not characteristically cough and scratch. These are "low" actions. Neither are they portrayed as alcoholics, however heartily they may drink toasts. Although Robinson may find a slight pathos in Miniver's predicament, he does not seriously praise the Middle Ages at the expense of modernity.

Some of the worst misinterpretations of tonality result from a failure to perceive irony. An ironic statement means something different from what it appears to mean; it undercuts, although it need not absolutely contradict, the literal sense. To miss the irony is thus to attribute to the poet an attitude he has implicitly denied. The following passage from John Dryden's *Absalom and Achitophel* (636–53) might conceivably be read as praise by an earnest student who lacked sensitivity. The subject is a historical personage disguised under the fictive name of Corah:

> What though his birth were base, yet comets rise
> From earthy vapors, ere they shine in skies.
> Prodigious actions may as well be done
> By weaver's issue, as by prince's son.
> This arch-attestor for the public good
> By that one deed ennobles all his blood . . . .
> Sunk were his eyes, his voice was harsh and loud,
> Sure signs he neither choleric was nor proud.
> His long chin proved his wit; his saintlike grace,
> A church vermilion and a Moses' face.
> His memory, miraculously great,
> Could plots exceeding man's belief repeat;
> Which therefore cannot be accounted lies,
> For human wit could never such devise.

The literal meaning of these lines is that Corah's humble birth is not to be held against him, that he was neither irascible nor proud, that he was witty, enjoyed God's grace, had a strong memory, and reported alarming plots against the state. None of this is necessarily discreditable; yet we understand clearly that Corah is an object of derision. How do we know?

We know because the tonality is again pervasively ironic. The likening of a man to a comet which has arisen from an earthy vapor does not impute unqualified praise. Although an attestor for the public good may be an authentic patriot, we are suspicious of an *arch*-attestor. The physical evidence of Corah's patience and humility consists of disagreeable eyes and an unpleasant voice. His possession of wit is an inference from an abnormally long chin. His saintlike grace is said to be "proved" by a red complexion and a resemblance to Moses; evidently his expression was somewhat fanatical. The comment about his memory suggests that he imagined sedition in remarks which only a neurotically fearful man would have bothered to remember.

When tonality is hard to sense, it may be helpful to ask oneself, "What poetic intention might have led to the producing of these lines?" The beginning of John Donne's "To the Countess of Bedford," in his *Letters to Several Personages,* may at first leave us uncertain whether the extravagant praise offered to the noble lady is intended seriously:

MADAM,

> Reason is our soul's left hand, Faith her right,
> By these we reach divinity, that's you;
> Their loves, who have the blessings of your light,
> Grew from their reason, mine from fair faith grew.
>
> But as, although a squint left-handedness
> Be ungracious, yet we cannot want that hand,
> So would I, not to increase, but to express
> My faith, as I believe, so understand.
>
> Therefore I study you first in your Saints,
> Those friends whom your election glorifies . . . .

Here the Countess is implicitly equated with Deity. Her glory is realized partly by rational thought, partly by faith that a lady in such an exalted station must be glorious. Persons in direct contact with her can prove her greatness by argument, whereas the poet, who implies that he does not know her intimately, must rely on trust. Her friends are spoken of as saints—persons blessed by her special favor, as God "elects" some human beings for salvation despite their faults.

All this is so hyperbolic, so extreme, that we may wonder whether Donne's intention was satirical. The answer is no: in the whole poem there is no flash of unmistakable rancor, no signal that the reader is expected to smile or curl his lip. Regretfully, we must conclude that an address which was intended to be complimentary has succeeded only in being fulsome.*

Rhetorical signals are of many kinds. In William Cowper's "The Sofa" (1–7), the style is comically inflated to indicate a playful intent.

> I sing the sofa. I, who lately sang
> Truth, Hope, and Charity, and touched with awe
> The solemn chords, and with a trembling hand,

---

* Some readers will dispute this conclusion. Antecedently, it is barely possible that Donne meant the poem as ironic exaggeration within a tradition of courtly compliment. Other evidence, however (including a large number of begging letters written by the poet to great persons), suggests that he hoped to win the Countess as a patron. Milton (almost certainly) and Jonson (probably, in view of his criticism of Donne's first "Anniversary") would have thought the comparison to God blasphemous.

> Escaped with pain from that advent'rous flight,
> Now seek repose upon an humbler theme.
> The theme though humble, yet august and proud
> Th' occasion—for the Fair commands the song.

The contrast of the sofa with Truth, Hope, and Charity, and of the "humbler theme" with one which demanded the trembling evocation of solemn chords indicates that the genre of this poem will be mock-epic. A sofa is not a proper "hero" for polysyllabic blank verse. Further, we can already detect specific parody. For centuries Virgil's *Aeneid* had been prefaced by lines which identified the author with the poet who had previously written pastorals ("I am he who formerly measured my song on a slender reed"), and Milton's *Paradise Regained* began, "I who erewhile the happy garden sung. . . ." The traditional movement was from pastoral to epic, from the less elevated poetic forms to the more elevated; Cowper reverses the order. The pretense that the request of a beautiful lady can dignify any subject is also playful. Although Cowper may have felt some modest pride that she asked him to write at all, her "command" hardly sufficed to make the occasion "august."

Oddly, perhaps, a satirical intention can often be recognized even when the object of satire is unidentified. "Art Review," by Kenneth Fearing, sounds ironic from the first lines:

> Recently displayed at the Times Square Station, a new
> Vandyke on the face-cream girl.
> (Artist unknown. Has promise, but lacks the brilliance
> shown by the great masters of the Elevated age.)
> The latest wood carving in a Whelan telephone booth,
> titled "O Mortal Fools WA 9–5090," shows two winged
> hearts above an ace of spades.
> (His meaning is not entirely clear, but this man will go far.)

Whether the poem makes fun of art criticism, or of modern art, or of people who deface signs and buildings may provoke a lively discussion, but the ironic tonality is unmistakable. Quite without rational analysis, we understand that the person who draws a beard on the face in an advertisement ought not to be discussed as a serious artist.

Not all problems of tonality involve irony. The following "Sonnet," by John Masefield, raises a quite different question:

Here in the self is all that man can know
Of Beauty, all the wonder, all the power,
All the unearthly color, all the glow,
Here in the self which withers like a flower;
Here in the self which fades as hours pass,
And droops and dies and rots and is forgotten,
Sooner, by ages, than the mirroring glass
In which it sees its glory still unrotten.
Here in the flesh, within the flesh, behind,
Swift in the blood and throbbing on the bone,
Beauty herself, the universal mind,
Eternal April wandering alone.
The god, the holy ghost, the atoning lord,
Here in the flesh, the never yet explored.

The sonnet quite clearly decries conventional theology and philosophy. God the Father, the Holy Ghost, and the Redeeming Christ exist "here in the flesh" and nowhere else; so too do Beauty and universal mind. But how is this meant? Is the poem basically an attack on traditional ideas, or is it basically an assertion of the sacredness of individuality and the human body? Is the poet more interested in destroying an old religion or in recommending a new one? Because no other means of answering the query are available, the decision must depend on a sensing of tone. Although the matter is debatable, the student may decide that the negative energy is stronger than the positive—that the poem is more energetically angry than enthusiastic. Or he may decide the contrary.

Problems of tonality have to do with a wide variety of possible moods. Anger, tenderness, impatience, dread, anticipation, contempt, hope, and a hundred other feelings may be an important part of the semantic burden. *How* the tonalities can be sensitively apprehended is hard to say, because the part of the mind which registers them is not the discursive reason. The reason is useful chiefly in explaining what has already been perceived, as it has been used in the present chapter. Yet the significance of tonality is not on that account dubious.

Exercises

1. Name the mood implied by the opening lines of Marvell's "To His Coy Mistress":

Had we but world enough, and time,
This coyness, Lady, were no crime.
We would sit down, and think which way
To walk, and pass our long love's day.
Thou by the Indian Ganges' side
Should'st rubies find; I by the tide
Of Humber would complain. I would
Love you ten years before the Flood;
And you should, if you please, refuse
Till the conversion of the Jews.

2. Thomas Bailey Aldrich's "Accomplices" is tonally ambiguous. Study the sonnet carefully and then try to decide whether the dominant mood is indignation or relief.

The soft new grass is creeping o'er the graves
　By the Potomac; and the crisp ground-flower
　Lifts its blue cup to catch the passing shower;
The pine-cone ripens, and the long moss waves
Its tangled gonfalons above our braves.
　Hark, what a burst of music from yon bower!
　The Southern nightingale that hour by hour
In its melodious summer madness raves.
Ah, with what delicate touches of her hand,
　With what sweet voices, Nature seeks to screen
The awful Crime of this distracted land—
　Sets her birds singing, while she spreads her green
Mantle of velvet where the murdered lie,
As if to hide the horror from God's eye.

The title, "Accomplices," suggests something bad, as do also the "raving" of the nightingale and the phrase "Nature seeks to screen/ The awful Crime." The tone of the first seven lines, however, and of such phrases as "delicate touches" and "sweet voices" in the latter half, implies pleasure. Which mood predominates?

3. Shakespeare's "Sonnet CXXX," on p. 167, is obviously satirical—but of what? Do not arrive hastily at an answer.

XI

THE IMPLIED SPEAKER

A second, and sometimes more convenient, way of focusing the attitudes embodied in poems is to consider the kind of person who might appropriately speak the lines. The beginning student tends to assume that the speaker is necessarily identical with the poet. If the poem sounds angry, the poet must have been angry when he wrote it. If it breathes tender love, the poet must have been thinking of a specific woman. If this were not so, the poem would be "insincere." This belief is so widespread that it deserves to be examined; and no better approach can be made than by attempting to differentiate the historical person whose name is attached to the poem as author from the fictive person—often called the *persona*—whose character and emotions can be glimpsed behind it.

75

First, however, it must be said emphatically that during most periods of history the poet has been assumed to be artist rather than autobiographer. The old English term for "poet" was "maker," and the Greek word *poiētēs* meant exactly the same thing. It was no more incumbent upon the poet to feel the emotions embodied in his work than it was for a sculptor to suffer pain while carving a statue of Laocoön being strangled by snakes. He worked within traditions, writing pastorals, epics, lyrics, or didactic poems in the forms and moods appropriate to those genres. When he composed sonnets, convention usually inspired him to become a lover; as a Juvenalian satirist he was so moved by indignation that he was unable to keep his meters smooth; as a writer of Pindaric odes he felt a divine afflatus from the Muse. Although at times he may have chosen a convention because it suited his mood, it is unwise to deny that his feelings may have been partly worked up for the occasion, as a Method actor tries to project himself into a role he is to play. He did not profess sincerity, in the student's sense of that much-abused word, and he did not expect to be read as an autobiographer.

Of course it would be silly to pretend that a poem never reflects traits of its author's character. After the Romantic Movement, which began in the late eighteenth century, expression sometimes became *self*-expression, so that the gap narrowed between what the poems said and what their writers "really" thought and felt. When Matthew Arnold, in a sonnet called "To a Friend," answered a question about what he had been reading, presumably he told the truth, or part of it. One need not assert that poems are wholly unlike their authors in order to warn students against assuming that every poem is a personal confession. Even the pre-Romantic Ben Jonson no doubt hoped that the friend he invited to supper (p. 186) would eat with him. Yet the pedagogical emphasis must fall on the discontinuity between life and art rather than upon the continuity, because it is here that the beginning reader is most likely to make mistakes. Although Arnold said that he had been reading Homer, Epictetus, and Sophocles, we ought not to imagine that he read nothing else; and persons who believe that Donne had all the amatory adventures implied by his poetry are aesthetically naïve. All the world, said Shakespeare, is a stage, and one man in his time plays many parts. The statement is pre-eminently true of writers, who would feel themselves intolerably limited if in their works they could present only what had actually happened to them or what they had really thought and felt before they sat down to compose. Like the novelist who has recently taken over a part of the subject matter which formerly belonged to poetry, the poet makes no necessary commitment to historical fact.

An excerpt from Pope will illustrate the technique of inferring the character of an implied speaker. The following passage is from *Moral Essays* ("Timon's Villa," 29–42).

> My Lord advances with majestic mien,
> Smit with the mighty pleasure to be seen.
> But soft—by regular approach—not yet.
> First through the length of yon hot terrace sweat;
> And when up ten steep slopes you've dragged your thighs,
> Just at his study door he'll bless your eyes.
> His study! with what authors is it stored?
> In books, not authors, curious is my Lord.
> To all their dated backs he turns you round;
> These Aldus printed, those Du Sueil has bound.
> Lo, some are vellum—and the rest as good,
> For all his Lordship knows; but they are wood.
> For Locke or Milton 'tis in vain to look;
> These shelves admit not any modern book.

The speaker (or, if one prefers, the fictive writer) of these lines thinks of himself, perhaps with justice, as a man of taste. He deplores presumption, vanity, ostentation. He has opinions about landscape architecture: terraces ought to offer protective shade, and the approach even to grand houses should be easy. He is perhaps not in very good training, since he objects to climbing several flights of steps. Although he values the Latin and Greek classics, he finds merit in modern authors as well. In his own view he is well educated, but without pedantry. No doubt his affection for good literature is sincere, for he is not much impressed by expensive bindings or fine print, and he feels scorn for book collectors who do not read. Besides all this, he is thoroughly well bred. His criticism is suave, urbane, controlled. He does not lose his temper, does not scream or shout. In company, he would probably express disapproval rather by ironic indirections than by forthright attack. We like him, and from the beginning we are inclined to accept his judgments.

How much of this might also be said of Alexander Pope? A

good deal, perhaps, but not all. Pope had his own vanity, if not quite the vanity of Timon. He was not only out of training, but was also a cripple, and he could not stand without being laced up in a corset; this physical disability is concealed in the passage. Although he may have read John Locke and certainly knew Locke's reputation, he was a less competent judge of philosophy than of Milton. His skill in the learned languages had been affected by his disbarment from the universities because he was a Catholic. No matter. What is aesthetically important is not the author but the persona. When our attention passes through the poetry to rest on the author, our interest is primarily biographical and only secondarily and derivatively literary.

The example will suggest that distinguishing between poets and their personae safeguards readers against committing the biographical fallacy. To assert of the poet whatever can be said of his fictive speakers, or to say of the speakers only what can truthfully be said of the poet, indicates a basic disorientation with art. The spheres of the poet's life and of his separate works overlap, but they seldom coincide perfectly.

The lack of congruence is especially striking when the poet presents attitudes of which he disapproves. In Browning's "The Bishop Orders His Tomb at St. Praxed's Church," a sixteenth-century Roman bishop speaks from his deathbed to his sons, whom for the sake of decorum he calls nephews. The monologue begins as follows:

> Vanity, saith the preacher, vanity!
> Draw round my bed: is Anselm keeping back?
> Nephews—sons mine . . . ah, God, I know not! Well—
> She, men would have to be your mother once,
> Old Gandolf envied me, so fair she was!
> What's done is done, and she is dead beside,
> Dead long ago, and I am Bishop since.
> And as she died, so must we die ourselves,
> And thence ye may perceive the world's a dream.
> Life, how and what is it? As here I lie
> In this state-chamber, dying by degrees,
> Hours and long hours in the dead night, I ask,
> "Do I live, am I dead?" Peace, peace seems all.
> St. Praxed's ever was the church for peace;
> And so, about this tomb of mine. I fought
> With tooth and nail to save my niche, ye know:

—Old Gandolf cozened me, despite my care;
Shrewd was that snatch from out the corner south
He graced his carrion with, God curse the same!

The speaker here quotes Ecclesiastes ("the preacher"); he asserts that life on earth is dreamlike in comparison with life in eternity; he has named one of his sons after Saint Anselm of Canterbury, who invented the ontological proof of God's existence; he praises peace; and his spiritual authority over a Roman Catholic diocese implies a strong piety. Yet in fact he is morally despicable. Because he was bound by an oath of celibacy, he ought not to have had sons. (That he begot them after becoming a priest is made clear by his pretense that they are nephews.) He won his mistress over the competition of the preceding bishop, Gandolf, whom he has evidently hated. Gandolf's acquisition of a choice spot within the church for a tomb he thinks to have been inspired by personal animosity; and his unwillingness to practice Christian forgiveness even as he himself approaches death is shown by the invoking of a curse on his rival's "carrion." After Gandolf's death, he has fought "tooth and nail" with other enemies—perhaps unscrupulously, and certainly with unbecoming selfishness—to obtain for his own tomb the best spot yet unoccupied within the church. As the monologue proceeds, we learn that he is a thief. Browning was fascinated, evidently, by the image of a worldly bishop of the Renaissance period who in a speech from his deathbed would reveal how little he was a true vicar of Christ. By attempting to characterize the speaker, we are helped to arrive at the core of the poem's meaning.

In the foregoing example the distance between poet and persona is maximal. The two are separated not only by vast differences of character but also by three centuries of time. In the following little poem by George Barker the difference is much less:

TO MY MOTHER

Most near, most dear, most loved and most far,
Under the window where I often found her
Sitting as huge as Asia, seismic with laughter,
Gin and chicken helpless in her Irish hand,
Irresistible as Rabelais, but most tender for
The lame dogs and hurt birds that surround her—
She is a procession no one can follow after
But be like a little dog following a brass band.

She will not glance up at the bomber, or condescend
To drop her gin and scuttle to a cellar,
But lean on the mahogany table like a mountain
Whom only faith can move, and so I send
O all my faith, and all my love to tell her
That she will move from mourning into morning.

The implied speaker of these lines reveals a good deal about himself while writing about his mother. He is capable of real affection and perhaps of deep love. Not every son would admire the mother he pictures. Although she sits "as huge as Asia" and shakes the earth with her laughter, he is not annoyed by her corpulency. Instead he takes it as a symbol of moral firmness. Neither does he criticize her fondness for gin or her hearty appetite, but rather notices power in the hands which hold tumbler and chicken leg. He finds her merriment as irresistible as the humor of the gusty French satirist Rabelais and contrasts her ponderous vitality with the tenderness she shows to helpless animals. Without envy, he feels himself inferior: "She is a procession no one can follow after/ But be like a little dog following a brass band." In the second section, he celebrates her (imagined?) imperturbability during a bombing raid: she scorns to take shelter and sits at the table with the lumpy immovability of a mountain. She inspires him not only with love but also with hope. While such women live, England will not succumb to Nazi savagery: "She will move from mourning into morning." In a word, he is the kind of man in whom the contemplation of such a mother produces such responses—this kind, and no other.

Is George Barker that man? Possibly—but, again, possibly not. I have chosen this last example because I know of the poet only what I can infer from the poem, and that is virtually nothing. I find the implied speaker very attractive. He is intelligent, perceptive, empathetic, articulate, and, like his mother, courageous. About the poet himself, I know only that he was capable of presenting this mother (whether his own I cannot tell) and this son (whether himself it is aesthetically irrelevant to guess). In real life he may, for all I know, be like hundreds of other artists who are less likable in a house or on the street than in the realm of ideal concepts and forms. As a social man, I hope that Mr. Barker is every bit as humane as his persona. As an ethical judge, I have no right to believe that he is not. As a literary historian, I should like to be able to trace some relationship between the man and his works. As a mere *reader,* however, I am satisfied with the poem alone, for it contains everything necessary for understanding and enjoyment.

The moral of this chapter is that, as a general rule, the drawing of factual biographical inferences from art works is perilous. At most, we can observe what the artist's mind is capable of imagining. On the purely aesthetic level, a work of art can best be contemplated as if suspended in an aesthetic universe of its own creation; and one exercise which can train us to hold it there is drill in the analysis of the implied speaker.

Exercises

1. If you have already studied Milton's "Lycidas," characterize the implied speaker of that poem in an essay of whatever length your instructor may specify.

2. If you have not already studied "Lycidas," prepare oral or written characterizations of the implied speakers of the following poems, or some of them, as the instructor may direct:

  (a) John Wilmot, Earl of Rochester, "The Maimed Debauchee" (p. 246).
  (b) John Donne, "The Flea" (p. 171).
  (c) John Oldham, "A Satire . . ." (p. 248).
  (d) Thomas Hardy, "The Ruined Maid" (p. 369).

XII

PROSODY

Prosody, or "1. the science or study of poetic meters and versification," is a subject concerning which every student of poetry must inform himself. Unfortunately, the principles are just now in dispute because of an attempt currently being made to test conventional assumptions by new linguistic methods and the analysis of taped readings. Under the circumstances, whatever is said must be regarded as tentative; but the principles by which most poets have thought themselves to be guided deserve explanation.

Prosody has been traditionally thought of in terms of *feet,* or repeated rhythmic patterns consisting of two or three syllables, and of *lines,* into which, usually, no more than six feet are combined. The feet, which will

82

be described in a moment, are of six kinds. Lines consist of from one to six feet and are called, respectively, *monometer, dimeter, trimeter, tetrameter, pentameter,* and *hexameter.* Any line—or "verse"—of poetry can be described roughly in terms of the kind of feet and the number of feet in the line: for example, iambic pentameter (five iambs to the line) or trochaic tetrameter (four trochees to the line). Illustrations will be offered later.

The rhythmic patterns within the feet are determined by the *relative prominence* of the syllables. In a foot of two syllables, the pattern may be any of the following. Relatively light prominence will be indicated by ˘ , relatively heavy prominence by − .*

iamb (or iambus): ˘ −   spondee: − −

trochee: − ˘   pyrrhic: ˘ ˘

Spondees and pyrrhic feet, in which there is no apparent difference of prominence, are occasional variants within the line and cannot set the rhythmic norm. Although trochaic rhythms are not uncommon, iambs are most usual.

Three-syllable feet consist of the *anapest* (˘ ˘ −) and the *dactyl* (− ˘ ˘). Other conceivable trisyllabic patterns are lacking: for example, ˘ − ˘ , the amphibrach, which appears in Latin and Greek lyrics.

The feet can be conveniently illustrated by single words, such as "aWAY" (second syllable stressed) for the iamb and "SOMEbody" (first of three syllables stressed) for the dactyl. Actually, however, the divisions of the line into feet proceed quite independently of the division into words, so that a single foot may consist of more than one word or of mere parts of words. In the phrase "Though actors cannot much of learning boast," the rhythmic norm is the iamb and every second syllable is relatively prominent, thus: "Though ACtors CANnot MUCH of LEARNing BOAST." A diagrammatic representation, or scansion, of the line would be written as follows (a vertical line being inserted to mark the end of each foot): ˘ − | ˘ − | ˘ − | ˘ − | ˘ − | . This representation suggests a reading in which the voice would alternate relatively stressed and relatively unstressed syllables, thus: "DiDA, diDA, diDA, diDA, diDA." If the pattern is superimposed upon the words, we obtain the following:

---

* An × is sometimes preferred for an unstressed syllable and a ⁄ for a stressed: thus, for the iamb, × ⁄ instead of ˘ − .

Though ac|tors can|not much| of learn|ing boast . . .

It will be observed that the first foot consists of "Though ac-,"
the second of "-tors can-," the third of "-not much," the fourth
of "of learn-," and the last of "-ing boast." It is important, therefore, to realize that the pattern of less and greater prominence
overrides the arrangement of the syllables in words.

A very great quantity of English poetry is written, like the example just given, in iambic pentameter. If the following lines are
read with fairly natural accentuation but in a rather singsong way,
the same pattern will emerge:

No his|tory |de ceived |him, for|he knew

Lit tle| of times|and ar|mies not|his own;

He nev|er felt|that peace|was but|a loan,

Had nev|er ques|tioned the| i dea|of gain.

Be yond|the head|lines once|or twice|he saw

The gath|er ing of|a pow|er by|the few

But could|not tell|their names;| he cast| his vote,

Dis trust|ing all|the e lect|ed but|not law.

(Karl Shapiro, "Elegy for a Dead Soldier," 73–80)

The pattern here is unusually regular. That some substitutions
occur should not disturb us, for absolute regularity would produce
rhythmic dullness. A parallel can be drawn with music. The
simplest pattern of a musical composition written in four-four time
would consist of measures containing four quarter-notes each, of
which the first would receive a primary accent and the third a
secondary accent. Yet such measures are rare. In the excerpt from
Shapiro's "Elegy," the following variations appear: in the first
foot of the second line, a trochee; in the second foot of the sixth
line and the third foot of the eighth, an anapest; and in the fourth
foot of the fourth line "idea" is read as a disyllable instead of—
as normally—a trisyllable. Alternatively, we could preserve the trisyllabic pronunciation and make the last foot an anapest, thus:

"i de|a of gain." Other variations are also possible. "Gathering," in line 6, could be read "gath'ring," and "the elected," in line 8, could be read "th' elected." But the basic pattern would be little changed by such modifications.

In reading aloud as an aid to scansion, the student should not allow his marking of the difference between greater and less prominence to result in serious distortion of the natural reading. Thus "When to the sessions of sweet silent thought" (Shakespeare, "Sonnet XXX") should not be read "When TO the SESSIONS OF sweet silent THOUGHT" simply because the meter is predominantly iambic. "When" should be stressed and "to" left unstressed; although the first foot then becomes trochaic, the iambic pattern remains quite adequately evident. But the line contains additional intricacies. If read in a less singsong manner and more like prose (as an actor, in contrast to a poet, might read it), "of" loses most of its stress and "sweet," as an important adjective, gains emphasis. Such a rendition would have to be scanned as follows:

When to | the ses | sions of | sweet si | lent thought . . . .

The third foot is now pyrrhic ($\smile\smile$) and the fourth, by way of compensation, has become spondaic ($-$ $-$). The atypical lightness of the third foot is made up by the atypical weight of the fourth. Whether this reading is acceptable will depend not only on views about the principles of scansion but also on tolerance of irregularities. A reading which to some persons seems to destroy the rhythm will seem to others merely to offer a pleasing relief from monotony.

So far the illustrations have been iambic. Here is an example of trochaic tetrameter (John Milton, *L'Allegro,* 33–34) :

Come, and | trip it | as you | go ^{x}
On the | light fan | tas tic | toe. ^{x}

Except for the omission of the final light syllable in each line (*catalexis,* indicated by $\times$), the pattern is quite regular.

Three-syllable measures are less common in English and often contain a relatively high proportion of two-syllable feet. Browning's "How They Brought the Good News from Ghent to Aix" (7–8) is a textbook example of anapests:

Not a word | to each oth | er; we kept | the great pace

Neck by neck, | stride by stride, | nev er chang|ing our pace.

Thomas Hood's "The Bridge of Sighs" (1–4) is in dactyls:

One more Un|for tu nate,

Wea ry of | breath, ˣ ˣ

Rash ly im|por tu nate,

Gone to her|death! ˣ ˣ

In the latter example, it will be noticed that the second foot in the second and fourth lines is incomplete. A longer poem in dactyls is Longfellow's *Evangeline:*

This is the | for est pri|me val; the | mur mur ing | pines and the | hem lock ˣ
Stand like | harp ers | hoar, with | beards that | rest on their | bos oms.ˣ

In the second line the tendency of English dactyls to become trochees is strikingly evident. The usual English line is iambic—an interesting fact, for the typical English word is accented on the first syllable, and a tendency is thus created for the divisions into feet to cut across the boundaries of individual words.

In writing traditional meters (other kinds of verse lie outside the scope of this chapter), the poet usually adheres to a chosen metrical pattern sufficiently for the dominant beat, however modified, never to sink out of the reader's consciousness. Sometimes, as in a sonnet, all the lines are of the same length. Again, they may vary according to some regular plan, as in the following excerpt from a ballad:

There lived | a wife | at Ush| er's Well,

And a wealth|y wife | was she;

She had | three stout | and stal|wart sons,

And sent | them o'er | the sea.

Here the first and third lines are iambic tetrameter and the second and fourth iambic trimeter. The resulting stanza, which appears frequently in ballads, is called *common ballad measure.* The poet who elects to write in this measure makes an implicit commitment to honor the pattern throughout the whole poem. Conventional patterns normally include a definite rhyme scheme (unless rhyme is eschewed altogether, as in blank verse). *Rhyme scheme* means that rhymes must occur regularly at expected points and cannot be inserted whenever the poet happens to think of words that sound alike. In the above example the second and fourth lines are rhymed, but the first and third are not.

The number of conventional stanza forms is relatively great. "Long ballad measure" resembles the stanza we have just examined, but has four lines of tetrameter instead of two of tetrameter and two of trimeter. "Short ballad measure" has four lines of trimeter. (The rhyme schemes may, however, vary within limits: for instance, the first and third lines may rhyme as well as the second and fourth.) Any four-line stanza, regardless of its metrical pattern, is called a *quatrain*.

These forms are comparatively simple. Others are more complicated. In the descriptions which follow, rhyming lines will be designated by the same letter of the alphabet. Thus a quatrain with alternating rhyme will be marked *abab*. Some of the more common stanzas are these:

Couplet: two lines of the same measure rhymed together—*aa, bb, cc,* and so on. Normally couplets are run together without stanza breaks.

Tercet (or *triplet*): three lines of the same measure rhymed together—*aaa, bbb, ccc,* and so forth.

Terza rima: consecutive three-line stanzas rhymed *aba, bcb, cdc,* and so on, all the lines being of the same measure.

Quatrain: a four-line stanza rhymed *abcb, abab, abba,* or *aaba.* Lines are not always—or even usually—all in the same measure.

Rhyme royal: a seven-line stanza of iambic pentameter rhymed *abab bcc.*

Ottava rima: an eight-line stanza of iambic pentameter rhymed *abab abcc.*

Spenserian stanza: a nine-line stanza, the first eight lines in iambic pentameter, the ninth in iambic hexameter (an *alexandrine*); the rhyme is *ababbcbcc.*

Sonnet: a fourteen-line pattern, almost always in iambic pentameter, which constitutes a complete poem (although a number of sonnets may be grouped together as a *sonnet sequence*). The two most common rhyme schemes are the following: the *Italian* or *Petrarchan,* rhymed *abbaabba* in the first eight lines or *octave,* and variously in the remaining six, the *sestet*—for example, *cdecde* or *cdcdcd*; and the *Shakespearean* or *English,* rhymed *ababcdcdefefgg.*

Many other stanzaic forms exist but need not be enumerated here. The stanzaic pattern of an ode may be especially intricate. Certain French forms—for example, the *triolet*—demand the repetition of whole lines at specified points.

It has been said that the responsibility of the poet who elects to write in stanzas is normally to continue repeating the pattern until his poem ends. Besides this, he ought usually to construct his syntax in such a way as to make the line-breaks in some degree functional; he ought not to fight his pattern. He need not make the end of every line coincide with the end of a unit of sense; *run-on lines* are common, as in the following excerpt from Keats' "Ode on a Grecian Urn" (38–40):

> And, little town, thy streets for evermore
> Will silent be; and not a soul to tell
> Why thou art desolate, can e'er return.

In spite of the carrying on of the sense from line to line (alternatively called *enjambment*), the terminal words of the lines will bear a certain stress, and the stanzaic form is not repudiated. The following arrangement, however, would be unskillful.

> And, little
> Town, thy streets for evermore will silent
> Be; and not a soul to tell why thou art
> Desolate . . .

Here the words are crammed into a framework they do not really fit.

In recent years poets have sometimes experimented with the violation of this principle. One purpose has been to shock expectation and thereby to secure exceptional vividness. Occasionally, as in the following passage by E. E. Cummings ("In Just-," 1–4) the visual structure runs so counter to the auditory one that it does not help but hinders:

> in Just-
> spring   when the world is mud-
> luscious the little
> lame balloonman . . . .

Possibly the lines are intended to be humorous. If so, appreciation of the humor requires awareness of the prosodical norm which has been playfully violated.

Stanzaic patterns, as a part of prosody, demanded brief consideration here; but we may now return to the subject of meters for the purpose of noting subtleties not included in the introductory discussion. Of these, the most important has to do with the discrimination of stressed and unstressed syllables.

The first line of Shakespeare's "Sonnet XXX" was earlier scanned like this:

When to | the ses | sions of | sweet si | lent thought . . . .

This marking illustrates a probable reading by persons who are not rhythmically insensitive but who enjoy maximum variation. The principle is now rather widely accepted, however, that in determining what syllables are stressed only the syllables *within each individual foot* ought to be considered. This may often mean that the prominent syllable in one foot has less emphasis than an unstressed syllable in another foot.

How scansion is affected by the principle can be illustrated by examination of a line from Browning's "The Bishop Orders His Tomb at St. Praxed's Church" (71): "One block, pure green as a pistachio-nut." Here "pure" may receive more stress than "nut," although "pure" is technically unstressed and "nut" technically stressed:

One block, | pure green | as a | pis tach | i o-nut.

The student is invited to read this line several times to see whether what was just said is not true. Possibly "One," which is technically unstressed, is also pronounced with more energy (or at a higher pitch, or both) than the technically stressed "nut." This is to say that the acoustic pattern of an oral reading need not follow closely the theoretical pattern of the meter. We *pretend* that the reading is "One BLOCK, pure GREEN as A pisTAchio NUT," whereas we actually *say* something nearer to "ONE BLOCK, PURE GREEN as a pisTAchio NUT." (The difficulty, of course, is that people read the line differently, so that scansion works with two sets of variables: unlike readings on one hand, and contrasting practices of scansion on the other.) In fact, however, the situation is more complicated than an alternation of capitalized and uncapitalized syllables can suggest. Several degrees of stress can be discriminated: "One" may be pronounced more strongly than "as" or "a" but less strongly than "block"; "as" may be stressed very lightly, but a trifle more strongly than "a"; and "nut," although given more prominence than either "as" or "a," may be pronounced less strongly than "One," which is technically unstressed.

If we now return to the line from Shakespeare, we may decide that "of" is a little more stressed than "-sions" and "si-" than "sweet," thus:

When to | the ses | sions of | sweet si | lent thought . . . .

Recognition of such subtleties is partly responsible for the chaotic state of metrical theory mentioned in the first paragraph. The development of electronic instruments by empirical metrists for the measurement of actual readings and new insights arrived at by structural linguists have brought many conventional assumptions about prosody into doubt. Four degrees of stress have been found instead of two; importance has been discovered in *juncture*, or differing acoustic phenomena produced in passing from one syllable of an utterance to the next (as in the easily recognized difference between "ice cream" and "I scream"); and so on. Yet a tentative conservatism in metrical theory, modified by an openness to whatever solid discoveries may be made in the future, is defensible and probably wise.

The chief practical disagreements among teachers have to do with the admission of spondees and pyrrhic feet, as in "of sweet silent thought." Some teachers will prefer the scansion offered first, others—probably more—the alternative one suggested later. The instructor, if he elects to introduce scansion into the course, will indicate his preference either by explicit statement or by his own practice.

Exercises

Scan the following passages in the anthology. In placing the symbols and the vertical lines, be careful to syllabify properly. Division into syllables is determined by the syllabic units in actual pronunciation, not by some arbitrary rule (as that every syllable ought to begin with a consonant if possible). Thus "city" is syllabified "cit-y," not "ci-ty." When in doubt, consult the dictionary, where the proper divisions will be marked.

1. The first four lines of John Gay's "The Toilette: A Town Eclogue" (p. 271).
2. Lines 8-11 of William Cowper's "The Sofa" (p. 287).
3. Lines 6-7 of Tennyson's "Tears, Idle Tears" (p. 336).
4. Lines 1-4 of Robert Frost's "Desert Places" (p. 385).
5. Lines 9-14 of Archibald MacLeish's "The End of the World" (p. 408).

XIII

FORM

Ideally, all the semantic and structural elements of poetry hitherto discussed achieve resolution within a *form*. As the term will be used here, a form is more than a structure, more even than a design. It is something which should be not only noticed but also apprehended as an important constituent of the meaning. Progress in the understanding and enjoyment of poetry involves, among other things, steadily deepening formal insights, until at last the appreciation of meaning becomes coincident with the perception of form. At every moment the form limits and shapes the poem's total reality. What is excluded from the aesthetic universe of the poem is kept out by the invisible line which marks the poem's boundaries, and what is admitted allows only such semantic expansion as does not generate units of significance which hang suspended. The Roman poet Lucretius imagined that atoms—the smallest particles of matter—were sometimes *hooked,* that is, had little projections which connected firmly with similar projections on other atoms. We may think of a perfectly formed poem as one in which no structural element, however small, remains unhooked and in which all the groups of elements which constitute substructures coalesce on a higher level into a unity like that of a body with distinct but cooperating organs. Such a form has both semantic and aesthetic aspects, as will be seen shortly.

So highly abstract an assertion needs illustration. We may experiment with a simple example—Robert Graves' "Flying Crooked," which, besides having submerged formal values, also has one small formal ambiguity.

> The butterfly, a cabbage-white,
> (His honest idiocy of flight)
> Will never now, it is too late,
> Master the art of flying straight,
> Yet has—who knows so well as I?—
> A just sense of how not to fly:
> He lurches here and here by guess
> And God and hope and hopelessness.
> Even the aerobatic swift
> Has not his flying-crooked gift.

Several problems appear immediately. What is the connection of "honest idiocy of flight" with a cabbage-white color, upon which the phrase seems to be a comment? To what sort of expertness does the poet lay claim by saying "Who knows so well as I?" Finally, and most important, does the poem have a metaphorical level of meaning, or is it concerned only with the butterfly? (I do not include "aerobatic" as problematical because it obviously combines elements of "aeronautical" and "acrobatic" and means "acrobatic in the air.") Although we have confronted similar problems before, this time we shall consider them explicitly in relation to form.

The claim to expertness may be considered first. Nobody realizes more clearly than the poet the butterfly's avoidance of wrong ways of flying. In another context, we might suspect that the speaker has an entomologist's understanding of insects. Here the supposition is prevented by the very next lines: "He lurches here and here by guess/ And God and hope and hopelessness." The language is so blatantly nonscientific that we recognize instinctively the exclusion of rigidly disciplined thought from a poem which focuses upon impressions. The poet's special knowledge must have some other source. As a man who contemplates a white butterfly's flight and expresses his observations in rhymed and metered lines, he presents himself to the reader chiefly as a poet. As such, by saying "Who knows so well as I?" he may imply a rueful sense of his own aesthetic fallibility in comparison with the butterfly's skill at avoiding catastrophe while swerving and darting about. The next two lines would then describe not only the butterfly's erratic course but also the poet's clumsy efforts to avoid taking up the wrong ideas and sensations among those thrown up by his creative imagination as he works at the very craft of which this lyric is one product. On the metaphorical level, "flying" would also mean "imaginative soaring" or "singing in a lofty strain"; and the final two lines of the poem—

> Even the aerobatic swift
> Has not his flying-crooked gift

—would suggest comfortingly that poets who write with more rapidity and assurance than he does are, in their own way, also inferior to the butterfly.

Is this reading too bold? Earlier the student was advised not to assume that poems about small subjects necessarily have some deeper meaning. The advice still stands. If scrutinized carefully, the tiniest happenings can be found to have intrinsic values upon which a contemplative mind may pause. In the present instance, however, we were forced to speculate by the recognition that "Who knows so well as I?" appeared to be unhooked, to remain in suspension rather than entering into chemical solution. In seeking for connections, we were led to reject notions which lay outside the aesthetic perimeter and to pick up hints which lay inside it. The interpretation gains credibility from the fact that the whole second half of the poem develops the metaphor we believed ourselves to have perceived. Nevertheless, the reading is not certainly but only probably correct. It is conceivable that the question may be a mere filler, inserted because of the need of a rhyme with "fly." If we delete the phrase, the poem makes perfect sense as centered sharply and finally on the butterfly. Nothing besides the question forces us to look beneath the surface meaning. On principle, however, we ought to take an apparently competent poem's aesthetic integrity for granted until we have failed repeatedly to account for all the formal elements. Here we have not failed.

As often happens, the solution of one formal problem has involved the solution of another. We no longer need to inquire whether the meaning has a metaphorical level as well as a literal one. That problems are interconnected in this way is one of the evidences that aesthetic form has a kind of organicity. The relation of "honest idiocy of flight" to "cabbage-white" remains, however, to be perceived.

In one sense, no problem exists; from the beginning we understand that the butterfly's color indicates somehow that he is dull but without guile. The uncertainty results from a curiosity about why. This time we are not helped by a search for suggestions within the poem's limits. We must go outside it—for example, by wondering whether "cabbage" is meant to remind us of "cabbage-head" or to imply that the butterfly is like a humble man in whose diet the lowly cabbage is a staple. But we cannot guess confidently, for the poem's form excludes the information which we must have in order to choose. Whether the failure is important every reader will have to decide for himself. It may be observed, however, that the "obscurity" charged against recent poetry often results from associations which exist *outside the poem* for the poet but not for his reader. Connotations give no trouble if they are sufficiently public to need no development. If they are private, the reader must speculate about them. He will be guided, of course, by formal considerations; but even if he feels sure of the implication he may wonder, as we do here, about its grounds.

Beyond all this, the metrical form of Graves' lyric has semantic value. The poem is about the darting, uncertain, apparently idiotic —but never catastrophic—flight of a butterfly and also about the haphazard, unsystematic way in which a poet's mind seeks to pull disparate aesthetic materials together into a work of art. That the poem's metrical form is skillfully controlled, that the description of seeming chaos is accomplished within a pattern which never falters rhythmically, syntactically, or in rhyme, qualifies the literal and metaphorical meaning in an important way. We have been told by indirection that the poet, in attempting to write, "lurches here and here by guess/ And God and hope and hopelessness."

On the prosodical level, as well as by its referential meanings, the lyric says that the poet is less inferior to the butterfly than he pretends. He has not blundered into self-destruction. His lurching guesses, aided perhaps by some power which rather possesses him than is possessed by him, have justified the hope which has alternated with hopelessness in his mind. We feel in the solid aesthetic structure of the piece the justification of a compositional method which would seem to foredoom his work to nullity.

Perhaps all aesthetic form suggests an ultimate orderliness beneath the chaotic surface of much experience. As we watch how the elements of a work of art snap into place, each reaching out to form meaningful union with others and the whole rounding itself into a miniature universe, free-floating and complete, yet analogically representative of some fragment of the everyday world in which we pass our less serenely contemplative hours, a deeplying part of the mind is reassured about life. Or, again—and the same response can be made to music—the perception of order is itself profoundly satisfying, healthfully invigorating; the conscious and unconscious halves of the psyche, ordinarily self-divided and in conflict with each other, come for a few minutes into joyful harmony, like a thousand instruments playing without discord. At any rate, the appreciation of form provides one of the richest pleasures of the adequately trained art-lover. The more complex and absorbing the form the better, provided only the mind is not fatigued into losing its hold. But the appreciation must be *responsible,* not arbitrary; a perception, not a creation. If it is not, works very different in quality will stimulate similar reactions, and the range of pleasure will be limited. Herein lies the justification of all the disciplinary exercises which have preceded the present chapter.

The development of such an appreciation may occur quickly in especially gifted persons but will come slowly for most. A preliminary stage is sensitivity to such schematic forms as that of the following stanza by Ben Jonson ("A Celebration of Charis," 103–12):

> Have you seen but a bright lily grow
> Before rude hands have touched it?
> Ha' you marked but the fall o' the snow
> Before the soil hath smutched it?
> Ha' you felt the wool of beaver?
> Or swan's down ever?

> Or have smelt o' the bud o' the brier
> Or the nard in the fire?
> Or have tasted the bag of the bee?
> O so white! O so soft! O so sweet is she!

The whiteness of the lily mentioned in the first two lines, the softness of the snow, of beaver fur, and of swan's down mentioned in the next four, and the sweetness of the brier bud, of the aromatic ointment called nard, and of honey mentioned in the following three are brought together in the same order in the final line: "O so white! O so soft! O so sweet is she!" Many beginning students will notice—and enjoy—the form of this lyric without help, and all can easily be brought to perceive it.

A similar plan is less apparent in the first four lines of Donne's "Holy Sonnet XIV":

> Batter my heart, three-personed God; for you
> As yet but knock, breathe, shine, and seek to mend;
> That I may rise and stand, o'erthrow me, and bend
> Your force to break, blow, burn and make me new.

Not every reader will observe that "break" is a more forcible extension of "knock," "blow" of "breathe," "burn" of "shine," and "make me new" of "mend." Yet the organizational plan is partly identical with that of the stanza from Jonson.

In Shelley's "Ode to the West Wind," a similar plan is expanded through four of the five sections. In the first three, the wind is described in terms of its action on leaves, clouds, and waves; in the fourth, the three images are twice put into close juxtaposition (43–45, 53):

> If I were a dead leaf thou mightest bear;
> If I were a swift cloud to fly with thee;
> A wave to pant beneath thy power . . .
>
> Oh! Lift me as a wave, a leaf, a cloud!

Recognition of the pattern in this poem requires a longer attention-span because the resolution does not begin till the forty-third line.

Structural patterns are of course almost infinitely variable. In Shelley's "Ode," we discover on rereading that the wish to disseminate revolutionary ideas in which the poem culminates is not brought in suddenly at the end but has been subtly suggested by what seemed at first a routine description of "nature." The leaves described in the first section—"Yellow, and black, and pale, and hectic red,/ Pestilent-stricken multitudes" (4–5)—are now discerned to suggest oppressed people of all four races, and the seeds that are blown to their "dark wintry bed" (6), where they will germinate in the spring, represent creative social ideals which, like the seeds, require time to blossom. In order to create a new social order, the revolutionary must undermine contemporary social institutions; like the wind to which he appeals, he is a "Destroyer and preserver" (14). "The dying year" in the second section (24) is also the completion of an imperfect cycle of social development, and "pumice," in the phrase "a pumice isle in Baiae's bay" (32), indicates both that the isle has a volcanic origin and that social creativity, like its natural counterpart, is sometimes violent.

The full appreciation of any complex form (if appreciation can ever be called "full") requires the gradual accumulation, or *funding,* as aestheticians sometimes call it, of quantities of initially discrete perceptions such as these. It goes without saying that every work has its special formal properties and that, except on a very abstract level, no two forms are identical. The structural resemblance—for instance, between two Petrarchan sonnets which are both about unsuccessful courtship and which both work out a metaphor of military siege—dissipates as the examination becomes more minute. Every poem is thus formally unique and requires the discrimination of properties which exist nowhere else in just this combination.

The subject of form ramifies in so many directions that an attempt to exhaust it would be hopeless. I conclude with some remarks on acoustic properties, or, as they are sometimes designated, sound patterns. And here the notes must be partly cautionary.

The importance of sound to poetry is clearly very great. Amateur poetry can often be recognized instantly as amateur because it sounds awkward. The rhythms halt or are monotonous, the rhymes are infelicitous, the meters are ill-adapted to the subjects. We say that the poetaster "has no ear." In contrast, the words set down by a skillful poet *sound right.* Yet the attempts which have been made to distinguish formally appropriate sound properties from formally inappropriate or distracting ones often raise serious questions.

For one thing, not much is achieved by simply noticing that one or two vowel or consonantal sounds are often repeated. Some teachers are especially fond of *alliteration* ("the commencement of two or more stressed syllables of a word group . . . with the same consonant sound or sound group . . .") , as in "The *princes* *portrayed* their *prowess* in battle." The real problem concerns what alliteration does for the poem in which it appears, and this is rarely easy to state. Again, sounds are often confused with spellings. It is not correct to say that Shakespeare's line ("Sonnet XXX"), "When to the sessions of sweet silent thought," contains five *s*'s, for the two *ss*'s of "sessions" are pronounced together as *sh,* which is phonetically distinct from *s,* and the terminal *s* is pronounced as a *z.* Similarly, in words like "God," "remove," "come," and "hoof" there are no *o*-sounds, for the first vowel, in the most common American pronunciation at least, is sounded as an *a,* and the other three vowels as three distinct varieties of *u.* In the same way, nothing intelligent can be said about the *ou* sounds in "rough," "though," "cough," "through," and "plough" (an English spelling of "plow") except that they are all different. Statements about phonetic similarities and identities should, indeed, be made only by persons who have a firm grounding in general or comparative linguistics. Finally, great çare should be used in assigning affective values to individual sounds. Comments about the brassy gurgle of *l* sounds, or the cheerfulness of the liquid *r*'s, or the relaxed indolence of the *m*'s and *n*'s, or the mental confusion implied by the dull *f*'s and *v*'s ordinarily describe impressions derived from individual readings instead of auditory values actually embodied in the lines. Trained linguists are almost unanimous in their scorn of such observations, and the student will do well to avoid them.

Some instances of *onomatopoeia,* or the adaptation of sound to sense (please note and master the spelling!), stand on a firmer basis. That onomatopoeia exists is beyond doubt; that, in general, any kind of poetic fitness is a formal good may be taken for granted. Moreover, even relatively insensitive ears can be made aware of clear examples of onomatopoeia—the tolling and clanging of Poe's *The Bells,* or the variations in this set of familiar lines by Pope:

> 'Tis not enough no harshness gives offence,
> The sound must seem an echo to the sense.
> Soft is the strain when Zephyr gently blows,
> And the smooth stream in smoother numbers flows;
> But when loud surges lash the sounding shore,
> The hoarse, rough verse should like the torrent roar.
> When Ajax strives some rock's vast weight to throw,

> The line too labors, and the words move slow.
> Not so, when swift Camilla scours the plain,
> Fliers o'er the unbending corn, and skims along the main.
>
> ("An Essay on Criticism," II, 164–73)

The intention here cannot be misunderstood; and the accomplishment is the more remarkable because, except for the alexandrine in the last line, it is achieved within the closed pentameter couplet.

The range of possible onomatopoeic effects is very wide. Keats begins "The Eve of St. Agnes" as follows:

> St. Agnes' Eve—Ah, bitter chill it was!
> The owl, for all his feathers, was a-cold;
> The hare limped trembling through the frozen grass . . . .

Because "limped" (pronounced "limpt") ends with the same consonant—technically, an alveolar plosive—with which the following word begins, a limp of sorts is introduced, or at least can be introduced by a cooperating reader, into a description of a limp. In "The Secular Masque" (45–52), by John Dryden, a speech by Mars imitates the sound of martial music:

> Inspire the vocal brass, inspire;
> The world is past its infant age.
> Arms and honor,
> Arms and honor,
> Set the martial mind on fire
> And kindle manly rage.
> Mars has looked the sky to red,
> And Peace, the lazy good, is fled.

The strong rhythm of a passage in Tennyson's "Ulysses" (58–59) suggests the regular beat of oars:

> Push off, and sitting well in order smite
> The sounding furrows . . . .

Other subtler effects are possible—some, indeed, so subtle as hardly to allow description. We must be careful, however, in discussing onomatopoeia, not to let our interpretations become fanciful.

The temptation to make fanciful judgments about sounds is often irresistible. Does the word "rigid" sound stiff, the word "tender" soft and melting, the word "tyranny" harsh? Perhaps we insensibly transfer to the acoustical properties an affective response to the meanings. The d and r of "tender" reappear in "rigid," the t and n in "tyranny." "Murmuring" seems onomatopoeic until we notice (with John Crowe Ransom) that "murdering" is identical except for one letter. And yet, as has been said, onomatopoeia undoubtedly has formal importance. We ought not to become so skeptical about particular instances that we cease to be able to perceive it where it is actually present.

The most valuable observations about form, however, are those which help to define meanings, not those which simply illustrate meanings already known to be present, interesting as the latter may be. If tension exists between two aspects of form—for example, designative meaning and tone, as when a horrible event is described blandly—the comment made on one aspect by the other cannot be missed if interpretation is not to go astray. Similarly, the meanings of isolated passages are modified by other passages which precede and follow. Every teacher has known students who are admirably perceptive of patches but miss the total meaning because they read from line to line instead of letting each new meaning be absorbed into a developing structure. Their readings are to adequate interpretations what a string of disconnected anecdotes about kings and generals is to history. The attainment of formal awareness is thus a process both of learning to *perceive more* and of *holding more perceptions in mind simultaneously,* so that each structural member can be seen in relation to every other.

Not every person is able to attain such an awareness on the higher levels, and some who have it in their contacts with one art do not have it in their contacts with others. Not everybody who can see paintings can hear music, and vice-versa. The experience of aesthetic form, however, when it can be attained, is a source of keen enjoyment as well as a cognitive achievement; and the enjoyment tends to be greater in proportion as the materials are richer.

Exercise

Write out a formal analysis of the following poem by Samuel Taylor Coleridge in which you show the poem's organicity, or lack of it, by attempting to bring all the formal elements into perfect harmony. In doing so, consider especially the aspects of form which were discussed in the preceding chapter—but you need not limit yourself to them.

TIME REAL AND IMAGINARY:
AN ALLEGORY

On the wide level of a mountain's head
(I knew not where, but 'twas some faery place),
Their pinions, ostrich-like, for sails outspread,
Two lovely children run an endless race,
    A sister and a brother!
    This far outstripped the other;
Yet ever runs she with reverted face,
And looks and listens for the boy behind;
    For he, alas! is blind.
O'er rough and smooth with even step he passed,
And knows not whether he be first or last.

XIV

THE HISTORICAL BACKGROUND

So far we have considered poems much as an amateur art-lover would study pictures if he had no guidance except that offered by a catalogue and a textbook entitled *What to Look For in Paintings*. But all the arts have a second dimension, the historical, with reference to which many disputes must be settled: a fact which is responsible for the heavy preponderance of "scholarship" over "criticism" in academic journals at a time when criticism enjoys unusual esteem. Upon the historical dimension we must therefore pause briefly.

Much that has already been said can be looked at afresh from this point of view. When we learn the sense of an archaic word by using the dictionary, we make a small historical discovery. The information that

Chaucer's "Hit am I" is a fourteenth-century syntactical equivalent of "It's I" (or the more recent "It's me") is easily accessible because historical grammar has been studied by specialists. The identification of allusions—to political events, to long-dead persons, to obscure books and authors, to classical deities—depends on a knowledge of history. Conventional symbols (the cross, the rose, the garden, the phoenix, the dove) are rooted in tradition. Every art work, although in one aspect timeless and self-subsistent, is also a product of historical conditions; and these must often be studied.

The conditioning of poems by their milieux is made especially intricate by the fact that no man's consciousness is limited to the events of his own period. When Dryden, in the long poem from which the portrait of Corah was drawn, described the rebellion of the Duke of Monmouth against James II, he did so in terms of the Biblical Absalom's struggle against David. A full understanding of the poem thus requires some knowledge not only of English politics circa 1680 but also of the Bible. The example is not unusual. Every poet learns a language which was not invented in his lifetime. He is surrounded by social institutions which have a long history. He absorbs attitudes and copies modes of behavior which are at some stage of a continuous development. The very techniques of his art are mostly traditional. A modern French poet sounds final e's which have been mute for a long time in ordinary speech. Accordingly, the ideal preparation for reading poetry would include learning everything that is known about the past—personalities, ideas, manners, traditions, conventions, and much else.

Since no man can achieve this goal, the usual recourse of professional readers is to specialize. Even so, the most distinguished scholars come far short of having a completely adequate background for the understanding of even a single poet. The best-equipped Miltonist is unable, besides acquiring a detailed knowledge of Milton's life and seventeenth-century English history, to study literary influences adequately by reading everything that Milton read in English, Latin, Greek, French, Italian, Hebrew, Aramaic, and Syriac. He does the best he can and hopes that by absorbing the results of other scholars' researches he can make up the worst of his deficiencies. The widest usefulness of professional scholarship is thus that it permits the gradual building up of historical—and aesthetic—insights which, through the medium of footnotes and introductions in textbooks, can enhance the ordinary reader's understanding and increase his enjoyment. Without such helps, most of us would often be puzzled by richly meaningful passages in poetry.

Among the innumerable strands which together constitute history, a few can be easily discriminated. We shall consider briefly biography, or the history of an individual human being, and then, in turn, political, intellectual, and social history. All are important for the serious reader of poetry, and any one (or more than one) may bear very heavily on a specific poem.

Biography is concerned with the events, conditions, thoughts, associations, and psychic states of a human existence. Because the question "What does this poem mean?" is easily transformed to "What did the poet have in mind?" problems of poetic meaning frequently invite biographical study. What, exactly, were the romantic disappointments of the hero in Tennyson's *Maud?* In attempting to solve the problem, we may look to Tennyson's history and discover the plot to have derived from the poet's own romantic entanglements.* Byron's closet drama *Manfred* raises a similar problem. The hero suffers remorse for an unspecified crime for which commentators have sought an explanation in the circumstances of Byron's voluntary exile from England. John Dryden wrote two long theological poems, of which the earlier, *Religio Laici,* is Anglican and the later, *The Hind and the Panther,* Roman Catholic. The reader who knows that in the interval a Catholic king, James II, had come to the throne may wish to learn whether the poet's religious convictions were sincere or time-serving. Important clues must be sought in records of Dryden's life.

Inquiries of other kinds may also lead to biographical study. Why is Milton's *Samson Agonistes* written in a barer, less highly colored style than his *Paradise Lost?* If we are tempted to reply that Milton developed toward greater stylistic simplicity, we must be sure of the order in which his poems were written. What was the Pre-Raphaelite Movement in nineteenth-century poetry? Although the question is basically aesthetic, it motivates research into biography in order that we may learn what the members of the

---

* A biographical study of *Maud* by Ralph Rader, entitled *Tennyson's Maud: The Biographical Genesis* (Berkeley: University of California Press, 1963), analyzes the problem in detail.

group thought they were doing. Questions about influences, methods of composition, and poetic intentions motivate a hunt for sources or a reading of preserved letters. The interest need not always be in events, or even in the poet's conscious thought-processes. We may become curious about emotional states and subconscious drives. Much ink has been expended on efforts to prove that Milton did or did not sympathize subconsciously with the Satan of his *Paradise Lost.*

The influence of political history is so obvious as hardly to need comment. Satires, especially, are often soaked in contemporary politics. Dryden's *Absalom and Achitophel,* mentioned above, is only one example. When Chaucer begins the "Envoy" of "The Complaint of Chaucer to His Purse" by writing "O conquerour of Brutes Albyon," it is interesting to learn not only that Brut, a great-grandson of the Trojan Aeneas, was thought to be the founder of the British race and that Albion—perhaps derived from Latin *albus,* "white" (the color of the chalk cliffs of Dover)—is an old name for England, but also that the "conquerour" was King Henry IV, who in 1399 acquired the throne by unseating Richard II. Also, we may value the discovery that the "Complaint," which because of this allusion can be dated in the last year or two of Chaucer's life, is perhaps the latest of his preserved poems. Again, poetic tributes are often written to persons whose fame has been obscured by time. If Marvell's "Horatian Ode Upon Cromwell's Return from Ireland" concerns a man about whom we already have some information, Milton's sonnet to "Fairfax, whose name in arms through Europe rings," may stimulate us to look for a footnote which will tell us something about the subject. Wordsworth and Coleridge wrote poems on the French Revolution; Thomas Hardy's "Channel Firing" relates to the First World War; in writing about Irish politics, Yeats alluded to persons about whom we must learn at least a little if the meaning is not to remain foggy.

A key to other poetic difficulties is found in social history, or the history of institutions and interpersonal relationships as these may have been affected by physical and political conditions. Nobody can read through H. D. Traill's *Social England,* or any similar work, without finding his appreciation of our older poetry wonderfully sharpened. The formal characteristics of Chaucer's poetry are partly determined by its relation to the court. Oliver Goldsmith's *The Deserted Village* reflects conditions resulting from the enclosure by country squires of the common pastures and wastelands formerly used by peasants. The financial success of Alexander Pope's translation of the *Iliad* and *Odyssey* was partly an effect of the aspirations to culture of the rising middle class. Thomas Hood's "The Song of the Shirt" is a nineteenth-century protest against working conditions in the textile industry. But, indeed, almost any bit of information about social history—the condition of seventeenth-century roads, the position of the wife in the medieval family, the passion of James I for hunting, even the introduction of coffee and the institution of the coffeehouse—has relevance to some piece of literature. The reader who knows little about social history is bound to miss literary hints which, by suggesting the continuity of literature with its social milieu, not only clarify meanings but also bear upon the fundamental nature of art. The proof is our feeling of disorientation when we read a work whose background is almost totally unfamiliar —for example, Lady Murasaki's eleventh-century Japanese novel, *The Tale of Genji*.

Intellectual history, which includes what has recently become known as the history of ideas, is at least equally important for the understanding of poetry. The idea of the Great Chain of Being, first explicated by A. O. Lovejoy in a notable book and then given wider currency by E. M. W. Tillyard's *The Elizabethan World Picture*, underlies much capital poetry of the pre-Romantic period. A famous speech by Ulysses in Shakespeare's *Troilus and Cressida* (I, iii), and much of Pope's *Essay on Man*, merely state explicitly concepts which are taken for granted elsewhere. Marjorie Nicolson's *The Breaking of the Circle* calls attention to a belief, virtually unchallenged from antiquity to the Renaissance, that the circle is the perfect form; and we remember innumerable circles in poems, which have now been given a new significance for us. Ernest Tuveson's *Millennium and Utopia* traces the gradual development, beginning in the seventeenth century, from an expectation of Christ's return to a hope for the perfection of earthly society. The rise of science, the emergence of democratic ideals, and the continuities and innovations of philosophical thought are other important strands in intellectual history. There is matter here, indeed, rather for a library of books than for a paragraph.

The most puzzling of all difficulties in the interpretation of poetry arise from doubts about the functioning of the minds of persons who lived long ago. Uneducated people suppose that all human beings perceive and think in a similar manner, but they are mistaken. No doubt the human constitution has altered little, if at all, since the beginning of history. No doubt, too, the fundamental human drives have always been relatively stable and the emotional responses to experience based on a similar body-chemistry. Yet the mature human character depends not only on native biological endowments but also on acculturation; and because of man's prolonged infancy the process of social adaptation normally continues till puberty and can continue throughout life. The ways in which the feelings are manifested, if not the feelings themselves, may cease to be recognizable; and the very bases of conscious thought, as anthropologists have shown, may be chosen from any part of a huge arc of cultural possibility. The remainder of the present chapter will be given over to the brief illustration of these statements.

The Song of Solomon, in the Bible, furnishes an excellent example. The second verse of the fourth chapter reads as follows: "Thy teeth are as flocks of sheep, that are shorn, which come up from the washing, all with twins, and there is none barren among them." * To a twentieth-century reader, the comparison of the teeth with sheep seems intended to emphasize the teeth's whiteness, and the remarks about the fertility of the sheep and the fact that all of them bear twins seem to be interesting irrelevancies—unless, perhaps, we reflect that teeth are paired or wonder whether the poet's erotic desire is responsible for the sexual tone of the imagery. For centuries, however, the verse was understood quite differently because of an exegetic tradition dating back at least as far as St. Augustine (d. A.D. 430). In a work called On Christian Doctrine, Augustine begins by explaining that there are men whose example helps the Church to extirpate superstition in those who seek divine truth. Such men, he continues, submit themselves to Holy Baptism, and as a result of that ritual they "conceive" by the Holy Spirit and produce a twofold fruit of charity. In The Song of Solomon, the holy men are pleasingly described as "the teeth of the Church, which cut off men from their errors and soften them so that they may be taken into the body of the Church." The men are likened to shorn

---

* I quote the Douay, or Catholic, version because it comes most directly from the Latin Vulgate, which was used by St. Augustine, whose interpretation of the passage is given below. The discussion at this point is based on D. W. Robertson, A Preface to Chaucer (Princeton, N.J.: Princeton University Press, 1962), p. 53.

sheep because in the washing of baptism they are cleansed of their sins; and none are barren because all bear the twin fruits of faith. Was St. Augustine's reading "correct" and the modern reading mistaken? The problem is so complicated that no simple answer can be given. Very possibly the Saint was misled by assumptions made in his period about the plurisignificance of every verse in Holy Scripture. Even so, it does not follow that the merely "sensitive" interpretation of the modern reader is more accurate. The biblical writer may have been working within a symbolic tradition which has been lost, or to which only specialists in Old Testament exegesis now possess the key. Anyhow, our interest may be less in what the author meant than in how the verse was understood by an English poet who alluded to it. Because Augustine's interpretation held currency for a thousand years, the chances are good that medieval references to the verse should be understood to assume his reading. This is to say that the historical context must be considered. The passage meant one thing to its author, other things to other people in other times and places.

The interpretation of our older literature is full of such pitfalls. Chaucer's works contain a whole nestful of examples. In "The Knight's Tale," for instance, Chaucer tells a story about two young men who fall in love with a beautiful young woman and carry their rivalry so far as to dispute her hand first in a duel and later, supported by a hundred knights each, in an elaborate tournament. The typical modern reader assumes that Chaucer wished to inspire sympathy for the lovers. He may have done so; but much evidence supports a very different reading. For one thing, from point to point the author drops in ludicrously inappropriate incidents and phrases. When the lovers are discovered fighting the duel, we are told that they stand in blood up to their ankles. Later the goddess Venus, who has been watching the tournament from "above," is so disappointed by Arcite's victory that she weeps tears which fall down into the amphitheater. When Arcite dies as the result of a fall from his horse, Chaucer writes, "His spirit chaunged hous and wente ther,/ As I cam nevere, I kan nat tellen wher." And there are other equally puzzling lines. Perhaps we are to regard the infatuation as silly and perhaps even sinful. According to medieval theology, the three stages of sin are very like the stages of love portrayed here: first an attractive object is noticed, next the mind becomes obsessed with the object's desirability, and finally the will assents to the thought of going to any lengths to possess the object. As D. W. Robertson has shown,* the stages were not only written about frequently but also were represented in much painting and sculpture. Did Chaucer count on his audience to recognize them as they followed his story? At this distance we can only guess, for the answer is not in the poem but in the poet's expectation of prepared mental states in his readers.

The same problem arises in Chaucer's *Troilus and Criseyde,* his most massive single achievement and one of the great long poems in English. But it arises also in connection with later writings. Lewis Carroll's *Alice in Wonderland* is an example from prose fiction. One interpretation is that the White Rabbit, the Red Queen, and the other actors in the story were meant to be recognized as caricatures of persons living in Oxford, where the author was a lecturer in mathematics. If so, the key to the intended interpretation was wholly outside the work. Much early poetry which now seems to be secular may have had religious meanings that have been obscured by changes in the thought patterns of readers. Rhetorical techniques which would have been instantly appreciated at a time when rhetoric was studied by every schoolboy are now missed or must be painfully explicated; and the use of a scholastic logic, as in Milton's *Paradise Regained,* is seldom recognized because university students no longer focus a major part of their attention on formal public disputation.

The moral of all this is that the professional study of poetry is highly complicated and sometimes even wearisome. Except for special purposes, college undergraduates cannot be expected to do more than acquire some idea of what it involves. Further, professors whose primary commitment is to literary history sometimes contort poetry because their aesthetic awareness is less highly developed than their knowledge of backgrounds. Nevertheless, a realization of the connection between backgrounds and meanings may help even the amateur to develop tolerance—and perhaps respect—for scholarship and to accept gratefully the discoveries of scholars which are offered him in footnotes and introductions.

---

* In *A Preface to Chaucer,* cited above.

XV

THE EVALUATION OF POETRY

This final chapter may not be assigned by the instructor if he does not care to open up the subject of evaluation or has views on it which differ from those expressed here. To some students, moreover, it may seem confusing rather than informative, in spite of the effort which has been made to keep it simple—for the orientation is philosophical, the conceptual structure aims at a certain rigor, and space will not admit liberal poetic illustrations. The discussion is offered to exceptionally capable undergraduates who may find pleasure or profit, or both, in tracing a complex problem a short distance toward its roots. Most disputes about poetic values fail to be resolved because the real grounds of difference are never brought to light. An attempt will be made here to uncover some of the hidden difficulties. A few minds, perhaps, will be first stimulated to develop a passionate interest in poetry by the discovery that art, of which poetry is a subdivision, can engage the best powers of the abstract reason as well as the aesthetic sensitivities.

It will be necessary to bear constantly in mind that *evaluate* is used exclusively in the sense "to appraise, estimate the value of." We shall not be interested in *appreciation,* if that word is understood to mean "relish, find personal pleasure in." The focus will be upon objective values accessible to all competent readers, not upon private likes and dislikes. I may "appreciate"—that is, respond positively to—a poetic description because it reminds me of a mountain setting in which I enjoyed a memorable picnic with a sweetheart. Nobody ought to argue me out of my enjoyment; but I ought not seriously to maintain that the poem is "good" because it sets me to reminiscing about a pleasurable incident in my individual past. The distinction betweeen what we like and what we recognize to be objectively good is, in fact, relatively easy to make. On occasion we have all said "It's good, but I don't like it" or "I like it, but it doesn't really amount to much." My liking for certain stage personalities does not involve the delusion that they act well. Throughout the discussion which follows, our attempt will be to discover value properties in poetry which are at least potentially present for readers besides ourselves.

Literary evaluation falls properly (although not always practically) within the larger discipline of value theory, or axiology—a discipline which becomes more complicated the longer one investigates it. One disquieting conclusion to which a century of philosophical study has led is the realization that no evaluation can be finally "proved." The value of an object cannot be established by the finding of specific properties in the object unless the properties have already been defined as valuable. Unfortunately, every definition of value properties appears to rest ultimately on an unprovable assumption. Arguments intended to establish the assumption regularly turn out to be circular. Hence there has arisen what value theorists have called a "crisis in the theory of value."

A nonliterary example will illustrate. A certain car, I may claim, is a very "good" car because it is unusually powerful and has expensive upholstery. Obviously, I assume that great power and expensive upholstery are unqualified values in an automobile. Both assumptions can be denied. Extremely high power, it can be said, is uselessly expensive in view of legal speed limits, and the cost of upholstery is less important than its attractiveness and durability. An effort to refute the objections can only substitute other value assumptions for the original one. Let us follow the second half of the problem a little farther. It may be urged that the ostentatious display of wealth in expensive upholstery is worth while because the enjoyment of superior economic success is good. This assertion, in turn, can be defended by the argument that members of a competitive society ought to accept the opportunities offered them for competition. But why should social norms be accepted rather than rejected? Presumably because we have already decided that social adjustment is itself an unqualified good. If the reason for this belief is questioned, the reply may be that adjustment is better than conflict. Here the reasoning becomes circular, for competition has been said to be the pattern of the society to which we must adjust.

The example is fairly typical. Every evaluation, whether of poetry or of something else, depends finally upon an "if." *If* this poem is good because it is pleasantly melodic, then pleasant melody must always be good in poetry. But this can be so only *if* poetry is conceived to be more nearly akin to music than—for instance—to picture or to thought; and an attempt to establish that thesis will involve a second affirmation which will reveal itself, upon inspection, to depend upon a third. The process is infinitely regressive.

Attempts to resolve the difficulty have usually involved an appeal to forget about logical proof and observe the choices which people actually make. In the end, this amounts to an assertion that we should take votes, should count noses. If, however, we attempt to settle poetic values so, we discover that Edgar Guest is a better writer than Robert Frost. Among moving-picture actresses, Elizabeth Taylor would currently be "best" because she draws the biggest audiences. And so on. Critics find such verdicts repellent and try to avoid them by saying that the only votes which should count are those of "good judges." A good judge of poetry, however, is one who values poems that we have previously decided were valuable. How else can we establish the fact that he has taste? But we began by attempting to learn how good literature can be distinguished from bad, and we cannot accept an answer which implies that we already know which works are good.*

---

* The problems sketched above are discussed in more detail in Chapters 8-11 of my *Elements of Critical Theory* (Berkeley: University of California Press, 1952).

No matter how hard we struggle, we are forced back in the end to an admission that no evaluative judgment is logically irrefutable. If I am told that Tennyson's *Idylls of the King* is technically accomplished, I may retort that its ethics is shallow. Praise of Browning's "The Grammarian's Funeral" as richly suggestive of the Renaissance interest in Greek scholarship may be countered by the assertion that the metrics are bad. And so always: whatever is praised in one aspect can be found bad in another. It might seem, accordingly, that the urge to evaluate should be controlled and our literary discussions kept rigorously factual.

Actually, there is no better reason to remain uncommitted in talking about literature than in facing other practical decisions which must be made daily. Although I cannot prove beyond cavil that one car is better than another, I must probably buy one in order to avoid traveling everywhere on foot or by bus. Moral principles are as difficult to justify as literary, yet I must frequently make moral choices—as, for instance, in deciding whether to discipline a child. Neither can uncertainty about the relative beauty of Chippendale and Regency furniture keep me from wanting chairs in my home. In judging literature, however, as in settling other problems, we want to act intelligently. To defend our judgments by saying merely "That's what I like" puts the matter beyond logic and begs the question of rational soundness. We must therefore see whether we can discover evaluative principles which at least are not intellectually disreputable.

A preliminary division may be made between *intrinsic* and *extrinsic* standards. The intrinsic judgment rests on the internal consistency of the object, the extrinsic judgment on the relation of the object to something external to it.

Throughout most of the preceding chapters our attention has been focused on the ways in which poetic parts fuse to produce wholes; therefore the discussion of intrinsic judgments can be kept brief. When all the parts are discovered to fit (usually to produce a meaning), so that the whole is tightly unified, the intrinsic judgment must be favorable. If the parts are found to pull against each other, an unfavorable verdict is entailed. Care must be taken, naturally, to interpret the work perceptively. If a contradiction between parts escapes notice, or if the resolution of an apparent contradiction is missed, the evaluation will not be sensitively responsive to the criterion. The chance that this may happen offers no theoretical difficulty, however, for factual error is always possible.

It will be observed that criticism of this kind grants the work its subject, its meaning, and, indeed, its total purpose. The assumption underlying the evaluative method is that art has no other responsibility than to become, triumphantly, whatever it aspires to be. In practice, most readers draw the line somewhere between acceptable and repugnant subjects. One critic may resent a poem which makes sexual promiscuity attractive and another become agitated when militant patriotism is praised (as by Kipling), but hardly anyone has unlimited tolerance. For the most part, however, undergraduate critics should avoid attacking a poem's subject, or at least should postpone attacking it until they have made the most perceptive examination they can of the way the parts of the work cooperate, or fail to cooperate, to produce a whole. An assault on a poetic subject typically shows disorientation. The student does not know how to discuss poetry as poetry, and therefore writes his essay on ethics or religion or politics instead. From a pedagogical point of view, this is evasive—like writing an ode to a frog for a zoology course.

Intrinsic evaluation can be recommended for at least two further reasons. The first is that the method offers protection against youthful prejudices. The college undergraduate, presumably, is at school because he wishes to have his understanding widened and deepened. The unprejudiced reading of good literature will help wonderfully toward this end—perhaps the more effectively in proportion as the subjects or attitudes are unfamiliar. Second, intrinsic criticism has been popular in literary circles for several decades and is likely to be well received by teachers. When the ignoring of prejudices comes hard, the student can console himself by reflecting that an intrinsic evaluation of a poem is not total. Nothing more than the work's success in attaining a limited end is appraised. The evaluation of the end is simply not attempted.

Here, strictly, the discussion of intrinsic criticism should end, for no judgment is actually intrinsic if it depends on information brought to the reading. By custom, however, any estimate of a writer's attainment of his purpose is spoken of as intrinsic. Even if the purpose is defined with the help of information discovered in a preface, in letters written by the author, or in some other external source, the willingness to let the writer determine the grounds of judgment sets the critic apart from persons who bring ready-made standards to their reading. In this broader sense, the intrinsic critic is any judge who, instead of making a priori demands on literature, accepts each work on terms relevant specifically to it.

When we move beyond internal standards, a bewildering variety of possibilities opens itself to view. To what besides its own ends should poetry be held accountable? Ultimately, perhaps, poetry is valuable for the same reasons as any other experience, whether or not the experience is distinctively aesthetic. Some very general term like "life enhancement" may suggest the deepest value of food, sleep, love, work, and poetry alike. For our purposes, however, it will be best to make a preliminary division between purely aesthetic and not-purely-aesthetic values and then to look briefly at each.

Purely aesthetic standards assume that art works, including poems and plays and novels, exist in an autonomous realm within which special values obtain. "Art," although it may touch on such other areas as politics and morality, ought to be considered merely as art. Traditionally the realm of art has been defined as that of beauty. But what kind of thing is beauty?

In the visual arts, beauty is widely believed to be mainly or wholly *sensory* in quality, its elements being line, shape, mass, color, texture, and the form which all five together produce. By this standard, ideas and narrative values are irrelevant. A painting like "The End of the Trail," which shows a disconsolate Indian sitting on a drooping horse, or "Old Shepherd's Chief Mourner," which portrays a grief-stricken dog pressing his chest against the coffin of a rustic whose piety is suggested by spectacles laid in a closed Bible, is pooh-poohed by the typical art critic because the real interest is in the subject. Attention, such a critic would say, ought not to be diverted from plastic forms to sentiments and thoughts. A picture entitled simply "Head of a Young Girl," or perhaps a nonobjective painting by Mondrian or Jackson Pollock, may from this point of view be thought far superior, in spite of an almost total lack of describable "meaning."

In poetry, some connection between beauty and meaning is unavoidable, because the basic aesthetic material of poetry—words—cannot wholly lack reference. None the less, sensory beauty can be especially prized. Critics who exclaim over alliteration, elaborate patterns of vowel and consonant sounds, rhythmic beauties, and other similar qualities implicitly accept the importance of sensory properties. A fondness for onomatopoeia suggests a relation between sound and meaning; but images are often highly sensory and may evoke pleasing word pictures. On the whole, however, the young critic will be wise not to focus his critical papers on sensory qualities considered in isolation but to relate these in some way to the aesthetic whole. Poetry is now rarely believed to consist basically of a stream of beautiful sound, and images are praised more for their meanings than for objective beauty.

In recent decades, aesthetic criticism has tended to abandon the traditional interest in beauty for a new emphasis on *expressiveness*. The theoretical justification of the shift is the opinion that art differs from nonart in attempting rather to *present* its meanings than to *reason them out*. From this angle, "The End of the Trail" and "Old Shepherd's Chief Mourner" look better because they make us understand something by nonlogical means. Technique continues to be important. If the brushwork is amateurish, it can be criticized as unexpressive; if the composition is awkward, it can be shown to detract from the meaning; and the meanings themselves can be judged sentimental. Yet the critical standard has been altered profoundly. Blandness is no longer encouraged, and pictures of shepherdesses in graceful postures are likely to seem trivial. Value is sought more in *impact:* the colors are more daring, the play of imagination is freer, and violence no longer is reproached as ugly.

The criticism of poetry has been much affected by the change. If the substance of art is percepts, a highly rational poem like Pope's *Essay on Man* hardly deserves to be classified as aesthetic. Such images as it contains tend to illustrate meanings which have already been explained discursively. Donne's poems, in contrast, use images to make statements that could not be expressed so effectively in any other way. Accordingly, Donne's reputation, which had been in eclipse for two and a half centuries, rose sharply, as did that of such odd (and often difficult) poets as Gerard Manley Hopkins, whose techniques had hitherto seemed merely eccentric. Criticism (often called "The New Criticism") began to concentrate more on images and to devalue logic to such an extent that Cleanth Brooks identified the language of poetry with that of paradox. By intention, the focus was still aesthetic; literature was to be criticized, said T. S. Eliot, as literature and not as another thing. But beauty was now subordinated to expressiveness, and expressiveness was thought to reside mainly in percepts, which functioned characteristically as metaphors and symbols.

Although it seems to be declining in popularity, the method is still viable. The student who attempts it can find models in the writings of Cleanth Brooks, Robert Penn Warren (who collaborated with Brooks on an influential textbook called *Understanding Poetry*), John Crowe Ransom, Allen Tate, and R. P. Blackmur. Many of the insights of the New Critics are permanently valuable; and in the foreseeable future there is unlikely to be a return to the belief that the fundamental responsibility of an art work is to be beautiful. The chief evaluative criteria are nondiscursiveness, perceptual richness, highly metaphorical quality, and complexity. Where these qualities are found in relative density, the evaluation is favorable. A danger is that the method may become showy—an exercise in critical ingenuity. Also, the critic who digs for submerged meanings is often not a man who does historical spadework enthusiastically, so that essays produced by members of the school have occasionally offered readings which were indignantly rejected by scholars whose knowledge of contemporary backgrounds was sounder.

The two aesthetic emphases so far mentioned are comparatively recent. As an autonomous intellectual discipline, aesthetics hardly predates the publication of two Latin treatises by Alexander Baumgarten in 1735 and 1750. The very term "aesthetics," meaning "a science of perception" in Baumgarten's use, has no earlier history. A further impetus was exerted in 1790 by the celebrated *Critique of Judgment* (*Kritik der Urteilskraft*) of Immanuel Kant. Kant argued that only a science of judgment (aesthetic and teleological, but especially the former) can bridge the gap between the two major divisions of philosophy, natural and moral. Knowledge of the natural world lies in the realm of the understanding and is theoretical; moral concepts lie in the realm of the reason and are practical. The sphere of delight, or the beautiful, lies midway between and engages the power of judgment. Like objects in the natural world, a work of art stimulates the senses; like moral drives, which spring from desire, it is related to subjective pleasure. The aesthetic realm is hence that of disinterested satisfaction. Thereafter aesthetics seemed to be a necessary part of any adequate world view, and every aspiring philosopher sought to round out his thought by adding a theory of art to his metaphysics, epistemology, and ethics. John Dewey's *Art as Experience* is a twentieth-century example. But prior to the mid-eighteenth century aesthetics scarcely had philosophical grounding except as it derived from Aristotle's *Poetics*, which borrowed its assumptions from a philosophy of archetypes (the view that sensory objects are imperfect realizations of eternal ideas). We shall recur to this classical theory in a moment. For the most part, the literary tradition was rhetorical and can be summed up by saying that literature was expected to *teach with delight* by means of well-understood persuasive techniques.

In view of what was said earlier about the relation of aesthetics to total philosophies, it is evident that aesthetic standards must vary along with broader philosophical commitments. According to Stephen C. Pepper,* there are only four relatively adequate philosophies at present, hence only four aesthetic systems which derive support from total world views.† *Mechanism,* which regards the whole universe as an immense machine, has generated a hedonistic type of aesthetics: the purpose of art is to *give pleasure. Contextualism* (or *pragmatism*) defines the aesthetic field as that of *voluntary vivid intuitions of quality,* "quality" being understood as "intuited wholeness or total character." ‡ Whereas expository prose is mainly analytic, creative literature gives us a sense of the feeling and flavor of actual experience. *Organicism* (historically known as *objective idealism*) emphasizes relatedness and therefore puts a special premium on the achievement of *tightly integrated form,* the special subject matter of art works being *feelings.* The approach recommended in Chapters I–XIII of the present text has been basically organistic. The fourth of the relatively adequate world views, *formism* (or *philosophical realism*), deserves a somewhat fuller description because it was dominant during the longest historical period—roughly from the beginnings of Western literature in Greece and Rome to the end of the eighteenth century.

Formism begins with perceptions of similarity and through them arrives easily at the idea of *norms.* The normal object is one which contains all the traits or characteristics present in all the members of its class and is in no important way eccentric. Abnormality comes to be associated with badness or disease; normality is equated with value. The processes of comparison and differentiation are fundamental in formist thought. A tree belongs to the vegetable kingdom because it shares with blades of grass and bushes characteristics not present in rocks or animals; but it differs from a blade of grass and

---

* *The Basis of Criticism in the Arts* (Cambridge, Mass.: Harvard University Press, 1945).

† My own *Elements of Critical Theory* covers some of the same ground in Chapter 10, "Orders of Evaluative Assumptions."

‡ For the phrase, see Stephen C. Pepper, *World-Hypotheses: A Study in Evidence* (Berkeley: University of California Press, 1948), p. 238.

a bush, which also belong to the vegetable kingdom, by having characteristics possessed only by other trees. Ultimately categories are generated for every conceivable sort of object, so that thinking involves the assigning of phenomena to appropriate pigeonholes.

Poetry is an "art" because it is an "imitation" or "representation" of something other than itself. (The Aristotelian word is *mimesis*.) It differs from the other arts—music, painting, sculpture—by using words as its medium. "Poetry" is itself, however, a relatively high-level abstraction. It can be subdivided into tragedy, comedy, epic, and lyric—and these, in turn, into still smaller categories. The evaluation of poems accordingly depends rather heavily on their typicality, or conformity to tendencies observable within their classes. Each poetic kind or genre has its own rules, and the good poem is one which has all the appropriate traits. In proportion as formist criticism is philosophical it tends, as has been said, to have traffic with *archetypal ideas* (as these were described by Plato and Aristotle). As the idea of a bed which pre-existed the making of particular beds is the standard for the judgment of beds, so an abstract notion of good tragedy is the standard for tragedies.

Such, very generally, are the aesthetic principles which accompanied the dominance of philosophical realism. They are historically, if not absolutely, relevant to the criticism of ancient poetry and of virtually all "learned" poetry, at least through the mid-eighteenth-century. With the emergence of Romanticism, formist principles began to be replaced by organicist; later, mechanist and contextualistic systems began to emerge. None of the four philosophies is dead, however, and all, according to Professor Pepper, are about equally credible. In Departments of English, the oldest of the four aesthetic systems is probably the most popular, for the academic study of literature tends to be historically oriented. An assignment which called upon the student to discuss whether Arthur Miller's *Death of a Salesman* was or was not "true" tragedy would raise few eyebrows. Specialists in the nineteenth and twentieth centuries, however, are likely, either consciously or unconsciously, to be organicists or contextualists.

So far we have considered only aesthetic standards (and those only very superficially). But poetry also makes statements about experience which can often be judged by nonliterary standards as "true" or "false," "moral" or "immoral," and so on; and aesthetic activity itself may in certain circumstances be less admirable than nonaesthetic. How are we to cope with these additional complications? How terribly involved the problems become when art is not considered to be a self-justifying activity can be suggested by an illustration. Let us imagine a ballerina who executes a step called *entrechat six* in an aesthetically praiseworthy manner. As art, the maneuver is unquestionably admirable; the journalistic critics will have nothing but praise for it. In the meantime, however—let us imagine, rather dramatically—the dancer's little son has been left in the care of a sadistic nurse who, while the ballet is being given, continues to lay the foundation for a neurosis which will cause the boy a lifetime of suffering. Also, the *entre-chat six* so enchants an impressionable young spectator that, when he next looks at his somewhat dumpy fiancée, he will draw comparisons unfavorable to her and finally terminate an engagement that offered both of them a unique opportunity for happiness. Are these and other similar consequences balanced, or overbalanced, by the aesthetic pleasure given a theaterful of people? Would it perhaps be better that the ballerina should give up her theatrical career altogether in order to care properly for her son? No act, aesthetic or other, is really isolated. It occurs within an individual life which is enmeshed within a social context of family, friends, and general public; and within this larger area nonaesthetic values are sure to be involved.

Recognition of the continuity of aesthetic with nonaesthetic experience has led to the production of criticism which, if aesthetically disoriented, has none the less strongly influenced literary practice. Jeremy Collier's *Short View of the Profaneness and Immorality of the English Stage* (1698) affected drama for decades. And good nonaesthetic criticism continues to be written. A perceptive essay by L. C. Knights has called Restoration comedy "trivial, gross, and dull"; a minor classic by Joseph Wood Krutch entitled "The Tragic Fallacy" laments the decay of a feeling that man is intrinsically admirable. No really valid claim can be made that art exists in a realm wholly its own. Nothing at all in human experience totally lacks connection with anything else.

In an introduction like the present one, nothing more can be done in this impossibly complicated situation than to offer a few practically helpful suggestions.

First, unless we want to play God we had better not worry about the ballerina's little son and the enchanted young spectator. The ultimate results of any single action may range from virtually nothing to a very great deal, and no human being can foresee them. Yet sometimes what is said by an art work about life may demand evaluation in its own right. The economics of Ezra Pound's *Cantos* or the morality of Shelley's *Queen Mab* is not immune to inspection. The poets themselves wanted their ideas to be taken seriously. When the focus of an evaluative essay is nonaesthetic, the reason should of course be that the work invites that kind of discussion; and the critic must use every possible means to insure that his thinking is responsible and informed. It goes without saying also that he should not reveal himself to be aesthetically imperceptive. When these conditions are met, however, no good objection can be made to a nonaesthetic, or not-wholly-aesthetic, focus. Art is praised, not despised, when it is recognized to have cognitive as well as aesthetic importance.

Second, the typical evaluative essay on a literary subject—and perhaps especially on a poem—will none the less address itself to a consideration of artistry. Every practical activity demands the drawing of a line somewhere. A surgeon who removes a set of infected tonsils does not attempt at the same time to fill cavities in the patient's teeth. The focusing of criticism on aesthetic values does not normally deny the relevance of other evaluative standards but merely specializes in one interest. For college undergraduates particularly, the aesthetic emphasis is good because it forces awareness to be concentrated on what is poetic about poetry instead of on matters which can best be studied in courses outside the English Department.

Third, the basis of total evaluation, if this is attempted, should ideally be a responsible theory of art; and such a theory has authority in proportion as it is corroborated by an entire philosophical system which accounts adequately for the total human experience. Aesthetic theories held by persons who are interested only in art, or knowledgeable only about art (for example, practicing poets, who often undervalue whatever they do not themselves attempt to do) tend to be philosophically naïve. In an academic environment, a certain naiveté is pardonable if it accompanies a really earnest effort to think problems through. Young people must be allowed to make errors while seeking to develop their capabilities. Yet the danger of making silly assumptions is very great, and the student who attempts total evaluations necessarily skates on very brittle ice.

Fourth, if partial rather than total evaluation is attempted, the safest criterion is one implied by the work under consideration. Magnanimity is shown by a willingness to allow a poet his choice of purpose and methods; and there is educational value in an intellectual resilience which allows the frequent shifting of horizons. An effort to discover whether a work has successfully achieved its aims requires both a sympathetic understanding of the purport and a sensitive analysis of technical means.

Fifth, other partial evaluations can be offered with reasonable safety provided they are made conditional on the soundness of an acknowledged standard. The evaluation can be explicitly linked to the standard in a form something like this: "If X is an aesthetic value, then this work has (or does not have) that kind of value." Sensory richness or vividness or organic unity or fidelity to the laws of a poetic genre or realistic accuracy can be praised *on condition that* the characteristic is a poetic good. Much the same kind of evaluation is implied by the commendation of a specific quality or trait without the explicit attaching of a condition, as in the sentence, "This lyric is beautifully melodic." The mark of such a conditional evaluation is simply the absence of a direct assertion that because the admired quality is present the poem *therefore* must be totally good. In the typical short paper likely to be assigned in English classes, evaluation seldom need go farther.

Finally, because "criticism" long ago ceased to contain lists of beauties and faults, evaluation may usually be avoided altogether in favor of technical exploration; and this choice is perhaps best of all. Few instructors will be dissatisfied with papers which show a lively concern about poetic traits, whether or not they include ringing statements about values. A careful analysis of *the way in which a total meaning is supported by the details of poetic structure* will feel, and sound, like criticism and will do more than any other invariable method to initiate the student gradually into an appreciative comprehension of poetry. Only it should be remembered steadily that the meaning need not be a "message." It may be an attitude, a feeling, a mood, or anything else in which the poet has found either momentary or enduring significance. A thousand poems which attempt nothing more than to "render" evanescent impressions may, in fact, do more to brighten and illuminate existence than an equal number of ponderously philosophical or damply moral poems about "problems." If the student attempts to perceive the special *whatness* of every poem he reads and also, within the limits of his native endowments, to understand *how* the whatness is achieved, he will be doing, perhaps, as much as any student can do to enrich his mind and life through the medium of poetry.

Part Two

AN ANTHOLOGY OF POEMS

Sir Thomas Wyatt (1503–1542)

MY GALLEY CHARGÈD WITH FORGETFULNESS

My galley chargèd with forgetfulness
Thorough sharp seas, in winter nights, doth pass
'Tween rock and rock; and eke mine enemy, alas,
That is my lord, steereth with cruelness;   4
And every hour a thought in readiness,
As though that death were light in such a case.
An endless wind doth tear the sail apace
Of forcèd sighs and trusty fearfulness;   8
A rain of tears, a cloud of dark disdain,
Hath done the wearèd cords great hinderance.
Wretched with error and eke with ignorance,
The stars be hid that led me to this pain;   12
Drownèd is reason that should me comfort,
And I remain despairing of the port.

(1557)

WHOSO LIST TO HUNT,
I KNOW WHERE IS AN HIND

Whoso list to hunt, I know where is an hind;
But as for me, alas, I may no more.
The vain travail hath wearied me so sore
I am of them that furdest come behind.   4
Yet may I, by no means, my wearied mind
Draw from the deer; but as she fleeth afore,
Fainting I follow, and leave off therefore,

WYATT. There are many textual cruxes in Wyatt. The texts given here are modernized from the holograph printed by Ewald Flügel in *Anglia,* xviii-xix (1896–97); but for their interest I indicate in the notes a few of the revisions made (probably not by Wyatt) for *Tottel's Miscellany* (1557).

MY GALLEY . . . 2 *thorough:* through. 3 *eke:* also. 5 *hour:* ms. owre; Tottel, oar. 10 *wearèd:* Tottel, wearied. 13 *comfort:* ms. confort; Tottel, consort.

WHOSO LIST . . . 1 *list:* likes. 4 *furdest:* furthest.

127

Since in a net I seek to hold the wind. 8
Who list her hunt, I put him out of doubt,
As well as I may spend his time in vain.
And graven with diamonds in letters plain
There is written, her fair neck round about, 12
Noli me tangere, for Caesar's I am,
And wild for to hold, though I seem tame.

(1557)

FAREWELL, LOVE, AND ALL THY LAWS FOREVER

Farewell, love, and all thy laws forever;
Thy baited hooks shall tangle me no more.
Senec and Plato call me from thy lore
To perfect wealth, my wit for to endeavor. 4
In blind error when I did perséver,
Thy sharp repulse, that pricketh aye so sore,
Hath taught me to set in trifles no store,
And scape forth, since liberty is lever. 8
Therefore, farewell; go trouble younger hearts,
And in me claim no more authority.
With idle youth go use thy property,
And thereon spend thy many brittle darts; 12
For hitherto, though I have lost all my time,
Me lusteth no lenger rotten boughs to climb.

(1557)

THEY FLEE FROM ME,
THAT SOMETIME DID ME SEEK

They flee from me, that sometime did me seek,
With naked foot stalking in my chamber.
I have seen them gentle, tame, and meek

---

13 *Noli me tangere:* Do not touch me. *Caesar's:* it has been speculated that the
object of Wyatt's love was Anne Boleyn, who became Henry VIII's second wife.

FAREWELL, LOVE . . . 3 *Senec and Plato:* Seneca, Roman Stoic philosopher
(d. A.D. 65); Plato, Greek philosopher (d. 347 B.C.). 6 *pricketh:* goads or pains.
8 *lever:* liever, preferable. 11 *property:* attribute or quality (of personality).
14 *Me lusteth:* I desire. *lenger:* longer.

128

That sometime they put themself in danger 5
That now are wild and do not remember
To take bread at my hand; and now they range,
Busily seeking with a continual change.

Thankèd be fortune, it hath been otherwise,
Twenty times better; but once, in special,
In thin array, after a pleasant guise, 10
When her loose gown from her shoulders did fall
And she me caught in her arms long and small,
Therewithal sweetly did me kiss,
And softly said, Dear heart, how like you this?

It was no dream; I lay broad waking. 15
But all is turned thorough my gentleness
Into a strange fashion of forsaking,
And I have leave to go, of her goodness,
And she also to use newfangleness.
But since that I so kindely am served, 20
I would fain know what she hath deserved.

(1557)

Henry Howard, Earl of Surrey (1517?–1547)

THE SOOTE SEASON,
THAT BUD AND BLOOM FORTH BRINGS

The sootë season, that bud and bloom forth brings,
With green hath clad the hill and eke the vale.
The nightingale with feathers new she sings;

THEY FLEE FROM ME . . . 10 *guise:* manner. 16 *turned thorough:* Tottel,
turned now through. (In any case, "thorough" means "through.") 17 *strange:*
Tottel, bitter. 20 *so kindely:* Tottel, I unkindly so. *kindely:* benevolently? according to her (my) nature? 21 Tottel, "How like you this, what hath she now
deserved?"

THE SOOTE SEASON . . . Both Wyatt and Surrey often adapted Italian poems.
The present sonnet seems to have been inspired by Petrarch's *Sonetto in Morte
XLII.* The adaptation here is very free; in contrast, the next sonnet follows
Petrarch's *Sonetto in Vita XCI* rather closely. Comparisons of the two with
their sources will suggest the wide variety of relationships between much Renais-
sance poetry and continental originals. 1 *sootë:* sweet.

The turtle to her make hath told her tale.   4
Summer is come, for every spray now springs.
The hart hath hung his old head on the pale;
The buck in brake his winter coat he flings;
The fishes float with new-repairèd scale;   8
The adder all her slough away she slings;
The swift swallow pursueth the flies small;
The busy bee her honey now she mings.
Winter is worn, that was the flowers' bale.   12
And thus I see among these pleasant things
Each care decays, and yet my sorrow springs.

(1557)

LOVE, THAT DOTH REIGN AND LIVE WITHIN MY THOUGHT

Love, that doth reign and live within my thought
And built his seat within my captive breast,
Clad in the arms wherein with me he fought,
Oft in my face he doth his banner rest.   4
But she that taught me love and suffer pain,
My doubtful hope and eke my hot desire
With shamefast look to shadow and refrain,
Her smiling grace converteth straight to ire.   8
And coward love, then, to the heart apace
Taketh his flight, where he doth lurk and plain
His purpose lost, and dare not shew his face.
For my lord's guilt thus faultless bide I pain,   12
Yet from my lord shall not my foot remove.
Sweet is the death that taketh end by love.

(1557)

---

4 *turtle:* turtledove. *make:* mate. 11 *mings:* either "mixes" (*mengs*) or "re-members."

LOVE, THAT DOTH REIGN . . . 10 *plain:* complain.

130

WYATT RESTETH HERE,
THAT QUICK COULD NEVER REST

Wyatt resteth here, that quick could never rest;
Whose heavenly gifts increasèd by disdain,
And virtue sank the deeper in his breast:
Such profit he by envy could obtain.   4

A head where wisdom mysteries did frame;
Whose hammers beat still in that lively brain
As on a stith, where that some work of fame
Was daily wrought to turn to Britain's gain.   8

A visage stern and mild, where both did grow
Vice to contemn, in virtue to rejoice;
Amid great storms, whom grace assurèd so,
To live upright, and smile at fortune's choice. 12

A hand that taught what might be said in rhyme;
That reft Chaucer the glory of his wit:
A mark the which, unparfited, for time,
Some may approach, but never none shall hit.   16

A tongue that served in foreign realms his king,
Whose courteous talk to virtue did enflame
Each noble heart; a worthy guide to bring
Our English youth, by travail, unto fame.   20

An eye whose judgment none affect could blind
Friends to allure, and foes to reconcile;
Whose piercing look did represent a mind
With virtue fraught, reposèd, void of guile.   24

A heart where dread was never so impressed
To hide the thought that might the truth advance;
In neither fortune lost, nor yet repressed,
To swell in wealth, or yield unto mischance.   28

A valiant corps, where force and beauty met;
Happy, alas, too happy, but for foes;
Livèd, and ran the race that nature set;
Of manhood's shape, where she the mold did lose. 32

WYATT RESTETH HERE . . . 1 *quick:* alive. 7 *stith:* stithy. 14 *reft:* bereft, deprived. 15 *unparfited, for time:* unperfected for lack of time. 21 *affect:* emotion. 27 *In . . . lost:* At a loss neither in good fortune nor in bad. 29 *corps:* (living) body.

But to the heavens that simple soul is fled,
Which left with such as covet Christ to know
Witness of faith that never shall be dead;
Sent for our health, but not receivèd so. 36

Thus, for our guilt, this jewel have we lost.
The earth his bones, the heavens possess his ghost.

(1557)

Sir Philip Sidney *(1554–1586)*

From ASTROPHEL AND STELLA

I

Loving in truth, and fain in verse my love to show,
That she, dear she, might take some pleasure of my pain;
Pleasure might cause her read, reading might make her know,
Knowledge might pity win, and pity grace obtain: 4
I sought fit words to paint the blackest face of woe,
Studying inventions fine her wits to entertain,
Oft turning others' leaves, to see if thence would flow
Some fresh and fruitful showers upon my sunburnt brain. 8
But words came halting forth, wanting invention's stay;
Invention, Nature's child, fled stepdame Study's blows,
And others' feet still seemed but strangers in my way.
Thus, great with child to speak, and helpless in my throes, 12
Biting my truant pen, beating myself for spite—
Fool! said my Muse to me. Look in thy heart, and write.

II

Not at the first sight, nor with a dribbèd shot,
Love gave the wound which, while I breathe, will bleed.
But known worth did in mine of time proceed,

I. 9 *stay:* support.

II. 1 *dribbèd:* falling short or going wild. 3 *mine of time:* a process of gradual
undermining? Other texts have "mind."

Till, by degrees, it had full conquest got. 4
I saw, and liked; I liked, but lovèd not;
I loved, but straight did not what love decreed.
At length to love's decrees I, forced, agreed,
Yet with repining at so partial lot. 8
Now even that footstep of lost liberty
Is gone; and now, like slave-born Muscovite,
I call it praise to suffer tyranny;
And now employ the remnant of my wit 12
To make myself believe that all is well,
While, with a feeling skill, I paint my hell.

IV

Virtue, alas, now let me take some rest.
Thou set'st a bate between my will and wit.
If vain love have my simple soul oppressed,
Leave what thou lik'st not; deal not thou with it. 4
Thy scepter use in some old Cato's breast.
Churches or schools are for thy seat more fit;
I do confess (pardon a fault confessed)
My mouth too tender is for thy hard bit. 8
But if that needs thou wilt usurping be
The little reason that is left in me,
And still the effect of thy persuasions prove,
I swear, my heart such one shall show to thee 12
That shrines in flesh so true a deity
That, virtue, thou thyself shalt be in love.

VIII

Love, born in Greece, of late fled from his native place,
Forced, by a tedious proof, that Turkish hardened heart
Is not fit mark to pierce with his fine-pointed dart,
And pleased with our soft peace, stayed here his flying race. 4
But finding these north climes too coldly him embrace,
Not used to frozen clips, he strave to find some part
Where with most ease and warmth he might employ his art.
At length he perched himself in Stella's joyful face, 8
Whose fair skin, beamy eyes, like morning sun on snow,
Deceived the quaking boy, who thought from so pure light

IV. 2 *bate:* conflict. 5 *Cato's breast:* Cato the Censor (234–149 B.C.) is used as an example of a morally rigorous man.

VIII. 6 *clips:* embraces. *strave:* strove.

Effects of lively heat must needs in nature grow.
But she, most fair, most cold, made him thence take his flight   12
To my close heart; where, while some firebrands he did lay,
He burnt unwares his wings, and cannot fly away.

XXXI

With how sad steps, O Moon, thou climb'st the skies!
How silently, and with how wan a face!
What! may it be that even in heavenly place
That busy archer his sharp arrows tries?   4
Sure, if that long-with-love-acquainted eyes
Can judge of love, thou feel'st a lover's case.
I read it in thy looks; thy languished grace
To me, that feel the like, thy state descries.   8
Then, even of fellowship, O Moon, tell me:
Is constant love deemed there but want of wit?
Are beauties there as proud as here they be?
Do they above love to be loved, and yet   12
Those lovers scorn whom that love doth possess?
Do they call virtue there ungratefulness?

XXXIX

Come sleep, O sleep, the certain knot of peace!
The baiting-place of wit, the balm of woe,
The poor man's wealth, the prisoner's release,
The indifferent judge between the high and low.   4
With shield of proof shield me from out the press
Of those fierce darts despair at me doth throw.
O make in me those civil wars to cease;
I will good tribute pay, if thou do so.   8
Take thou of me smooth pillows, sweetest bed,
A chamber deaf to noise and blind to light,
A rosy garland and a weary head;
And if these things, as being thine by right,   12
Move not thy heavy grace, thou shalt in me,
Livelier than elsewhere, Stella's image see.

XLI

Having this day my horse, my hand, my lance
Guided so well that I obtained the prize

XXXIX. 2 *baiting-place:* a stopping-place on a journey.   5 *press:* throng.

134

Both by the judgment of the English eyes
And of some sent from that sweet enemy, France,   4
Horsemen my skill in horsemanship advance,
Townfolks my strength; a daintier judge applies
His praise to sleight which from good use doth rise;
Some lucky wits impute it but to chance;   8
Others, because of both sides I do take
My blood from them who did excel in this,
Think nature me a man-at-arms did make.
How far they shoot awry! The true cause is,   12
Stella looked on, and from her heavenly face
Sent forth the beams which made so fair my race.

(1591)

XLI. 5 *advance:* praise. 6 *daintier:* more discriminating. 7 *use:* practice.

Edmund Spenser *(1552?–1599)*

From THE SHEPHERD'S CALENDAR: OCTOBER

Ægloga decima.

Argument

In Cuddie is set out the perfect pattern of a poet, which, finding no maintenance of his state and studies, complaineth of the contempt of poetry, and the causes thereof: specially

---

ARGUMENT: summary. Besides the *Argument,* early editions contain notes by E. K. (unidentified), the more interesting or useful of which will be entered in their proper places below. ἐνθουσιασμός: inspiration (our word "enthusiasm"). *The English Poet:* not extant. E. K.'s first note reads as follows: "This eclogue is made in imitation of Theocritus's xvi. Idilion [i.e., idyl], wherein he reproved the tyran Hiero of Syracuse for his nigardise [niggardliness] toward poets, in whom is the power to make men immortal for their good deeds, or shameful for their naughty life. And the like also is in Mantuan [1448–1516—a neo-Latin writer of eclogues]. The style hereof, as also that in Theocritus, is more lofty than the rest, and applied to the height of poetical wit." An *eclogue* was a "pastoral" poem in which the poet and his companions were represented as shepherds and shepherdesses.

136

having been in all ages, and even amongst the most barbarous, always of singular account and honor, and being indeed so worthy and commendable an art—or rather no art, but a divine gift and heavenly instinct not to be gotten by labor and learning, but adorned with both, and poured into the wit by a certain ἐνθουσιασμός and celestial inspiration, as the author hereof elsewhere at large discourseth, in his book called *The English Poet,* which book, being lately come to my hands, I mind also by God's grace upon further advisement to publish.

Pierce   Cuddie

Cuddie, for shame! Hold up thy heavy head,
And let us cast with what delight to chase
And weary this long ling'ring Phoebus' race.
Whilom thou wont the shepherd's lads to lead
In rhymes, in riddles, and in bidding base:
Now they in thee, and thou in sleep, art dead.   6

Cuddie

Piers, I have pipèd erst so long with pain
That all mine oaten reeds been rent and wore;
And my poor muse hath spent her sparèd store,
Yet little good hath got, and much less gain.
Such pleasance makes the grasshopper so poor
And ligge so laid, when winter doth her strain.   12

The dapper ditties that I wont devise
To feed youth's fancy, and the flocking fry,
Delighten much: what I the bet forthy?
They han the pleasure, I a slender prize.
I beat the bush, the birds to them do fly.
What good thereof to Cuddie can arise?   18

Piers

Cuddie, the praise is better than the prize,

---

1 *Cuddie:* "I doubt whether by Cuddie be specified the author self, or some other" (E. K.). 2 *cast:* consider. 3 *Phoebus' race:* the passage of the sun across the sky; a day. 4 *Whilom:* formerly. 5 *bidding base:* prisoner's base (a game). 7 *pipèd:* played on my pipe, composed poems. *erst:* hitherto. 12 *ligge so laid:* lie so exhausted, subdued. 13 *dapper ditties:* pretty songs. 14 *flocking fry:* "a bold metaphor, forced from the spawning fishes. For the multitude of young fish be called the fry" (E. K.). 15 *the bet forthy:* the better therefore.

137

The glory eke much greater than the gain.
Oh, what an honor is it to restrain
The lust of lawless youth with good advice,
Or prick them forth with pleasance of thy vein,
Whereto thou list their trainèd wills entice! 24

Soon as thou gin'st to set thy notes in frame,
Oh, how the rural routs to thee do cleave!
Seemeth thou dost their soul of sense bereave,
All as the shepherd that did fetch his dame
From Pluto's baleful bow'r withouten leave:
His music's might the hellish hound did tame. 30

Cuddie

So praisen babes the peacock's spotted train,
And wondren at bright Argus' blazing eye.
But who rewards him e'er the more forthy,
Or feeds him once the fuller by a grain?
Sik praise is smoke, that sheddeth in the sky;
Sik words been wind, and wasten soon in vain. 36

Piers

Abandon then the base and viler clown;
Lift up thyself out of the lowly dust
And sing of bloody Mars, of wars, of justs.
Turn thee to those that wield the awful crown:
To doubted knights, whose woundless armor rusts
And helms unbruisèd wexen daily brown. 42

There may thy muse display her flutt'ring wing
And stretch herself at large from East to West,

---

20 *eke:* also. 21–22 *restrain . . . advice:* "This place seemeth to conspire with Plato, who in his first book *De Legibus* [*Concerning the Laws*] saith that the first invention of poetry was of very virtuous intent" (E. K.). 23 *prick:* goad, urge. *vein:* poetic vein. 24 *trainèd:* allured. 26 *routs:* crowds. 28–29 *shepherd . . . bow'r:* "Orpheus: of whom is said, that by his excellent skill in music and poetry he recovered his wife Eurydice from hell" (E. K.). 31–32 *peacock's . . . eye:* "of Argus is before said, that Juno to him committed her husband Jupiter's paragon [paramour] Io, because he [Argus] had an hundred eyes; but afterward Mercury, with his music lulling Argus asleep, slew him and brought Io away, whose eyes it is said that Juno for his eternal memory placed in her bird the peacock's tail" (E. K.). 33 *forthy:* therefore. 35 *sik:* such. *sheddeth in:* pours into. 37 *clown:* rustic fellow. 39 *justs:* jousts. 41 *doubted:* redoubted. *woundless . . . rusts:* because it is unused. 42 *wexen . . . brown:* become dark.

138

Whether thou list in fair Eliza rest,
Or, if thee please in bigger notes to sing,
Advance the worthy whom she loveth best,
That first the white bear to the stake did bring. 48

And when the stubborn stroke of stronger stounds
Has somewhat slacked the tenor of thy string,
Of love and lustihead tho mayst thou sing,
And carol loud, and lead the millers' round,
All were Eliza one of thilk same ring.
So mought our Cuddie's name to Heaven sound. 54

Cuddie

Indeed, the Romish Tityrus, I hear,
Through his Maecenas left his oaten reed,
Whereon he erst had taught his flocks to feed
And labored lands to yield the timely ear,
And eft did sing of wars and deadly dread,
So as the heavens did quake his verse to hear. 60

But ah, Maecenas is yclad in clay,
And great Augustus long ago is dead;
And all the worthies liggen wrapped in lead
That matter made for poets on to play.
For ever, who in derring-do were dread,
The lofty verse of them was lovèd aye. 66

But after virtue gan for age to stoop,
And mighty manhood brought a bed of ease,
The vaunting poets found nought worth a pease
To put in press among the learnèd troupe.

---

45 *list:* likest. *Eliza:* Queen Elizabeth. 48 *That first . . . did bring:* "he meaneth
(as I guess) the most honorable and renowned the Earl of Leicester" (E. K.).
Leicester's escutcheon was a bear and ragged staff. 49 *stounds:* bewilderment,
troubles. 50 *slacked:* "that is, when thou changest thy verse from stately discourse to matter of more pleasance and delight" (E. K.). 51 *tho:* then. 52
millers' round: "a kind of dance" (E. K.). 53 *All:* although. *thilk:* this. 54
mought: might. 55 *Romish Tityrus:* "well known to be Virgil, who by Maecenas'
means was brought into the favor of the Emperor Augustus, and by him moved
to write in loftier kind than he erst had done" (E. K.). 57–59: these three lines
allude, respectively, to Virgil's *Eclogues,* his *Georgics,* and his *Aeneid.* 61 *yclad:*
clad. The *y-* is a decayed form of *ge-,* the sign of the past participle in Old
English. 63 *liggen:* lie. 64 *on to play:* to pipe songs about. 65 *derring-do:*
daring deeds. *dread:* dreadful. 67–72: "he showeth the cause of contempt of
poetry to be idleness and baseness of mind" (E. K.). 69 *pease:* pea. 70 *in
press:* into practice.

Tho gan the streams of flowing wits to cease,
And sun-bright honor penned in shameful coop. 72

And if that any buds of poesy
Yet of the old stock gan to shoot again,
Or it men's follies mote be forced to feign
And roll with rest in rhymes of ribaldry,
Or, as it sprung, it wither must again.
Tom Piper makes us better melody. 78

Piers

O peerless poesy, where is then thy place?
If nor in prince's palace thou do sit
(And yet is prince's palace the most fit),
Ne brest of baser birth doth thee embrace.
Then make thee wings of thine aspiring wit,
And, whence thou cam'st, fly back to heaven apace. 84

Cuddie

Ah, Percy, it is all too weak and wan
So high to soar, and make so large a flight.
Her piecèd pinions been not so in plight.
For Colin fits such famous flight to scan;
He, were he not with love so ill bedight,
Would mount as high, and sing as soote as swan. 90

Piers

Ah, fon, for love does teach him climb so high,
And lifts him up out of the loathsome mire.
Such immortal mirror as he doth admire
Would raise one's mind above the starry sky
And cause a caitive corage to aspire;
For lofty love doth loathe a lowly eye. 96

---

75 *Or:* either. *mote:* must. 78 *Tom . . . melody:* "An ironical sarcasmus, spoken
in derision of these rude wits which make more account of a rhyming ribald
than of skill grounded upon learning or judgment" (E. K.). 82 *Ne:* nor.
87 *piecèd pinions:* patched-up wings. 88 *Colin:* another shepherd-poet. *fits:*
befits. *scan:* attempt. 89 *bedight:* afflicted, pained. 90 *sing . . . swan:* "it is
said of the learned that the swan a little before her death singeth most pleasantly" (E. K.). *soote:* sweetly. 91 *fon:* fool. 93 *immortal mirror:* "Beauty, which
is an excellent object of poetical spirits" (E. K.). 95 *caitive corage:* cowardly
heart.

Cuddie

All otherwise the state of poet stands;
For lordly love is such a tyran fell
That where he rules, all power he doth expel.
The vaunted verse a vacant head demands,
Ne wont with crabbèd care the muses dwell.
Unwisely weaves, that takes two webs in hand. 102

Whoever casts to compass weighty prize,
And thinks to throw out thund'ring words of threat,
Let pour in lavish cups and thrifty bits of meat,
For Bacchus' fruit is friend to Phoebus wise.
And when with wine the brain begins to sweat,
The numbers flow as fast as spring doth rise. 108

Thou ken'st not, Percy, how the rhyme should rage.
Oh, if my temples were distained with wine,
And girt in garlands of wild ivy twine,
How I could rear the muse on stately stage
And teach her tread aloft in buskin fine,
With quaint Bellona in her equipage! 114

But ah, my corage cools ere it be warm;
Forthy, content us in this humble shade.
Where no such troublous tides han us assayed,
Here we our slender pipes may safely charm. 118

Piers

And when my gates shall han their bellies laid,
Cuddie shall have a kid to store his farm.

Cuddie's Emblem:
Agitante calescimus illo, etc.

(1579)

---

100 *The vaunted . . . demands:* Mantuan, *vacuum curis divina cerebrum poscit* (the goddess demands a brain empty of cares). 102 *that:* he who. 105 *thrifty:* causing to thrive, nourishing. The idea seems to be that the epic poet should drink deeply and eat heartily. 108 *numbers:* meters, rhythms. 109 *ken'st:* knowest. 110 *Oh, if my:* "He seemeth here to be ravished with a poetical fury" (E. K.). *distained:* stained. 111 *ivy twine:* twisted ivy, which was "dedicated to Bacchus" (E. K.). 113 *buskin:* a high shoe worn in ancient tragedy. 114 *quaint:* strange. *Bellona:* goddess of war. *equipage:* train. 115 *corage:* heart. 117 *tides:* times. 118 *charm:* play charms or songs on. 119 *when . . . laid:* when my goats have borne their young. *Emblem:* motto. *Agitante . . . etc.:* we grow warm when he [the god of poetry] stirs us. "Hereby is meant, as also in the whole course of this ecloque, that poetry is a divine instinct and unnatural rage, passing the reach of common reason" (E. K.).

141

From AMORETTI

XV

Ye tradeful merchants, that with weary toil
  Do seek most precious things to make your gain,
  And both the Indias of their treasures spoil:
  What needeth you to seek so far in vain?   4
For lo, my love doth in herself contain
  All this world's riches that may far be found.
  If sapphires, lo, her eyes be sapphires plain;
  If rubies, lo, her lips be rubies sound;   8
If pearls, her teeth be pearls both pure and round;
  If ivory, her forehead ivory ween;
  If gold, her locks are finest gold on ground;
  If silver, her fair hands are silver sheen.   12
But that which fairest is, but few behold:
  Her mind, adorned with virtues manifold.

XVI

One day as I unwarily did gaze
  On those fair eyes, my love's immortal light,
  The whiles my stonished heart stood in amaze
  Through sweet illusion of her looks' delight,   4
I mote perceive how in her glancing sight
  Legions of loves with little wings did fly,
  Darting their deadly arrows fiery bright
  At every rash beholder passing by.   8
One of those archers closely I did spy
  Aiming his arrow at my very heart:
  When suddenly, with twinkle of her eye,
  The damsel broke his mistended dart.   12
Had she not so done, sure I had been slain;
  Yet, as it was, I hardly scaped with pain.

XVIII

The rolling wheel that runneth often round
  The hardest steel in tract of time doth tear;

XV. 3 *Indias:* India and the West Indies.   11 *on ground:* in basic substance?
On a "base" of natural hair?   12 *sheen:* shining.

XVI. 5 *mote:* might, could.

XVIII. 2 *tract:* course.

And drizzling drops that often do redound
The firmest flint doth in continuance wear.
Yet cannot I with many a dropping tear
And long entreaty soften her hard heart,
That she will once vouchsafe my plaint to hear,
Or look with pity on my painful smart.
But when I plead, she bids me play my part;
And when I weep, she says tears are but water;
And when I sigh, she says I know the art;
And when I wail, she turns herself to laughter.
So do I weep, and wail, and plead in vain,
Whiles she as steel and flint doth still remain.

XXX

My love is like to ice, and I to fire.
How comes it, then, that this her cold so great
Is not dissolved through my so hot desire,
But harder grows the more I her entreat?
Or how comes it that my exceeding heat
Is not delayed by her heart frozen cold,
But that I burn much more in boiling sweat,
And feel my flames augmented manifold?
What more miraculous thing may be told,
That fire, which all things melts, should harden ice,
And ice, which is congealed with senseless cold,
Should kindle fire by wonderful device?
Such is the pow'r of love in gentle mind
That it can alter all the course of kind.

LIII

The panther, knowing that his spotted hide
Doth please all beasts, but that his looks them fray,
Within a bush his dreadful head doth hide
To let them gaze whilst he on them may prey.
Right so my cruel fair with me doth play;
For with the goodly semblant of her hue
She doth allure me to mine own decay,
And then no mercy will unto me shew.
Great shame it is, thing so divine in view,

XXX. 11 *senseless:* without feeling. 14 *kind:* nature.
LIII. 2 *fray:* frighten. 6 *semblant:* semblance. 8 *shew:* show.

143

Made for to be the world's most ornament,
To make the bait her gazers to imbrue;
Good shames to be to ill an instrument.   12
But mercy doth with beauty best agree,
    As in their Maker ye them best may see.

LXVIII

Most glorious Lord of Life, that on this day
    Didst make thy triumph over death and sin;
    And, having harrowed Hell, didst bring away
    Captivity, thence captive, us to win: 4
This joyous day, dear Lord, with joy begin,
    And grant that we for whom Thou didest die,
    Being with Thy dear blood clean washed from sin,
    May live forever in felicity;   8
And that Thy love we, weighing worthily,
    May likewise love Thee for the same again;
    And for Thy sake that all like dear didst buy,
    With love may one another entertain.   12
So let us love, dear love, like as we ought:
    Love is the lesson which the Lord us taught.

LXXV

One day I wrote her name upon the strand,
    But came the waves and washèd it away.
    Again I wrote it with a second hand,
    But came the tide, and made my pains his prey.   4
Vain man, said she, that dost in vain assay
    A mortal thing so to immortalize;
    For I myself shall, like to this, decay,
    And eke my name be wipèd out likewise.   8
Not so, quod I. Let baser things devise
    To die in dust, but you shall live by fame.
    My verse your virtues rare shall eternize,
    And in the heavens write your glorious name,   12
Where, whenas death shall all the world subdue,
    Our love shall live, and later life renew.

                                        (1595)

LXVIII. 3 *harrowed Hell:* the phrase "He descended into Hell," in the Apostles'
Creed, was interpreted to mean that between the crucifixion and the resurrection Christ removed from Hell to Heaven all the virtuous people who had died
before His redemptive mission. 11 *like dear:* at equally great cost.

PROTHALAMION

1

Calm was the day, and through the trembling air
Sweet-breathing Zephyrus did softly play—
A gentle spirit, that lightly did delay
Hot Titan's beams, which then did glister fair;
When I, whom sullen care,   5
Through discontent of my long fruitless stay
In prince's court, and expectation vain
Of idle hopes, which still do fly away
Like empty shadows, did afflict my brain,
Walked forth to ease my pain   10
Along the shore of silver-streaming Thames,
Whose rutty bank, the which his river hems,
Was painted all with variable flowers,
And all the meads adorned with dainty gems
Fit to deck maidens' bow'rs   15
And crown their paramours
Against the bridal day, which is not long.
    Sweet Thames, run softly, till I end my song.

2

There, in a meadow by the river's side,
A flock of nymphs I chancèd to espy—   20
All lovely daughters of the flood thereby,
With goodly greenish locks all loose untied
As each had been a bride;
And each one had a little wicker basket
Made of fine twigs entrailèd curiously,   25
In which they gathered flowers to fill their flasket;
And with fine fingers cropped full fetisly
The tender stalks on high.
Of every sort which in that meadow grew

PROTHALAMION: marriage-song. The occasion was the marriage of two sisters, Lady Elizabeth and Lady Katherine Somerset, daughters of the Earl of Worcester, to Henry Gilford and William Peter (or Petre). 2 *Zephyrus:* the west wind. 4 *Titan's:* the sun's. *glister:* glitter. 8 *still:* continually. 12 *rutty:* root-filled? 13 *variable:* various. 23 *As:* as if. 25 *entrailèd:* entwined. 26 *flasket:* a longish basket. 27 *fetisly:* neatly, skillfully.

They gathered some: the violet pallid blue, 30
The little daisy, that at evening closes,
The virgin lily, and the primrose true,
With store of vermeil roses,
To deck their bridegrooms' posies
Against the bridal day, which was not long. 35
    Sweet Thames, run softly, till I end my song.

3

With that I saw two swans of goodly hue
Come softly swimming down along the Lea.
Two fairer birds I yet did never see.
The snow which doth the top of Pindus strew 40
Did never whiter shew;
Nor Jove himself, when he a swan would be
For love of Leda, whiter did appear.
Let Leda was, they say, as white as he.
Yet not so white as these, nor nothing near; 45
So purely white they were
That even the gentle stream, the which them bare,
Seemed foul to them, and bade his billows spare
To wet their silken feathers, lest they might
Soil their fair plumes with water not so fair 50
And mar their beauties bright,
That shone as heaven's light
Against their bridal day, which was not long.
    Sweet Thames, run softly, till I end my song.

4

Eftsoons the nymphs, which now had flowers their fill, 55
Ran all in haste to see that silver brood
As they came floating on the crystal flood;
Whom when they saw, they stood amazèd still
Their wondering eyes to fill.
Them seemed they never saw a sight so fair, 60
Of fowls so lovely that they sure did deem
Them heavenly born, or to be that same pair
Which through the sky draw Venus' silver team;

---

33 *vermeil:* vermilion. 38 *Lea:* a former tributary of the Thames at Greenwich.
40 *Pindus:* a mountain range in Greece. 41 *shew:* show. 42–43: Jove transformed himself to a swan in order to rape Leda. 48 *to:* in comparison with.
55 *Eftsoons:* soon afterward.

146

For sure they did not seem
To be begot of any earthly seed, 65
But rather angels, or of angels' breed.
Yet were they bred of summer's heat, they say,
In sweetest season, when each flower and weed
The earth did fresh array.
So fresh they seemed as day— 70
Even as their bridal day, which was not long.
　Sweet Thames, run softly, till I end my song.

5

Then forth they all out of their baskets drew
Great store of flowers, the honor of the field,
That to the sense did fragrant odors yield; 75
All which upon those goodly birds they threw,
And all the waves did strew,
That like old Peneus' waters they did seem,
When, down along by pleasant Tempe's shore,
Scattered with flow'rs, through Thessaly they stream; 80
That they appear, through lilies' plenteous store,
Like a bride's chamber floor.
Two of those nymphs, meanwhile, two garlands bound
Of freshest flow'rs which in that mead they found;
The which presenting, all in trim array, 85
Their snowy foreheads therewithal they crowned
Whilst one did sing this lay,
Prepared against that day—
Against their bridal day, which was not long.
　Sweet Thames, run softly, till I end my song. 90

6

Ye gentle birds, the world's fair ornament
And heaven's glory, whom this happy hour
Doth lead unto your lovers' blissful bower:
Joy may you have, and gentle hearts' content,
Of your loves' couplement. 95
And let fair Venus, that is Queen of Love,

___

67 *summer's heat:* a pun on *Somerset.* The *ea* of *heat* was then pronounced like
the *ea* in modern *head.* 78 *That:* so that. *Peneus:* ancient name for the Salambria
River, in Thessaly. 79 *Tempe's:* Tempe was a valley of the Peneus which lay
between Mt. Olympus and Mt. Ossa. 81 *That:* so that. 86 *Their:* the swans'.
95 *couplement:* coupling, union.

147

With her heart-quelling son, upon you smile;
Whose smile, they say, hath virtue to remove
All love's dislike, and friendship's faulty guile
Forever to assoil. 100
Let endless peace your steadfast hearts accord,
And blessèd plenty wait upon your board;
And let your bed with pleasures chaste abound,
That fruitful issue may to you afford
Which may your foes confound 105
And make your joys redound
Upon your bridal day, which is not long.
   Sweet Thames, run softly, till I end my song.

7

So ended she; and all the rest around
To her redoubled that her undersong, 110
Which said their bridal day should not be long.
And gentle Echo from the neighbor ground
Their accents did resound.
So forth those joyous birds did pass along
Adown the Lea, that to them murmured low, 115
As he would speak, but that he lacked a tongue;
Yet did by signs his glad affection show,
Making his stream run slow.
And all the fowl which in his flood did dwell
Gan flock about these twain, that did excel 120
The rest so far as Cynthia doth shend
The lesser stars. So they, enrangèd well,
Did on those two attend
And their best service lend
Against their wedding day, which was not long. 125
   Sweet Thames, run softly, till I end my song.

8

At length they all to merry London came—
To merry London, my most kindly nurse,
That to me gave this life's first native source;
Though from another place I take my name, 130
An house of ancient fame.

---

97 *son:* Cupid. 110 *undersong:* refrain. 121 *Cynthia:* the Moon Goddess. *shend:* shame. 122 *enrangèd:* lined up. 130 *from . . . name:* the Spencers of Althorpe, near Northampton.

There when they came, whereas those bricky tow'rs,
The which on Thames' broad agèd back do ride,
Where now the studious lawyers have their bow'rs,
There whilom wont the Templar Knights to bide, 135
Till they decayed through pride;
Next whereunto there stands a stately place
Where oft I gainèd gifts and goodly grace
Of that great lord, which therein wont to dwell,
Whose want too well now feels my friendless case— 140
But ah! here fits not well
Old woes, but joys, to tell
Against the bridal day, which is not long.
Sweet Thames, run softly, till I end my song.

9

Yet therein now doth lodge a noble Peer, 145
Great England's glory and the world's wide wonder,
Whose dreadful name late through all Spain did thunder,
And Hercules' two pillars, standing near,
Did make to quake and fear:
Fair branch of honor, flower of chivalry, 150
That fillest England with thy triumph's fame,
Joy have thou of thy noble victory,
And endless happiness of thine own name
That promiseth the same;
That through thy prowess and victorious arms 155
Thy country may be freed from foreign harms
And great Eliza's glorious name may ring
Through all the world, filled with thy wide alarms,
Which some brave muse may sing
To ages following 160
Upon the bridal day, which is not long.
Sweet Thames, run softly, till I end my song.

10

From those high towers, this noble lord issuing
Like radiant Hesper when his golden hair

---

132 *bricky tow'rs:* of the Temple, whose history Spenser summarizes briefly.
135 *whilom:* formerly. 137 *stately place:* earlier, of the Earl of Leicester,
Spenser's patron; at this time, of the Earl of Essex, just returned (line 147) from
a military expedition to Cadiz. 148 *Hercules' two pillars:* cliffs on either side
of the Straits of Gibraltar. 157 *Eliza's:* Queen Elizabeth's. 164 *Hesper:* the
Evening Star (Venus).

In th' Ocean' billows he hath bathèd fair, 165
Descended to the river's open viewing,
With a great train ensuing.
Above the rest were goodly to be seen
Two gentle knights of lovely face and feature,
Beseeming well the bower of any queen, 170
With gifts of wit and ornaments of nature
Fit for so goodly stature,
That like the twins of Jove they seemed in sight,
Which deck the baldric of the heavens bright.
They two, forth pacing to the river's side, 175
Received those two fair brides, their loves' delight;
Which at th' appointed tide
Each one did make his bride
Against their bridal day, which is not long.
Sweet Thames, run softly, till I end my song. 180

(1596)

Christopher Marlowe (1564–1593)

From HERO AND LEANDER

On Hellespont, guilty of true love's blood,
In view, and opposite, two cities stood—
Sea-borderers, disjoined by Neptune's might—
The one Abydos, the other Sestos hight.
At Sestos Hero dwelt: Hero the fair, 5
Whom young Apollo courted for her hair,

---

173 *twins of Jove:* Castor and Pollux, sons of Leda (lines 42–43, above) who became a constellation. 174 *baldric:* belt; here, the zodiac.

HERO AND LEANDER. Marlowe's 818-line poem, of which the first 90 lines are printed here, was left unfinished. George Chapman supplied a sequel. Seeing Hero at a festival in Sestos, Leander fell in love with her and persuaded her to break her vow of chastity; he swam the Hellespont (the Dardanelles) every night from his home in Abydos, just across the strait, to visit her. When he drowned, Hero threw herself also into the waves. 3 *by Neptune's might:* that is, by a branch of the sea. 4 *hight:* was called.

And offered as a dower his burning throne,
Where she should sit for men to gaze upon.
The outside of her garments were of lawn,
The lining purple silk, with gilt stars drawn; 10
Her wide sleeves green, and bordered with a grove
Where Venus in her naked glory strove
To please the careless and disdainful eyes
Of proud Adonis that before her lies.
Her kirtle blue, whereon was many a stain 15
Made with the blood of wretched lovers slain.
Upon her head she ware a myrtle wreath,
From whence her veil reached to the ground beneath.
Her veil was artificial flowers and leaves,
Whose workmanship both man and beast deceives. 20
Many would praise the sweet smell as she passed,
When 'twas the odor which her breath forth cast;
And there for honey bees have sought in vain,
And, beat from thence, have lighted there again.
About her neck hung chains of pebble stone, 25
Which, lightened by her neck, like diamonds shone.
She ware no gloves, for neither sun nor wind
Would burn or parch her hands, but, to her mind,
Or warm or cool them, for they took delight
To play upon those hands, they were so white. 30
Buskins of shells all silvered usèd she,
And branched with blushing coral to the knee,
Where sparrows perched, of hollow pearl and gold,
Such as the world would wonder to behold.
Those with sweet water oft her handmail fills, 35
Which as she went would chirrup through the bills.
Some say for her the fairest Cupid pined,
And, looking in her face, was strooken blind.
But this is true: so like was one the other,
As he imagined Hero was his mother, 40
And oftentimes into her bosom flew,
About her naked neck his bare arms threw,
And laid his childish head upon her breast
And, with still panting rocked, there took his rest.
So lovely fair was Hero, Venus' nun, 45
As nature wept, thinking she was undone,

9 *lawn:* a thin cloth. 15 *kirtle:* skirt. 19 *artificial:* artful. 26 *lightened:* lighted.
28 *to her mind:* as she wished. 31 *Buskins:* half-boots. 38 *strooken:* struck.
40 *his mother:* Venus. 44 *still:* constant. 45 *Venus' nun:* Hero was priestess
of Aphrodite. 46 *As:* that.

Because she took more from her than she left,
And of such wondrous beauty her bereft.
Therefore, in sign her treasure suffered wrack,
Since Hero's time hath half the world been black. 50
Amorous Leander, beautiful and young,
Whose tragedy divine Musæus sung,
Dwelt at Abydos; since him dwelt there none
For whom succeeding times make greater moan.
His dangling tresses that were never shorn, 55
Had they been cut, and unto Colchos borne,
Would have allured the vent'rous youth of Greece
To hazard more than for the Golden Fleece.
Fair Cynthia wished his arms might be her sphere:
Grief makes her pale, because she moves not there. 60
His body was as straight as Circe's wand;
Jove might have sipped out nectar from his hand.
Even as delicious meat is to the taste,
So was his neck in touching, and surpassed
The white of Pelops' shoulder. I could tell ye 65
How smooth his breast was, and how white his belly,
And whose immortal fingers did imprint
That heavenly path, with many a curious dint,
That runs along his back; but my rude pen
Can hardly blazon forth the loves of men, 70
Much less of powerful gods. Let it suffice
That my slack muse sings of Leander's eyes,
Those orient cheeks and lips, exceeding his
That leapt into the water for a kiss
Of his own shadow, and, despising many, 75
Died ere he could enjoy the love of any.
Had wild Hippolytus Leander seen,
Enamored of his beauty had he been.
His presence made the rudest peasant melt
That in the vast uplandish country dwelt. 80

---

49 *wrack:* ruin, destruction. 52 *Musæus:* Greek poet of the sixth century B.C. who wrote a poem on Hero and Leander. 56 *Colchos:* Colchis, where Jason found the Golden Fleece. 59 *Cynthia:* Artemis or Diana, goddess of the moon. 61 *Circe:* enchantress who delayed the return home of Odysseus and his companions from Troy. 63 *meat:* food. 65 *The white of Pelops' shoulder:* after Pelops (whose name the Peloponnesus bears) was served to the gods as food, he was revived and furnished by Demeter with an ivory shoulder. 70 *blazon:* spread abroad, proclaim. 73–74 *exceeding his . . . kiss:* that of Narcissus, who fell in love with his own image in a pool. 77 *Hippolytus:* son of Theseus and the Amazon, Hippolyta; he resisted the suit of his stepmother, Phaedra, and is "wild" because of his averseness to love.

152

The barbarous Thracian soldier, moved with nought,
Was moved with him, and for his favor sought.
Some swore he was a maid in man's attire,
For in his looks were all that men desire—
A pleasant smiling cheek, a speaking eye, 85
A brow for love to banquet royally.
And such as knew he was a man would say,
Leander, thou art made for amorous play.
Why art thou not in love, and loved of all?
Though thou be fair, yet be not thine own thrall. 90

(1598)

Samuel Daniel (1562–1619)

From DELIA

I

Unto the boundless ocean of thy beauty
Runs this poor river, charged with streams of zeal,
Returning thee the tribute of my duty,
Which here my love, my youth, my plaints reveal. 4
Here I unclasp the book of my charged soul,
Where I have cast th' accounts of all my care;
Here have I summed my sighs, here I enroll
How they were spent for thee: look what they are. 8
Look on the dear expenses of my youth,
And see how just I reckon with thine eyes.
Examine well thy beauty with my truth,
And cross my cares ere greater sums arise. 12
Read it, sweet maid, though it be done but slightly.
Who can shew all his love, doth love but lightly.

DELIA. Texts and numbering are based on the 1592 version as edited by A. C. Sprague (1930). I. 5 *charged:* burdened. 6 *cast:* cast up, added. 10 *just I reckon:* accurately I compute. 12 *cross:* cross out, cancel?

153

III

If so it hap this offspring of my care,
These fatal anthems, sad and mournful songs,
Come to their view, who like afflicted are,
Let them yet sigh their own, and moan my wrongs.   4
　But untouched hearts, with unaffected eye,
Approach not to behold so great distress;
Clear-sighted, you soon note what is awry,
Whilst blinded ones mine errors never guess.   8
　You blinded souls, whom youth and errors lead,
You outcast eaglets, dazzled with your sun—
Ah, you, and none but you, my sorrows read;
You best can judge the wrongs that she hath done: 12
　That she hath done, the motive of my pain,
　Who, whilst I love, doth kill me with disdain.

IX

If this be love, to draw a weary breath,
Paint on floods, till the shore cry to th' air;
With downward looks, still reading on the earth
The sad memorials of my love's despair: 4
　If this be love, to war against my soul,
Lie down to wail, rise up to sigh and grieve me;
The never-resting stone of care to roll,
Still to complain my griefs, and none relieve me;   8
　If this be love, to clothe me with dark thoughts,
Haunting untrodden paths to wail apart;
My pleasures, horror; music, tragic notes;
Tears in my eyes, and sorrow at my heart: 12
　If this be love, to live a living death,
　Oh, then love I, and draw this weary breath.

(1592)

IX. 3 *still:* continually. 7 *stone . . . roll:* like Sisyphus, doomed to roll a
stone in Hades.

154

Michael Drayton *(1563–1631)*

From IDEA, IN SIXTY-THREE SONNETS

VI

How many paltry, foolish, painted things,
That now in coaches trouble ev'ry street,
Shall be forgotten, whom no poet sings,
Ere they be well wrapped in their winding sheet! 4
Where I to thee eternity shall give
When nothing else remaineth of these days;
And queens hereafter shall be glad to live
Upon the alms of thy superfluous praise. 8
Virgins and matrons, reading these my rhymes,
Shall be so much delighted with thy story
That they shall grieve they lived not in these times
To have seen thee, their sex's only glory. 12
   So shalt thou fly above the vulgar throng,
   Still to survive in my immortal song.

IX

As other men, so I myself do muse
Why in this sort I wrest invention so,
And why these giddy metaphors I use,
Leaving the path the greater part do go. 4
I will resolve you: I am lunatic;
And ever this in madmen you shall find:
What they last thought of, when the brain grew sick,
In most distraction they keep that in mind. 8
Thus, talking idly in this bedlam fit,
Reason and I, you must conceive, are twain.
'Tis nine years now since first I lost my wit;
Bear with me, then, though troubled be my brain. 12
   With diet and correction, men distraught—
   Not too far past—may to their wits be brought.

IX. 9 *bedlam:* wild, insane. Bedlam, or the Hospital of St. Mary of Bethlehem, was a London madhouse.

XLIV

Whilst thus my pen strives to eternize thee,
Age rules my lines with wrinkles in my face,
Where, in the map of all my misery,
Is modeled out the world of my disgrace. 4
Whilst, in despite of tyrannizing times,
Medea-like, I make thee young again,
Proudly thou scorn'st my world-outwearing rhymes,
And murther'st virtue with thy coy disdain. 8
And though in youth my youth untimely perish
To keep thee from oblivion and the grave,
Ensuing ages yet my rhymes shall cherish,
Where I, entombed, my better part shall save. 12
  And though this earthly body fade and die,
  My name shall mount upon eternity.

LXI

Since there's no help, come, let us kiss and part.
Nay—I have done; you get no more of me.
And I am glad, yea, glad with all my heart,
That thus so cleanly I myself can free. 4
Shake hands forever, cancel all our vows;
And, when we meet at any time again,
Be it not seen in either of our brows
That we one jot of former love retain. 8
Now, at the last gasp of love's latest breath,
When, his pulse failing, Passion speechless lies;
When Faith is kneeling by his bed of death,
And Innocence is closing up his eyes: 12
  Now, if thou would'st, when all have given him over,
  From death to life thou might'st him yet recover.

(1619)

XLIV. 6 *Medea-like:* Medea rejuvenated a ram by boiling it in a cauldron.
LXI. 9 *latest:* last.

Sir Walter Ralegh (1552?–1618)

A VISION
UPON THIS CONCEIT OF THE *FAIRY QUEEN*

Methought I saw the grave where Laura lay
Within that temple where the vestal flame
Was wont to burn; and, passing by that way
To see that buried dust of living fame,   4
Whose tomb fair love, and fairer virtue, kept,
All suddenly I saw the Fairy Queen;
At whose approach the soul of Petrarch wept,
And from thenceforth those graces were not seen,   8
For they this Queen attended, in whose stead
Oblivion laid him down on Laura's hearse.
Hereat the hardest stones were seen to bleed,
And groans of buried ghosts the heavens did pierce: 12
   Where Homer's sprite did tremble all for grief,
   And cursed th' access of that celestial thief.

(1590)

THE NYMPH'S REPLY TO THE SHEPHERD

If all the world and love were young,
And truth in every shepherd's tongue,
These pretty pleasures might me move
To live with thee and be thy love.   4

Time drives the flocks from field to fold,
When rivers rage and rocks grow cold,
And Philomel becometh dumb;
The rest complains of cares to come.   8

A Vision . . . A commendatory sonnet published with Spenser's *Fairy Queen*.
conceit: fiction. 1 *Laura:* the subject of Petrarch's sonnets. 13 *sprite:* spirit.

The Nymph's Reply . . . An antipastoral, aimed especially at Marlowe's "The
Passionate Shepherd to His Love." 7 *Philomel:* the nightingale. Philomela was
turned into a nightingale when she was pursued by Tereus, whose rape of her
she had punished by serving his son's flesh to him at dinner.

The flowers do fade, and wanton fields
To wayward winter reckoning yields.
A honey tongue, a heart of gall,
Is fancy's spring, but sorrow's fall. 12

Thy gowns, thy shoes, thy beds of roses,
Thy cap, thy kirtle, and thy posies,
Soon break, soon wither, soon forgotten—
In folly ripe, in reason rotten. 16

Thy belt of straw and ivy buds,
Thy coral clasps and amber studs—
All these in me no means can move
To come to thee and be thy love. 20

But could youth last, and love still breed;
Had joys no date, nor age no need:
Then these delights my mind might move
To live with thee and be thy love. 24

(1600)

THESE VERSES FOLLOWING WERE MADE BY SIR WALTER RALEGH THE NIGHT BEFORE HE DIED, AND LEFT AT THE GATEHOUSE

Even such is time, which takes in trust
Our youth, our joys, and all we have,
And pays us but with age and dust;
Who, in the dark and silent grave, 4
When we have wandered all our ways,
Shuts up the story of our days;
And from which earth and grave and dust
The Lord shall raise me up, I trust.

(1628)

---

14 *kirtle:* skirt or gown. 18 *studs:* buttons or fasteners. 21 *still:* continually.

158

William Shakespeare (1564–1616)

From LOVE'S LABOR'S LOST (V, ii)

When icicles hang by the wall,
  And Dick the shepherd blows his nail;
And Tom bears logs into the hall,
  And milk comes frozen home in pail;
When blood is nipped, and ways be foul: 5
Then nightly sings the staring owl,
    Tu-whit, tu-who!
  A merry note,
While greasy Joan doth keel the pot.

When all aloud the wind doth blow,   10
  And coughing drowns the parson's saw;
And birds sit brooding in the snow,
  And Marian's nose looks red and raw;
When roasted crabs hiss in the bowl:
Then nightly sings the staring owl,   15
    Tu-whit, tu-who!
  A merry note,
While greasy Joan doth keel the pot.

          (1594–95)

From AS YOU LIKE IT (V, iii)

It was a lover and his lass,
  With a hey, and a ho, and a hey nonino,
That o'er the green cornfield did pass
  In the springtime, the only pretty ring-time;
When birds do sing, hey ding-a-ding-ding,
Sweet lovers love the spring.   6

And therefore take the present time,
  With a hey, and a ho, and a hey nonino,
For love is crownèd with the prime.

LOVE'S LABOR'S LOST. 9 *keel:* cool by stirring. 11 *saw:* saying—that is, a sermon. 14 *crabs:* crab apples.

AS YOU LIKE IT. 3 *cornfield:* field of grain.

In springtime, the only pretty ring-time,
When birds do sing, hey ding-a-ding-ding,
Sweet lovers love the spring. 12

Between the acres of the rye,
    With a hey, and a ho, and a hey nonino,
These pretty country folks would lie.
    In springtime, the only pretty ring-time,
When birds do sing, hey ding-a-ding-ding,
Sweet lovers love the spring. 18

This carol they began that hour,
    With a hey, and a ho, and a hey nonino,
How that a life was but a flower.
    In springtime, the only pretty ring-time,
When birds do sing, hey ding-a-ding-ding,
Sweet lovers love the spring. 24

(1599?)

From CYMBELINE (IV, ii)

Fear no more the heat o' th' sun,
    Nor the furious winter's rages;
Thou thy worldly task hast done,
    Home art gone, and ta'en thy wages.
Golden lads and girls all must,
As chimney-sweepers, come to dust. 6

Fear no more the frown o' th' great;
    Thou art past the tyrant's stroke.
Care no more to clothe and eat;
    To thee the reed is as the oak.
The scepter, learning, physic, must
All follow this, and come to dust. 12

Fear no more the lightning flash,
    Nor th' all-dreaded thunder-stone;
Fear not slander, censure rash;
    Thou hast finished joy and moan.
All lovers young, all lovers must
Consign to thee, and come to dust. 18

(1609–10)

CYMBELINE. 14 *thunder-stone:* thunderbolt. 15 *censure:* judgment. 18 *consign:* agree, submit.

160

SONNETS

I

From fairest creatures we desire increase,
That thereby beauty's rose might never die,
But, as the riper should by time decease,
His tender heir might bear his memory.   4
But thou, contracted to thine own bright eyes,
Feed'st thy light's flame with self-substantial fuel,
Making a famine where abundance lies:
Thyself thy foe, to thy sweet self too cruel.   8
Thou, that art now the world's fresh ornament
And only herald to the gaudy spring,
Within thine own bud buriest thy content,
And, tender churl, mak'st waste in niggarding.   12
    Pity the world, or else this glutton be:
    To eat the world's due, by the grave and thee.

XV

When I consider everything that grows
Holds in perfection but a little moment;
That this huge stage presenteth nought but shows
Whereon the stars in secret influence comment;   4
When I perceive that men as plants increase,
Cheerèd and checked ev'n by the selfsame sky,
Vaunt in their youthful sap, at height decrease,
And wear their brave state out of memory: 8
Then the conceit of this inconstant stay
Sets you most rich in youth before my sight,
Where wasteful time debateth with decay,
To change your day of youth to sullied night;   12
    And, all in war with time for love of you,
    As he takes from you, I engraft you new.

XVIII

Shall I compare thee to a summer's day?
Thou art more lovely and more temperate.

I. 5 *contracted:* bound by contract; betrothed.   6 *self-substantial:* self-sustaining.   12 *churl:* miser.

XV. 8 *brave:* handsome, splendid.   9 *conceit:* conception, thought.

161

Rough winds do shake the darling buds of May,
And summer's lease hath all too short a date. 4
Sometime too hot the eye of heaven shines,
And often is his gold complexion dimmed;
And every fair from fair sometime declines,
By chance, or nature's changing course, untrimmed. 8
But thy eternal summer shall not fade,
Nor lose possession of that fair thou ow'st;
Nor shall death brag thou wand'rest in his shade,
When in eternal lines to time thou grow'st. 12
  So long as men can breathe or eyes can see,
  So long lives this, and this gives life to thee.

XXXIII

Full many a glorious morning have I seen
Flatter the mountain tops with sovereign eye,
Kissing with golden face the meadows green,
Gilding pale streams with heavenly alchemy; 4
Anon permit the basest clouds to ride
With ugly rack on his celestial face,
And from the fórlorn world his visage hide,
Stealing unseen to west with this disgrace. 8
Even so my sun one early morn did shine
With all-triumphant splendor on my brow;
But out, alack! He was but one hour mine;
The region cloud hath masked him from me now. 12
  Yet him for this my love no whit disdaineth.
  Suns of the world may stain, when heaven's sun staineth.

LV

Not marble nor the gilded monuments
Of princes shall outlive this pow'rful rhyme;
But you shall shine more bright in these contents
Than unswept stone, besmeared with sluttish time. 4
When wasteful war shall statues overturn,
And broils root out the work of masonry,
Nor Mars's sword nor war's quick fire shall burn
The living record of your memory. 8

XVIII. 8 *untrimmed:* deprived of beauty. 10 *that fair thou ow'st:* that fairness thou ownest.

XXXIII. 6 *rack:* wind-driven clouds. 11 *out, alack!:* an emphatic way of saying "Alas!" "Out!" is itself an exclamation of irritation.

'Gainst death and all-oblivious enmity
Shall you pace forth; your praise shall still find room
Even in the eyes of all posterity
That wear this world out to the ending doom.
  So, till the Judgment that yourself arise,
  You live in this, and dwell in lovers' eyes.

12

LXIV

When I have seen by time's fell hand defaced
The rich, proud cost of outworn, buried age;
When sometime lofty towers I see down-rased,
And brass eternal slave to mortal rage;
When I have seen the hungry ocean gain
Advantage on the kingdom of the shore,
And the firm soil win of the wat'ry main,
Increasing store with loss, and loss with store;
When I have seen such interchange of state,
Or state itself confounded to decay,
Ruin hath taught me thus to ruminate,
That time will come and take my love away.
  This thought is as a death, which cannot choose
  But weep, to have that which it fears to lose.

4

8

12

LXV

Since brass, nor stone, nor earth, nor boundless sea,
But sad mortality o'ersways their power,
How, with this rage, shall beauty hold a plea,
Whose action is no stronger than a flower?
Oh, how shall summer's honey breath hold out
Against the wrackful siege of batt'ring days,
When rocks impregnable are not so stout,
Nor gates of steel so strong, but time decays?
O fearful meditation! Where, alack,
Shall time's best jewel from time's chest lie hid?
Or what strong hand can hold his swift foot back?
Or who his spoil of beauty can forbid?
  Oh, none! unless this miracle have might,
  That in black ink my love may still shine bright.

4

8

12

LV. 13 *Judgment:* at the Day of Doom.
LXIV. 10 *state:* stateliness.
LXV. 1 *Since brass:* since there is neither brass. 6 *wrackful:* destructive.

163

LXVI

Tired with all these, for restful death I cry:
As, to behold desert a beggar born;
And needy nothing trimmed in jollity;
And purest faith unhappily forsworn; 4
And gilded honor shamefully misplaced;
And maiden virtue rudely strumpeted;
And right perfection wrongfully disgraced;
And strength by limping sway disablèd; 8
And art made tongue-tied by authority;
And folly—doctor-like—controlling skill;
And simple truth miscalled simplicity;
And captive good attending captain ill— 12
   Tired with all these, from these would I be gone,
   Save that, to die, I leave my love alone.

LXXIII

That time of year thou may'st in me behold
When yellow leaves, or none, or few, do hang
Upon those boughs which shake against the cold—
Bare, ruined choirs where late the sweet birds sang. 4
In me thou see'st the twilight of such day
As after sunset fadeth in the west;
Which by and by black night doth take away,
Death's second self, that seals up all in rest. 8
In me thou see'st the glowing of such fire
That on the ashes of his youth doth lie,
As the deathbed whereon it must expire,
Consumed with that which it was nourished by. 12
   This thou perceiv'st, which makes thy love more strong
   To love that well which thou must leave ere long.

XCIV

They that have pow'r to hurt and will do none;
That do not do the thing they most do show;
Who, moving others, are themselves as stone,
Unmovèd, cold, and to temptation slow: 4

LXVI. 8 *disablèd:* tetrasyllabic.
LXXIII. 10 *his:* its.

They rightly do inherit heaven's graces,
And husband nature's riches from expense.
They are the lords and owners of their faces—
Others but stewards of their excellence. 8
The summer's flow'r is to the summer sweet,
Though to itself it only live and die.
But if that flow'r with base infection meet,
The basest weed outbraves his dignity. 12
   For sweetest things turn sourest by their deeds:
   Lilies that fester smell far worse than weeds.

CVI

When in the chronicle of wasted time
I see descriptions of the fairest wights,
And beauty making beautiful old rhyme,
In praise of ladies dead and lovely knights, 4
Then, in the blazon of sweet beauty's best—
Of hand, of foot, of lip, of eye, of brow—
I see their ántique pen would have expressed
Even such a beauty as you master now. 8
So all their praises are but prophecies
Of this our time, all you prefiguring;
And—for they looked but with divining eyes—
They had not skill enough your worth to sing. 12
   For we, which now behold these present days,
   Have eyes to wonder, but lack tongues to praise.

CX

Alas, 'tis true I have gone here and there
And made myself a motley to the view;
Gored mine own thoughts, sold cheap what is most dear,
Made old offenses of affections new. 4
Most true it is that I have looked on truth
Askance and strangely; but, by all above,
These blenches gave my heart another youth,
And worse essays proved thee my best of love. 8

XCIV. 12 *outbraves:* makes a finer show than.

  CVI. 2 *wights:* persons. 5 *blazon:* proclamation. 8 *master:* possess. 11 *divining eyes:* the foreseeing eyes of a diviner.

  CX. 2 *motley:* that is, a jester. 4 *Made . . . new:* offended old friends by making new ones. 7 *blenches:* shrinkings aside. 8 *essays:* trials.

Now all is done, have what shall have no end!
Mine appetite I never more will grind
On newer proof, to try an older friend—
A god in love, to whom I am confined.   12
    Then give me welcome, next my heaven the best,
    Even to thy pure and most, most loving breast.

CXVI

Let me not to the marriage of true minds
Admit impediments. Love is not love
Which alters when it alteration finds,
Or bends with the remover to remove.   4
Oh, no! It is an ever-fixèd mark
That looks on tempests and is never shaken;
It is the star to every wand'ring bark,
Whose worth's unknown, although his height be taken.   8
Love's not time's fool, though rosy lips and cheeks
Within his bending sickle's compass come.
Love alters not with his brief hours and weeks,
But bears it out even to the edge of doom.   12
    If this be error, and upon me proved,
    I never writ, nor no man ever loved.

CXXIX

Th' expense of spirit in a waste of shame
Is lust in action; and, till action, lust
Is perjured, murd'rous, bloody, full of blame;
Savage, extreme, rude, cruel, not to trust;   4
Enjoyed no sooner but despisèd straight;
Past reason hunted, and, no sooner had,
Past reason hated, as a swallowed bait
On purpose laid to make the taker mad: 8
Mad in pursuit, and in possession so;
Had, having, and in quest to have, extreme;
A bliss in proof, and, proved, a very woe;
Before, a joy proposed; behind, a dream.   12
    All this the world well knows; yet none knows well
    To shun the heaven that leads men to this hell.

CXVI. 4 *bends . . . remove:* changes its course to go away with a person who
has deflected its love. 8 *height be taken:* elevation be computed with a sextant.
12 *bears it out:* endures.

CXXX

My mistress' eyes are nothing like the sun;
Coral is far more red than her lips' red.
If snow be white, why, then, her breasts are dun;
If hairs be wires, black wires grow on her head. 4
I have seen roses damasked, red and white,
But no such roses see I in her cheeks;
And in some perfumes is there more delight
Than in the breath that from my mistress reeks. 8
I love to hear her speak; yet well I know
That music hath a far more pleasing sound.
I grant I never saw a goddess go;
My mistress, when she walks, treads on the ground. 12
 And yet, by heaven, I think my love as rare
 As any she belied with false compare.

CXXXVIII

When my love swears that she is made of truth
I do believe her, though I know she lies,
That she might think me some untutored youth,
Unlearnèd in the world's false subtilties. 4
Thus, vainly thinking that she thinks me young,
Although she knows my days are past the best,
Simply I credit her false-speaking tongue;
On both sides thus is simple truth suppressed. 8
But wherefore says she not she is unjust?
And wherefore say not I that I am old?
Oh, love's best habit is in seeming trust,
And age in love loves not to have years told. 12
 Therefore I lie with her and she with me;
 And, in our faults, by lies we flattered be.

(1609)

CXXX. 5 *damasked:* colored like a damask rose.
CXXXVIII. 3 *That:* so that. 7 *Simply:* foolishly. 12 *told:* counted.

167

Thomas Campion (1567–1620)

WHEN TO HER LUTE CORINNA SINGS

When to her lute Corinna sings,
Her voice revives the leaden strings,
And doth in highest notes appear
As any challenged echo clear;
But when she doth of mourning speak,
Ev'n with her sighs the strings do break.　6

And, as her lute doth live or die,
Led by her passion, so must I;
For when of pleasure she doth sing,
My thoughts enjoy a sudden spring;
But if she doth of sorrow speak,
Ev'n from my heart the strings do break.　12

(1601)

ROSE-CHEEKED LAURA, COME

Rose-cheeked Laura, come!
Sing thou smoothly with thy beauty's
Silent music, either other
Sweetly gracing.　4

ROSE-CHEEKED LAURA, COME. One of Campion's experiments in "quantitative" verse, in which the length of the syllables, and not stress or accent, is rhythmically significant. The "long" syllable is supposed to require approximately twice as long as the "short" syllable to pronounce. A syllable is long "by nature" if the vowel is long (that is, if it requires a relatively long time to pronounce, like the *a* in *father*); it is long "by position" if the vowel is followed by two or more consonants (like *from* in the phrase "From consent"). The system is borrowed from Greek and Latin prosody and does not really suit English verse, but Campion achieves interesting effects with it. In this poem, according to the author, the second and third lines of each stanza "consist of four feet, the first of either of them being a spondee [long-long] or troche [long-short], the other three only troches. The fourth and last verse [or line] is made of two troches." Campion's explanation of the first line is confusing.

168

Lovely forms do flow
From consent divinely framed;
Heav'n is music, and thy beauty's
      Birth is heavenly.   8

These dull notes we sing
Discords need for helps to grace them;
Only beauty purely loving
      Knows no discord,   12

But still moves delight,
Like clear springs renewed by flowing—
Ever perfect, ever in them-
      Selves eternal.   16

(1602)

THERE IS A GARDEN IN HER FACE

There is a garden in her face,
Where roses and white lilies grow;
  A heav'nly paradise is that place,
Wherein all pleasant fruits do flow.
  There cherries grow, which none may buy
  Till "Cherry-ripe!" themselves do cry.   6

Those cherries fairly do enclose
Of orient pearl a double row;
  Which when her lovely laughter shows,
They look like rosebuds filled with snow.
  Yet them nor peer nor prince can buy,
  Till "Cherry-ripe!" themselves do cry.   12

Her eyes like angels watch them still;
Her brows like bended bows do stand,
  Threat'ning with piercing frowns to kill
All that attempt with eye or hand
  Those sacred cherries to come nigh,
  Till "Cherry-ripe!" themselves do cry.   18

(ca. 1617)

John Donne (1572–1631)

THE CANONIZATION

For Godsake hold your tongue, and let me love;
  Or chide my palsy, or my gout;
My five gray hairs, or ruined fortune flout.
  With wealth your state, your mind with arts improve;
    Take you a course, get you a place,   5
    Observe His Honor, or His Grace,
  Or the King's reàl, or his stampèd face
  Contémplate; what you will, approve,
    So you will let me love.

Alas, alas, who's injured by my love?   10
  What merchants' ships have my sighs drowned?
Who says my tears have overflowed his ground?
  When did my colds a forward spring remove?
    When did the heats which my veins fill
    Add one more to the plaguy bill?   15
  Soldiers find wars, and lawyers find out still
  Litigious men, which quarrels move,
    Though she and I do love.

Call us what you will, we are made such by love.
  Call her one, me another fly;   20
We're tapers too, and at our own cost die.
  And we in us find th' eagle and the dove.
    The Phœnix riddle hath more wit
    By us; we too, being one, are it.
  So to one neutral thing both sexes fit: 25
  We die and rise the same, and prove
    Mysterious by this love.

THE CANONIZATION. 5 *take you a course:* decide on a course of action? go
riding? *place:* position, at court or elsewhere. 6 *Honor . . . Grace:* courtesy
titles used of nobles or persons in high position. 7 *stampèd face:* on coins.
13 *forward:* well-advanced. 15 *plaguy bill:* list of deaths from the plague.
21 *tapers:* candles. 22 *eagle . . . dove:* symbols of strength and mildness. 25 *one
neutral thing:* in the *Symposium* (189–90), Plato wrote of an aboriginal human
form which was sexless because it united masculinity and femininity. 26 *die:*
have sexual intercourse.

We can die by it, if not live by love;
And if unfit for tombs and hearse
Our legend be, it will be fit for verse. 30
    And if no piece of chronicle we prove,
        We'll build in sonnets pretty rooms.
        As well a well-wrought urn becomes
The greatest ashes, as half-acre tombs.
    And by these hymns, all shall approve 35
    Us canonized for love,

And thus invoke us: You whom reverend love
    Made one another's hermitage;
You, to whom love was peace, that now is rage;
    Who did the whole world's soul contract, and drove 40
        Into the glasses of your eyes
        (So made such mirrors, and such spies,
That they did all to you epitomize)
    Countries, towns, courts: Beg from above
    A pattern of your love! 45

                                    (1633)

THE FLEA

Mark but this flea, and mark in this
How little that which thou deni'st me is.
It sucked me first, and now sucks thee;
And in this flea, our two bloods mingled be.
Thou know'st that this cannot be said 5
A sin, nor shame, nor loss of maidenhead.
    Yet this enjoys before it woo,
    And, pampered, swells with one blood made of two:
    And this, alas, is more than we would do.

O stay, three lives in one flea spare, 10
Where we almost, yea, more than married are.
This flea is you and I, and this
Our marriage bed and marriage temple is.

---

30 *legend:* technical for "life of a saint." 31 *chronicle:* history. 33 *becomes:*
befits. 40–41 *drove . . . your eyes:* concentrated, as by a convex lens, into your
eyes.

Though parents grudge, and you, we're met
And cloistered in these living walls of jet. 15
  Though use make you apt to kill me,
  Let not, to that, self-murder added be,
  And sacrilege—three sins in killing three.

Cruel and sudden, hast thou since
Purpled thy nail in blood of innocence? 20
Wherein could this flea guilty be,
Except in that drop which it sucked from thee?
Yet thou triumph'st, and say'st that thou
Find'st not thyself, nor me, the weaker now.
  'Tis true; then learn how false fears be: 25
  Just so much honor, when thou yield'st to me,
  Will waste, as this flea's death took life from thee.
                                        (1633)

A VALEDICTION: FORBIDDING MOURNING

As virtuous men pass mildly away,
  And whisper to their souls to go,
Whilst some of their sad friends do say
  The breath goes now, and some say no; 4

So let us melt, and make no noise,
  No tear-floods, nor sigh-tempests move.
'Twere profanation of our joys
  To tell the laity our love. 8

Moving of th' earth brings harms and fears;
  Men reckon what it did and meant.
But trepidation of the spheres,
  Though greater far, is innocent. 12

Dull sublunary lovers' love,
  Whose soul is sense, cannot admit
Absence, because it doth remove
  Those things which elemented it. 16

THE FLEA. 16 *use:* habit.

A VALEDICTION . . . 11 *trepidation:* an agitation of the eighth sphere in the Ptolemaic system, invented to account for phenomena really caused by the earth's unsteadiness on its axis. 14 *sense:* sensation.

But we, by a love so much refined
   That ourselves know not what it is,
Inter-assured of the mind,
   Care less eyes, lips, and hands to miss.   20

Our two souls, therefore, which are one,
   Though I must go, endure not yet
A breach, but an expansïon,
   Like gold to airy thinness beat.   24

If they be two, they are two so
   As stiff twin compasses are two:
Thy soul, the fixed foot, makes no show
   To move, but doth if th' other do.   28

And though it in the center sit,
   Yet, when the other far doth roam,
It leans, and hearkens after it,
   And grows erect as that comes home.   32

Such wilt thou be to me, who must,
   Like th' other foot, obliquely run;
Thy firmness makes my circle just,
   And makes me end where I begun.   36

(1633)

THE ECSTASY

Where, like a pillow on a bed,
   A pregnant bank swelled up, to rest
The violet's reclining head,
   Sat we two, one another's best.   4
Our hands were firmly cementèd
   With a fast balm, which thence did spring;
Our eye-beams twisted, and did thread
   Our eyes upon one double string.   8

---

23 *A breach:* a break. 23–24: Cf. Donne's *Biathanatos:* "that precious nature of gold, that a little quantity thereof . . . will be brought to cover 10,000 times as much as of any other metal." 26 *compasses:* the draftsman's compass.

THE ECSTASY. *Ecstasy:* a "standing out" of the soul from the body, thought to occur when the mind was intensely concentrated on God, music, and so forth. 2 *pregnant:* fertile, teeming (on one level). 7 *eye-beams:* rays thought to emanate from the eyes.

173

So to intergraft our hands, as yet
  Was all the means to make us one,
And pictures in our eyes to get
  Was all our propagatïon.   12
As 'twixt two equal armies Fate
  Suspends uncertain victory,
Our souls (which, to advance their state,
  Were gone out) hung 'twixt her and me.   16
And whilst our souls negotiate there,
  We like sepulchral statues lay;
All day the same our postures were,
  And we said nothing all the day.   20
If any, so by love refined
  That he soul's language understood,
And by good love were grown all mind,
  Within convenient distance stood,   24
He (though he knew not which soul spake,
  Because both meant, both spake the same)
Might thence a new concoction take,
  And part far purer than he came.   28
This ecstasy doth unperplex—
  We said—and tell us what we love.
We see by this it was not sex;
  We see, we saw not what did move.   32
But as all several souls contain
  Mixture of things, they know not what,
Love these mixed souls doth mix again,
  And makes both one, each this and that.   36
A single violet transplant:
  The strength, the color, and the size
(All which before was poor and scant)
  Redoubles still, and multiplies.   40
When love with one another so
  Interinanimates two souls,
That abler soul which thence doth flow
  Defects of loneliness controls.   44
We then, who are this new soul, know
  Of what we are composed and made;
For th' atomies of which we grow
  Are souls, whom no change can invade.   48

---

11 *pictures:* tiny images on the cornea of what is seen. *get:* beget. 15 *advance:* improve. 18 *sepulchral statues:* statues on tombs. 27 *concoction:* something "cooked up" from a variety of ingredients. 47 *atomies:* atoms or particles.

But O alas! so long, so far,
   Our bodies why do we forbear?
They're ours, though they're not we; we are
   The intelligences, they the sphere.   52
We owe them thanks, because they thus
   Did us, to us, at first convey,
Yielded their forces, sense, to us,
   Nor are dross to us, but allay.   56
On man heaven's influence works not so
   But that it first imprints the air:
So soul into the soul may flow,
   Though it to body first repair.   60
As our blood labors to beget
   Spirits as like souls as it can,
Because such fingers need to knit
   That subtle knot which makes us man,   64
So must pure lovers' souls descend
   To affections, and to faculties
Which sense may reach and apprehend:
   Else a great prince in prison lies.   68
To our bodies turn we then, that so
   Weak men on love revealed may look.
Love's mysteries in souls do grow,
   But yet the body is his book.   72
And if some lover, such as we,
   Have heard this dialogue of one,
Let him still mark us; he shall see
   Small change, when we're to bodies gone.   76

(1633)

SATIRE III

Kind pity chokes my spleen; brave scorn forbids
Those tears to issue which swell my eyelids.
I must not laugh, nor weep sins, and be wise.
Can railing, then, cure these worn maladies?

---

52 *intelligences:* guardian angels of planets. 55 *sense:* sensation (which comes through the sense organs). 56 *allay:* alloy. 57 *heaven's influence:* astrological forces. 61 *blood:* (sexual) passion. 66 *affections:* feelings.

   SATIRE III. 1 *spleen:* thought to be the seat of various emotions, including mirth and melancholy.

Is not our mistress, fair religïon,   5
As worthy of all our souls' devotïon
As virtue was to the first blinded age?
Are not heaven's joys as valiant to assuage
Lusts as earth's honor was to them? Alas,
As we do them in means, shall they surpass   10
Us in the end; and shall thy father's spirit
Meet blind philosophers in heaven, whose merit
Of strict life may be imputed faith, and hear
Thee, whom he taught so easy ways, and near
To follow, damned? O if thou dar'st, fear this;   15
This fear great courage, and high valor, is.
Dar'st thou aid mutinous Dutch, and dar'st thou lay
Thee in ships' wooden sepulchers, a prey
To leaders' rage, to storms, to shot, to dearth?
Dar'st thou dive seas, and dungeons of the earth?   20
Hast thou courageous fire to thaw the ice
Of frozen North discoveries? and, thrice
Colder than salamanders, like divine
Children in th' oven, fires of Spain, and the line,
Whose countries limbecs to our bodies be,   25
Canst thou for gain bear? And must every he
Which cries not "Goddess!" to thy mistress, draw
Or eat thy poisonous words? Courage of straw!
O desperate coward, wilt thou seem bold, and
To thy foes and His (who made thee to stand   30
Sentinel in His world's garrison) thus yield,
And for forbidden wars leave th' appointed field?
Know thy foes: the foul Devil, whom thou
Strivest to please, for hate, not love, would allow
Thee fain his whole realm to be quit; and as   35
The world's all parts wither away and pass,
So the world's self, thy other loved foe, is
In her decrepit wane; and thou, loving this,
Dost love a withered and worn strumpet. Last,

---

7 *blinded age:* the pre-Christian period.   10 *them:* the ancients.   23 *salamanders:* supposed, because of their extreme coldness (Pliny), to be able to live in fire. 23–24 *divine/ Children in th' oven:* Shadrach, Meshach, and Abednego; for the story see *Daniel 3.*   24 *fires of Spain:* Spanish artillery fire. An alternative interpretation, "the fires of the Inquisition," seems inappropriate to "gain," in line 26. *the line:* the equator.   25 *limbecs:* alembics, used for distillation. Apparently the thought is that perspiration resembles drops collecting in a retort.   35 *quit:* requited, paid back (in exchange for your soul).   38 *wane:* the world was thought to be in its last age.

Flesh (itself's death), and joys which flesh can taste, 40
Thou lovest; and thy fair goodly soul, which doth
Give this flesh power to taste joy, thou dost loathe.
Seek true religion. O where? Mirreus,
Thinking her unhoused here, and fled from us,
Seeks her at Rome—there, because he doth know 45
That she was there a thousand years ago.
He loves her rags so, as we here obey
The state-cloth where the Prince sat yesterday.
Crantz to such brave loves will not be enthralled,
But loves her only, who at Géneva is called 50
Religïon, plain, simple, sullen, young,
Contemptuous, yet unhandsome: as among
Lecherous humors there is one that judges
No wenches wholesome but coarse country drudges.
Graius stays still at home here, and because 55
Some preachers—vile ambitious bawds—and laws
Still new, like fashions, bid him think that she
Which dwells with us is only perfect, he
Embraceth her whom his godfathers will
Tender to him, being tender, as wards still 60
Take such wives as their guardians offer, or
Pay values. Careless Phrygius doth abhor
All, because all cannot be good, as one
Knowing some women whores, dares marry none.
Graccus loves all as one, and thinks that so 65
As women do in divers countries go
In divers habits, yet are still one kind,
So doth, so is, religion; and this blind-
ness too much light breeds; but unmovèd thou
Of force must one—and, forced, but one—allow: 70
And the right. Ask thy father which is she;
Let him ask his. Though truth and falsehood be
Near twins, yet truth a little elder is.
Be busy to seek her. Believe me this:
He's not of none, nor worst, that seeks the best. 75
To adore, or scorn, an image, or protest,

---

43 ff. *Mirreus, Crantz,* and so on: names for persons who exemplify particular
religious attitudes. 50 *her . . . at Géneva:* the Calvinist (or Presbyterian)
Church. 53 *humors:* temperaments. 57 *still:* continually. 57–58 *she/ Which
dwells with us:* the Anglican Church. 60 *tender:* young. 62 *Pay values:* stand
the consequences; pay a forfeit. 67 *habits:* modes of dress. *kind:* species. 76 *protest:* become a Protestant? make a fuss over nonessentials?

May all be bad. Doubt wisely; in strange way
To stand inquiring right, is not to stray;
To sleep, or run wrong, is. On a huge hill,
Craggèd and steep, Truth stands, and he that will 80
Reach her, about must, and about must go,
And what the hill's suddenness resists, win so;
Yet strive so, that before age, death's twilight,
Thy soul rest, for none can work in that night.
To will implies delay, therefore now do. 85
Hard deeds, the body's pains, hard knowledge too
The mind's endeavors reach; and mysteries
Are like the sun, dazzling, yet plain to all eyes.
Keep the truth which thou hast found. Men do not stand
In so ill case here, that God hath with his hand 90
Signed kings' blank-charters to kill whom they hate;
Nor are they vicars, but hangmen, to Fate.
Fool and wretch! wilt thou let thy soul be tied
To man's laws, by which she shall not be tried
At the last day? Oh, will it then boot thee 95
To say a Philip, or a Gregory,
A Harry, or a Martin taught thee this?
Is not this excuse for mere contraries
Equally strong? Cannot both sides say so?
That thou mayest rightly obey power, her bounds know. 100
Those passed, her nature and name is changed; to be
Then humble to her is idolatry.
As streams are, power is; those blest flowers that dwell
At the rough stream's calm head, thrive and do well;
But having left their roots and themselves given 105
To the stream's tyrannous rage, alas, are driven
Through mills, and rocks, and woods, and at last, almost
Consumed in going, in the sea are lost.
So perish souls, which more choose men's unjust
Power from God claimed, than God himself to trust. 110

(1633)

---

77 *in strange way:* on a strange road. 81 *about:* round-about, by circuitous ways. 82 *suddenness:* steepness. 85 *will:* intend (to do something). 91 *blank-charters: cartes blanches,* warrants with the details left blank. *whom:* whomever. 92 *vicars:* persons authorized to perform the responsibilities of others. 95 *last day:* the Last Judgment. *boot:* profit. 96–97 *Philip, Gregory, Harry, Martin:* King Philip of Spain, Pope Gregory, King Henry VIII, Martin Luther.

From HOLY SONNETS

VII

At the round earth's imagined corners, blow
Your trumpets, angels, and arise, arise
From death, you numberless infinities
Of souls, and to your scattered bodies go: 4
All whom the flood did, and fire shall, o'erthrow;
All whom war, dearth, age, agues, tyrannies,
Despair, law, chance hath slain; and you whose eyes
Shall behold God and never taste death's woe.   8
But let them sleep, Lord, and me mourn a space;
For, if above all these my sins abound,
'Tis late to ask abundance of Thy grace
When we are there. Here, on this lowly ground,   12
Teach me how to repent: for that's as good
As if Thou 'dst sealed my pardon with Thy blood.

X

Death, be not proud, though some have callèd thee
Mighty and dreadful, for thou art not so.
For those whom thou think'st thou dost overthrow
Die not, poor death; nor yet canst thou kill me.   4
From rest and sleep, which but thy pictures be,
Much pleasure; then from thee much more must flow;
And soonest our best men with thee do go,
Rest of their bones, and soul's delivery.   8
Thou 'rt slave to fate, chance, kings, and desperate men,
And dost with poison, war, and sickness dwell;
And poppy or charms can make us sleep as well
And better than thy stroke. Why swell'st thou then?   12
One short sleep past, we wake eternally,
And death shall be no more: Death, thou shalt die.

XI

Spit in my face, you Jews, and pierce my side;
Buffet and scoff, scourge and crucify me,

VII. 5 *fire:* at the Last Judgment. 6 *dearth:* famine.
X. 11 *poppy:* òpium or laudanum. 12 *swell'st:* with pride.

179

For I have sinned and sinned, and only He
Who could do no iniquity hath died. 4
But by my death cannot be satisfied
My sins, which pass the Jews' impiety:
They killed once an inglorious Man, but I
Crucify Him daily, being now glorified. 8
O let me then His strange love still admire.
Kings pardon, but He bore our punishment.
And Jacob came clothed in vile harsh attire
But to supplant, and with gainful intent. 12
God clothed Himself in vile man's flesh, that so
He might be weak enough to suffer woe.

XIV

Batter my heart, Three-Personed God, for you
As yet but knock, breathe, shine, and seek to mend.
That I may rise and stand, o'erthrow me, and bend
Your force to break, blow, burn and make me new. 4
I, like an usurped town, to another due,
Labor to admit you, but O! to no end.
Reason, your viceroy in me, me should defend,
But is captíved, and proves weak or untrue. 8
Yet dearly I love you, and would be lovèd fain,
But am betrothed unto your enemy.
Divorce me, untie or break that knot again.
Take me to you, imprison me; for I— 12
Except you enthrall me—never shall be free;
Nor ever chaste, except you ravish me.

XVIII

Show me, dear Christ, Thy spouse, so bright and clear.
What! is it she which on the other shore
Goes richly painted? or which, robbed and tore,
Laments and mourns in Germany and here? 4
Sleeps she a thousand, then peeps up one year?
Is she self-truth, and errs? now new, now outwore?

XI. 6 *pass:* surpass. 9 *admire:* wonder at. 11 *Jacob:* when he disguised
himself to obtain Esau's blessing; see *Genesis 27.*

XIV. 9. Donne intended the *y* of *dearly* and the *ou* of *you* to be elided.

XVIII. 1 *spouse:* the church is the "bride" of Christ. 3 *tore:* torn. 6 *outwore:* outworn.

Doth she, and did she, and shall she evermore
On one, on seven, or on no hill appear? 8
Dwells she with us, or, like adventuring knights,
First travel we to seek and then make love?
Betray, kind Husband, Thy spouse to our sights,
And let mine amorous soul court Thy mild Dove, 12
Who is most true and pleasing to Thee then,
When she's embraced and open to most men.

(1633)

HYMN TO GOD MY GOD, IN MY SICKNESS

Since I am coming to that holy room
  Where, with Thy choir of saints for evermore
I shall be made Thy music, as I come
  I tune the instrument here at the door,
  And what I must do then, think here before. 5

Whilst my physicians by their love are grown
  Cosmographers, and I their map, who lie
Flat on this bed, that by them may be shown
  That this is my southwest discovery—
  Per fretum febris, by these straits to die; 10

I joy that, in these straits, I see my West;
  For, though their currents yield return to none,
What shall my West hurt me? As West and East
  In all flat maps (and I am one) are one,
  So death doth touch the resurrection. 15

Is the Pacific Sea my home? Or are
  The Eastern riches? Is Jerusalem?
Anyan, and Magellan, and Gibraltar,
  All straits, and none but straits, are ways to them,
  Whether where Japhet dwelt, or Cham, or Sem. 20

---

8 *on one, on seven, or on no hill:* at Wittenberg, where Luther began the Reformation; at Rome; at Geneva. 10 *travel:* with a pun on "travail." 12 *Dove:* the Holy Spirit.

HYMN . . . 9 *southwest discovery:* of a passage to the East. 10 *per fretum febris:* Lat., by the straits of fever. *straits:* neck of water; also difficulty, distress. 11 *West:* death, the Happy Isles of ancient legend, and Heaven. 18 *Anyan:* Bering (Straits). 20 *Japhet, Cham* (Ham), *Sem* (Shem): sons of Noah from whom descended the people of Europe, Africa, and Asia.

We think that Paradise and Calvary,
  Christ's cross and Adam's tree, stood in one place.
Look, Lord, and find both Adams met in me.
  As the first Adam's sweat surrounds my face,
  May the last Adam's blood my soul embrace.   25

So, in His purple wrapped, receive me, Lord;
  By these His thorns give me His other crown.
And, as to others' souls I preached Thy word,
  Be this my text, my sermon, to mine own:
  Therefore that He may raise, the Lord throws down.   30

(1633)

William Browne (1591?–1643?)

VENUS BY ADONIS' SIDE

Venus by Adonis' side
Crying kissed, and kissing cried;
Wrung her hands and tore her hair
For Adonis lying there.   4

Stay, quoth she, O stay and live!
Nature surely doth not give
To the earth her sweetest flowers
To be seen but some few hours.   8

On his face, still as he bled,
For each drop a tear she shed,
Which she kissed or wiped away,
Else had drowned him where he lay.   12

---

23 *both Adams:* Christ was often called "Second Adam." 24 *sweat:* "in the sweat of thy face shalt thou eat bread" (*Genesis 3:19*). 27 *other crown:* immortality.

VENUS BY ADONIS' SIDE. *Adonis:* beloved of Venus, or Aphrodite. He was killed by a boar.

182

Fair Proserpina, quoth she,
Shall not have thee yet from me,
Nor thy soul to fly begin
While my lips can keep it in.   16

Here she closed again. And some
Say Apollo would have come
To have cured his wounded limb,
But that she had smothered him.   20

(1616)

ON THE DEATH OF MARIE,
COUNTESS OF PEMBROKE

Underneath this sable hearse
Lies the subject of all verse:
Sidney's sister, Pembroke's mother.
Death, ere thou hast slain another
Fair, and learned, and good as she,
Time shall throw a dart at thee.   6

Marble piles let no man raise
To her name for after-days.
Some kind woman, born as she,
Reading this, like Niobe
Shall turn marble, and become
Both her mourner and her tomb.   12

(1623)

---

13 *Proserpina:* Queen of Hades.   17 *closed:* embraced him.
On the Death of . . . 3 *Sidney's:* Sir Philip Sidney's. *Pembroke's:* the Earl of
Pembroke's.   10 *Niobe:* a conventional figure of grief. She wept so excessively
that even when Zeus, in pity, turned her to stone the tears continued to flow.

Ben Jonson (1572?–1637)

ON SOMETHING THAT WALKS SOMEWHERE

At court I met it, in clothes brave enough
To be a courtier, and looks grave enough
To seem a statesman. As I near it came,
It made me a great face. I asked the name;
A lord! it cried, buried in flesh and blood;   5
And such from whom let no man hope least good,
For I will do none; and as little ill,
For I will dare none. Good lord, walk dead still.

(1616)

TO WILLIAM CAMDEN

Camden, most reverend head, to whom I owe
All that I am in arts, all that I know
(How nothing's that!); to whom my country owes
The great renown and name wherewith she goes:
Than thee the age sees not that thing more grave,   5
More high, more holy, that she more would crave.
What name, what skill, what faith hast thou in things!
What sight in searching the most antique springs!
What weight, and what authority in thy speech!
Man scarce can make that doubt but thou canst teach.   10
Pardon free truth, and let thy modesty,
Which conquers all, be once overcome by thee.
Many of thine this better could than I;
But, for their powers, accept my piety.

(1616)

To WILLIAM CAMDEN. Camden was a great antiquarian and Jonson's teacher
at Westminster School. 10: *Man . . . teach:* You can teach men how to resolve
almost any doubt that they may have. 14 *for:* in exchange for.

184

ON MY FIRST DAUGHTER

Here lies, to each her parents' ruth,
Mary, the daughter of their youth.
Yet all Heaven's gifts being Heaven's due,
It makes the father less to rue,
At six months' end she parted hence   5
With safety of her innocence;
Whose soul Heaven's Queen (whose name she bears),
In comfort of her mother's tears,
Hath placed amongst her virgin train;
Where, while that severed doth remain,   10
This grave partakes the fleshly birth—
Which cover lightly, gentle earth.

(1616)

ON MY FIRST SON

Farewell, thou child of my right hand, and joy;
My sin was too much hope of thee, loved boy.
Seven years thou wert lent to me, and I thee pay,
Exacted by thy fate, on the just day.
Oh, I could loose all father now! For why   5
Will man lament the state he should envy,
To have so soon scaped world's and flesh's rage,
And, if no other misery, yet age?
Rest in soft peace, and, asked, say here doth lie
Ben Jonson his best piece of poetry;   10
For whose sake, henceforth, all his vows be such
As what he loves may never like too much.

(1616)

ON MY FIRST SON. 5 *loose:* let loose, give vent to. (Or, possibly, lose.)   10 *Ben Jonson his:* a common, though unhistorical, form of the possessive.   12 *like:* please.

TO FINE LADY WOULD-BE

Fine Madame Would-be, wherefore should you fear,
That love to make so well, a child to bear?
The world reputes you barren; but I know
Your 'pothecary, and his drug says no.
Is it the pain affrights? That's soon forgot.   5
Or your complexion's loss? You have a pot
That can restore that. Will it hurt your feature?
To make amends, you're thought a wholesome creature.
What should the cause be? Oh, you live at court,
And there's both loss of time and loss of sport   10
In a great belly. Write, then, on thy womb,
Of the not born, yet buried: Here's the tomb.

                                        (1616)

INVITING A FRIEND TO SUPPER

Tonight, grave sir, both my poor house and I
Do equally desire your company;
Not that we think us worthy such a guest,
But that your worth will dignify our feast
With those that come; whose grace may make that seem   5
Something, which else could hope for no esteem.
It is the fair acceptance, Sir, creates
The entertainment perfect—not the cates.
Yet shall you have, to rectify your palate,
An olive, capers, or some better salad   10
Ush'ring the mutton, with a short-legged hen,
If we can get her, full of eggs, and then
Lemons, and wine for sauce. To these, a cony
Is not to be despaired of, for our money;
And, though fowl now be scarce, yet there are clarks, 15
The sky not falling, think we may have larks.
I'll tell you more, and lie, so you will come:
Of partridge, pheasant, woodcock, of which some

INVITING A FRIEND . . . 8 *cates:* delicacies. 10 *capers:* buds of the *capperis spinosa,* used as a garnish. 13 *cony:* rabbit. 15 *clarks:* clerks, learned men.

186

May yet be there; and godwit, if we can;
Knat, rail, and ruff, too. Howsoe'er, my man 20
Shall read a piece of Virgil, Tacitus,
Livy, or of some better book to us,
Of which we'll speak our minds amidst our meat;
And I'll profess no verses to repeat.
To this, if aught appear which I not know of, 25
That will the pastry, not my paper, show of.
Digestive cheese and fruit there sure will be;
But that which most doth take my Muse and me
Is a pure cup of rich canary wine,
Which is the Mermaid's now, but shall be mine. 30
Of which had Horace or Anacreon tasted,
Their lives—as do their lines—till now had lasted.
Tobacco, nectar, or the Thespian spring
Are all but Luther's beer, to this I sing.
Of this we will sup free, but moderately. 35
And we will have no Pooly or Parrot by;
Nor shall our cups make any guilty men,
But, at our parting, we will be as when
We innocently met. No simple word
That shall be uttered at our mirthful board 40
Shall make us sad next morning, or affright
The liberty that we'll enjoy tonight.

(1616)

EPITAPH ON S. P., A CHILD
OF QUEEN ELIZABETH'S CHAPEL

Weep with me, all you that read
    This little story;
And know, for whom a tear you shed,
    Death's self is sorry. 4

---

19 *godwit:* a shore bird. 20 *Knat, rail:* other birds. *ruff:* a fish. *man:* servant.
21 *Shall read:* in Latin, of course. 23 *meat:* food. 24 *profess:* promise. 25 *To
this:* along with this. 28 *take:* charm, captivate. 30 *Mermaid's:* that is, belongs
to the Mermaid Tavern. 31 *Horace or Anacreon:* the Latin poet Horace (65–8
B.C.) often praised wine; the Greek Anacreon (d. ca. 478 B.C.) wrote drinking
songs. 33 *nectar:* the drink of the gods. *Thespian spring:* a spring sacred to the
Muses. 34 *all but:* nearly the same as. *to:* in comparison with. 36 *Pooly or
Parrot:* besides suggesting "Polly Parrot," the words may allude to Robert Poley,
who witnessed Christopher Marlowe's violent death, and a man named Parrot.

   EPITAPH . . . *S. P.:* Salomon Pavey, a child actor who had parts in several of
Jonson's plays.

187

'Twas a child that so did thrive
　　In grace and feature
As Heaven and Nature seemed to strive
　　Which owned the creature.　　　　8
Years he numbered scarce thirteen
　　When Fates turned cruel;
Yet three filled zodiacs had he been
　　The stage's jewel,　　　　12
And did act—what now we moan—
　　Old men so duly,
As, sooth, the Parcae thought him one,
　　He played so truly.　　　　16
So, by error, to his fate
　　They all consented;
But viewing him since (alas, too late),
　　They have repented,　　　　20
And have sought, to give new birth,
　　In baths to steep him.
But, being so much too good for earth,
　　Heaven vows to keep him.　　　　24

　　　　　　(1616)

TO CELIA

Come, my Celia, let us prove,
While we may, the sports of love.
Time will not be ours forever;
He at length our good will sever.
Spend not then his gifts in vain.　　　5
Suns that set may rise again;
But if once we lose this light,
'Tis with us perpetual night.
Why should we defer our joys?
Fame and rumor are but toys.　　　10

---

10 *Fates:* the three Fates spun, drew out, and cut the thread of human lives.
11 *zodiacs:* that is, years. 15 *sooth:* truly. *Parcae:* the Fates. 21–22 *to give . . .
steep him:* Medea restored a butchered ram to life by boiling it in a cauldron
and promised, falsely, to do the same with Pelias.

　To CELIA. Like many of Jonson's poems, this is in part an adaptation of a
Latin original (Catullus, *Veronensis Liber* 5). 10 *Fame:* reputation. *toys:* trivialities.

Cannot we delude the eyes
Of a few poor household spies,
Or his easier ears beguile,
So removèd by our wile?
'Tis no sin love's fruit to steal,   15
But the sweet theft to reveal.
To be taken, to be seen—
These have crimes accounted been.

(1616)

A LITTLE SHRUB GROWING BY

Ask not to know this man. If fame should speak
His name in any metal, it would break.
Two letters were enough the plague to tear
Out of his grave, and poison every ear.
A parcel of court dirt, a heap, a mass   5
Of all vice hurled together, there he was;
Proud, false, and treacherous, vindictive, all
That thought can add—unthankful, the lay-stall
Of putrid flesh alive; of blood, the sink.
And so I leave to stir him, lest he stink.   10

(1640)

AN ODE: TO HIMSELF

Where dost thou careless lie,
    Buried in ease and sloth?
Knowledge that sleeps doth die;
And this security,
    It is the common moth
That eats on wits and arts, and oft destroys them both.   6

Are all th' Aonian springs
    Dried up? Lies Thespia waste?

A LITTLE SHRUB . . . 2 *metal:* mineral. 3 *were:* would be. 8 *lay-stall:* dung
pit. 9 *sink:* sewer.

AN ODE . . . 4 *security:* freedom from care. 7 *Aonian springs:* at the foot of
Mt. Helicon, in Greece; sacred to the Muses. 8 *Thespia:* a town on Mt. Helicon,
thought of here as the abode of poets.

Doth Clarius' harp want strings,
That not a nymph now sings?
  Or droop they as disgraced
To see their seats and bowers by chatt'ring pies defaced?   12

If hence thy silence be,
  As 'tis too just a cause,
Let this thought quicken thee:
Minds that are great and free
  Should not on fortune pause.
'Tis crown enough to virtue still, her own applause.   18

What though the greedy fry
  Be taken with false baits
Of worded balladry
And think it poesy?
  They die with their conceits,
And only piteous scorn upon their folly waits.   24

Then take in hand thy lyre;
  Strike in thy proper strain.
With Japhet's line, aspire
Sol's chariot for new fire
  To give the world again.
Who aided him, will thee, the issue of Jove's brain.   30

And, since our dainty age
  Cannot endure reproof,
Make not thyself a page
To that strumpet the stage,
  But sing high and aloof,
Safe from the wolf's black jaw and the dull ass's hoof.   36

(1640)

---

9 *Clarius':* Apollo's. Apollo had a shrine at Klaros, in Asia Minor. 12 *pies:*
magpies. 19 *fry:* the crowd (of common people). 23 *They . . . conceits:* they die
together with their ideas. "Conceit" was a noun from "conceive." 27 *Japhet's
line:* Prometheus, son of Iapetus, stole fire from heaven. 28 *Sol's:* the sun's.

Robert Herrick *(1591–1674)*

THE ARGUMENT OF HIS BOOK

I sing of brooks, of blossoms, birds, and bowers;
Of April, May, of June, and July flowers.
I sing of maypoles, hock-carts, wassails, wakes;
Of bridegrooms, brides, and of their bridal cakes.
I write of youth, of love, and have access,   5
By these, to sing of cleanly wantonness.
I sing of dews, of rains, and, piece by piece,
Of balm, of oil, of spice, and ambergris.
I sing of time's trans–shifting; and I write
How roses first came red, and lilies white.   10
I write of groves, of twilights, and I sing
The court of Mab, and of the Fairy King.
I write of Hell; I sing—and ever shall—
Of Heaven, and hope to have it after all.

(1648)

WHEN HE WOULD HAVE HIS VERSES READ

In sober mornings, do not thou rehearse
The holy incantation of a verse;
But when that men have both well drunk and fed,
Let my enchantments then be sung, or read.
When laurel spurts i' th' fire, and when the hearth   5
Smiles to itself and gilds the roof with mirth;

ARGUMENT: subject matter. 3 *hock-carts:* the last carts—usually decorated—which brought in the harvest. *wassails:* drinkings of healths, especially on Christmas Eve, Twelfth Night, and New Year's Eve. *wakes:* the eves (sometimes including the whole preceding day) of festivals, mostly religious in origin. 6 *wantonness:* undisciplined conduct. 8 *balm:* used as an ointment and as a perfume. 12 *Mab:* wife of Oberon, the fairy king (as in Shakespeare's *A Midsummer Night's Dream*).

191

When up the thyrse is raised, and when the sound
Of sacred orgies flies, a round! a round!
When the rose reigns, and locks with ointments shine,
Let rigid Cato read these lines of mine. 10

(1648)

DELIGHT IN DISORDER

A sweet disorder in the dress
Kindles in clothes a wantonness.
A lawn about the shoulders thrown
Into a fine distraction;
An erring lace, which here and there 5
Enthralls the crimson stomacher;
A cuff neglectful, and thereby
Ribands to flow confusedly;
A winning wave, deserving note,
In the tempestuous petticoat; 10
A careless shoestring, in whose tie
I see a wild civility:
Do more bewitch me than when art
Is too precise in every part.

(1648)

CORINNA'S GOING A-MAYING

Get up, get up, for shame! The blooming morn
Upon her wings presents the god unshorn.
    See how Aurora throws her fair
    Fresh-quilted colors through the air;
    Get up, sweet slug-abed, and see 5
    The dew bespangling herb and tree.

WHEN HE WOULD . . . 7 *thyrse:* thyrsus, a staff carried by Dionysus (Bacchus)
and his votaries. 8 *round:* a song sung by persons who begin at different times.
10 *Cato:* Cato the Censor (234–149 B.C.), a rigid moralist.

DELIGHT IN DISORDER. 2 *wantonness:* pleasant wildness. 3 *lawn:* a sheer cloth.
5 *erring:* wandering, straying. 6 *stomacher:* an article of dress worn over the
stomach. 8 *Ribands:* ribbons.

CORINNA'S GOING A-MAYING. 2 *god unshorn:* Phoebus (or Helios), the sun-god.
3 *Aurora:* goddess of the dawn. 5 *slug-abed:* sluggard in bed.

Each flower has wept and bowed towárd the east
Above an hour since, yet you not dressed.
 Nay, not so much as out of bed?
 When all the birds have matins said   10
 And sung their thankful hymns, 'tis sin,
 Nay, profanation, to keep in;
Whenas a thousand virgins on this day
Spring sooner than the lark to fetch in May.

Rise, and put on your foliage, and be seen   15
To come forth, like the springtime, fresh and green,
 And sweet as Flora. Take no care
 For jewels for your gown or hair.
 Fear not; the leaves will strew
 Gems in abundance upon you.   20
Besides, the childhood of the day has kept,
Against you come, some orient pearls unwept;
 Come, and receive them while the light
 Hangs on the dew-locks of the night,
 And Titan, on the eastern hill,   25
 Retires himself, or else stands still
Till you come forth. Wash, dress, be brief in praying;
Few beads are best, when once we go a-Maying.

Come, my Corinna, come; and, coming, mark
How each field turns a street, each street a park   30
 Made green, and trimmed with trees. See how
 Devotion gives each house a bough
 Or branch. Each porch, each door, ere this,
 An ark, a tabernacle, is,
Made up of white-thorn neatly interwove,   35
As if here were those cooler shades of love.
 Can such delights be in the street
 And open fields, and we not see 't?
 Come, we'll abroad; and let's obey
 The proclamation made for May,   40
And sin no more, as we have done, by staying.
But, my Corinna, come, let's go a-Maying.

---

10 *matins:* morning prayer.   14 *fetch in May:* perform rites to induce the coming
of May; or, perhaps, to gather hawthorn in honor of May.   17 *Flora:* goddess
of flowers.   25 *Titan:* Helios, one of the Titans, or primordial Greek deities
later succeeded by the dynasty of Zeus: a sun-god.   28 *beads:* prayers said on
the beads of the rosary.   30 *turns:* turns into, becomes.   34 *ark:* a basket with a
cover; also a holy object, like the Ark of the Covenant, the most sacred religious
symbol of the early Jews.   35 *white-thorn:* hawthorn.

There's not a budding boy or girl, this day,
But is got up, and gone to bring in May.
   A deal of youth, ere this, is come   45
   Back, and with white-thorn laden home.
   Some have dispatched their cakes and cream
   Before that we have left to dream;
And some have wept, and wooed, and plighted troth,
And chose their priest, ere we can cast off sloth.   50
   Many a green gown has been given,
   Many a kiss, both odd and even;
   Many a glance, too, has been sent
   From out the eye, love's firmament;
Many a jest told of the key's betraying   55
This night, and locks picked, yet we're not a-Maying.

Come, let us go while we are in our prime,
And take the harmless folly of the time.
   We shall grow old apace, and die
   Before we know our liberty.
   Our life is short, and our days run   60
   As fast away as does the sun;
And, as a vapor, or a drop of rain,
Once lost, can ne'er be found again,
   So when or you or I are made   65
   A fable, song, or fleeting shade,
   All love, all liking, all delight
   Lies drowned with us in endless night.
Then, while time serves, and we are but decaying,
Come, my Corinna, come, let's go a-Maying.   70

                         (1648)

UPON JULIA'S SWEAT

   Would ye oil of blossoms get?
   Take it from my Julia's sweat.
   Oil of lilies and of spike—
   From her moisture take the like
   Let her breathe, or let her blow:
   All rich spices thence will flow.   6
            (1648)

---

48 *left:* ceased. 51 *Many a . . . given:* " 'to give a woman a green gown': to roll
her, in sport, on the grass, so that her dress is stained with green" (*Oxford
English Dictionary*). 65 *or . . . or:* either . . . or.
  UPON JULIA'S SWEAT. 3 *spike:* spikenard, an aromatic substance.

HIS PRAYER FOR ABSOLUTION

For those my unbaptizèd rhymes,
Writ in my wild unhallowed times;
For every sentence, clause and word
That's not inlaid with Thee, my Lord:
Forgive me, God, and blot each line   5
Out of my book, that is not Thine.
But if, 'mongst all, Thou find'st here one
Worthy Thy benedictïon,
That one, of all the rest, shall be
The glory of my work, and me.   10

(1648)

George Herbert *(1593–1633)*

HUMILITY

I saw the Virtues sitting hand in hand
In sev'ral ranks upon an azure throne,
Where all the beasts and fowl by their command
Presented tokens of submissïon.
Humility, who sat the lowest there   5
          To execute their call,
When by the beasts the presents tendered were,
          Gave them about to all.

The angry Lion did present his paw,
Which by consent was giv'n to Mansuetude.   10
The fearful Hare her ears, which by their law
Humility did reach to Fortitude.
The jealous Turkey brought his coral chain;

HUMILITY. 3 *beasts and fowl:* representatives of man's lower or animal nature.
10 *Mansuetude:* Mildness. 12 *reach:* hand. 13 *coral chain:* comb or wattle,
or both.

195

That went to Temperance.
On Justice was bestowed the Fox's brain, 15
Killed in the way, by chance.

At length, the Crow bringing the Peacock's plume
(For he would not), as they beheld the grace
Of that brave gift, each one began to fume
And challenge it, as proper to his place, 20
Till they fell out; which, when the beasts espied,
They leapt upon the throne;
And if the Fox had lived to rule their side,
They had deposed each one.

Humility, who held the plume, at this 25
Did weep so fast that the tears, trickling down,
Spoiled all the train; then, saying "Here it is
For which ye wrangle," made them turn their frown
Against the beasts. So, jointly bandying,
They drive them soon away; 30
And then amerced them, double gifts to bring
At the next Session-Day.

(1633)

PEACE

Sweet Peace, where dost thou dwell? I humbly crave,
Let me once know.
I sought thee in a secret cave
And asked if Peace were there.
A hollow wind did seem to answer, No; 5
Go seek elsewhere.

I did, and, going, did a rainbow note.
Surely, thought I,
This is the lace of Peace's coat;
I will search out the matter. 10
But while I looked, the clouds immediately
Did break and scatter.

---

18 *he would not:* the Peacock did not wish to. 21 *fell out:* quarreled. 23 *the Fox:* noted for his shrewdness. 29 *bandying:* banding together? exchanging words?

Then went I to a garden and did spy
A gallant flower,
The Crown Imperial. Sure, said I, 15
Peace at the root must dwell.
But when I digged, I saw a worm devour
What showed so well.

At length I met a rev'rend good old man,
Whom when for Peace 20
I did demand, he thus began:
There was a prince of old
At Salem dwelt, who lived with good increase
Of flock and fold.

He sweetly lived; yet sweetness did not save 25
His life from foes.
But after death out of his grave
There sprang twelve stalks of wheat;
Which many, wond'ring at, got some of those
To plant and set. 30

It prospered strangely, and did soon disperse
Through all the earth;
For they that taste it do rehearse
That virtue lies therein—
A secret virtue bringing peace and mirth 35
By flight of sin.

Take of this grain, which in my garden grows,
And grows for you.
Make bread of it; and that repose
And peace, which ev'rywhere 40
With so much earnestness you do pursue,
Is only there.

(1633)

PEACE. 15 *Crown Imperial:* a handsome flower (fritillary). 23 *Salem:* Mel-chizedek, King of Salem (*Genesis 14:18*), was one of the Old Testament "types" of Christ.

197

ARTILLERY

As I one ev'ning sat before my cell,
Methoughts a star did shoot into my lap.
I rose and shook my clothes, as knowing well
That from small fires comes oft no small mishap.
      When suddenly I heard one say,   5
      "Do as thou usest, disobey;
        Expel good motions from thy breast,
Which have the face of fire, but end in rest."

I, who had heard of music in the spheres,
But not of speech in stars, began to muse;   10
But turning to my God, whose ministers
The stars and all things are: If I refuse,
      Dread Lord, said I, so oft my good,
      Then I refuse not ev'n with blood
        To wash away my stubborn thought;   15
For I will do, or suffer, what I ought.

But I have also stars, and shooters too,
Born where thy servants both artilleries use.
My tears and prayers night and day do woo
And work up to Thee; yet Thou dost refuse.   20
      Not but I am (I must say still)
      Much more obliged to do Thy will
        Than Thou to grant mine; but because
Thy promise now hath ev'n set Thee Thy laws.

Then we are shooters both, and Thou dost deign   25
To enter combat with us, and contest
With Thine own clay. But I would parley fain:
Shun not my arrows—and behold my breast.
      Yet, if Thou shunnest, I am Thine.
      I must be so, if I am mine.   30
      There is no articling with Thee:
I am but finite, yet Thine infinitely.

                             (1633)

ARTILLERY. 2 *Methoughts:* it seemed to me.   7 *motions:* impulses (with a pun).
9 *music in the spheres:* tradition held that the revolutions of the heavenly bodies
in their orbits produced a music inaudible to man.   17 *shooters:* shooting stars.
31 *articling:* reaching agreements by compromise.

THE PULLEY

When God at first made man,
Having a glass of blessings standing by,
Let us, said He, pour on him all we can;
Let the world's riches, which dispersèd lie,
 Contract into a span.   5

 So strength first made a way;
Then beauty flowed, then wisdom, honor, pleasure.
When almost all was out, God made a stay,
Perceiving that alone of all His treasure
 Rest in the bottom lay.   10

 For if I should (said He)
Bestow this jewel also on my creature,
He would adore my gifts instead of me,
And rest in Nature, not the God of Nature.
 So both should losers be.   15

 Yet let him keep the rest,
But keep them with repining restlessness.
Let him be rich and weary, that, at least,
If goodness lead him not, yet weariness
 May toss him to my breast.   20

       (1633)

THE ELIXIR

Teach me, my God and King,
 In all things Thee to see,
And what I do in anything,
 To do it as for Thee.   4

Not rudely, as a beast,
 To run into an action;
But still to make Thee prepossessed,
 And give it his perfection.   8

THE ELIXIR. 7 *still to make Thee prepossessed:* "always to give Thee a prior claim" (Hutchinson). 8 *his:* its.

A man that looks on glass
On it may stay his eye;
Or, if he pleaseth, through it pass,
And then the heav'n espy. 12

All may of Thee partake.
Nothing can be so mean
Which with His tincture ("For Thy sake")
Will not grow bright and clean. 16

A servant, with this clause,
Makes drudgery divine.
Who sweeps a room as for Thy laws
Makes that, and th' action, fine. 20

This is the famous stone
That turneth all to gold:
For that which God doth touch and own
Cannot for less be told. 24

(1633)

---

15 *His (his?):* its? *tincture:* infusion or impregnation. 19 *Who:* whoever. 21
stone: philosopher's stone, which turned everything it touched to gold. 24 *told:*
counted.

Francis Quarles (1592–1644)

From EMBLEMS, DIVINE AND MORAL

Book I, Emblem xv

Debilitata fides : Terras Astræa reliquit

EMBLEM XV. The "emblem" was an illustrated poem, poem and illustration being expected to reinforce and comment upon each other. The form, which perhaps developed from the Horatian doctrine that a poem is like a picture ("*Ut pictura, poësis*"—*Ars Poetica*, line 316), achieved immense popularity. Spenser's *Shepherd's Calendar*—see "October" in the present text—is an early example. The poem is usually preceded by a Scriptural quotation and concluded by an epigram. The text given here is taken from the 1643 edition.

The devil is come unto you, having great wrath,
because he knoweth that he hath but a short time.

Lord, canst Thou see and suffer? Is Thy hand
  Still bound to th' peace? Shall earth's black Monarch take
A full possession of Thy wasted land?
    Oh, will Thy slumb'ring vengeance never wake
    Till full-aged, law-resisting custom shake   5
The pillars of Thy right by false command?
    Unlock Thy clouds, great Thund'rer, and come down;
    Behold whose temples wear Thy sacred crown.
Redress, redress our wrongs; revenge, revenge Thy own.

See how the bold Usurper mounts the seat   10
  Of royal Majesty; how, overstrawing
Perils with pleasure, pointing ev'ry threat
    With bugbear death, by torments overawing
    Thy frighted subjects, or by favors drawing
Their tempted hearts to his unjust retreat.   15
    Lord, canst Thou be so mild? And he so bold?
    Or can Thy flocks be thriving, when the fold
Is governed by a fox? Lord, canst Thou see and hold?

That swift-winged advocate, that did commence
  Our welcome suits before the King of Kings;   20
That sweet ambassador, that hurries hence
    What airs th' harmonious soul or sighs or sings,
    See how she flutters with her idle wings;
Her wings are clipped, and eyes put out by sense.
    Sense-conquering faith is now grown blind and cold,   25
    And basely cravened, that in times of old
Did conquer Heav'n itself, do what th' Almighty could.

Behold how double Fraud does scourge and tear
  Astræa's wounded sides, plowed up and rent
With knotted cords, whose fury has no care.   30
    See how she stands a pris'ner to be sent,
    A slave, into eternal banishment,
I know not whither, O I know not where.
    Her patent must be canceled in disgrace,
    And sweet-lipped Fraud, with her divided face,   35
Must act Astræa's part, must take Astræa's place.

---

11 *overstrawing:* strewing over. 18 *hold:* hold off, be patient. 22 *or . . . or:*
either . . . or. 24 *sense:* sensations coming through the sense organs. 26
cravened: made cowardly. 29 *Astræa's:* Astræa was goddess of justice. 34 *patent:*
a writ conveying authority.

Faith's pinions clipped? And fair Astræa gone?
Quick-seeing Faith now blind? And Justice see?
Has Justice now found wings? And has Faith none?
What do we here, who would not wish to be
Dissolved from earth, and with Astræa flee
From this blind dungeon to that sun-bright throne?
Lord, is Thy scepter lost, or laid aside?
Is Hell broke loose, and all her fiends untied?
Lord, rise and rouse, and rule and crush their furious pride!

40

45

Petr. Rav. in Math:

The Devil is the author of evil, the fountain of wickedness, the adversary of the truth, the corrupter of the world, man's perpetual enemy; he planteth snares, diggeth ditches, spurreth bodies; he goadeth souls, he suggesteth thoughts, belcheth anger, exposeth virtues to hatred, maketh vices beloved, soweth errors, nourisheth contention, disturbeth peace, and scattereth affections.

Macar:

Let us suffer with those that suffer, and be crucified with those that are crucified, that we may be glorified with those that are glorified.

Savanar:

If there be no enemy, no fight; if no fight, no victory; if no victory, no crown.

Epig. 15

My soul, sit thou a patient looker-on;
Judge not the play before the play is done.
Her plot has many changes: every day
Speaks a new scene. The last act crowns the play.

(1635)

Petr. Rav. Peter Chrysologus (406–450), Bishop of Ravenna? Macar. Macarius, Bishop of Vinnitza, who objected to the Roman Catholic handling of confession and absolution? (*Ante-Nicene Fathers*, III, 667.) Savanar. Probably Savonarola (1452–1498), a precursor of the Reformation.

Thomas Carew (1594?–1640)

AN ELEGY UPON THE DEATH OF THE DEAN OF PAUL'S, DR. JOHN DONNE

Can we not force from widowed poetry,
Now thou art dead (great Donne), one elegy
To crown thy hearse? Why yet dare we not trust,
Though with unkneaded dough-baked prose, thy dust,
Such as the unscissored churchman from the flower   5
Of fading rhetoric, short-lived as his hour,
Dry as the sand that measures it, should lay
Upon thy ashes on the funeral day?
Have we no voice, no tune? Didst thou dispense,
Through all our language, both the words and sense?   10
'Tis a sad truth: the pulpit may her plain
And sober Christian precepts still retain;
Doctrines it may, and wholesome uses, frame,
Grave homilies, and lectures; but the flame
Of thy brave soul—that shot such heat and light   15
As burnt our earth, and made our darkness bright,
Committed holy rapes upon our will,
Did through the eye the melting heart distill,
And the deep knowledge of dark truths so teach
As sense might judge, what fancy could not reach—   20
Must be desired forever. So the fire
That fills with spirit and heat the Delphic choir,
Which, kindled first by thy Promethean breath,
Glowed here awhile, lies quenched now in thy death.

AN ELEGY . . . *Paul's:* St. Paul's Cathedral, in London. 3–8 *Why . . . funeral day?:* The syntax is obscure. The sense may be something like this: "Why have we not yet dared to entrust to (that is, bestow upon, give to) your corpse some tribute, though in such crude prose as the shaggy-haired preacher might speak over your ashes at the funeral—prose whose rhetorical ornaments would not outlive the funeral service, and as dry as the sand in his hourglass?" 9 *dispense:* distribute. "Was it you who enriched our language with words and gave it meaning?" 13 *uses:* habits, practices. 17 *rapes:* seizures. 20 *sense:* sensation, as of sight and hearing. *fancy:* imagination. The thought is, "Your preaching caused us to image what our reason was incapable of understanding." 22 *Delphic choir:* choir of priests which chanted oracles in Apollo's temple at Delphi. 23 *Promethean:* Prometheus was a Titan who stole fire from heaven for man's use.

204

The Muses' garden, with pedantic weeds 25
O'erspread, was purged by thee; the lazy seeds
Of servile imitation thrown away,
And fresh invention planted. Thou didst pay
The debts of our penurious bankrupt age:
Licentious thefts, that make poetic rage 30
A mimic fury, when our souls must be
Possessed, or with Anacreon's ecstasy,
Or Pindar's, not their own. The subtle cheat
Of sly exchanges, and the juggling feat
Of two-edged words, or whatsoever wrong 35
By ours was done the Greek or Latin tongue,
Thou hast redeemed, and opened us a mine
Of rich and pregnant fancy, drawn a line
Of masculine expression, which had good
Old Orpheus seen, or all the ancient brood 40
Our superstitious fools admire, and hold
Their lead more precious than thy burnished gold,
Thou hadst been their exchequer, and no more
They each in other's dust had raked for ore.
Thou shalt yield no precédence but of time 45
And the blind fate of language, whose tuned chime
More charms the outward sense. Yet thou may'st claim
From so great disadvantage greater fame,
Since to the awe of thy imperious wit
Our stubborn language bends, made only fit, 50
With her tough, thick-ribbed hoops, to gird about
Thy giant fancy, which had proved too stout
For their soft, melting phrases. As in time
They had the start, so did they cull the prime
Buds of invention many a hundred year, 55
And left the rifled fields, besides the fear
To touch their harvest. Yet from those bare lands
Of what is purely thine, thy only hands
(And that thy smallest work) have gleanèd more
Than all those times and tongues could reap before. 60
But thou art gone, and thy strict laws will be

27 *imitation:* of the ancient Greek and Latin poets. 32–33 *or . . . Or:* either . . . or. *Anacreon, Pindar:* Greek poets. Anacreon (born ca. 560 B.C.) was best known for drinking-songs and love-poems; Pindar (born ca. 522 B.C.) was famed for his odes. 34 *sly exchanges:* the borrowing of poetic phrases with slight changes. 35 *two-edged words:* puns? words with different meanings in Latin (or Greek) and English? 40 *Orpheus:* a mythical Greek poet. 59 *smallest work:* that is, Donne did his chief work as an Anglican priest.

Too hard for libertines in poetry.
They will repeal the goodly exiled train
Of gods and goddesses, which in thy just reign
Were banished nobler poems. Now, with these, 65
The silenced tales o' the *Metamorphoses*
Shall stuff their lines, and swell the windy page;
Till verse, refined by thee, in this last age
Turn ballad rhyme, or those old idols be
Adored again, with new apostasy. 70
Oh, pardon me, that break with untuned verse
The reverent silence that attends thy hearse,
Whose awful, solemn murmurs were to thee,
More than these faint lines, a loud elegy;
That did proclaim in a dumb eloquence 75
The death of all the arts, whose influence,
Grown feeble, in these panting numbers lies
Gasping short-winded accents, and so dies.
So doth the swiftly turning wheel not stand
In th' instant we withdraw the moving hand, 80
But some small time maintain a faint, weak course
By virtue of the first impulsive force.
And so, whilst I cast on thy funeral pile
Thy crown of bays, oh, let it crack awhile
And spit disdain, till the devouring flashes 85
Suck all the moisture up, then turn to ashes.
I will not draw the envy to engross
All thy perfections, or weep all our loss.
Those are too numerous for an elegy,
And this too great to be expressed by me. 90
Though every pen should share a distinct part,
Yet art thou theme enough to tire all art.
Let others carve the rest; it shall suffice
I on thy tomb this epitaph incise:
    Here lies a king, that ruled as he thought fit 95
    The universal monarchy of wit.
    Here lie two flamens, and both those the best:
    Apollo's first, at last the true God's priest.

                                            (1633)

---

63 *repeal:* call back. 66 *Metamorphoses:* a long, mythological poem by Ovid (d.
ca. A.D. 17). 69 *old idols:* the gods and goddesses mentioned in line 64. 77 *numbers:* rhythms. 84 *crown of bays:* an award for poetic achievement. 87 *engross:*
set down formally. 96 *universal monarchy:* whole kingdom. 97 *flamens:* priests.
98 *Apollo's . . . priest:* Donne's early poetry (*Apollo's*) was amatory, his later
poetry (*the true God's*) devotional.

INGRATEFUL BEAUTY THREATENED

Know, Celia, since thou art so proud,
  'Twas I that gave thee thy renown.
Thou hadst, in the forgotten crowd
  Of common beauties, lived unknown,
Had not my verse exhaled thy name
And, with it, imped the wings of fame.   6

That killing power is none of thine;
  I gave it to thy voice and eyes.
Thy sweets, thy graces, all are mine;
  Thou art my star, shin'st in my skies.
Then dart not from thy borrowed sphere
Lightning on him that fixed thee there.   12

Tempt me with such affrights no more,
  Lest what I made, I uncreate.
Let fools thy mystic forms adore;
  I'll know thee in thy mortal state.
Wise poets that wrapped truth in tales
Knew her themselves, through all her veils.   18

(1640)

INGRATEFUL . . . 6 *imped:* mended the feathers of. 11 *sphere:* each star moved in its special sphere, or orbit. 15 *mystic forms:* the forms of the soul, thought by Plato to determine the qualities of the body.

Richard Crashaw (1612?–1649)

THE FLAMING HEART:

Upon the Book and Picture of the Seraphical Saint Teresa (As She Is Usually Expressed With a Seraphim Beside Her)

Well-meaning readers! you that come as friends
And catch the precious name this piece pretends,
Make not too much haste to admire
That fair-cheeked fallacy of fire.
That is a Seraphim, they say;   5
And this the great Teresia.
Readers, be ruled by me, and make
Here a well-placed and wise mistake.
You must transpose the picture quite,
And spell it wrong to read it right.   10
Read HIM for her, and her for him;
And call the Saint the seraphim.
   Painter, what didst thou understand,
To put her dart into his hand?
See, even the years and size of him   15
Shows this the mother Seraphim.
This is the mistress-flame; and, duteous, he
Her happy fireworks, here, comes down to see.
O most poor-spirited of men!
Had thy cold pencil kissed her pen,   20
Thou could'st not so unkindly err,
To show us this faint shade for her.

THE FLAMING HEART. St. Theresa, a Spanish mystic (1515–82; canonized 1622), was an object of special devotion to Crashaw. The "Book" of the subtitle was almost certainly the English translation (1642) of a Spanish *Vida*, or *Life*. The "Picture" evidently showed the Saint with an angel who sometimes visited her— a seraph, she thought, because he seemed "all in a fire." (*Seraph* means "one who burns.") The angel bore a golden dart tipped with fire, which he thrust into her heart to make it "wholy inflamed with a great loue of Almightye God" (quoted in Martin's edition of Crashaw, p. 437). 2 *pretends:* offers (*praetendere*); or the modern meaning? 3 *admire:* wonder at. 4 *fallacy:* deceit. 17 *mistress-flame:* variant of "master-flame." 20 *pen:* her mss. were valued highly by Philip II of Spain. 21 *unkindly:* unnaturally.

Why, man, this speaks pure mortal frame,
And mocks with female frost love's manly flame.
One would suspect thou meant'st to paint
Some weak, inferior, woman saint.   25
But had thy pale-faced purple took
Fire from the burning cheeks of that bright book,
Thou would'st on her have heaped up all
That could be found seraphical: 30
Whate'er this youth of fire wears fair—
Rosy fingers, radiant hair,
Glowing cheek, and glistering wings—
All those fair and flagrant things.
But, before all, that fiery dart   35
Had filled the hand of this great heart.
    Do then as equal right requires;
Since his the blushes be, and hers the fires,
Resume and rectify thy rude design:
Undress thy seraphim into mine.   40
Redeem this injury of thy art;
Give him the veil, give her the dart.
    Give him the veil, that he may cover
The red cheeks of a rivaled lover;
Ashamed that our world, now, can show   45
Nests of new seraphims here below.
    Give her the dart, for it is she
(Fair youth) shoots both thy shaft and thee.
Say, all ye wise and well-pierced hearts
That live and die amidst her darts,   50
What is 't your tasteful spirits do prove
In that rare life of her, and love?
Say, and bear witness. Sends she not
A seraphim at every shot?
What magazines of immortal arms there shine!   55
Heav'n's great artillery in each love-spun line.
Give, then, the dart to her who gives the flame;
Give him the veil, who kindly takes the shame.
    But if it be the frequent fate
Of worst faults to be fortunate;   60

---

26 *inferior, woman:* one of Theresa's confessors called her "a bearded man" (because of her strong character and organizational ability?). 28 *burning cheeks:* was the book bound in red? 34 *flagrant:* blazing. 42 *veil:* Theresa was a Carmelite nun. 51 *tasteful:* endowed with good taste. *prove:* approve, commend. 60 *worst . . . fortunate:* Adam's sin was said to be fortunate *(felix culpa)* because it motivated Christ's redemptive mission.

If all's prescription, and proud wrong
Hearkens not to a humble song;
For all the gallantry of him,
Give me the suff'ring seraphim.
His be the bravery of all those bright things: 65
The glowing cheeks, the glistering wings,
The rosy hand, the radiant dart.
Leave her alone the flaming heart.
  Leave her that; and thou shalt leave her
Not one loose shaft, but love's whole quiver.   70
For in love's field was never found
A nobler weapon than a wound.
Love's passives are his activ'st part;
The wounded is the wounding heart.
O heart! the equal poise of love's both parts,   75
Big alike with wounds and darts,
Live in these conquering leaves; live all the same,
And walk through all tongues one triumphant flame.
Live here, great heart, and love and die and kill,
And bleed and wound; and yield and conquer still.   80
Let this immortal life, where'er it comes,
Walk in a crowd of loves and martyrdoms.
Let mystic deaths wait on 't, and wise souls be
The love-slain witnesses of this life of thee.
O sweet incendiary! show here thy art.   85
Upon this carcass of a hard, cold heart
Let all thy scattered shafts of light, that play
Among the leaves of thy large books of day,
Combined against this breast, at once break in
And take away from me myself and sin.   90
This gracious robbery shall thy bounty be;
And my best fortunes, such fair spoils of me.
O thou undaunted daughter of desires!
By all thy dow'r of lights and fires;
By all the eagle in thee, all the dove;   95
By all thy lives and deaths of love;
By thy large draughts of intellectual day,
And by thy thirsts of love more large than they;
By all thy brim-filled bowls of fierce desire;
By thy last morning's draught of liquid fire;   100

61 *prescription:* written down in advance, hence unchangeable. 65 *bravery:* fine show. 95 *eagle . . . dove:* symbols of strength and mildness. 100 *draught:* from the fire-tipped lance?

By the full kingdom of that final kiss
That seized thy parting soul, and sealed thee His;
By all the heav'ns thou hast in Him
(Fair sister of the seraphim);
By all of Him we have in thee: 105
Leave nothing of myself in me.
• Let me so read thy life, that I
Unto all life of mine may die.

(1642)

Sir John Suckling *(1609–1642)*

'TIS NOW, SINCE I SAT DOWN BEFORE

'Tis now, since I sat down before
   That foolish fort, a heart
(Time strangely spent!), a year and more;
   And still I did my part;   4

Made my approaches, from her hand
   Unto her lip did rise;
And did already understand
   The language of her eyes;   8

Proceeded on with no less art—
   My tongue was engineer.
I thought to undermine the heart
   By whispering in the ear.   12

When this did nothing, I brought down
   Great cannon-oaths and shot
A thousand thousand to the town;
   And still it yielded not.   16

I then resolved to starve the place
   By cutting off all kisses,
Praising, and gazing on her face,
   And all such little blisses.   20

211

To draw her out and from her strength,
  I drew all batteries in,
And brought myself to lie at length
  As if no siege had been.   24

When I had done what man could do,
  And thought the place mine own,
The enemy lay quiet too,
  And smiled at all was done.   28

I sent to know from whence and where
  These hopes and this relief.
A spy informed, Honor was there,
  And did command in chief.   32

March, march! quoth I; the word straight give;
  Let's lose no time, but leave her.
That giant upon air will live,
  And hold it out forever.   36

To such a place our camp remove
  As will no siege abide.
I hate a fool that starves her love
  Only to feed her pride.   40

                    (1646)

'Tis now . . . 23 *lie:* lodge, sojourn.

212

John Milton (1608–1674)

LYCIDAS

In this monody the author bewails a learned friend, unfortunately drowned in his passage from Chester on the Irish Seas, 1637. And by occasion foretells the ruin of our corrupted clergy, then in their height.

Yet once more, O ye laurels, and once more
Ye myrtles brown, with ivy never sere,
I come to pluck your berries harsh and crude,
And with forced fingers rude
Shatter your leaves before the mellowing year. 5
Bitter constraint, and sad occasion dear,
Compels me to disturb your season due;
For Lycidas is dead, dead ere his prime—
Young Lycidas, and hath not left his peer.
Who would not sing for Lycidas? He knew 10
Himself to sing, and build the lofty rhyme.
He must not float upon his wat'ry bier
Unwept, and welter to the parching wind,
Without the meed of some melodious tear.
   Begin then, Sisters of the sacred well, 15
That from beneath the seat of Jove doth spring;
Begin, and somewhat loudly sweep the string.
Hence with denial vain and coy excuse.
So may some gentle Muse
With lucky words favor my destined urn, 20
And as he passes turn
And bid fair peace be to my sable shroud.
For we were nursed upon the self-same hill,
Fed the same flock, by fountain, shade, and rill.

LYCIDAS. A pastoral name for Edward King, a contemporary of Milton's at Cambridge. King, who was preparing for the ministry, appears to have been a good scholar and a poet of sorts. 1–2 *laurels, myrtles, ivy:* evergreens which symbolize poetic fame. 2 *brown:* dark (Italian, *bruno*). 3 *crude:* raw, unripe. 6 *dear:* hard, grievous (from a different source than "dear," *precious*). 15 *Sisters:* the Muses. *sacred well:* the Pierian Spring, at the foot of Mt. Olympus. 24 *Fed the same flock:* in pastorals, the poet was traditionally represented as a shepherd.

Together both, ere the high lawns appeared 25
Under the opening eyelids of the morn,
We drove afield, and both together heard
What time the gray-fly winds her sultry horn;
Batt'ning our flocks with the fresh dews of night,
Oft till the star that rose at ev'ning bright 30
Toward heav'n's descent had sloped his westering wheel.
Meanwhile the rural ditties were not mute,
Tempered to th' oaten flute;
Rough satyrs danced, and fauns with cloven heel
From the glad sound would not be absent long; 35
And old Damœtas loved to hear our song.
But O the heavy change, now thou art gone—
Now thou art gone, and never must return!
Thee, shepherd, thee the woods and desert caves,
With wild thyme and the gadding vine o'ergrown, 40
And all their echoes mourn.
The willows and the hazel copses green
Shall now no more be seen
Fanning their joyous leaves to thy soft lays.
As killing as the canker to the rose, 45
Or taint-worm to the weanling herds that graze,
Or frost to flowers that their gay wardrobe wear
When first the white-thorn blows:
Such, Lycidas, thy loss to shepherd's ear.
Where were ye, Nymphs, when the remorseless deep 50
Closed o'er the head of your loved Lycidas?
For neither were ye playing on the steep
Where your old bards, the famous Druids, lie,
Nor on the shaggy top of Mona high,
Nor yet where Deva spreads her wizard stream. 55
Ay me, I fondly dream!
Had ye been there—for what could that have done?

---

28 *winds:* blows. 29 *batt'ning:* fattening. 30 *star . . . bright:* Venus. 33 *oaten flute:* pipe made of an oat-straw. 36 *Damœtas:* a tutor at Cambridge? 40 *gadding:* straying. 41 *mourn:* pronounced to rhyme with *turn* in line 38. 44 *lays:* songs, poems. 45 *canker:* cankerworm, a type of caterpillar. 46 *taint-worm:* thought to lurk where animals might feed. *weanling:* recently weaned. 48 *white-thorn:* hawthorn. *blows:* blooms. 53 *Druids:* poet-priests of the ancient Druidic religion of the Celts. 54 *Mona:* Anglesey, an island off the northwest coast of Wales. 55 *Deva:* the River Dee, which flows through northern Wales into the Irish Sea. *wizard:* the Dee had "divinity" above all other Welsh rivers (Camden). 56 *fondly:* foolishly.

214

What could the Muse herself that Orpheus bore,
The Muse herself, for her enchanting son,
Whom universal nature did lament, 60
When by the rout that made the hideous roar
His gory visage down the stream was sent,
Down the swift Hebrus to the Lesbian shore?
   Alas! What boots it, with uncessant care,
To tend the homely, slighted shepherd's trade 65
And strictly meditate the thankless Muse?
Were it not better done, as others use,
To sport with Amaryllis in the shade,
Or with the tangles of Neæra's hair?
Fame is the spur that the clear spirit doth raise— 70
That last infirmity of noble mind—
To scorn delights and live laborious days;
But the fair guerdon when we hope to find,
And think to burst out into sudden blaze,
Comes the blind Fury with th' abhorrèd shears 75
And slits the thin-spun life. But not the praise,
Phœbus replied, and touched my trembling ears.
Fame is no plant that grows on mortal soil,
Nor in the glistering foil
Set off to th' world, nor in broad rumor lies; 80
But lives and spreads aloft by those pure eyes
And perfect witness of all-judging Jove.
As he pronounces lastly on each deed,
Of so much fame in Heav'n expect thy meed.
   O Fountain Arethuse, and thou honored flood, 85
Smooth-sliding Mincius, crowned with vocal reeds,
That strain I heard was of a higher mood.
But now my oat proceeds
And listens to the Herald of the Sea

58–63 *Muse . . . shore:* Calliope, the muse of epic poetry, was the mother of
Orpheus, a Thracian poet, who was torn to pieces by wild Thracian women. His
head was thrown into the Hebrus River and finally came ashore at Lesbos.
64 *boots:* profits. 65 *shepherd's trade:* the art of poetry. 66 *meditate:* attend
to, study. 67 *use:* are accustomed (to do). 75 *Fury:* Atropos (a Fate, not a
Fury), who cut the thread of life spun by Clotho and drawn out by Lachesis.
77 *Phœbus:* god—among other things—of poetry. *touched . . . ears:* to attract
attention, as in Virgil's sixth *Eclogue, 3–5.* 79 *glistering:* glittering. *foil:* a thin
sheet of metal set behind a jewel to increase its brilliance. 85 *Fountain Arethuse:*
in Sicily, near the birthplace of Theocritus, a famous Greek pastoral poet.
86 *Mincius:* a river near the birthplace of Virgil, the most celebrated Roman
writer of pastorals. 87 *strain:* of music. 88 *oat:* oaten reed, as in line 33 above.
89 *Herald of the Sea:* Triton, son of Neptune.

215

That came in Neptune's plea. 90
He asked the waves, and asked the felon winds,
What hard mishap hath doomed this gentle swain?
And questioned every gust of rugged wings
That blows from off each beakèd promontory.
They knew not of his story; 95
And sage Hippotades their answer brings,
That not a blast was from his dungeon strayed.
The air was calm, and on the level brine
Sleek Panope with all her sisters played.
It was that fatal and perfidious bark, 100
Built in th' eclipse, and rigged with curses dark,
That sunk so low that sacred head of thine.

Next Camus, reverend sire, went footing slow,
His mantle hairy and his bonnet sedge,
Inwrought with figures dim, and on the edge 105
Like to that sanguine flower inscribed with woe.
Ah, who hath reft, quoth he, my dearest pledge?
Last came, and last did go,
The pilot of the Galilean lake.
Two massy keys he bore of metals twain. 110
(The golden opes, the iron shuts amain.)
He shook his mitered locks and stern bespake:
How well could I have spared for thee, young swain,
Enow of such as for their bellies' sake
Creep, and intrude, and climb into the fold! 115
Of other care they little reck'ning make
Than how to scramble at the shearers' feast
And shove away the worthy bidden guest.
Blind mouths! that scarce themselves know how to hold
A sheep-hook, or have learned ought else the least 120
That to the faithful herdman's art belongs!

---

90 *in Neptune's plea:* to plead "Not guilty" on behalf of Neptune. 96 *Hippotades:* Æolus, son of Hippotas and god of the winds. He is *sage* because he invented navigation. 99 *Panope . . . sisters:* sea-nymphs or Nereids. 100 *fatal:* ill-fated. 103 *Camus:* the personified River Cam, from which Cambridge is named. 106 *sanguine . . . woe:* the hyacinth is *sanguine,* or bloody (purple), because it sprang from the blood of Hyacinthus, accidentally slain by Apollo. Its markings were thought to spell AI (alas). 109–12 *pilot:* Saint Peter, a fisherman of Galilee. *keys:* those of Heaven (and Hell?), given Peter by Christ (*Matthew 16:19*). *mitered:* the miter is the bishop's headdress: St. Peter was thought to have been the first Bishop of Rome. 115 *fold:* the Church. 119 *Blind mouths:* the opposite of "one who sees" [*episkopos,* bishop] and "one who feeds" [*pastor*] (Ruskin). 120 *sheep-hook:* the shepherd's crook; the bishop's crozier.

216

What recks it them? What need they? They are sped.
And when they list, their lean and flashy songs
Grate on their scrannel pipes of wretched straw.
The hungry sheep look up, and are not fed, 125
But swoll'n with wind, and the rank mist they draw,
Rot inwardly, and foul contagion spread,
Besides what the grim Wolf with privy paw
Daily devours apace, and nothing said.
But that two-handed engine at the door 130
Stands ready to smite once, and smite no more.
   Return, Alpheus, the dread voice is past
That shrunk thy streams; return, Sicilian Muse,
And call the vales, and bid them hither cast
Their bells and flow'rets of a thousand hues. 135
Ye valleys low, where the mild whispers use
Of shades, and wanton winds, and gushing brooks,
On whose fresh lap the swart star sparely looks:
Throw hither all your quaint enameled eyes
That on the green turf suck the honeyed show'rs 140
And purple all the ground with vernal flow'rs.
Bring the rathe primrose, that forsaken dies,
The tufted crow-toe, and pale jessamine,
The white pink, and the pansy freaked with jet,
The glowing violet, 145
The musk rose, and the well-attired woodbine,
With cowslips wan that hang the pensive head,
And every flower that sad embroidery wears.
Bid amaranthus all his beauty shed,
And daffadillies fill their cups with tears, 150
To strew the laureate hearse where Lycid lies.
For so, to interpose a little ease,
Let our frail thoughts dally with false surmise.
Ay me! whilst thee the shores and sounding seas
Wash far away, where'er thy bones are hurled: 155
Whether beyond the stormy Hebrides,

---

122 *recks:* concerns. *are sped:* have prospered. 124 *scrannel:* thin, squeaky.
128 *Wolf:* probably the Roman Catholic Church, which at this time was making
converts at the English court. 130 *two-handed engine:* one of the most famous
cruxes in English literature. Probably the executioner's two-handed sword or axe.
132 *Alpheus:* a river in Arcady. The river-god loved Arethusa (line 85). 133
Sicilian Muse: the pastoral muse who inspired Theocritus. 136 *use:* visit, resort.
138 *swart star:* Sirius, which blackened vegetation during the heat of summer.
142 *rathe:* early. 144 *freaked:* streaked. 149 *amaranthus:* a fabulous "unfading"
flower—or a real one.

Where thou perhaps under the whelming tide
Visit'st the bottom of the monstrous world;
Or whether thou, to our moist vows denied,
Sleep'st by the fable of Bellerus old,   160
Where the great vision of the guarded mount
Looks toward Namancos and Bayona's hold.
Look homeward Angel, now, and melt with ruth.
And, O ye dolphins, waft the hapless youth.
 Weep no more, woeful shepherds, weep no more,   165
For Lycidas, your sorrow, is not dead,
Sunk though he be beneath the wat'ry floor.
So sinks the day-star in the ocean bed,
And yet anon repairs his drooping head,
And tricks his beams, and with new-spangled ore   170
Flames in the forehead of the morning sky.
So Lycidas sunk low, but mounted high
Through the dear might of Him that walked the waves;
Where other groves, and other streams along,
With nectar pure his oozy locks he laves,   175
And hears the unexpressive nuptial song
In the blessed kingdoms meek of joy and love.
There entertain him all the saints above,
In solemn troops and sweet societies,
That sing, and singing in their glory move,   180
And wipe the tears forever from his eyes.
Now, Lycidas, the shepherds weep no more;
Henceforth thou art the genius of the shore
In thy large recompense, and shalt be good
To all that wander in that perilous flood.   185
 Thus sang the uncouth swain to th' oaks and rills
While the still morn went out with sandals gray.
He touched the tender stops of various quills,
With eager thought warbling his Doric lay.

---

158 *monstrous world:* world of monsters. 160 *fable of Bellerus:* fabled Bellerus, a giant from whom Land's End, in Cornwall (Bellerium), was thought to be named. 161 *great vision:* of St. Michael, thought to guard St. Michael's Mount, at the tip of Cornwall. 162 *Namancos . . . Bayona's* (strong)*hold:* in north-west Spain. 163 *ruth:* pity. 164 *waft:* as in Greek legend a dolphin brought ashore the corpse of Palæmon. 168 *day-star:* the sun. 169 *repairs:* restores. 170 *tricks:* adorns. 176 *unexpressive:* inexpressible. *nuptial song:* for the marriage of the Lamb, Christ (*Revelations 14:3–4 and 19:9*). 183 *genius of the shore:* local divinity (*genius loci*). 184 *good:* propitious. 186 *uncouth:* unknown or rustic. 188 *quills:* reeds (of the shepherd's pipe). 189 *Doric:* the dialect in which Greek pastoral poetry was written.

And now the sun had stretched out all the hills, 190
And now was dropped into the western bay.
At last he rose, and twitched his mantle blue:
Tomorrow to fresh woods, and pastures new.

(1638)

SONNETS

XVIII

Avenge, O Lord, Thy slaughtered Saints, whose bones
  Lie scattered on the Alpine mountains cold—
  Ev'n them who kept Thy truth so pure of old,
  When all our fathers worshiped stocks and stones, 4
Forget not: in Thy book record their groans
  Who were Thy sheep, and in their ancient fold
  Slain by the bloody Piemontese, that rolled
  Mother with infant down the rocks. Their moans 8
The vales redoubled to the hills, and they
  To Heav'n. Their martyred blood and ashes sow
  O'er all th' Italian fields where still doth sway
The triple tyrant, that from these may grow 12
  A hundredfold, who, having learnt Thy way,
  Early may fly the Babylonian woe.

(1673)

XIX

When I consider how my light is spent,
  Ere half my days in this dark world and wide,
  And that one talent which is death to hide
  Lodged with me useless, though my soul more bent 4
To serve therewith my Maker, and present
  My true account, lest He returning chide:

XVIII. The Waldenses (or Vaudois) were Italian members of a heterodox, hence "Protestant," religious sect which originated in the twelfth century. On April 24, 1655, they were cruelly attacked by the Duke of Savoy. 12 *triple tyrant:* the Pope, who wears a triple tiara. 14 *Babylonian:* Papal—a common parallelism.

XIX. 1 *light is spent:* Milton became completely blind in 1651. 3 *one talent:* see the parable in *Matthew 25:14–30.* 4 *bent:* inclined.

219

Doth God exact day-labor, light denied?
I fondly ask; but patience, to prevent
That murmur, soon replies: God doth not need
Either man's work or His own gifts. Who best
Bear His mild yoke, they serve Him best. His state
Is kingly. Thousands at His bidding speed
And post o'er land and ocean without rest;
They also serve who only stand and wait.

(1673)

XXIII

Methought I saw my late espousèd saint
Brought to me like Alcestis from the grave,
Whom Jove's great son to her glad husband gave,
Rescued from death by force, though pale and faint.
Mine, as whom washed from spot of childbed taint
Purification in the Old Law did save,
And such as yet once more I trust to have
Full sight of her in Heaven without restraint,
Came vested all in white, pure as her mind.
Her face was veiled, yet, to my fancied sight,
Love, sweetness, goodness in her person shined
So clear, as in no face with more delight.
But oh! as to embrace me she inclined,
I waked, she fled, and day brought back my night.

(1673)

8 *fondly:* foolishly. 12 *Thousands:* of angels.

XXIII. 1 *late-espousèd saint:* usually taken to be Milton's second wife, Katherine Woodcock, who died in 1658, some weeks after giving birth to a daughter. 2 *Alcestis:* restored after death to her husband, Admetus, by Hercules ("Jove's great son") in Euripides' play *Alcestis.* 5 *whom:* one whom. 6 *Old Law:* Jewish ritual law, which required that the mother of a daughter undergo a term of purification lasting sixty-six days (*Leviticus 12:1–5*). 10 *veiled:* it is probable that Milton never saw his second wife, but Alcestis also was veiled when restored to Admetus.

PARADISE LOST

From Book I

Of man's first disobedience, and the fruit
Of that forbidden tree, whose mortal taste
Brought death into the world, and all our woe,
With loss of Eden, till one greater Man
Restore us, and regain the blissful seat,   5
Sing Heav'nly Muse, that on the secret top
Or Oreb, or of Sinai, didst inspire
That shepherd, who first taught the chosen seed
In the beginning how the heav'ns and earth
Rose out of Chaos; or if Sion Hill   10
Delight thee more, and Siloa's brook that flowed
Fast by the Oracle of God, I thence
Invoke thy aid to my advent'rous song,
That with no middle flight intends to soar
Above th' Aonian Mount, while it pursues   15
Things unattempted yet in prose or rhyme.
And chiefly Thou, O Spirit, that dost prefer
Before all temples th' upright heart and pure,
Instruct me, for Thou know'st; Thou from the first
Wast present, and with mighty wings outspread   20
Dove-like sat'st brooding on the vast abyss
And mad'st it pregnant: what in me is dark
Illumine, what is low raise and support,
That to the heighth of this great argument
I may assert Eternal Providence,   25
And justify the ways of God to men.
    Say first, for Heav'n hides nothing from thy view,
Nor the deep tract of Hell—say first what cause
Moved our grand parents in that happy state,
Favored of Heav'n so highly, to fall off   30

PARADISE LOST, BOOK I (Lines 1–49). 2 *mortal:* deadly. 4 *one greater Man:*
Christ. 6 *Heav'nly Muse:* Urania, the muse of astronomy, identified by Milton
with the Holy Spirit. 7 *Oreb* (Horeb) . . . *Sinai:* alternative names for the
mountain on which Moses—"That shepherd" of line 8—received the Ten Commandments. 10 *Sion:* Zion, the hill in Jerusalem on which the Temple was
built. 11 *Siloa's brook:* Shiloah, a brook on Zion. 12 *Oracle of God:* the
Temple. 15 *Aonian Mount:* Helicon, sacred to the Muses. 21 *sat'st brooding:*
during the Creation. 24 *argument:* subject matter. 29 *grand parents:* Adam
and Eve.

From their Creator, and transgress His will
For one restraint, lords of the world besides?
Who first seduced them to that foul revolt?
Th' infernal Serpent: he it was, whose guile,
Stirred up with envy and revenge, deceived   35
The mother of mankind, what time his pride
Had cast him out from Heav'n, with all his host
Of rebel angels, by whose aid aspiring
To set himself in glory above his peers,
He trusted to have equaled the Most High,   40
If He opposed, and with ambitious aim
Against the throne and monarchy of God
Raised impious war in Heav'n and battle proud,
With vain attempt. Him the Almighty Power
Hurled headlong, flaming, from th' ethereal sky,   45
With hideous ruin and combustion, down
To bottomless perdition, there to dwell
In adamantine chains and penal fire,
Who durst defy th' Omnipotent to Arms.

(1667)

From Book VIII

He ended, or I heard no more, for now
My earthly by his Heav'nly overpower'd,
Which it had long stood under, strained to the heighth
In that celestial colloquy sublime
As with an object that excels the sense,   5
Dazzled and spent, sunk down and sought repair
Of sleep, which instantly fell on me, called
By nature as in aid, and closed mine eyes.
Mine eyes He closed, but open left the cell
Of fancy, my internal sight, by which,   10
Abstract as in a trance, methought I saw,

---

32 *one restraint:* the prohibition against eating the fruit of the Tree of Knowledge. 34 *Serpent:* Satan. 35–36 *envy . . . pride:* two of the Seven Deadly Sins. 37 *cast him out from Heav'n:* the belief that Satan and other angels had been ejected from Heaven was deduced mostly from *Revelation 12:7–9.* 41 *ambitious:* with a bad sense, as in Shakespeare's *Julius Caesar.* 46 *ruin:* fall, as in Latin *ruina.* 47 *there:* in Hell.

Paradise Lost, book viii (Lines 452–559). Adam is describing to the Archangel Raphael God's response to his request for a suitable companion. 2 *earthly . . . Heav'nly:* earthly nature; Heavenly nature. 6 *spent:* exhausted. 11 *abstract:* withdrawn.

222

Though sleeping, where I lay, and saw the Shape
Still glorious before Whom awake I stood;
Who, stooping, opened my left side, and took
From thence a rib, with cordial spirits warm 15
And life-blood streaming fresh. Wide was the wound,
But suddenly with flesh filled up and healed.
The rib He formed and fashioned with His hands;
Under His forming hands a creature grew,
Man-like, but different sex, so lovely fair 20
That what seemed fair in all the world seemed now
Mean, or in her summed up, in her contained
And in her looks, which from that time infused
Sweetness into my heart, unfelt before,
And into all things from her air inspired 25
The spirit of love and amorous delight.
She disappeared and left me dark; I waked
To find her, or forever to deplore
Her loss, and other pleasures all abjure.
When out of hope, behold her not far off 30
Such as I saw her in my dream, adorned
With what all Earth or Heaven could bestow
To make her amiable. On she came,
Led by her Heav'nly Maker, though unseen,
And guided by His voice, nor uninformed 35
Of nuptial sanctity and marriage rites.
Grace was in all her steps, Heav'n in her eye,
In every gesture dignity and love.
I, overjoyed, could not forbear aloud:
    This turn hath made amends; Thou hast fulfilled 40
Thy words, Creator bounteous and benign,
Giver of all things fair; but fairest this
Of all Thy gifts, nor enviest. I now see
Bone of my bone, flesh of my flesh, myself
Before me; Woman is her name, of Man 45
Extracted. For this cause he shall forgo
Father and mother, and to his wife adhere;
And they shall be one flesh, one heart, one soul.
    She heard me thus, and, though divinely brought,
Yet innocence and virgin modesty, 50
Her virtue and the conscience of her worth,
That would be wooed, and not unsought be won,

---

15 *cordial:* of the heart. 43 *enviest:* nor dost Thou envy. 51 *conscience:* consciousness.

223

Not obvious, not obtrusive, but, retired,
The more desirable—or, to say all,
Nature herself, though pure of sinful thought, 55
Wrought in her so, that, seeing me, she turned.
I followed her; she what was honor knew,
And with obsequious majesty approved
My pleaded reason. To the nuptial bow'r
I led her blushing like the morn; all Heav'n 60
And happy constellations on that hour
Shed their selectest influence; the Earth
Gave sign of gratulation, and each hill.
Joyous the birds; fresh gales and gentle airs
Whispered it to the woods, and from their wings 65
Flung rose, flung odors from the spicy shrub,
Disporting, till the amorous bird of night
Sung spousal, and bid haste the evening star
On his hilltop, to light the bridal lamp.
Thus I have told thee all my state, and brought 70
My story to the sum of earthly bliss
Which I enjoy, and must confess to find
In all things else delight indeed, but such
As, used or not, works in the mind no change,
Nor vehement desire: these delicacies 75
I mean of taste, sight, smell, herbs, fruits, and flow'rs,
Walks, and the melody of birds. But here
Far otherwise, transported I behold,
Transported touch; here passion first I felt,
Commotion strange; in all enjoyments else 80
Superior and unmoved, here only weak
Against the charm of beauty's powerful glance.
Or nature failed in me, and left some part
Not proof enough such object to sustain,
Or, from my side subducting, took perhaps 85
More than enough; at least on her bestowed
Too much of ornament, in outward show
Elaborate, of inward less exact.
For well I understand in the prime end
Of nature her th' inferior, in the mind 90
And inward faculties, which most excel,

---

53 *obvious:* Latin *obvia,* in the way; hence not forward or coquettish. 55 *though pure:* though Eve was pure. 62 *influence:* astrological influence. 63 *gratulation:* joy. 67 *bird:* the nightingale. 68 *star:* Venus. 83–85 *Or . . . Or:* either . . . or. 85 *subducting:* taking away.

224

In outward also her resembling less
His image who made both, and less expressing
The character of that dominion giv'n
O'er other creatures. Yet when I approach   95
Her loveliness, so absolute she seems
And in herself complete, so well to know
Her own, that what she wills to do or say
Seems wisest, virtuousest, discreetest, best.
All higher knowledge in her presence falls   100
Degraded; Wisdom in discourse with her
Loses, discount'nanced, and like folly shows.
Authority and reason on her wait,
As one intended first, not after made
Occasionally; and, to consúmmate all,   105
Greatness of mind and nobleness their seat
Build in her loveliest, and create an awe
About her, as a guard angelic placed.

(1667)

PARADISE REGAINED

From Book IV

So saying, he took—for still he knew his power
Not yet expir'd—and to the wilderness
Brought back the Son of God, and left Him there,
Feigning to disappear. Darkness now rose
As daylight sunk, and brought in low'ring night,   5
Her shadowy offspring; unsubstantial both,
Privation mere of light and absent day.
Our Savior, meek and with untroubled mind
After his airy jaunt, though hurried sore,
Hungry and cold betook Him to His rest,   10
Wherever, under some concourse of shades,
Whose branching arms thick intertwined might shield
From dews and damps of night His sheltered head.

---

96 *absolute:* finished, perfect. 101 *Degraded:* placed on a lower step.

PARADISE REGAINED, BOOK IV (Lines 394–438). After Christ has withstood the
temptations of the bread and the kingdoms (for which see *Luke 4:1–13*), the
Devil returns Him to the wilderness. 9 *airy jaunt:* aerial journey. A *jaunt* was
a jogging or fatiguing trip.

But sheltered slept in vain, for at His head
The Tempter watched, and soon with ugly dreams 15
Disturbed His sleep; and either tropic now
'Gan thunder, and both ends of heav'n; the clouds
From many a horrid rift abortive poured
Fierce rain with lightning mixed, water with fire
In ruin reconciled; nor slept the winds 20
Within their stony caves, but rushed abroad
From the four hinges of the world, and fell
On the vexed wilderness, whose tallest pines,
Though rooted deep as high, and sturdiest oaks,
Bowed their stiff necks, loaden with stormy blasts, 25
Or torn up sheer. Ill wast Thou shrouded then,
O patient Son of God, yet only stood'st
Unshaken. Nor yet stayed the terror there:
Infernal ghosts, and Hellish furies, round
Environed Thee; some howled, some yelled, some shrieked, 30
Some bent at Thee their fiery darts, while Thou
Sat'st unappalled in calm and sinless peace.
Thus passed the night so foul till morning fair
Came forth with pilgrim steps in amice gray;
Who with her radiant finger stilled the roar 35
Of thunder, chased the clouds, and laid the winds
And grisly specters, which the Fiend had raised
To tempt the Son of God with terrors dire.
And now the sun with more effectual beams
Had cheered the face of Earth, and dried the wet 40
From drooping plant or dropping tree; the birds,
Who all things now behold more fresh and green,
After a night of storm so ruinous,
Cleared up their choicest notes in bush and spray
To gratulate the sweet return of morn. 45

(1671)

---

16 *either tropic:* of Cancer or Capricorn; more loosely, both parts of the sky.
18 *abortive:* prematurely or fruitlessly. 20 *ruin:* Latin *ruina,* fall. *reconciled:*
water and fire were thought to be antagonistic elements. 22 *hinges:* the *cardines*
(hinges) after which the four cardinal points of the compass are named.
34 *amice:* an ecclesiastical hood lined with gray fur. 44 *spray:* branch. 45
gratulate: rejoice at.

Andrew Marvell *(1621–1678)*

TO HIS COY MISTRESS

Had we but world enough, and time,
This coyness, Lady, were no crime.
We would sit down and think which way
To walk, and pass our long love's day.
Thou by the Indian Ganges' side   5
Should'st rubies find; I by the tide
Of Humber would complain. I would
Love you ten years before the Flood;
And you should, if you please, refuse
Till the conversion of the Jews.   10
My vegetable love should grow
Vaster than empires, and more slow.
An hundred years should go to praise
Thine eyes, and on thy forehead gaze;
Two hundred to adore each breast;   15
But thirty thousand to the rest.
An age at least to every part;
And the last age should show your heart.
For, Lady, you deserve this state;
Nor would I love at lower rate.   20
　But at my back I always hear
Time's wingèd chariot hurrying near;
And yonder all before us lie
Deserts of vast eternity.
Thy beauty shall no more be found;   25
Nor, in thy marble vault, shall sound
My echoing song; then worms shall try
That long-preserved virginity,
And your quaint honor turn to dust,
And into ashes all my lust.   30
The grave's a fine and private place;
But none, I think, do there embrace.

To His Coy Mistress. *Coy:* reserved, modest.   7 *Humber:* Hull, where Marvell
lived, stands on the Humber Estuary.   19 *state:* stateliness; dignified treatment.

Now, therefore, while the youthful hue
Sits on thy skin like morning dew,
And while thy willing soul transpires
At every pore with instant fires, 35
Now let us sport us while we may;
And now, like am'rous birds of prey,
Rather at once our Time devour
Than languish in his slow-chapped pow'r. 40
Let us roll all our strength and all
Our sweetness, up into one ball,
And tear our pleasures, with rough strife,
Thorough the iron gates of life.
Thus, though we cannot make our sun 45
Stand still, yet we will make him run.

(1681)

THE GARDEN

How vainly men themselves amaze
To win the palm, the oak, or bays,
And their uncessant labors see
Crowned from some single herb or tree, 4
Whose short and narrow-vergèd shade
Does prudently their toils upbraid;
While all flow'rs and all trees do close
To weave the garlands of repose. 8

Fair Quiet, have I found thee here,
And Innocence, thy sister dear!
Mistaken long, I sought you then
In busy companies of men. 12
Your sacred plants, if here below,
Only among the plants will grow.
Society is all but rude
To this delicious solitude. 16

No white nor red was ever seen
So am'rous as this lovely green.

35 *transpires:* breathes forth. 36 *instant fires:* fires contained in it (Latin *instare,* to stand within). 40 *slow-chapped:* slow-jawed. 44 *thorough:* through.

THE GARDEN. 2 *palm, oak, bays:* symbols, respectively, of success in war, government, and poetry. 7 *close:* come together, unite. 16 *To:* in comparison with.

228

Fond lovers, cruel as their flame,
Cut in these trees their mistress' name. 20
Little, alas, they know or heed
How far these beauties hers exceed!
Fair trees! wheres'e'r your barks I wound,
No name shall but your own be found. 24

When we have run our passion's heat,
Love hither makes his best retreat.
The gods that mortal beauty chase
Still in a tree did end their race. 28
Apollo hunted Daphne so,
Only that she might laurel grow;
And Pan did after Syrinx speed
Not as a nymph, but for a reed. 32

What wondrous life in this I lead!
Ripe apples drop about my head;
The luscious clusters of the vine
Upon my mouth do crush their wine. 36
The nectarine and curious peach
Into my hands themselves do reach;
Stumbling on melons, as I pass,
Ensnared with flow'rs, I fall on grass. 40

Meanwhile the mind, from pleasure less,
Withdraws into its happiness:
The mind, that ocean where each kind
Does straight its own resemblance find. 44
Yet it creates, transcending these,
Far other worlds, and other seas;
Annihilating all that's made
To a green thought in a green shade. 48

Here at the fountain's sliding foot,
Or at some fruit-tree's mossy root,
Casting the body's vest aside,
My soul into the boughs does glide. 52
There like a bird it sits, and sings,

---

28 *Still:* always. 29–32 *Apollo . . . reed:* when Daphne was pursued by Apollo
she prayed to the gods for help and was turned into a laurel tree. Similarly,
Syrinx escaped Pan, a god of shepherds and hunters, by being turned into a
reed, of which Pan later made a shepherd's pipe. 37 *curious:* requiring care.
43–44 *Mind . . . find:* that is, the mind contains innate ideas of everything that
has actual existence. 44 *straight:* straightway. 51 *vest:* vestment or vesture.

229

Then whets and combs its silver wings;
And, till prepared for longer flight,
Waves in its plumes the various light.   56

Such was that happy garden-state
While man there walked without a mate.
After a place so pure and sweet,
What other help could yet be meet?   60
But 'twas beyond a mortal's share
To wander solitary there.
Two Paradises 'twere in one
To live in Paradise alone.   64

How well the skillful gard'ner drew
Of flow'rs and herbs this dial new!
Where, from above, the milder sun
Does through a fragrant zodiac run;   68
And, as it works, th' industrious bee
Computes its time as well as we.
How could such sweet and wholesome hours
Be reckoned but with herbs and flow'rs?   72

(1681)

Henry Vaughan (1621–1695)

THE SHOWER

'Twas so, I saw thy birth; that drowsy lake
From her faint bosom breathed thee, the disease
Of her sick waters, and infectious ease.
　　　　But now, at even,
　　　　Too gross for heaven,
Thou fall'st in tears, and weep'st for thy mistake.   6

---

54 *whets:* preens. 60 *help . . . meet:* Eve was created as a help meet (fitting) for Adam. 66 *dial:* sundial. 68 *zodiac:* path, course (like the zodiac in the heavens). 70 *time:* perhaps with a pun on *thyme.* 72 *reckoned:* computed.

230

Ah, it is so with me; oft have I pressed
Heaven with a lazy breath, but, fruitless, this
Pierced not. Love only can with quick access
   Unlock the way,
   When all else stray—
The smoke and exhalations of the breast.   12

Yet if, as thou dost melt, and with thy train
Of drops make soft the earth, my eyes could weep
O'er my hard heart, that's bound up and asleep,
   Perhaps at last—
   Some such show'rs past—
My God would give a sunshine after rain.   18

      (1650)

THE WORLD

I saw Eternity the other night
Like a great ring of pure and endless light,
  All calm as it was bright;
And round beneath it, Time in hours, days, years,
  Driv'n by the spheres,   5
Like a vast shadow moved, in which the world
  And all her train were hurled.
The doting lover in his quaintest strain
  Did there complain;
Near him, his lute, his fancy, and his flights   10
  (Wit's sour delights),
With gloves, and knots, the silly snares of pleasure.
  Yet his dear treasure
All scattered lay, while he his eyes did pour
  Upon a flow'r.   15

The darksome statesman, hung with weights and woe,
Like a thick midnight fog, moved there so slow
  He did nor stay nor go.
Condemning thoughts, like sad eclipses, scowl
  Upon his soul,
And clouds of crying witnesses without   20
  Pursued him with one shout.

THE WORLD. 5 *Driv'n ... spheres:* that is, time is measured by the movements
of the heavenly bodies. 8 *quaintest:* most artful. 12 *knots:* love-knots. 16
darksome: secretive. 18 *nor ... nor:* neither ... nor.

231

Yet digged the mole, and, lest his ways be found,
  Worked underground,
Where he did clutch his prey (but One did see 25
  That policy).
Churches and altars fed him; perjuries
  Were gnats and flies.
It rained about him blood and tears, but he
  Drank them as free. 30

The fearful miser on a heap of rust
(Sat pining all his life there) did scarce trust
  His own hands with the dust,
Yet would not place one piece above, but lives
  In fear of thieves. 35
Thousands there were as frantic as himself,
  And hugged each one his pelf.
The downright epicure placed heav'n in sense,
  And scorned pretence,
While others, slipped into a wide excess, 40
  Said little less.
The weaker sort slight, trivial wares enslave,
  Who think them brave;
And poor, despisèd Truth sat counting by
  Their victory. 45

Yet some, who all this while did weep and sing,
And sing and weep, soared up into the ring;
  But most would use no wing.
O fools! said I, thus to prefer dark night
  Before true light; 50
To live in grots and caves, and hate the day
  Because it shews the way—
The way which from this dead and dark abode
  Leads up to God;
A way where you might tread the sun, and be 55
  More bright than he.
But as I did their madness so discuss,
  One whispered thus:
This ring the Bridegroom did for none provide
  But for his bride. 60

---

26 *policy:* stratagem. 34 *above:* in plain sight. 38 *in sense:* in what can be
sensed. 43 *brave:* splendid, showy. 44 *counting by:* reckoning up, observing.
52 *shews:* shows. 59 *Bridegroom:* Christ. 60 *bride:* the Church.

232

[I] John 2:16–17:

All that is in the world, the lust of the flesh, the lust of the eyes, and the pride of life, is not of the Father, but is of the world.

And the world passeth away, and the lusts thereof, but he that doth the will of God abideth forever.

(1650)

Abraham Cowley (1618–1667)

ANACREONTICS

Drinking

The thirsty earth soaks up the rain
And drinks, and gapes for drink again.
The plants suck in the earth, and are
With constant drinking fresh and fair.
The sea itself, which one would think   5
Should have but little need of drink,
Drinks ten thousand rivers up,
So filled that they o'erflow the cup.
The busy sun (and one would guess,
By's drunken, fiery face, no less)   10
Drinks up the sea, and, when h'as done,
The moon and stars drink up the sun.
They drink and dance by their own light;
They drink and revel all the night.
Nothing in nature's sober found,   15
But an eternal health goes round.
Fill up the bowl then, fill it high,
Fill all the glasses there; for why
Should every creature drink but I?
Why, man of morals, tell me why?   20

(1656)

ANACREONTICS: poems modeled on those of the Greek Anacreon (b. ca. 560 B.C.) —especially drinking songs.

THE WISH

Well, then; I now do plainly see
This busy world and I shall ne'er agree.
The very honey of all earthly joy
    Does of all meats the soonest cloy;   4
    And they, methinks, deserve my pity,
Who for it can endure the stings,
The crowd, and buzz, and murmurings
    Of this great hive, the City.   8

Ah, yet, ere I descend to th' grave,
May I a small house and large garden have,
And a few friends, and many books—both true,
    Both wise, and both delightful too!   12
    And since love ne'er will from me flee,
A mistress moderately fair
And good, as guardian angels are:
    Only beloved, and loving me!   16

O fountains, when in you shall I
Myself, eased of unpeaceful thoughts, espy?
O fields! O woods! when, when shall I be made
    The happy tenant of your shade?   20
    Here's the spring-head of pleasure's flood,
Where all the riches lie that she
    Has coined and stamped for good.   23

Pride and ambition here
Only in far-fetched metaphors appear.
Here nought but winds can hurtful murmurs scatter,
    And nought but echo flatter.   27
    The gods, when they descended, hither
From Heav'n did always choose their way;
And therefore we may boldly say
    That 'tis the way, too, thither.   31

How happy here should I
And one dear She live, and embracing die!
She who is all the world, and can exclude,
    In deserts, solitude.   35

THE WISH. 4 *meats:* food.

234

I should have then this only fear,
Lest men, when they my pleasures see,
Should hither throng to live like me,
    And so make a city here.

39

(1647)

Sir John Denham (1615–1669)

From COOPER'S HILL

Thames, the most loved of all the ocean's sons,
By his old sire, to his embraces runs,
Hasting to pay his tribute to the sea,
Like mortal life to meet eternity.
Though with those streams he no resemblance hold, 5
Whose foam is amber, and their gravel gold,
His genuine, and less guilty, wealth t' explore,
Search not his bottom, but survey his shore,
O'er which he kindly spreads his spacious wing
And hatches plenty for th' ensuing spring; 10
Nor then destroys it with too fond a stay,
Like mothers which their infants overlay;
Nor with a sudden and impetuous wave,
Like prófuse kings, resumes the wealth he gave.
No unexpected inundations spoil 15
The mower's hopes, nor mock the plowman's toil;
But God-like his unwearied bounty flows:
First loves to do, then loves the good he does.
Nor are his blessings to his banks confined,
But free, and common as the sea or wind; 20
When he to boast, or to disperse his stores—
Full of the tributes of his grateful shores—
Visits the world, and in his flying towers
Brings home to us, and makes both Indies ours;
Finds wealth where 'tis, bestows it where it wants, 25
Cities in deserts, woods in cities plants,

COOPER'S HILL, lines 161–92. 12 *overlay:* accidentally smother in bed. 14 *re-sumes:* takes back. 24 *Indies:* India (or the East Indies) and the West Indies.

235

So that to us no thing, no place, is strange,
While his fair bosom is the world's exchange.
O could I flow like thee, and make thy stream
My great example, as it is my theme!
Though deep, yet clear; though gentle, yet not dull;   30
Strong without rage, without o'erflowing full.

(1668)

Edmund Waller (1606–1687)

TO THE KING, ON HIS NAVY

Where'er thy navy spreads her canvas wings,
Homage to thee, and peace to all, she brings.
The French and Spaniard, when thy flags appear,
Forget their hatred, and consent to fear.
So Jove from Ida did both hosts survey,   5
And, when he pleased to thunder, part the fray.
Ships heretofore in seas like fishes sped—
The mighty still upon the smaller fed.
Thou on the deep imposest nobler laws,
And by that justice hast removed the cause   10
Of those rude tempests which, for rapine sent,
Too oft, alas! involved the innocent.
Now shall the ocean, as thy Thames, be free
From both those fates, of storms and piracy;
But we most happy, who can fear no force   15
But winged troops, or Pegasean horse.
'Tis not so hard for greedy foes to spoil
Another nation as to touch our soil.
Should nature's self invade the world again,

To the King . . . According to G. Thorn Drury, Waller's nineteenth-century editor, this poem may have been written as early as 1627, when the Duke of Buckingham was equipping a large fleet. He believed that lines 3–4 refer to an agreement of April, 1627, between the French and Spaniards. 16 *Pegasean:* Pegasus was a winged horse ridden by Bellerophon in subduing the Chimæra. Waller may also have been thinking, however, of a griffin-horse which played an important part in Ludovico Ariosto's *Orlando Furioso* (1532), a famous Italian epic of the Renaissance.

And o'er the center spread the liquid main, 20
Thy power were safe, and her destructive hand
Would but enlarge the bounds of thy command.
Thy dreadful fleet would style thee lord of all,
And ride in triumph o'er the drownèd ball.
Those towers of oak o'er fertile plains might go, 25
And visit mountains where they once did grow.
    The world's Restorer never could endure
That finished Babel should those men secure
Whose pride designed that fabric to have stood
Above the reach of any second flood. 30
To thee, his chosen, more indulgent, He
Dares trust such power with so much piety.

(1686)

OF THE LAST VERSES IN THE BOOK

When we for age could neither read nor write,
The subject made us able to indite;
The soul, with nobler resolutions decked,
The body stooping, does herself erect.
No mortal parts are requisite to raise
Her that, unbodied, can her Maker praise.
    The seas are quiet when the winds give o'er;
So calm are we when passions are no more.
For then we know how vain it was to boast
Of fleeting things, so certain to be lost. 10
Clouds of affection from our younger eyes
Conceal that emptiness which age descries.
    The soul's dark cottage, battered and decayed,
Lets in new light through chinks that time has made.
Stronger by weakness, wiser men become 15
As they draw near to their eternal home.
Leaving the old, both worlds at once they view
That stand upon the threshold of the new.

. . . . *Miratur limen Olympi*—Virgil

(1686)

27–30 *The world's . . . flood:* For the story of Babel see *Genesis 11:1–9.*

OF THE LAST VERSES . . . The "Book" is the edition of Waller's poems published
in 1686. 11 *affection:* feeling. *Miratur limen Olympi:* [Daphne] "marvels at
Heaven's threshold" (Virgil, *Eclogue V,* 56).

237

John Dryden *(1631–1700)*

MAC FLECKNOE

All human things are subject to decay,
And, when fate summons, monarchs must obey.
This Flecknoe found, who, like Augustus, young
Was called to empire, and had governed long:
In prose and verse was owned, without dispute, 5
Through all the realms of nonsense, absolute.
The aged Prince, now flourishing in peace,
And blessed with issue of a large increase,
Worn out with business, did at length debate
To settle the succession of the state; 10
And, pond'ring which of all his sons was fit
To reign, and wage immortal war with wit,
Cried, " 'Tis resolved! For nature pleads that he
Should only rule who most resembles me.
Sh——— alone my perfect image bears, 15
Mature in dullness from his tender years.
Sh——— alone, of all my sons, is he
Who stands confirmed in full stupidity.
The rest to some faint meaning make pretense,
But Sh——— never deviates into sense. 20
Some beams of wit on other souls may fall,
Strike through, and make a lucid interval;
But Sh———'s genuine night admits no ray;
His rising fogs prevail upon the day.
Besides, his goodly fabric fills the eye, 25
And seems designed for thoughtless majesty:
Thoughtless as monarch oaks that shade the plain
And, spread in solemn state, supinely reign.
Heywood and Shirley were but types of thee,

MAC FLECKNOE: "Son of Flecknoe." Richard Flecknoe was an incompetent Irish poet who died about 1678. He is used here as a type of the dull poet. 3 *Augustus, young:* Augustus became Emperor of Rome at the age of thirty-two. 15 *Sh———:* [Thomas] Shadwell, 1642(?)–1692, a dramatist of some ability, but a bad poet. Dryden had been feuding with him for several years about literary matters. 29 *Heywood and Shirley:* Thomas Heywood and James Shirley, dramatists who died, respectively, in 1641 and 1666.

Thou last great prophet of tautology. 30
Even I, a dunce of more renown than they,
Was sent before but to prepare thy way,
And, coarsely clad in Norwich drugget, came
To teach the nations in thy greater name.
My warbling lute, the lute I whilom strung 35
When to King John of Portugal I sung,
Was but the prelude to that glorious day
When thou on silver Thames did'st cut thy way
With well-timed oars before the royal barge,
Swelled with the pride of thy celestial charge 40
And big with hymn, commander of an host;
The like was ne'er in *Epsom* blankets tossed.
Methinks I see the new Arion sail,
The lute still trembling underneath thy nail.
At thy well-sharpened thumb, from shore to shore 45
The treble squeaks for fear, the bases roar.
Echoes from Pissing Alley Sh———! call;
And Sh———! they resound from A—— Hall.
About thy boat the little fishes throng,
As at the morning toast that floats along. 50
Sometimes, as prince of thy harmonious band,
Thou wield'st thy papers in thy threshing hand.
St. André's feet ne'er kept more equal time,
Not ev'n the feet of thy own *Psyche's* rhyme,
Though they in number, as in sense, excel; 55
So just, so like tautology, they fell,
That, pale with envy, Singleton forswore ⎫
The lute and sword which he in triumph bore, ⎬
And vowed he ne'er would act Villerius more." ⎭
Here stopped the good old sire, and wept for joy 60
In silent raptures of the hopeful boy.
All arguments, but most his plays, persuade
That for anointed dullness he was made.

---

32 *sent before:* as John the Baptist was sent before Christ to prepare His way.
33 *Norwich drugget:* a coarse cloth. Shadwell came from Norwich. 36 *King
John of Portugal:* Shadwell had bragged of visiting him. 42 *Epsom blankets:*
one of Shadwell's plays was called *Epsom Wells;* in another a character named
Sir Samuel Hearty was tossed in a blanket. 43 *Arion:* a mythical Greek singer
who was saved from drowning by an appreciative dolphin. 47 *Pissing Alley:*
two lanes in London were called so. 48 *A—— Hall:* Aston Hall. 50 *morning
toast:* sewage. 53 *St. André:* a contemporary dancer. 54 *Psyche:* an opera by
Shadwell for which St. André was choreographer. 55 *in number:* in rhythm;
perhaps also in quantity? 57 *Singleton:* John Singleton, an opera singer. 59
Villerius: a character in Davenant's early opera, *The Siege of Rhodes.*

239

Close to the walls which fair Augusta bind
(The fair Augusta, much to fears inclined),   65
An ancient fabric, raised to inform the sight,
There stood of yore, and Barbican it hight;
A watchtower once, but now (so fate ordains)
Of all the pile an empty name remains.
From its old ruins brothel houses rise,   70
Scenes of lewd loves, and of polluted joys,
Where their vast courts the mother-strumpets keep,
And, undisturbed by watch, in silence sleep.
Near these a nursery erects its head,
Where queens are formed, and future heroes bred;   75
Where unfledged actors learn to laugh and cry,⎫
Where infant punks their tender voices try,   ⎬
And little Maximins the gods defy.   ⎭
Great Fletcher never treads in buskins here,
Nor greater Jonson dares in socks appear.   80
But gentle Simkin just reception finds
Amidst this monument of vanished minds:
Pure clinches the suburbian muse affords,
And Panton waging harmless war with words.
Here Flecknoe, as a place to fame well known,   85
Ambitiously designed his Sh————'s throne;
For ancient Dekker prophesied long since   ⎫
That in this pile should reign a mighty prince, ⎬
Born for a scourge of wit, and flail of sense; ⎭
To whom true dullness should some *Psyches* owe,   90
But worlds of *Misers* from his pen should flow;
Humorists and hypocrites it should produce—
Whole Raymond families, and tribes of Bruce.
Now Empress Fame had published the renown
Of Sh————'s coronation through the town.   95

---

64 *Augusta:* London. The fears are perhaps of Popish plots. 67 *hight:* was
called. 73 *watch:* the police; also "waking." 74 *nursery:* school for actors;
specifically, one founded by Lady Davenant in 1671. 75 *queens:* with a pun on
queans, prostitutes. 77 *punks:* strumpets. 78 *Maximins:* roles like that of the
ranting Maximin in Dryden's own *Tyrannic Love* (1670). 79 *Fletcher:* John
Fletcher (d. 1625), a writer of tragedies. *buskins:* high shoes worn in ancient
tragedy. 80 *Jonson:* Ben Jonson (d. 1637), best known as a writer of comedies.
socks: light shoes worn in ancient comedy. 81 *Simkin:* a name meaning "simple-
ton." 83 *clinches:* puns. 84 *Panton:* an English shortening of Pantalone (a
buffoon in Italian comedies). 87 *Dekker:* Thomas Dekker (d. 1632), poet and
dramatist ridiculed by Jonson. 90–93 *some Psyches . . . Bruce:* allusions to
Shadwell's plays, *Psyche* and *The Miser,* and to characters in *The Humorist*
and *The Virtuoso.*

Roused by report of fame, the nations meet
From near Bunhill and distant Watling Street.
No Persian carpets spread th' imperial way,
But scattered limbs of mangled poets lay.
From dusty shops neglected authors come, 100
Martyrs of pies, and relics of the bum.
Much Heywood, Shirley, Ogilby there lay,
But loads of Sh——— almost choked the way.
Bilked stationers for yeomen stood prepared,
And H————— was captain of the guard. 105
The hoary Prince in majesty appeared,
High on a throne of his own labors reared.
At his right hand our young Ascanius sate—
Rome's other hope, and pillar of the state.
His brows thick fogs, instead of glories, grace, 110
And lambent dullness played around his face.
As Hannibal did to the altars come,
Sworn by his sire a mortal foe to Rome,
So Sh——— swore—nor should his vow be vain—
That he till death true dullness would maintain, 115
And in his father's right, and realm's defense,
Ne'er to have peace with wit, nor truce with sense.
The King himself the sacred unction made,
As king by office, and as priest by trade.
In his sinister hand, instead of ball, 120
He placed a mighty mug of potent ale.
Love's Kingdom to his right he did convey—
At once his scepter and his rule of sway,
Whose righteous lore the Prince had practiced young,
And from whose loins recorded *Psyche* sprung. 125
His temples, last, with poppies were o'erspread,
That, nodding, seemed to consecrate his head.
Just at that point of time, if fame not lie,
On his left hand twelve reverend owls did fly.

---

97 *Bunhill . . . Watling Street:* Bunhill lay within a quarter of a mile; Watling
Street was "distant" by a little more than half a mile. 101 *Martyrs . . . bum:*
that is, their printed works had been used to wrap meat pies and as toilet paper.
"Bum" is short for "bottom." 102 *Ogilby:* a translator of Homer and Virgil.
104 *for:* in place of. 105 *H———:* Herringman, who had published Shadwell's
plays. He was also Dryden's publisher until 1678 or 1679. 108 *Ascanius:* son of
Aeneas and "Rome's other hope" (*spes altera Romae, Aeneid* XII, 168). 118 *unction:* anointing with oil. 120 *sinister:* Latin for "left." *ball:* a symbol of power
over the world. 122 *Love's Kingdom:* a "pastoral tragicomedy" by Flecknoe.
126 *poppies:* the source of opium. 129 *On his left hand . . . fly:* birds on the
left were a "sinister" omen.

241

So Romulus, 'tis sung, by Tiber's brook 130
Presage of sway from twice six vultures took.
Th' admiring throng loud acclamations make,
And omens of his future empire take.
The sire then shook the honors of his head,
And from his brows damps of oblivion shed 135
Full on the filial dullness; long he stood, ⎫
Repelling from his breast the raging god. ⎬
At length burst out in this prophetic mood: ⎭
   "Heavens bless my son; from Ireland let him reign
To far Barbadoes on the western main.
Of his dominion may no end be known, 140
And greater than his father's be his throne.
Beyond *Love's Kingdom* let him stretch his pen."
He paused, and all the people cried, "Amen!"
Then thus continued he: "My son, advance 145
Still in new impudence, new ignorance.
Success let others teach; learn thou from me
Pangs without birth, and fruitless industry.
Let *Virtuosos* in five years be writ,
Yet not one thought accuse thy toil of wit. 150
Let gentle George in triumph tread the stage,
Make Dorimant betray, and Loveit rage.
Let Cully, Cockwood, Fopling, charm the pit,
And in their folly shew the writer's wit.
Yet still thy fools shall stand in thy defense 155
And justify their author's want of sense.
Let 'em be all by thy own model made
Of dullness, and desire no foreign aid,
That they to future ages may be known
Not copies drawn, but issue of thy own. 160
Nay, let thy men of wit too be the same—
All full of thee, and differing but in name.
But let no alien S-dl-y interpose
To lard with wit thy hungry *Epsom* prose.
And when false flowers of rhetoric thou would'st cull, 165

---

134 *honors of his head:* an elegant periphrasis for "hair." 137 *Repelling . . .
God:* instead of inviting possession by the spirit of poetry, Flecknoe resists it.
149 *Virtuosos: The Virtuoso* was another play by Shadwell. 151 *George:* George
Etherege, 1634(?)–1691(?), one of the best of the Restoration playwrights. 152–
53 *Dorimant . . . Fopling:* the names are of characters in Etherege's plays.
163 *S-dl-y:* Sir Charles Sedley, a Restoration rake and wit. Dryden suggests that
he had touched up Shadwell's *Epsom Wells* as well as writing the prologue.
165 *flowers of rhetoric:* rhetorical figures.

242

Trust nature; do not labor to be dull!
But write thy best, and top, and in each line
Sir Formal's oratory will be thine.
Sir Formal, though unsought, attends thy quill,
And does thy northern dedications fill. 170
Nor let false friends seduce thy mind to fame
By arrogating Jonson's hostile name.
Let Father Flecknoe fire thy mind with praise,
And Uncle Ogilby thy envy raise.
Thou art my blood, where Jonson has no part; 175
What share have we in nature or in art?
Where did his wit on learning fix a brand,
And rail at arts he did not understand?
Where made he love in Prince Nicander's vein,
Or swept the dust in *Psyche*'s humble strain? 180
Where sold he bargains, whip-stitch, kiss my arse?
Promised a play, and dwindled to a farce?
When did his muse from Fletcher scenes purloin,
As thou whole Eth'rege dost transfuse to thine?
But, so transfused as oil on water's flow, 185
His always floats above, thine sinks below.
This is thy province, this thy wondrous way,
New humors to invent for each new play.
This is that boasted bias of thy mind,
By which one way—to dullness—'tis inclined; 190
Which makes thy writings lean on one side still,
And, in all changes, that way bends thy will.
Nor let thy mountain belly make pretense
Of likeness; thine's a tympany of sense.
A tun of man in thy large bulk is writ, 195
But sure thou 'rt but a kilderkin of wit.
Like mine, thy gentle numbers feebly creep;
Thy tragic muse gives smiles, thy comic, sleep.
With whate'er gall thou sett'st thyself to write,
Thy inoffensive satires never bite. 200

---

168 *Sir Formal:* Sir Formal Trifle, in *The Virtuoso.* 170 *northern dedications:* Shadwell had frequently dedicated his plays to the Duke and Duchess of Newcastle. 179 *Prince Nicander:* the heroine's suitor in *Psyche.* 181 *sold he bargains:* to "sell bargains" was to reply coarsely to an innocent question, as here in the phrase "Kiss my arse." "Whip-stitch" is a nonsense-word frequently used in *The Virtuoso.* 188 *humors:* eccentricities of character. Shadwell prided himself on following Jonson in inventing new humors. 189 *bias:* a bump on a bowling ball which influenced its course. 194 *tympany:* a drum, which is noisy but empty. The "likeness" is a reference to Jonson's similar corpulence. 195 *tun:* large cask. 196 *kilderkin:* a smallish keg. 197 *numbers:* rhythms.

In thy felonious heart, though venom lies,
It does but touch thy Irish pen, and dies.
Thy genius calls thee not to purchase fame
In keen iambics, but mild anagram.
Leave writing plays, and choose for thy command   205
Some peaceful province in acrostic-land.
There thou may'st wings display and altars raise,
And torture one poor word ten thousand ways.
Or, if thou would'st thy diff'rent talents suit,
Set thy own songs, and sing them to thy lute."   210
He said, but his last words were scarcely heard, ⎫
For Bruce and Longvil had a trap prepared,   ⎬
And down they sent the yet declaiming bard.   ⎭
Sinking, he left his drugget robe behind,
Borne upwards by a subterranean wind.   215
The mantle fell to the young prophet's part,
With double portion of his father's art.

(1682)

TO THE MEMORY OF MR. OLDHAM

Farewell, too little and too lately known,
Whom I began to think and call my own;
For sure our souls were near allied, and thine
Cast in the same poetic mold with mine.
One common note on either lyre did strike,   5
And knaves and fools we both abhorred alike.
To the same goal did both our studies drive;
The last set out the soonest did arrive.

202 *Irish:* the Irish were thought to be boorish and uncultured. Cf. line 139 above.
204–207 *anagram . . . acrostic:* in an anagram the letters of a word are rearranged to make a new word; in an acrostic the first letters of successive lines spell out a name or word; poems—like Herbert's *Easter Wings* and *The Altar*—were sometimes forced to produce odd forms on the page. Dryden recommends that Shadwell busy himself with such aesthetic trivialities. 212 *Bruce, Longvil:* characters in *The Virtuoso* who spring a trapdoor on which Sir Formal has stood ranting. 214–216 *he left . . . mantle fell:* similarly, Elisha picked up the mantle left behind when Elijah was borne up to heaven by a whirlwind (*2 Kings 2:9–13*).

OLDHAM: John Oldham (1653–1683), with whose *Remains* this poem was published. 8 *The last . . . arrive:* Oldham's *Satires upon the Jesuits,* written in 1679, preceded Dryden's great satires.

244

Thus Nisus fell upon the slippery place,
While his young friend performed and won the race. 10
O early ripe! to thy abundant store,
What could advancing age have added more?
It might—what nature never gives the young—
Have taught the numbers of thy native tongue.
But satire needs not those, and wit will shine 15
Through the harsh cadence of a rugged line.
A noble error, and but seldom made:
When poets are by too much force betrayed.
Thy generous fruits, though gathered ere their prime,
Still shewed a quickness; and maturing time 20
But mellows what we write to the dull sweets of rhyme.
Once more, hail and farewell! Farewell, thou young,
But ah, too short, Marcellus of our tongue,
Thy brows with ivy and with laurels bound.
But fate and gloomy night encompass thee around. 25

(1684)

Charles Sackville, Earl of Dorset *(1638–1706)*

SONG: CORYDON BENEATH A WILLOW

Corydon, beneath a willow,
    By a murmuring current laid,
His arm reclined, the lover's pillow,
    Thus addressed the charming maid: 4

O my Sacharissa, tell,
    How could Nature take delight
That a heart so hard should dwell
    In a frame so soft and white? 8

---

9 *Nisus:* in games described in the *Aeneid,* Nisus slipped in the blood of sacrificed steers but contrived, by tripping up the runner in second place, to cause his friend Euryalus to win the race (*Aeneid* V, 315–339). 14 *numbers:* rhythms, meters. 20 *shewed:* showed. 23 *Marcellus:* a "type" of frustrated promise. Marcellus, nephew and heir to the Emperor Augustus, died at the age of twenty.

Could you feel but half the anguish,
  Half the tortures, that I bear,
How for you I daily languish,
  You'd be kind as you are fair.   12

See the fire that in me reigns;
  Oh, behold the burning man!
Think I feel my dying pains,
  And be cruel if you can.   16

With her conquest pleased, the dame
  Cried, with an insulting look,
Yes, I fain would quench your flame—
  She spoke, and pointed to the brook.   20

(1749)

John Wilmot, Earl of Rochester (1647–1680)

THE MAIMED DEBAUCHEE

As some brave admiral, in former war
  Deprived of force, but pressed with courage still,
Two rival fleets appearing from afar,
  Crawls to the top of an adjacent hill,   4

From whence, with thoughts full of concern, he views
  The wise and daring conduct of the fight,
And each bold action to his mind renews—
  His present glory and his past delight;   8

From his fierce eyes flashes of rage he throws,
  As from black clouds when lightning breaks away;
Transported, thinks himself amidst his foes,
  And, absent, yet enjoys the bloody day: 12

So, when my days of impotence approach,
  And I'm by love and wine's unlucky chance
Driv'n from the pleasing billows of debauch
  On the dull shore of lazy temperance,   16

246

My pains at last some respite shall afford,
  While I behold the battles you maintain;
When fleets of glasses sail around the board,
  From whose broadsides volleys of wit shall rain.　　　20

Nor shall the sight of honorable scars,
  Which my too forward valor did procure,
Frighten new-listed soldiers from the wars.
  Past joys have more than paid what I endure.　　　24

Should some brave youth—worth being drunk—prove nice,
  And from his fair inviter meanly shrink,
'Twould please the ghost of my departed vice
  If, at my counsel, he repent and drink.　　　28

Or should some cold-complexioned sot forbid,
  With his dull morals, our night's brisk alarms,
I'll fire his blood by telling what I did
  When I was strong and able to bear arms.　　　32

I'll tell of whores attacked their lords at home,
  Bawds' quarters beaten up, and fortress won;
Windows demolished, watches overcome,
  And handsome ills by my contrivance done.　　　36

With tales like these I will such heat inspire
  As to important mischief shall incline.
I'll make him long some ancient church to fire,
  And fear no lewdness they're called to by wine.　　　40

Thus, statesman-like, I'll saucily impose,
  And, safe from danger, valiantly advise;
Sheltered in impotence, urge you to blows,
  And, being good for nothing else, be wise.　　　44

(1691)

The Maimed Debauchee. 23 *new-listed:* newly enlisted? newly entered on the
draft lists?　25 *nice:* foolishly particular, squeamish.　35 *watches:* the police.

247

John Oldham (1653–1683)

A SATIRE ADDRESSED TO A FRIEND
THAT IS ABOUT TO LEAVE THE UNIVERSITY
AND COME ABROAD IN THE WORLD

If you're so out of love with happiness
To quit a college life and learnèd ease,
Convince me first, and some good reasons give,
What methods and designs you'll take to live.
For such resolves are needful in the case   5
Before you tread the world's mysterious maze.
Without the premises, in vain you'll try
To live by systems of philosophy.
Your Aristotle, Cartès, and Le Grand,
And Euclid, too, in little stead will stand.   10
 How many men of choice and noted parts,
Well fraught with learning, languages, and arts,
Designing high preferment in their mind,
And little doubting good success to find,
With vast and towering thoughts have flocked to town, 15
But to their cost soon found themselves undone!
Now to repent, and starve at leisure, left,
Of misery's last comfort, hope, bereft.
 These failed for want of good advice, you cry,
Because at first they fixed on no employ.   20
Well then, let's draw the prospect and the scene
To all advantage possibly we can.
The world lies now before you; let me hear
What course your judgment counsels you to steer:
Always considered, that your whole estate   25
And all your fortune lies beneath your hat.
Were you the son of some rich usurer
That starved and damned himself to make his heir,

A SATIRE . . . 9 *Cartès:* René Descartes, French philosopher (1596–1650). *Le Grand:* Antoine Le Grand, Franciscan missionary to England and author of several philosophical works in the Restoration period. 13 *preferment:* appointment to a position.

248

Left nought to do but to inter the sot,
And spend with ease what he with pains had got, 30
'Twere easy to advise how you might live;
Nor would there need instruction then to give.
But you, that boast of no inheritance
Save that small stock which lies within your brains,
Learning must be your trade; and, therefore, weigh 35
With heed how you your game the best may play.
Bethink yourself awhile, and then propose
What way of life is fitt'st for you to choose.
  If you for orders and a gown devise,
Consider only this, dear friend of mine: 40
The church is grown so overstocked of late,
That if you walk abroad you'll hardly meet
More porters now than parsons in the street.
At every corner they are forced to ply
For jobs of hawkering divinity; 45
And half the number of the sacred herd
Are fain to stroll and wander unpreferred.
  If this, or thoughts of such a weighty charge,
Make you resolve to keep yourself at large
For want of better opportunity, 50
A school must your next sanctuary be.
Go, wed some grammar-Bridewell, and a wife,
And there beat Greek and Latin for your life.
With birchen scepter there command at will,
Greater than Busby's self, or Doctor Gill. 55
But who would be to the vile drudgery bound
Where there so small encouragement is found?
Where you, for recompense of all your pains,
Shall hardly reach a common fiddler's gains?
For when you've toiled and labored all you can 60
To dung and cultivate a barren brain,
A dancing-master shall be better paid,
Though he instructs the heels, and you the head.
To such indulgence are kind parents grown,
That nought costs less in breeding than a son. 65
Nor is it hard to find a father now

---

39 *orders:* clerical orders—that is, ordination as an (Anglican) priest. *gown:* the priest's cassock. 45 *hawkering:* hawking, selling in the streets. 52 *grammar-Bridewell:* a school like Bridewell prison, in London. 55 *Busby:* Richard Busby (d. 1695), master of Westminster School. *Doctor Gill:* probably the younger Alexander Gill (d. 1642), master of St. Paul's school at the time Milton was in attendance.

Shall more upon a setting-dog allow,
And with a freer hand reward the care
Of training up his spaniel, than his heir.
    Some think themselves exalted to the sky   70
If they light in some noble family.
Diet, a horse, and thirty pounds a year,
Besides the advantage of his lordship's ear,
The credit of the business, and the state,
Are things that in a youngster's sense sound great.   75
Little the inexperienced wretch does know
What slavery he oft must undergo
Who, though in silken scarf and cassock dressed,
Wears but a gayer livery at best.
When dinner calls, the implement must wait,   80
With holy words to consecrate the meat,
But hold it for a favor seldom known
If he be deigned the honor to sit down.
Soon as the tarts appear, Sir Crape, withdraw!
Those dainties are not for a spiritual maw.   85
Observe your distance, and be sure to stand
Hard by the cistern, with your cap in hand.
There for diversion you may pick your teeth
Till the kind voider comes for your relief.
For mere board wages such their freedom sell—   90
Slaves to an hour, and vassals to a bell.
And if the enjoyment of one day be stole,
They are but prisoners out upon parole.
Always the marks of slavery remain,
And they, though loose, still drag about their chain.   95
    And where's the mighty prospect after all—
A chaplainship served up, and seven years' thrall?
The menial thing, perhaps, for a reward
Is to some slender benefice preferred,
With this proviso bound, that he must wed   100
My lady's antiquated waiting maid,
In dressing only skilled, and marmalade.
    Let others, who such meannesses can brook,
Strike countenance to every great man's look.
Let those that have a mind, turn slaves to eat,   105
And live contented by another's plate.

---

74 *state:* stateliness. 80 *implement:* tool—which the cleric is regarded as being in this situation. *wait:* be in attendance. 81 *meat:* food. 84 *Sir Crape:* an illusion to the black cassock. 87 *cap in hand:* a posture of deference. 89 *voider:* one who clears the table.

I rate my freedom higher, nor will I
For food and raiment truck my liberty.
But, if I must to my last shifts be put
To fill a bladder and twelve yards of gut,   110
Rather with counterfeited wooden leg
And my right arm tied up, I'll choose to beg.
I'll rather choose to starve at large than be
The gaudiest vassal to dependency.

              (1683)

William Walsh (1663–1708)

THE DESPAIRING LOVER

Distracted with care
For Phyllis the fair,
Since nothing could move her,
Poor Damon, her lover,
Resolves in despair   5
No longer to languish
Nor bear so much anguish,
But, mad with his love,
To a precipice goes,
Where a leap from above   10
Would soon finish his woes.

When in rage he came there,
Beholding how steep
The sides did appear,
And the bottom how deep,   15
His torments projecting
And sadly reflecting
That a lover forsaken
A new love may get,
But a neck, when once broken,   20
Can never be set,

---

108 *truck:* barter in exchange.

And that he could die
Whenever he would,
But that he could live
But as long as he could;   25
How grievous soever
The torment might grow,
He scorned to endeavor
To finish it so,
But bold, unconcerned   30
At thoughts of the pain,
He calmly returned
To his cottage again.

(1736)

Matthew Prior *(1664–1721)*

CHLOE HUNTING

Behind her neck her comely tresses tied,
Her iv'ry quiver graceful by her side,
A-hunting Chloe went; she lost her way,
And through the woods, uncertain, chanced to stray.
Apollo, passing by, beheld the maid,   5
And, Sister dear, bright Cynthia, turn, he said;
The hunted hind lies close in yonder brake.
Loud Cupid laughed to see the god's mistake,
And, laughing, cried, Learn better, great divine,
To know thy kindred, and to honor mine.   10
Rightly advised, far hence thy sister seek,
Or on Mæander's bank, or Latmus' peak.
But in this nymph my friend, my sister know;
She draws my arrows, and she bends my bow.

CHLOE HUNTING. 6 *Cynthia:* another name for Diana. 12 *Or . . . or:* either
. . . or. *Mæander:* a river (modern Menderes) in Asia Minor. *Latmus:* a mountain
range in Caria, in Asia Minor, where Selene, the moon-goddess—here equated
with Cynthia—came to gaze on the sleeping Endymion.

Fair Thames she haunts, and ev'ry neighb'ring grove 15
Sacred to soft recess and gentle love.
Go, with thy Cynthia hurl the pointed spear
At the rough boar, or chase the flying deer.
I and my Chloe take a nobler aim;
At human hearts we fling, nor ever miss the game. 20

(1718)

A LOVER'S ANGER

As Chloe came into the room t' other day,
I peevish began: Where so long could you stay?
In your lifetime you never regarded your hour;
You promised at two, and, pray look, child, 'tis four.
A lady's watch needs neither figures nor wheels; 5
'Tis enough that 'tis loaded with baubles and seals.
A temper so heedless no mortal can bear—
Thus far I went on with a resolute air.
Lord bless me! said she. Let a body but speak.
Here's an ugly hard rosebud fall'n into my neck; 10
It has hurt me, and vexed me to such a degree—
See here, for you never believe me; pray see
On the left side my breast what a mark it has made.
So saying, her bosom she careless displayed.
That seat of delight I with wonder surveyed, 15
And forgot ev'ry word I designed to have said.

(1718)

253

Jonathan Swift (1667–1745)

PHYLLIS, OR THE PROGRESS OF LOVE

Desponding Phyllis was endued
With ev'ry talent of a prude.
She trembled when a man drew near;
Salute her, and she turned her ear.
If o'er against her you were placed,   5
She durst not look above your waist.
She'd rather take you to her bed
Than let you see her dress her head.
In church you heard her through the crowd
Repeat the absolution loud;   10
In church, secure behind her fan,
She durst behold that monster, man;
There practised how to place her head,
And bit her lips to make them red,
Or, on the mat devoutly kneeling,   15
Would lift her eyes up to the ceiling
And heave her bosom, unaware,
For neighb'ring beaux to see it bare.
   At length a lucky lover came
And found admittance from the dame.   20
Suppose all parties now agreed,
The writings drawn, the lawyer fee'd,
The vicar and the ring bespoke:
Guess how could such a match be broke?
See, then, what mortals place their bliss in!   25
Next morn betimes the bride was missing.
The mother screamed, the father chid;
Where can this idle wench be hid?
No news of Phyl. The bridegroom came,
And thought his bride had skulked for shame,   30
Because her father used to say
The girl had such a bashful way.
   Now John the butler must be sent
To learn the way that Phyllis went.

PHYLLIS . . . 10 *Repeat the absolution:* a curious passage, since the clergyman pronounces the absolution alone after the congregation have repeated the general confession in chorus.

The groom was wished to saddle Crop, 35
For John must neither light nor stop,
But find her, whereso'er she fled,
And bring her back alive or dead.
See here again the devil to do:
For truly John was missing too. 40
The horse and pillion both were gone:
Phyllis, it seems, was fled with John.
Old madam, who went up to find
What papers Phyl had left behind,
A letter on the toilet sees: 45
To my much honored Father, these. . . .
('Tis always done, romances tell us,
When daughters run away with fellows)
Filled with the choicest commonplaces
By others used in the like cases. 50
That, long ago a fortune-teller
Exactly said what now befell her,
And in a glass had made her see
A serving-man of low degree.
It was her fate, must be forgiven, 55
For marriages are made in Heaven;
His pardon begged, but, to be plain,
She'd do't if 'twere to do again.
Thank God, 'twas neither shame nor sin,
For John was come of honest kin. 60
Love never thinks of rich and poor;
She'd beg with John from door to door.
Forgive her, if it be a crime;
She'll never do 't another time.
She ne'er before in all her life 65
Once disobeyed him, maid nor wife.
One argument she summed up all in—
The thing was done and past recalling;
And therefore hoped she would recover
His favor when his passion's over. 70
She valued not what others thought her,
And was his most obedient daughter.
　　Fair maidens all, attend the Muse,
Who now the wand'ring pair pursues.
Away they rode in homely sort, 75

41 *pillion:* a cushion placed behind the saddle for a woman to ride on.　45
toilet: dressing table.　75 *homely sort:* domestic fashion.

255

Their journey long, their money short;
The loving couple well bemired,
The horse and both the riders tired,
Their victuals bad, their lodging worse.
Phyl cried, and John began to curse. 80
Phyl wished that she had strained a limb
When first she ventured out with him.
John wished that he had broke a leg
When first for her he quitted Peg.
But what adventures more befell 'em, 85
The Muse has now not time to tell 'em:
How Johnny wheedled, threat'ned, fawned,
Till Phyllis all her trinkets pawned;
How oft she broke her marriage vows
In kindness, to maintain her spouse, 90
Till swains unwholesome spoiled the trade—
For now the surgeon must be paid,
To whom those perquisites are gone
In Christian justice due to John.
When food and raiment now grew scarce, 95
Fate put a period to the farce,
And with exact poetic justice:
For John is landlord, Phyllis hostess.
They keep, at Stains, the old Blue Boar—
Are cat and dog, and rogue and whore. 100

(1727)

MARY THE COOK-MAID'S LETTER TO DR. SHERIDAN

Well, if ever I saw such another man since my mother bound
my head—
You a gentleman! Marry, come up; I wonder where you were
bred?

---

91 *unwholesome:* afflicted with venereal disease. 92 *surgeon:* physician. 96
period: end.

MARY THE COOK-MAID'S LETTER. Thomas Sheridan (d. 1738) was head of a
boys' school in Dublin, where Swift was Dean of St. Patrick's Cathedral. The
poem is supposed to be Mary's indignant retort to some joking verses by Sheridan
in reply to a piece by Swift which began, "Tom, for a goose you keep but base
quills" (that is, write with bad pens). 2 *Marry, come up:* an expression of indignation.

I am sure such words does not become a man of your cloth.
I would not give such language to a dog, faith and troth.
Yes, you called my master a knave: fie, Mr. Sheridan!
          'Tis a shame   5
For a parson, who should know better things, to come out
          with such a name.
Knave in your teeth, Mr. Sheridan—'tis both a shame and
          a sin.
And the Dean my master is an honester man than you and
          all your kin.
He has more goodness in his little finger than you have in
          your whole body.
My master is a parsonable man, and not a spindle-shanked
          hoddy-doddy.   10
And now, whereby I find you would fain make an excuse,
Because my master one day in anger called you goose,
Which, and I am sure I have been his servant four years
          since October,
And he never called me worse than sweetheart drunk or sober.
Not that I know his Reverence was ever concerned to my
          knowledge,   15
Though you and your come-rogues keep him out so late in
          your college.
You say you will eat grass on his grave: a Christian
          eat grass!
Whereby you now confess yourself to be a goose or an ass.
But that's as much as to say that my master should die
          before ye—
Well, well, that's as God pleases, and I don't believe
          that's a true story;   20
And so say I told you so, and you may go tell my master;
          what care I?
And I don't care who knows it; 'tis all one to Mary.
Everybody knows that I love to tell truth and shame the
          devil.
I am but a poor servant, but I think gentlefolks should be
          civil.
Besides, you found fault with our vittles one day that
          you was here.   25

---

3 *man of your cloth:* that is, a clergyman. 10 *parsonable:* error for "personable"? (But Swift was a parson.) *hoddy-doddy:* a dumpy, short person. 15 *concerned:* "concerned in liquor, that is, drunk" (Harold Williams). 16 *come-rogues:* comrogues, fellow-rogues. 17 *You say . . . eat grass:* the last line of Sheridan's piece was "I'll feed on the grass that grows on your grave."

257

I remember it was upon a Tuesday, of all days in the year.
And Saunders the man says you are always jesting and mocking;
Mary, said he one day, as I was mending my master's stocking,
My master is so fond of that minister that keeps the school;
I thought my master a wise man, but that man makes him a
     fool.   30
Saunders, said I, I would rather than a quart of ale
He would come into our kitchen, and I would pin a dish-clout
     to his tail.
And now I must go and get Saunders to direct this letter,
For I write but a sad scrawl, but my sister Marget, she
     writes better.
Well, but I must run and make the bed before my master comes
     from prayers;   35
And see now, it strikes ten, and I hear him coming upstairs;
Whereof I could say more to your verses, if I could write
     written hand.
And so I remain in a civil way, your servant to command,
        Mary.

          (1732)

Alexander Pope (1688–1744)

From AN ESSAY ON CRITICISM

Part I

'Tis hard to say if greater want of skill
Appear in writing, or in judging, ill.
But, of the two, less dang'rous is th' offense
To tire our patience, than mislead our sense.
Some few in that, but numbers err in this: 5
Ten censure wrong for one who writes amiss.

---

27 *Saunders:* Swift's name for his servant (though the real name was Alexander
McGee). 32 *dish-clout:* dishrag, dishcloth. 33 *direct:* address. 35 *prayers:*
morning prayer or matins.

 An Essay on Criticism. 6 *censure:* judge.

A fool might once himself alone expose;
Now one in verse makes many more in prose.
    'Tis with our judgments as our watches—none
Go just alike, yet each believes his own.   10
In poets as true genius is but rare,
True taste as seldom is the critic's share;
Both must alike from Heav'n derive their light,
These born to judge, as well as those to write.
Let such teach others who themselves excel,   15
And censure freely who have written well.
Authors are partial to their wit, 'tis true;
But are not critics to their judgment too?
    Yet if we look more closely, we shall find
Most have the seeds of judgment in their mind;   20
Nature affords at least a glimm'ring light;
The lines, though touched but faintly, are drawn right.
But as the slightest sketch, if justly traced, ⎫
Is by ill coloring but the more disgraced,   ⎬
So by false learning is good sense defaced.   ⎭   25
Some are bewildered in the maze of schools,
And some made coxcombs nature meant but fools.
In search of wit, these lose their common sense,
And then turn critics in their own defense.
Each burns alike, who can, or cannot, write,   30
Or with a rival's, or an eunuch's, spite.
All fools have still an itching to deride,
And fain would be upon the laughing side.
If Maevius scribble in Apollo's spite,
There are, who judge still worse than he can write.   35
    Some have at first for wits, then poets, passed,
Turned critics next, and proved plain fools at last.
Some neither can for wits nor critics pass,
As heavy mules are neither horse nor ass.
Those half-learn'd witlings, num'rous in our isle   40
As half-formed insects on the banks of Nile—
Unfinished things, one knows not what to call,
Their generation's so equivocal—
To tell 'em would a hundred tongues require,
Or one vain wit's, that might a hundred tire.   45

34 *Maevius:* a bad poet, contemporary with Virgil and Horace. 35 *There are:*
there are some. 41 *half-formed . . . Nile:* "insects" included worms, snails, and
so on. The mud left by the receding Nile was thought, when shone upon by
the sun, to generate small creatures spontaneously. 43 *generation:* manner of
birth. 44 *tell:* count.

But you who seek to give and merit fame,
And justly bear a critic's noble name,
Be sure yourself and your own reach to know:
How far your genius, taste, and learning go.
Launch not beyond your depth, but be discreet,   50
And mark that point where sense and dullness meet.
    Nature to all things fixed the limits fit,
And wisely curbed proud man's pretending wit.
As on the land, while here the ocean gains,
In other parts it leaves wide sandy plains,   55
Thus in the soul, while memory prevails,
The solid pow'r of understanding fails;
Where beams of warm imagination play,
The memory's soft figures melt away.
One science only will one genius fit,   60
So vast is art, so narrow human wit:
Not only bounded to peculiar arts,
But oft, in those, confined to single parts.
Like kings we lose the conquests gained before
By vain ambitions still to make them more.   65
Each might his sev'ral province well command,
Would all but stoop to what they understand.
    First follow NATURE, and your judgment frame
By her just standard, which is still the same.
Unerring Nature, still divinely bright,   70
One clear, unchanged, and universal light,
Life, force, and beauty must to all impart—
At once the source, and end, and test of art.
Art from that fund each just supply provides,
Works without show, and without pomp presides.   75
In some fair body thus th' informing soul
With spirits feeds, with vigor fills the whole,
Each motion guides, and ev'ry nerve sustains;
Itself unseen, but in th' effect remains.
Some, to whom Heav'n in wit has been profuse,   80
Want as much more, to turn it to its use;
For wit and judgment often are at strife,
Though meant each other's aid, like man and wife.
'Tis more to guide than spur the Muse's steed,
Restrain his fury, than provoke his speed;   85

_____

60 *science:* branch of knowledge. 65 *still:* always. 66 *sev'ral:* separate. 78
nerve: muscle. 81 *Want:* lack.

260

The wingèd courser, like a gen'rous horse,
Shows most true mettle when you check his course.
    Those RULES of old discover'd, not devised,
Are Nature still, but Nature methodized;
Nature, like Liberty, is but restrained   90
By the same laws which first herself ordained.
    Hear how learn'd Greece her useful rules indites,
When to repress, and when indulge, our flights.
High on Parnassus' top her sons she showed,
And pointed out, those arduous paths they trod;   95
Held from afar, aloft, th' immortal prize,
And urged the rest by equal steps to rise.
Just precepts thus from great examples giv'n:
She drew from them what they derived from Heav'n.
The gen'rous critic fanned the poet's fire,   100
And taught the world, with reason to admire.
Then criticism the muse's handmaid proved,
To dress her charms, and make her more beloved;
But following wits from that intention strayed:
Who could not win the mistress, wooed the maid.   105
Against the poets their own arms they turned,
Sure to hate most the men from whom they learned.
So modern 'pothecaries, taught the art
By doctors' bills to play the doctor's part,
Bold in the practice of mistaken rules,   110
Prescribe, apply, and call their masters fools.
Some on the leaves of ancient authors prey;
Nor time nor moths e'er spoiled so much as they.
Some dryly plain, without invention's aid,
Write dull receipts how poems may be made.   115
These leave the sense, their learning to display,
And those explain the meaning quite away.
    You then, whose judgment the right course would steer,
Know well each ancient's proper character:
His fable, subject, scope in ev'ry page,   120
Religion, country, genius of his age.
Without all these at once before your eyes,
Cavil you may, but never criticize.

_____

86 *wingèd courser:* Pegasus, a symbol of poetic inspiration. *gen'rous:* nobly born
(Latin *generosus*). 88 RULES: laid down by Aristotle in his *Poetics,* by Horace
in his *Ars Poetica,* and by other such "authorities." 94 *Parnassus:* a mountain
in Greece, sacred to the Muses. 109 *bills:* prescriptions. 113 *Nor:* neither.
115 *receipts:* recipes. 120 *fable:* plot.

261

Be Homer's works your study and delight;
Read them by day, and meditate by night. 125
Thence form your judgment, thence your maxims bring,
And trace the Muses upward to their spring.
Still with itself compared, his text peruse;
And let your comment be the Mantuan Muse.
When first young Maro in his boundless mind 130
A work to outlast immortal Rome designed,
Perhaps he seemed above the critic's law,
And but from nature's fountains scorned to draw;
But when to examine ev'ry part he came,
Nature and Homer were, he found, the same. 135
Convinced, amazed, he checks the bold design;
And rules as strict his labored work confine
As if the Stagirite o'erlooked each line.
Learn hence for ancient rules a just esteem:
To copy Nature is to copy them. 140
Some beauties yet no precepts can declare,
For there's a happiness as well as care.
Music resembles poetry: in each
Are nameless graces which no methods teach,
And which a master-hand alone can reach. 145
If, where the rules not far enough extend
(Since rules were made but to promote their end),
Some lucky license answers to the full
Th' intent proposed, that license is a rule.
Thus Pegasus, a nearer way to take, 150
May boldly deviate from the common track.
Great wits sometimes may gloriously offend,
And rise to faults true critics dare not mend;
From vulgar bounds with brave disorder part,
And snatch a grace beyond the reach of art— 155
Which, without passing through the judgment, gains
The heart, and all its end at once attains.
In prospects, thus, some objects please our eyes
Which out of Nature's common order rise:
The shapeless rock, or hanging precipice. 160
But though the ancients thus their rules invade
(As kings dispense with laws themselves have made),

---

129 *Let . . . Muse:* let Virgil's *Aeneid* be your commentary. (Virgil was born near Mantua.) 130 *Maro:* Virgil (Publius Vergilius Maro). 133 *but:* except. 138 *Stagirite:* Aristotle, born at Stagira in 384 B.C. 142 *happiness:* good luck. 154 *brave:* making a splendid appearance. 158 *prospects:* scenic views.

Moderns, beware! Or if you must offend
Against the precept, ne'er transgress its end.
Let it be seldom, and compelled by need, 165
And have, at least, their precedent to plead.
The critic else proceeds without remorse—
Seizes your fame, and puts his laws in force.
　I know there are, to whose presumptuous thoughts
Those freer beauties, ev'n in them, seem faults. 170
Some figures monstrous and misshaped appear,
Considered singly, or beheld too near;
Which, but proportioned to their light, or place,
Due distance reconciles to form and grace.
A prudent chief not always must display 175
His pow'rs in equal ranks and fair array,
But with th' occasion and the place comply;
Conceal his force—nay, seem sometimes to fly.
Those oft are stratagems which errors seem;
Nor is it Homer nods, but we that dream. 180
　Still green with bays each ancient altar stands,
Above the reach of sacrilegious hands;
Secure from flames, from envy's fiercer rage,
Destructive war, and all-involving age.
See, from each clime the learn'd their incense bring; 185
Hear in all tongues consenting paeans ring!
In praise so just, let ev'ry voice be joined,
And fill the gen'ral chorus of mankind!
Hail, bards triumphant, born in happier days,
Immortal heirs of universal praise! 190
Whose honors with increase of ages grow,
As streams roll down, enlarging as they flow!
Nations unborn your mighty names shall sound,
And worlds applaud that must not yet be found!
O may some spark of your celestial fire 195
The last, the meanest of your sons inspire,
That on weak wings, from far, pursues your flights,
Glows while he reads, but trembles as he writes,
To teach vain wits a science little known:
To admire superior sense, and doubt their own! 200

(1711)

---

181 *bays:* laurels.

263

From THE RAPE OF THE LOCK

Canto III

Close by those meads forever crowned with flow'rs,
Where Thames with pride surveys his rising tow'rs,
There stands a structure of majestic frame,
Which from the neighb'ring Hampton takes its name.
Here Britain's statesmen oft the fall foredoom   5
Of foreign tyrants, and of nymphs at home;
Here thou, Great Anna! whom three realms obey,
Dost sometimes council take—and sometimes tea.
  Hither the heroes and the nymphs resort
To taste awhile the pleasures of a court.   10
In various talk th' instructive hours they passed:
Who gave the ball, or paid the visit last.
One speaks the glory of the British Queen,
And one describes a charming Indian screen;
A third interprets motions, looks, and eyes;   15
At ev'ry word a reputation dies.
Snuff, or the fan, supply each pause of chat,
With singing, laughing, ogling, and all that.
  Meanwhile, declining from the noon of day,
The sun obliquely shoots his burning ray;   20
The hungry judges soon the sentence sign,
And wretches hang, that jurymen may dine.
The merchant from th' Exchange returns in peace,
And the long labors of the toilet cease.
Belinda now, whom thirst of fame invites,   25
Burns to encounter two advent'rous knights,
At omber singly to decide their doom,

RAPE OF THE LOCK. A mock-heroic poem in which a trivial incident is treated as though it had epic importance. Robert, Lord Petre—a descendant of the William Peter whose marriage Spenser had celebrated in the *Prothalamion*—had, without permission, cut off a lock of Miss Arabella Fermor's hair, and the families had become estranged. Pope's intent in this satire was to "laugh them together again." In Canto I Belinda is warned by her guardian sylph, Ariel, of an impending calamity; she then prepares for the day's flirtations. In Canto II she is protected by a troop of sylphs (comic reductions of Milton's epic angels) as she takes a pleasure ride on the Thames. Canto III contains the epic combat, depicted here as a card game. 3 *structure:* Hampton Court Palace. 7 *Anna:* Queen Anne. 27 *omber:* a card game. The declarer, called "omber" (from Spanish *hombre,* man), had to win more tricks than either of his two opponents.

And swells her breast with conquests yet to come.
Strait the three bands prepare in arms to join—
Each band the number of the Sacred Nine. 30
Soon as she spreads her hand, th' aërial guard
Descend, and sit on each important card.
First Ariel perched upon a Matadore;
Then each, according to the rank they bore.
For sylphs, yet mindful of their ancient race, 35
Are, as when women, wondrous fond of place.
    Behold, four kings, in majesty revered,
With hoary whiskers and a forky beard;
And four fair queens, whose hands sustain a flow'r,
Th' expressive emblem of their softer pow'r; 40
Four knaves in garbs succinct, a trusty band—
Caps on their heads, and halberds in their hand;
And parti-colored troops, a shining train,
Draw forth to combat on the velvet plain.
    The skillful nymph reviews her force with care: 45
Let spades be trumps! she said, and trumps they were.
    Now move to war her sable Matadores,
In show like leaders of the swarthy Moors.
Spadillio first, unconquerable lord!
Led off two captive trumps, and swept the board. 50
As many more Manillio forced to yield,
And marched a victor from the verdant field.
Him Basto followed, but his fate, more hard,
Gained but one trump and one plebeian card.
With his broad saber next, a chief in years, 55
The hoary majesty of spades appears;
Puts forth one manly leg, to sight revealed;
The rest, his many-colored robe concealed.
The rebel knave, who dares his prince engage,
Proves the just victim of his royal rage. 60

---

29 *Strait*: straightway. 29–30 *the three . . . Nine*: each of the three players held nine cards, the rest being dealt to the widow, or "stock." (The eights, nines, and tens were not used.) 30 *Sacred Nine*: the nine muses. 31 *aërial guard*: of protective sylphs. 33 *Matadore*: one of the three highest trumps, of which two were always the ace of spades and the ace of clubs. 35–36 *sylphs . . . when women*: in Canto I, the poet has explained that the sylphs were formerly coquettish women. 41 *knaves*: jacks. *succinct*: girded up, belted. 43 *parti-colored*: of various colors. 46 *Let spades be trumps*: since Belinda had the right to declare trumps, she sat at the right of the dealer. 49 *Spadillio*: the ace of spades. 51 *Manillio*: the second highest trump; in a spade contract, the deuce of spades. 53 *Basto*: the third highest trump, always the ace of clubs.

Ev'n mighty Pam, that kings and queens o'erthrew,
And mowed down armies in the fights of Loo,
Sad chance of war! now, destitute of aid,
Falls undistinguished by the victor spade.
   Thus far both armies to Belinda yield; 65
Now to the Baron fate inclines the field.
His warlike Amazon her host invades,
Th' imperial consort of the crown of spades.
The club's black tyrant first her victim died,
Spite of his haughty mien and barb'rous pride. 70
What boots the regal circle on his head,
His giant limbs in state unwieldy spread?
That long behind he trails his pompous robe,
And, of all monarchs, only grasps the globe?
   The Baron now his diamonds pours apace: 75
Th' embroidered king, who shows but half his face,
And his refulgent queen, with pow'rs combined,
Of broken troops an easy conquest find.
Clubs, diamonds, hearts, in wild disorder seen,
With throngs promiscuous strow the level green. 80
Thus, when dispersed, a routed army runs,
Of Asia's troops, and Africa's sable sons.
With like confusion different nations fly,
Of various habit and of various dye.
The pierced battalions disunited fall 85
In heaps on heaps; one fate o'erwhelms them all.
   The knave of diamonds tries his wily arts
And wins (O shameful chance!) the queen of hearts.
At this, the blood the virgin's cheek forsook;
A livid paleness spreads o'er all her look. 90
She sees, and trembles at th' approaching ill,
Just in the jaws of ruin, and codille.
And now, as oft in some distempered state,
On one nice trick depends the gen'ral fate.
An ace of hearts steps forth; the king unseen 95
Lurked in her hand, and mourned his captive queen.
He springs to vengeance with an eager pace

61–62 *Pam . . . Loo:* the jack of clubs—always highest trump in the game of loo.
67 *Amazon:* one of a nation of female warriors who lived near the Black Sea; any
warlike woman. 80 *strow:* strew. 84 *habit:* dress. *dye:* color. 87–88 *knave . . .
hearts:* as is apparent from what immediately follows, at this point Belinda
held only the king and queen of hearts. 92 *codille:* the declarer is given codille,
or defeat, when either opponent takes more tricks than he does. 95–98 *the
king . . . ace:* when a red suit was not trumps, the three red face-cards outranked
the ace.

266

And falls like thunder on the prostrate ace.
The nymph exulting fills with shouts the sky;
The walls, the woods, and long canals reply. 100
   O thoughtless mortals! ever blind to fate,
Too soon dejected, and too soon elate!
Sudden these honors shall be snatched away,
And cursed forever this victorious day.
   For lo! the board with cups and spoons is crowned, 105
The berries crackle, and the mill turns round.
On shining altars of Japan they raise
The silver lamp; the fiery spirits blaze.
From silver spouts the grateful liquors glide,
While China's earth receives the smoking tide. 110
At once they gratify their scent and taste,
And frequent cups prolong the rich repast.
Strait hover round the Fair her airy band;
Some, as she sipped, the fuming liquor fanned;
Some o'er her lap their careful plumes displayed, 115
Trembling, and conscious of the rich brocade.
Coffee, which makes the politician wise,
And see through all things with his half-shut eyes,
Sent up in vapors to the Baron's brain
New stratagems, the radiant lock to gain. 120
Ah, cease, rash youth! desist ere 'tis too late.
Fear the just gods, and think of Scylla's fate!
Changed to a bird, and sent to flit in air,
She dearly pays for Nisus' injured hair.
   But when to mischief mortals bend their will, 125
How soon they find fit instruments of ill!
Just then Clarissa drew with tempting grace
A two-edged weapon from her shining case.
So ladies in romance assist their knight,
Present the spear, and arm him for the fight. 130
He takes the gift with rev'rence, and extends
The little engine on his fingers' ends.
This just behind Belinda's neck he spread,
As o'er the fragrant steams she bends her head.

---

106 *mill:* coffee mill. 107 *altars of Japan:* lacquered (*japanned*) tables. 108
spirits: of the spirit lamps used to brew the coffee. 110 *China's earth:* porcelain cups. 120 *radiant lock:* in Canto II, 19–20, 29–30, we have been told
that "This nymph, to the destruction of mankind,/ Nourished two locks, which
graceful hung behind . . . Th' adventurous Baron the bright locks admired;/
He saw, he wished, and to the prize aspired." 122–24 *Scylla . . . hair:* for
stealing a magical lock of hair from her father, Scylla was ultimately transformed
to a bird. 127 *Clarissa:* a guest at the party. 132 *engine:* device.

Swift to the lock a thousand sprites repair; 135
A thousand wings, by turns, blow back the hair,
And thrice they twitched the diamond in her ear.
Thrice she looked back, and thrice the foe drew near.
Just in that instant anxious Ariel sought
The close recesses of the virgin's thought. 140
As on the nosegay in her breast reclined
He watched th' ideas rising in her mind,
Sudden he viewed, in spite of all her art,
An earthly lover lurking at her heart.
Amazed, confused, he found his pow'r expired, 145
Resigned to fate, and with a sigh retired.
   The peer now spreads the glitt'ring forfex wide
To enclose the lock; now joins it, to divide.
Ev'n then, before the fatal engine closed,
A wretched sylph too fondly interposed. 150
Fate urged the shears, and cut the sylph in twain;
But airy substance soon unites again.
The meeting points the sacred hair dissever
From the fair head, forever and forever!
   Then flashed the living lightning from her eyes, 155
And screams of horror rend th' affrighted skies.
Not louder shrieks to pitying Heav'n are cast
When husbands, or when lap-dogs, breathe their last,
Or when rich china vessels, fall'n from high,
In glitt'ring dust and painted fragments lie! 160
   Let wreaths of triumph now my temples twine,
The victor cried; the glorious prize is mine!
While fish in streams, or birds delight in air,
Or in a coach and six the British fair;
As long as *Atalantis* shall be read, 165
Or the small pillow grace a lady's bed;
While visits shall be paid on solemn days,
When numerous wax-lights in bright order blaze;
While nymphs take treats, or assignations give,
So long my honor, name, and praise shall live! 170
   What time would spare, from steel receives its date,
And monuments, like men, submit to fate.
Steel could the labor of the gods destroy

---

147 *forfex:* shears.   150 *fondly:* an old meaning was "foolishly."   165 *Atalantis:*
a *roman à clef,* or scandalous romance which presented fashionable persons
under a thin disguise. It was written by Mary Manley and published in 1709.
168 *wax-lights:* used in upper-class drawing rooms and in churches.   173 *labor of
the gods:* the walls of Troy were said to have been built by Apollo and Poseidon.

And strike to dust th' imperial tow'rs of Troy.
Steel could the works of mortal pride confound,   175
And hew triumphal arches to the ground.
What wonder, then, fair nymph, thy hairs should feel
The conqu'ring force of unresisted steel?

(1714)

From EPISTLES TO SEVERAL PERSONS
(MORAL ESSAYS)

Timon's Villa

At Timon's Villa let us pass a day,
Where all cry out, "What sums are thrown away!"
So proud, so grand, of that stupendous air
Soft and agreeable come never there.
Greatness, with Timon, dwells in such a draught   5
As brings all Brobdignag before your thought.
To compass this, his building is a town,
His pond an ocean, his parterre a down.
Who but must laugh, the master when he sees,
A puny insect, shiv'ring at a breeze!   10
Lo, what huge heaps of littleness around!
The whole, a labored quarry above ground.
Two Cupids squirt before; a lake behind
Improves the keenness of the northern wind.
His gardens next your admiration call: 15
On ev'ry side you look, behold the wall!
No pleasing intricacies intervene;
No artful wildness to perplex the scene.
Grove nods at grove, each alley has a brother,
And half the platform just reflects the other.   20

TIMON'S VILLA. From *Epistle IV, To Richard Boyle, Earl of Burlington,* lines
99–168. The intention of this part of the *Epistle* is "to comprise the principles
of a false taste of magnificence, and to exemplify what was said before, that
nothing but good sense can attain it" (Pope). Pope denied vigorously the charge
of certain contemporaries that the satire was aimed at the Duke of Chandos,
whose estate at Edgware in some ways resembled Timon's, claiming that his
fictive personage was "collected from twenty different absurdities and impro-
prieties and was never the picture of any one human creature." 5 *draught:*
draft. 6 *Brobdignag:* a land of gigantic people, described in Book II of Jona-
than Swift's *Gulliver's Travels.* 7 *compass:* encompass, attain. 8 *parterre:* flower
bed. 20 *platform:* terrace.

The suff'ring eye inverted nature sees—
Trees cut to statues, statues thick as trees;
With here a fountain, never to be play'd,
And there a summer-house that knows no shade.
Here Amphitrite sails through myrtle bow'rs;   25
There gladiators fight—or die—in flow'rs.
Unwatered see the drooping sea horse mourn,
And swallows roost in Nilus' dusty urn.
    My Lord advances with majestic mien,
Smit with the mighty pleasure to be seen.   30
But soft—by regular approach—not yet.
First through the length of yon hot terrace sweat;
And when up ten steep slopes you've dragged your thighs,
Just at his study door he'll bless your eyes.
His study! with what authors is it stored?   35
In books, not authors, curious is my Lord.
To all their dated backs he turns you round;
These Aldus printed, those Du Sueil has bound.
Lo, some are vellum—and the rest as good,
For all his Lordship knows; but they are wood.   40
For Locke or Milton, 'tis in vain to look;
These shelves admit not any modern book.
    And now the chapel's silver bell you hear,
That summons you to all the pride of pray'r.
Light quirks of music, broken and uneven,   45
Make the soul dance upon a jig to Heaven.
On painted ceilings you devoutly stare,
Where sprawl the saints of Verrio or Laguerre:
On gilded clouds in fair expansion lie,
And bring all Paradise before your eye.   50
To rest, the cushion and soft Dean invite,
Who never mentions Hell to ears polite.
    But hark! the chiming clocks to dinner call.
A hundred footsteps scrape the marble hall;
The rich buffet well-colored serpents grace,   55
And gaping Tritons spew to wash your face.

---

25 *Amphitrite:* wife of the sea-god Poseidon.   28 *Nilus':* the Nile's.   31 *soft:* not
so fast!   36 *curious:* inquisitive.   38 *Aldus, Du Sueil:* famous printers—the first
a Renaissance Venetian, the second an eighteenth-century Frenchman.   41 *Locke:*
John Locke (1632–1704), a much-admired English philosopher.   45 *quirks:* odd
musical phrases.   48 *Verrio, Laguerre:* near-contemporary painters who worked
in England.   52 *never mentions Hell:* "a reverend Dean preaching at court
threatened the sinner with punishment in 'a place which he thought it not
decent to name in so polite an assembly'" (Pope).   56 *Tritons:* minor sea-gods.

Is this a dinner? this a genial room?
No—'tis a temple, and a hecatomb;
A solemn sacrifice, performed in state.
You drink by measure, and to minutes eat. 60
So quick retires each flying course, you'd swear
Sancho's dread doctor and his wand were there.
Between each act the trembling salvers ring,
From soup to sweet wine, and God Bless the King!
In plenty starving, tantalized in state, 65
And cómplaisantly helped to all I hate.
Treated, caressed, and tired, I take my leave,
Sick of his civil pride from morn to eve.
I curse such lavish cost and little skill,
And swear no day was ever passed so ill. 70

(1731)

John Gay (1685–1732)

THE TOILETTE: A TOWN ECLOGUE

Now twenty springs had clothed the Park with green,
Since Lydia knew the blossom of fifteen.
No lovers now her morning hours molest,
And catch her at her toilette half undressed;
The thund'ring knocker wakes the street no more; 5
No chairs, no coaches crowd her silent door;
Her midnights once at cards and hazard fled,
Which now, alas! she dreams away in bed.
Around her wait Shocks, monkeys, and macaws,
To fill the place of fops and perjured beaus; 10

---

57 *genial:* cheerful (tasteful?). 62 *Sancho's dread doctor:* in Cervantes' *Don Quixote,* Sancho, the Don's servant, is prevented from eating by an enchanter-physician who makes every dish put before him disappear on the excuse that it is bad for his health. 63 *salver:* platter.

THE TOILETTE . . . 1 *Park:* St. James' Park, in London. 4 *toilette:* dressing table. 6 *chairs:* sedan chairs. 7 *hazard:* a game played with dice. 9 *Shocks:* dogs; cf. Pope, *The Rape of the Lock, I, 115.*

271

In these she views the mimicry of man,
And smiles when grinning Pug gallánts her fan.
When Poll repeats, the sounds deceive her ear,
For sounds like his once told her Damon's care.
With these alone her tedious mornings pass; 15
Or at the dumb devotion of her glass
She smoothes her brow and frizzles forth her hairs,
And fancies youthful dress gives youthful airs.
With crimson wool she fixes ev'ry grace,
That not a blush can discompose her face. 20
Reclined upon her arm, she pensive sate,
And cursed th' inconstancy of youth too late.
    O Youth! O spring of life, forever lost!
No more my name shall reign the fav'rite toast;
On glass no more the di'mond grave my name, 25
And rhymes misspelled record a lover's flame.
Nor shall side-boxes watch my restless eyes,
And, as they catch the glance, in rows arise
With humble bows, nor white-gloved beaus encroach
In crowds behind, to guard me to my coach. 30
Ah, hapless nymph! Such conquests are no more,
For Chloe's now what Lydia was before!
    'Tis true, this Chloe boasts the peach's bloom;
But does her nearer whisper breathe perfume?
I own her taper shape is formed to please— 35
Yet if you saw her unconfined by stays!
She doubly to fifteen may make pretense;
Alike we read it in her face and sense.
Her reputation! But that never yet
Could check the freedoms of a young coquet. 40
Why will ye then, vain fops, her eyes believe?
Her eyes can, like your perjured tongues, deceive.
    What shall I do? How spend the hateful day?
At chapel shall I wear the morn away?
Who there frequents at these unmodish hours 45
But ancient matrons with their frizzled tow'rs,
And gray religious maids? My presence there
Amid that sober train would own despair;
Nor am I yet so old; nor is my glance
As yet fixed wholly to devotion's trance. 50

---

12 *gallánts:* to "gallant a fan" was "to break it with design, on purpose to have
the favor to present a better." 19 *crimson wool:* powder puff? a kind of rouge?
20 *that:* so that. 27 *side-boxes:* boxes at the theater. 35 *own:* confess. 36 *stays:*
a corset. 40 *coquet:* lady-killer. 46 *tow'rs:* high-piled coiffures.

Strait then I'll dress, and take my wonted range
Through ev'ry Indian shop, through all the Change,
Where the tall jar erects his costly pride,
With antic shapes in China's azure dyed.
There careless lies the rich brocade unrolled; 55
Here shines a cabinet with burnished gold.
But then remembrance will my grief renew:
'Twas there the raffling dice false Damon threw.
The raffling dice to him decide the prize.
'Twas there he first conversed with Chloe's eyes; 60
Hence sprung th' ill-fated cause of all my smart:
To me the toy he gave, to her his heart.
But soon thy perj'ry in the gift was found;
The shiver'd China dropped upon the ground—
Sure omen that thy vows would faithless prove. 65
Frail was thy present, frailer is thy love.
    O happy Poll, in wiry prison pent!
Thou ne'er hast known what love or rivals meant.
And Pug with pleasure can his fetters bear,
Who ne'er believed the vows that lovers swear. 70
How am I cursed! Unhappy and forlorn
With perjury, with love, and rival's scorn!
False are the loose coquet's inveigling airs;
False is the pompous grief of youthful heirs;
False is the cringing courtier's plighted word; 75
False are the dice when gamesters stamp the board;
False is the sprightly widow's public tear.
Yet these, to Damon's oaths, are all sincere.
    Fly from perfidious man—the sex disdain;
Let servile Chloe wear the nuptial chain. 80
Damon is practiced in the modish life—
Can hate, and yet be civil to, a wife.
He games, he swears, he drinks, he fights, he roves;
Yet Chloe can believe he fondly loves.
Mistress and wife can well supply his need— 85
A miss for pleasure, and a wife for breed.
But Chloe's air is unconfined and gay,
And can perhaps an injured bed repay.
Perhaps her patient temper can behold
The rival of her love adorned with gold, 90
Powdered with di'monds; free from thought and care,

51 *Strait:* straightway. 52 *Change:* Exchange, the mercantile section of London.
62 *toy:* trifle. 76 *board:* floor. 78 *to:* in comparison with.

273

A husband's sullen humors she can bear.
Why are these sobs? And why these streaming eyes?
Is love the cause? No—I the sex despise.
I hate, I loathe his base, perfidious name. 95
Yet if he should but feign a rival flame?
But Chloe boasts and triumphs in my pains:
To her he's faithful, 'tis to me he feigns.
  Thus love-sick Lydia raved. Her maid appears;
A bandbox in her steady hand she bears. 100
How well this riband's gloss becomes your face,
She cries, in raptures; Then, so sweet a lace!
How charmingly you look! So bright, so fair!
'Tis to your eyes the headdress owes its air.
Strait Lydia smiled; the comb adjusts her locks, 105
And at the playhouse Harry keeps her box.

(1716)

Samuel Johnson (1709–1784)

From THE VANITY OF HUMAN WISHES:

The Tenth Satire of Juvenal Imitated

Let observation, with extensive view,
Survey mankind from China to Peru;
Remark each anxious toil, each eager strife,
And watch the busy scenes of crowded life.
Then say how hope and fear, desire and hate, 5
O'erspread with snares the clouded maze of fate,
Where wav'ring man, betrayed by vent'rous pride
To tread the dreary paths without a guide,
As treach'rous phantoms in the mist delude,
Shuns fancied ills, or chases airy good; 10

---

101 *riband:* ribbon.
  THE TENTH SATIRE . . . , lines 1–70. *Juvenal:* Decimus Junius Juvenalis (ca. A.D.
60–140), Roman satirical poet.

How rarely reason guides the stubborn choice,
Rules the bold hand, or prompts the suppliant voice;
How nations sink, by darling schemes oppressed,
When vengeance listens to the fool's request.
Fate wings with ev'ry wish th' afflictive dart, 15
Each gift of nature, and each grace of art.
With fatal heat impetuous courage glows;
With fatal sweetness elocution flows.
Impeachment stops the speaker's pow'rful breath,
And restless fire precipitates on death. 20
   But, scarce observed, the knowing and the bold
Fall in the gen'ral massacre of gold—
Wide-wasting pest! that rages unconfined,
And crowds with crimes the records of mankind.
For gold his sword the hireling ruffian draws; 25
For gold the hireling judge distorts the laws.
Wealth heaped on wealth nor truth nor safety buys;
The dangers gather as the treasures rise.
   Let hist'ry tell, where rival kings command
And dubious title shakes the madded land, 30
When statutes glean the refuse of the sword,
How much more safe the vassal than the lord.
Low skulks the hind beneath the rage of pow'r,
And leaves the wealthy traitor in the Tow'r.
Untouched his cottage, and his slumbers sound, 35
Though confiscation's vultures hover round.
   The needy traveler, serene and gay,
Walks the wild heath, and sings his toil away.
Does envy seize thee? Crush th' upbraiding joy;
Increase his riches, and his peace destroy. 40
Now fears in dire vicissitude invade;
The rustling brake alarms, and quiv'ring shade.
Nor light nor darkness bring his pain relief;
One shews the plunder, and one hides the thief.
   Yet still one gen'ral cry the skies assails, 45
And gain and grandeur load the tainted gales.
Few know the toiling statesman's fear or care,
Th' insidious rival, and the gaping heir.
   Once more, Democritus, arise on earth

20 *precipitates:* hastens. 27 *nor . . . nor:* neither . . . nor. 34 *Tow'r:* the
Tower of London, used as a prison. 41 *vicissitude:* change, alteration. 42 *brake:*
thicket. 44 *shews:* shows. 49 *Democritus:* Greek philosopher (ca. 460–370 B.C.)
who laughed at human miseries. But he was also a serious thinker who tried to
reduce superstition by teaching that the physical basis of matter was atomic.

With cheerful wisdom and instructive mirth. 50
See motley life in modern trappings dressed,
And feed with varied fools th' eternal jest:
Thou who could'st laugh where want enchained caprice,
Toil crushed conceit, and man was of a piece;
Where wealth unloved without a mourner died, 55
And scarce a sycophant was fed by pride;
Where ne'er was known the form of mock debate,
Or seen a new-made mayor's unwieldy state;
Where change of fav'rites made no change of laws,
And senates heard, before they judged, a cause; 60
How wouldst thou shake at Britain's modish tribe,
Dart the quick taunt, and edge the piercing gibe—
Attentive, truth and nature to descry,
And pierce each scene with philosophic eye!
To thee were solemn toys or empty shew 65
The robes of pleasure and the veils of woe.
All aid the farce, and all thy mirth maintain,
Whose joys are causeless, or whose griefs are vain.
Such was the scorn that filled the sage's mind,
Renewed at ev'ry glance on humankind. 70

(1749)

Thomas Gray (1716–1771)

ELEGY WRITTEN IN A COUNTRY CHURCHYARD

The curfew tolls the kneel of parting day;
    The lowing herd wind slowly o'er the lea.
The plowman homeward plods his weary way,
    And leaves the world to darkness, and to me. 4

Now fades the glimmering landscape on the sight,
    And all the air a solemn stillness holds,
Save where the beetle wheels his droning flight
    And drowsy tinklings lull the distant folds; 8

---

54 *of a piece:* all of one kind, undivided. 56 *sycophant:* flatterer. 61 *modish:* distracted by changing fashions. 62 *edge:* give a sharp edge to. 65 *toys:* trifles.
    ELEGY . . . 8 *folds:* pens for animals.

Save that from yonder ivy-mantled tow'r
    The moping owl does to the moon complain
Of such as, wand'ring near her secret bow'r,
    Molest her ancient, solitary reign.   12

Beneath those rugged elms, that yew-tree's shade,
    Where heaves the turf in many a mould'ring heap,
Each in his narrow cell forever laid,
    The rude forefathers of the hamlet sleep.   16

The breezy call of incense-breathing morn,
    The swallow twitt'ring from the straw-built shed,
The cock's shrill clarion, or the echoing horn,
    No more shall rouse them from their lowly bed.   20

For them no more the blazing hearth shall burn,
    Or busy housewife ply her evening care;
No children run to lisp their sire's return,
    Or climb his knees the envied kiss to share.   24

Oft did the harvest to their sickle yield;
    Their furrow oft the stubborn glebe has broke.
How jocund did they drive their team afield!
    How bowed the woods beneath their sturdy stroke!   28

Let not ambition mock their useful toil,
    Their homely joys and destiny obscure,
Nor grandeur hear with a disdainful smile
    The short and simple annals of the poor.   32

The boast of heraldry, the pomp of pow'r,
    And all that beauty, all that wealth e'er gave,
Awaits alike th' inevitable hour:
    The paths of glory lead but to the grave.   36

Nor you, ye proud, impute to these the fault
    If mem'ry o'er their tomb no trophies raise,
Where through the long-drawn aisle and fretted vault
    The pealing anthem swells the note of praise.   40

Can storied urn or animated bust
    Back to its mansion call the fleeting breath?
Can honor's voice provoke the silent dust,
    Or flatt'ry soothe the dull, cold ear of death?   44

---

26 *glebe:* soil. 30 *homely:* domestic. 39 *fretted:* ornamented, as with frets
(geometrical designs within a border).

277

Perhaps in this neglected spot is laid
   Some heart once pregnant with celestial fire;
Hands that the rod of empire might have swayed,
   Or waked to ecstasy the living lyre.   48

But knowledge to their eyes her ample page,
   Rich with the spoils of time, did ne'er unroll.
Chill penury repressed their noble rage,
   And froze the genial current of the soul.   52

Full many a gem of purest ray serene
   The dark, unfathomed caves of ocean bear.
Full many a flower is born to blush unseen,
   And waste its sweetness on the desert air.   56

Some village Hampden, that with dauntless breast
   The little tyrant of his fields withstood,
Some mute, inglorious Milton, here may rest,
   Some Cromwell guiltless of his country's blood.   60

Th' applause of list'ning senates to command,
   The threats of pain and ruin to despise,
To scatter plenty o'er a smiling land
   And read their hist'ry in a nation's eyes,   64

Their lot forbade: nor circumscribed alone
   Their growing virtues, but their crimes confined;
Forbade to wade through slaughter to a throne,
   And shut the gates of mercy on mankind;   68

The struggling pangs of conscious truth to hide,
   To quench the blushes of ingenuous shame,
Or heap the shrine of luxury and pride
   With incense kindled at the muse's flame.   72

Far from the madding crowd's ignoble strife,
   Their sober wishes never learned to stray.
Along the cool, sequestered vale of life
   They kept the noiseless tenor of their way.   76

Yet ev'n these bones from insult to protect
   Some frail memorial still erected nigh,
With uncouth rhymes and shapeless sculpture decked,
   Implores the passing tribute of a sigh.   80

---

51 *rage:* enthusiasm, energy. 52 *genial:* native, inborn. 53 *serene:* clear, unblemished. 57 *Hampden:* John Hampden (1595–1643), who resisted arbitrary measures taken by the government of Charles I. He was a first cousin of Oliver Cromwell. 69 *conscious:* known. 73 *madding:* acting madly. 78 *still:* always.

Their name, their years, spelt by th' unlettered muse,
The place of fame and elegy supply;
And many a holy text around she strews,
That teach the rustic moralist to die. 84

For who, to dumb forgetfulness a prey,
This pleasing, anxious being e'er resigned,
Left the warm precincts of the cheerful day,
Nor cast one longing, ling'ring look behind? 88

On some fond breast the parting soul relies;
Some pious drops the closing eye requires.
Ev'n from the tomb the voice of nature cries;
Ev'n in our ashes live their wonted fires. 92

For thee, who, mindful of th' unhonored dead,
Dost in these lines their artless tale relate,
If chance, by lonely contemplation led,
Some kindred spirit shall inquire thy fate, 96

Haply some hoary-headed swain may say,
"Oft have we seen him at the peep of dawn
Brushing with hasty steps the dews away
To meet the sun upon the upland lawn. 100

"There at the foot of yonder nodding beech
That wreathes its old, fantastic roots so high
His listless length at noontide would he stretch,
And pore upon the brook that babbles by. 104

"Hard by yon wood, now smiling as in scorn,
Mutt'ring his wayward fancies, he would rove,
Now drooping, woeful wan, like one forlorn—
Or crazed with care, or crossed in hopeless love. 108

"One morn I missed him on the customed hill,
Along the heath and near his fav'rite tree.
Another came; nor yet beside the rill,
Nor up the lawn, nor at the wood, was he. 112

"The next, with dirges due, in sad array,
Slow through the church-way path we saw him borne.
Approach and read (for thou canst read) the lay
Graved on the stone beneath yon agèd thorn." 116

---

108 *Or . . . or:* either . . . or. 115 *lay:* a short narrative or lyric poem.

THE EPITAPH

Here rests his head upon the lap of earth
 A youth to fortune and to fame unknown.
Fair science frowned not on his humble birth,
 And melancholy marked him for her own. 120

Large was his bounty, and his soul sincere.
 Heav'n did a recompense as largely send:
He gave to mis'ry all he had, a tear;
 He gained from Heav'n—'twas all he wished—a friend. 124

No farther seek his merits to disclose,
 Or draw his frailties from their dread abode
(There they alike in trembling hope repose),
 The bosom of his Father and his God. 128

(1751)

Oliver Goldsmith (1728?–1774)

THE DESERTED VILLAGE

Near yonder copse, where once the garden smiled,
And still where many a garden flower grows wild;
There, where a few torn shrubs the place disclose,
The village preacher's modest mansion rose.
A man he was to all the country dear, 5
And passing rich with forty pounds a year.
Remote from towns he ran his godly race,
Nor e'er had changed, nor wished to change, his place.
Unpracticed he to fawn or seek for power
By doctrines fashioned to the varying hour; 10
Far other aims his heart had learned to prize,

---

119 *science:* knowledge, learning.

THE DESERTED VILLAGE, lines 137–218. The poem from which this passage is an excerpt laments the decay of formerly idyllic villages, caused partly by the rise of industrialism and partly by the enclosure of common pastures and waste-lands by the squires. 4 *mansion:* dwelling place, house.

More skilled to raise the wretched than to rise.
His house was known to all the vagrant train;
He chid their wanderings, but relieved their pain.
The long-remembered beggar was his guest, 15
Whose beard, descending, swept his aged breast;
The ruined spendthrift, now no longer proud,
Claimed kindred there, and had his claims allowed;
The broken soldier, kindly bade to stay,
Sat by his fire, and talked the night away; 20
Wept o'er his wounds, or, tales of sorrow done,
Shouldered his crutch, and shewed how fields were won.
Pleased with his guests, the good man learned to glow,
And quite forgot their vices in their woe;
Careless their merits or their faults to scan, 25
His pity gave ere charity began.
    Thus to relieve the wretched was his pride;
And e'en his failings leaned to virtue's side.
But in his duty prompt at every call,
He watched and wept, he prayed and felt for all; 30
And, as a bird each fond endearment tries
To tempt its new-fledged offspring to the skies,
He tried each art, reproved each dull delay,
Allured to brighter worlds, and led the way.
    Beside the bed where parting life was laid, 35
And sorrow, guilt, and pain by turns dismayed,
The reverend champion stood. At his control,
Despair and anguish fled the struggling soul;
Comfort came down the trembling wretch to raise,
And his last faltering accents whispered praise. 40
    At church, with meek and unaffected grace,
His looks adorned the venerable place.
Truth from his lips prevailed with double sway,
And fools who came to scoff remained to pray.
The service past, around the pious man, 45
With steady zeal, each honest rustic ran;
E'en children followed, with endearing wile,
And plucked his gown to share the good man's smile.
His ready smile a parent's warmth expressed;
Their welfare pleased him, and their cares distressed. 50
To them his heart, his love, his griefs were given,
But all his serious thoughts had rest in heaven:

14 *wanderings:* strayings from virtue. 21 *done:* finished. 22 *shewed:* showed.
30 *watched:* stayed awake, sat up.

281

As some tall cliff that lifts its awful form
Swells from the vale, and midway leaves the storm,
Though round its breast the rolling clouds are spread, 55
Eternal sunshine settles on its head.
  Beside yon straggling fence that skirts the way,
With blossomed furze unprofitably gay,
There, in his noisy mansion, skilled to rule,
The village master taught his little school. 60
A man severe he was, and stern to view;
I knew him well, and every truant knew.
Well had the boding tremblers learned to trace
The day's disasters in his morning face;
Full well they laughed with counterfeited glee 65
At all his jokes, for many a joke had he;
Full well the busy whisper circling round
Conveyed the dismal tidings when he frowned.
Yet he was kind, or, if severe in aught,
The love he bore to learning was in fault. 70
The village all declared how much he knew:
'Twas certain he could write, and cipher too;
Lands he could measure, terms and tides presage,
And e'en the story ran that he could gauge.
In arguing, too, the parson owned his skill; 75
For e'en though vanquished, he could argue still,
While words of learned length, and thundering sound,
Amazed the gazing rustics ranged around;
And still they gazed, and still the wonder grew,
That one small head could carry all his knew. 80

(1770)

---

73 *Lands . . . presage:* he knew surveying and could compute the due days for
rents and feast days such as Whitsuntide and All Hallows' Eve. 74 *story:* rumor.
gauge: compute liquid and dry measures. 75 *owned:* confessed.

282

William Collins *(1721–1759)*

ODE TO EVENING

If aught of oaten stop, or pastoral song,
May hope, chaste Eve, to soothe thy modest ear,
    Like thy own solemn springs,
    Thy springs and dying gales;   4

O nymph reserved, while now the bright-haired sun
Sits in yon western tent, whose cloudy skirts,
    With brede ethereal wove,
    O'erhang his wavy bed;   8

Now air is hushed, save where the weak-eyed bat
With short, shrill shriek flits by on leathern wing,
    Or where the beetle winds
    His small but sullen horn,   12

As oft he rises 'midst the twilight path,
Against the pilgrim borne in heedless hum:
    Now teach me, maid composed,
    To breathe some softened strain,   16

Whose numbers, stealing through thy dark'ning vale,
May not unseemly with its stillness suit,
    As, musing slow, I hail
    Thy genial, loved return!   20

For when thy folding-star arising shews
His paly circlet, at his warning lamp
    The fragrant Hours, and elves
    Who slept in flow'rs the day,   24

And many a nymph who wreathes her brows with sedge
And sheds the fresh'ning dew, and, lovelier still,
    The pensive Pleasures sweet,
    Prepare thy shadowy car.   28

ODE TO EVENING. 1 *aught of oaten stop:* that is, any shepherd's pipe. 7 *brede:* embroidery. 11 *winds:* blows, sounds. 17 *numbers:* meters, rhythms. 21 *folding-star:* Venus, the evening star, which by rising indicates that the flocks should be folded or penned. *shews:* shows. 28 *car:* cart, chariot.

Then lead, calm vot'ress, where some sheety lake
Cheers the lone heath, or some time-hallowed pile
   Or upland fallows gray
   Reflect its last cool gleam.   32

But when chill, blust'ring winds, or driving rain,
Forbid my willing feet, be mine the hut
   That from the mountain's side
   Views wilds, and swelling floods,   36

And hamlets brown, and dim-discovered spires,
And hears their simple bell, and marks, o'er all,
   Thy dewy fingers draw
   The gradual, dusky veil.   40

While Spring shall pour his show'rs, as oft he wont,
And bathe thy breathing tresses, meekest Eve;
   While Summer loves to sport
   Beneath thy ling'ring light;   44

While sallow Autumn fills thy lap with leaves,
Or Winter, yelling through the troublous air,
   Affrights thy shrinking train
   And rudely rends thy robes: 48

So long, sure-found beneath the sylvan shed,
Shall Fancy, Friendship, Science, rose-lipped Health,
   Thy gentlest influence own,
   And hymn thy fav'rite name!   52

                    (1746)

---

29 *vot'ress:* votaress, a woman who has taken a vow. 37 *dim-discovered:* dimly
revealed. 50 *Science:* knowledge, learning.

Christopher Smart *(1722–1771)*

From REJOICE IN THE LAMB [JUBILATE AGNO]

For I will consider my cat Jeoffry.

For he is the servant of the Living God, duly and daily serving Him.

For at the first glance of the glory of God in the east he worships in his way.

For is this done by wreathing his body seven times round with elegant quickness.

For then he leaps up to catch the musk, which is the blessing of God upon his prayer. 5

For he rolls upon prank to work it in.

For having done duty and received blessing he begins to consider himself.

For this he performs in ten degrees.

For first he looks upon his fore-paws to see if they are clean.

For secondly he kicks up behind to clear away there. 10

For thirdly he works it upon stretch with the fore-paws extended.

For fourthly he sharpens his paws by wood.

For fifthly he washes himself.

For sixthly he rolls upon wash.

For seventhly he fleas himself, that he may not be interrupted upon the beat. 15

For eighthly he rubs himself against a post.

For ninthly he looks up for his instructions.

For tenthly he goes in quest of food.

For having considered God and himself he will consider his neighbor.

For if he meets another cat he will kiss her in kindness. 20

REJOICE IN THE LAMB: XIX, lines 51–60, XX, lines 1–24. This curious work was written while Smart was confined in a madhouse. The theme is praise of God in terms of His works; the content is "a panorama of the thoughts, or, more correctly, of the stream of ideas, which flowed through his mind" (William Force Stead). Though composed between 1759 and 1763, the ms. was first published in the present century. 5 *musk:* musk seeds? a musk-ball? 6 *upon prank:* prankishly? 11 *works it upon stretch:* stretches? plays with the musk while stretched out?

285

For when he takes his prey he plays with it to give it [a] chance.
For one mouse in seven escapes by his dallying.
For when his day's work is done his business more properly
begins.
For [he] keeps the Lord's watch in the night against the Ad-
versary.
For he counteracts the powers of darkness by his electrical skin
and glaring eyes.   25
For he counteracts the Devil, who is death, by brisking about
the life.
For in his morning orisons he loves the sun and the sun loves
him.
For he is of the tribe of Tiger.
For the cherub cat is a term of the angel Tiger.
For he has the subtlety and hissing of a serpent, which in good-
ness he suppresses.   30
For he will not do destruction if he is well fed, neither will he
spit without provocation.
For he purrs in thankfulness when God tells him he's a good
cat.
For he is an instrument for the children to learn benevolence
upon.
For every house is incomplete without him and a blessing is
lacking in the spirit.

(Written 1759–63)

24 *Adversary:* Satan.

William Cowper (1731–1800)

From THE TASK

Book I, *The Sofa*

I sing the sofa. I, who lately sang
Truth, Hope, and Charity, and touched with awe
The solemn chords, and with a trembling hand,
Escaped with pain from that advent'rous flight,
Now seek repose upon an humbler theme.   5
The theme though humble, yet august and proud
Th' occasion—for the Fair commands the song.
    Time was, when clothing sumptuous or for use,
Save their own painted skins, our sires had none.
As yet black breeches were not, satin smooth,   10
Or velvet soft, or plush with shaggy pile;
The hardy chief upon the rugged rock
Washed by the sea, or on the grav'ly bank
Thrown up by wintry torrents roaring loud,
Fearless of wrong, reposed his weary strength.   15
Those barb'rous ages past, succeeded next
The birthday of invention; weak at first,
Dull in design, and clumsy to perform.
Joint-stools were then created; on three legs
Upborne they stood: three legs upholding firm   20
A massy slab, in fashion square or round.
On such a stool immortal Alfred sat,
And swayed the scepter of his infant realms;

The Sofa, lines 1–88. "The history of the following production is briefly this:
A lady, fond of blank verse, demanded a poem of that kind from the author,
and gave him the SOFA for a subject. He obeyed; and, having much leisure, connected another subject with it; and, pursuing the train of thought to which his
situation and turn of mind led him, brought forth at length, instead of the
trifle which he at first intended, a serious affair—a volume!" (Cowper) Subsequent books are on "The Time-Piece," "The Garden," "The Winter Evening,"
"The Winter Morning Walk," and "The Winter Walk at Noon." 1–2 *lately
sang . . . Charity:* three of the moral satires which comprised Cowper's *Table-
Talk* (1782). 11 *pile:* surface of looped or cut strands, as on a carpet. 19 *Joint-
stools:* stools "joined," or fitted together, by a joiner or carpenter. 22 *Alfred:*
Alfred the Great (848?–900), Saxon king of England.

And such in ancient halls and mansions drear
May still be seen; but perforated sore, 25
And drilled in holes, the solid oak is found,
By worms voracious eating through and through.
   At length a generation more refined
Improved the simple plan; made three legs four,
Gave them a twisted form vermicular, 30
And o'er the seat, with plenteous wadding stuffed,
Induced a splendid cover, green and blue,
Yellow and red, of tap'stry richly wrought,
And woven close, or needle-work sublime.
There might ye see the piony spread wide, 35
The full-blown rose, the shepherd and his lass,
Lap-dog and lambkin with black staring eyes,
And parrots with twin cherries in their beak.
   Now came the cane from India, smooth and bright
With nature's varnish; severed into stripes 40
That interlaced each other, these supplied
Of texture firm a lattice-work, that braced
The new machine, and it became a chair.
But restless was the chair; the back erect
Distressed the weary loins, that felt no ease; 45
The slipp'ry seat betrayed the sliding part
That pressed it, and the feet hung dangling down,
Anxious in vain to find the distant floor.
These for the rich: the rest, whom fate had placed
In modest mediocrity, content 50
With base materials, sat on well-tanned hides,
Obdúrate and unyielding, glassy smooth,
With here and there a tuft of crimson yarn,
Or scarlet crewel, in the cushion fixed;
If cushion might be called what harder seemed 55
Than the firm oak of which the frame was formed.
No want of timber then was felt or feared
In Albion's happy isle. The lumber stood
Pond'rous and fixed by its own massy weight.
But elbows still were wanting; these, some say, 60
An alderman of Cripplegate contrived;
And some ascribe th' invention to a priest
Burly and big, and studious of his ease.

---

30 *vermicular:* wormlike; sinuously curving. 32 *Induced:* drew on. 35 *piony:*
peony. 40 *stripes:* strips. 43 *machine:* device. 54 *crewel:* a worsted yarn used
for embroidery. 58 *Albion:* England. 61 *Cripplegate:* at first one of the gates
in the ancient wall about London; later a section of London.

But, rude at first, and not with easy slope
Receding wide, they pressed against the ribs   65
And bruised the side, and, elevated high,
Taught the raised shoulders to invade the ears.
Long time elapsed or e'er our rugged sires
Complained, though incommodiously pent in
And ill at ease behind. The ladies first   70
'Gan murmur, as became the softer sex.
Ingenious fancy, never better pleased
Than when employed to accommodate the fair,
Heard the sweet moan with pity, and devised
The soft settee; one elbow at each end,   75
And in the midst an elbow, it received—
United yet divided, twain at once.
So sit two kings of Brentford on one throne;
And so two citizens who take the air,
Close-packed, and smiling, in a chaise and one.   80
But relaxation of the languid frame
By soft recumbency of outstretched limbs
Was bliss reserved for happier days. So slow
The growth of what is excellent; so hard
To attain perfection in this nether world.   85
Thus first necessity invented stools,
Convenience next suggested elbow-chairs,
And luxury th' accomplished sofa last.

                                          (1785)

George Crabbe (1754–1832)

From THE VILLAGE

The village life, and every care that reigns
O'er youthful peasants and declining swains;
What labor yields, and what, that labor past,
Age, in its hour of languor, finds at last;

---

78 *kings of Brentford:* Brentford was a shabby place upstream of London. The
two kings were apparently an old joke. 80 *and one:* with one horse.

What forms the real picture of the poor, 5
Demands a song: the muse can give no more.
Fled are those times, if e'er such times were seen,
When rustic poets praised their native green.
No shepherds now, in smooth, altérnate verse,
Their country's beauty, or their nymphs', rehearse. 10
Yet still for these we frame the tender strain:
Still in our lays fond Corydons complain,
And shepherds' boys their amorous pains reveal—
The only pains, alas! they never feel.
On Mincio's banks, in Caesar's bounteous reign, 15
If Tityrus found the golden age again,
Must sleepy bards the flattering dream prolong,
Mechanic echoes of the Mantuan song?
From truth and nature shall we widely stray,
Where Virgil, not where fancy, leads the way? 20
Yes, thus the muses sing of happy swains,
Because the muses never knew their pains.
They boast their peasants' pipes; but peasants now
Resign their pipes and plod behind the plow,
And few amid the rural tribe have time 25
To number syllables and play with rhyme.
Save honest Duck, what son of verse could share
The poet's rapture and the peasant's care?
Or the great labors of the field degrade
With the new peril of a poorer trade? 30
From one chief cause these idle praises spring:
That themes so easy few forbear to sing.
They ask no thought, require no deep design,
But swell the song and liquefy the line.
The gentle lover takes the rural strain; 35
A nymph his mistress, and himself a swain.
With no sad scenes he clouds his tuneful prayer,
But all, to look like her, is painted fair.
I grant indeed that fields and flocks have charms
For him that gazes or for him that farms; 40

THE VILLAGE, lines 1–54. 5 *real picture:* Crabbe is reacting against the ideal-
ized picture of village life given by Goldsmith in *The Deserted Village.*
12 *Corydons:* rustics given names out of the classic pastoral tradition. 15 *Mincio:*
a river near Mantua, mentioned by Virgil and associated with him. 16 *Tityrus:*
Virgil—actually, a speaker in Virgil's first *Eclogue.* 18 *Mantuan:* Virgilian, since
Virgil was born at Mantua. 20 *fancy:* obviously not "irresponsible play of the
imagination." 26 *number:* count, or arrange in metrical form. 27 *Duck:*
Stephen Duck (1705–1756), a rural poet patronized by Caroline, George II's
queen.

But when amid such pleasing scenes I trace
The poor, laborious natives of the place,
And see the midday sun, with fervid ray,
On their bare heads and dewy temples play,
While some, with feebler hands and fainter hearts,   45
Deplore their fortune, yet sustain their parts,
Then shall I dare these real ills to hide
In tinsel trappings of poetic pride?
  No—cast by fortune on a frowning coast,
Which can no groves nor happy valleys boast,   50
Where other cares than those the muse relates,
And other shepherds, dwell with other mates;
By such examples taught, I paint the cot
As truth will paint it, and as bards will not.

(1783)

Robert Burns *(1759–1796)*

TO A MOUSE

Wee, sleekit, cow'rin', tim'rous beastie,
O what a panic's in thy breastie!
Thou need na start awa sae hasty,
   Wi' bickering brattle.
I wad be laith to rin an' chase thee
   Wi' murdering pattle!   6

I'm truly sorry man's dominion
Has broken Nature's social union,
An' justifies that ill opinion
   Which makes thee startle
At me, thy poor, earth-born companion
   An' fellow-mortal.   12

I doubt na, whiles, but thou may thieve;
What then? Poor beastie, thou maun live!

---

49 *frowning coast:* Crabbe is thinking of Aldeburgh, a fishing village on the Suffolk coast where he was born. 53 *cot:* cottage.

To a Mouse. 1 *sleekit:* sleek. 4 *bickering brattle:* hurrying scamper. 5 *laith:* loath. 6 *pattle:* a stick used to scrape earth from the plowshare. 13 *whiles:* sometimes. 14 *maun:* must.

A daimen-icker in a thrave
       'S a sma' request.
I'll get a blessin' wi' the lave,
       And never miss 't!   18

Thy wee bit housie, too, in ruin!
Its silly wa's the win's are strewin',
An' naething, now, to big a new ane
       O' foggage green!
An' bleak December's winds ensuin',
       Baith snell an' keen!   24

Thou saw the fields laid bare and waste
An' weary winter comin' fast,
An' cozie here, beneath the blast,
       Thou thought to dwell;
Till crash! the cruel coulter passed
       Out-through thy cell.   30

That wee bit heap o' leaves an' stibble
Has cost thee mony a weary nibble!
Now thou's turned out, for a' thy trouble,
       But house or hald,
To thole the winter's sleety dribble
       An' cranreuch cauld!   36

But, mousie, thou art no thy lane
In proving foresight may be vain.
The best-laid schemes o' mice an' men
       Gang aft a-gley,
An' lea'e us nought but grief an' pain
       For promised joy.   42

Still thou art blest compared wi' me:
The present only toucheth thee,
But och! I backward cast my e'e
       On prospects drear,
An' forward tho' I canna see,
       I guess an' fear!   48

(1786)

---

15 *daimen-icker in a thrave:* a "thrave" is twenty-four sheaves; "daimen" means "a few," and "icker" is an ear of grain. 17 *lave:* remainder. 20 *wa's:* walls. *win's:* winds. 21 *big:* build. *ane:* one. 22 *foggage:* forage. 24 *baith:* both. *snell:* sharp. 31 *stibble:* stubble. 34 *But:* without. *hald:* hold, as in "household." 35 *thole:* suffer, endure. 36 *cranreuch:* frost. *cauld:* cold. 37 *thy lane:* alone. 40 *gang aft a-gley:* go often askew. 45 *e'e:* eye.

YE FLOWERY BANKS

Ye flowery banks o' bonie Doon,
  How can ye blume sae fair?
How can ye chant, ye little birds,
  And I sae fu' of care?   4

Thou'll break my heart, thou bonie bird,
  That sings upon the bough;
Thou minds me o' the happy days
  When my fause luve was true.   8

Thou'll break my heart, thou bonie bird,
  That sings beside thy mate;
For sae I sat, and sae I sang,
  And wist na o' my fate.   12

Aft hae I roved by bonie Doon
  To see the woodbine twine;
And ilka bird sang o' its luve,
  And sae did I o' mine.   16

Wi' lightsome heart I pu'd a rose
  Frae aff its thorny tree;
And my fause luver staw my rose,
  But left the thorn wi' me.   20

(1808)

YE FLOWERY BANKS. 1 *Doon:* a river in Ayr County, Scotland. 8 *fause:* false.
12 *wist na:* knew not. 13 *Aft:* oft. 14 *woodbine:* honeysuckle. 15 *ilka:* every.
19 *staw:* stole.

William Blake (1757–1827)

INTRODUCTION
TO SONGS OF INNOCENCE

Piping down the valleys wild,
Piping songs of pleasant glee,
On a cloud I saw a child,
And he, laughing, said to me,   4

"Pipe a song about a lamb!"
So I piped with merry cheer.
"Piper, pipe that song again!"
So I piped; he wept to hear.   8

"Drop thy pipe, thy happy pipe;
Sing thy songs of happy cheer!"
So I sung the same again,
While he wept with joy to hear.   12

"Piper, sit thee down and write
In a book, that all may read!"
So he vanished from my sight,
And I plucked a hollow reed,   16

And I made a rural pen,
And I stained the water clear,
And I wrote my happy songs
Every child may joy to hear.   20

(1789)

THE LAMB

Little lamb, who made thee?
Dost thou know who made thee?
Gave thee life, and bid thee feed
By the stream and o'er the mead,
Gave thee clothing of delight,   5

294

Softest clothing, woolly, bright;
Gave thee such a tender voice,
Making all the vales rejoice?
   Little lamb, who made thee?
   Dost thou know who made thee?   10

   Little lamb, I'll tell thee;
   Little lamb, I'll tell thee.
He is callèd by thy name,
For He calls himself a lamb.
He is meek, and He is mild;   15
He became a little child.
I, a child, and thou, a lamb—
We are callèd by His name.
   Little lamb, God bless thee!
   Little lamb, God bless thee!   20

(1789)

THE ECHOING GREEN

The sun does arise
And make happy the skies;
The merry bells ring
To welcome the spring.
The skylark and thrush,   5
The birds of the bush,
Sing louder around
To the bells' cheerful sound,
While our sports shall be seen
On the echoing green.   10

Old John, with white hair,
Does laugh away care
Sitting under the oak
Among the old folk.
They laugh at our play;   15
And soon they all say,
"Such, such were the joys
When we all, girls and boys,
In our youth-time were seen
On the echoing green."   20

295

Till the little ones, weary,
No more can be merry;
The sun does descend,
And our sports have an end.
Round the laps of their mothers 25
Many sisters and brothers,
Like birds in their nest,
Are ready for rest,
And sport no more seen
On the darkening green. 30

(1789)

THE TIGER

Tiger, tiger, burning bright
In the forests of the night,
What immortal hand or eye
Could frame thy fearful symmetry? 4

In what distant deeps or skies
Burnt the fire of thine eyes?
On what wings dare he aspire?
What the hand dare seize the fire? 8

And what shoulder, and what art,
Could twist the sinews of thy heart?
And when thy heart began to beat,
What dread hand, and what dread feet? 12

What the hammer? What the chain?
In what furnace was thy brain?
What the anvil? What dread grasp
Dare its deadly terrors clasp? 16

When the stars threw down their spears
And watered heaven with their tears,
Did He smile His work to see?
Did He who made the lamb make thee? 20

Tiger, tiger, burning bright
In the forests of the night,
What immortal hand or eye
Dare frame thy fearful symmetry? 24

(1794)

296

AH, SUNFLOWER!

Ah, sunflower, weary of time,
Who countest the steps of the sun
Seeking after that sweet, golden clime
Where the traveler's journey is done;   4

Where the youth pined away with desire,
And the pale virgin, shrouded in snow,
Arise from their graves and aspire
Where my sunflower wishes to go.   8

(1794)

William Wordsworth (1770–1850)

LINES COMPOSED A FEW MILES
ABOVE TINTERN ABBEY, ON REVISITING
THE BANKS OF THE WYE DURING A TOUR
JULY 13, 1798

Five years have passed; five summers, with the length
Of five long winters! and again I hear
These waters, rolling from their mountain springs
With a soft inland murmur. Once again
Do I behold these steep and lofty cliffs,   5
That on a wild, secluded scene impress
Thoughts of more deep seclusion, and connect
The landscape with the quiet of the sky.
The day is come when I again repose
Here, under this dark sycamore, and view   10
These plots of cottage-ground, these orchard tufts,
Which, at this season, with their unripe fruits,
Are clad in one green hue, and lose themselves

'Mid groves and copses. Once again I see
These hedge-rows, hardly hedge-rows, little lines   15
Of sportive wood run wild; these pastoral farms,
Green to the very door; and wreaths of smoke
Sent up, in silence, from among the trees,
With some uncertain notice, as might seem,
Of vagrant dwellers in the houseless woods,   20
Or of some hermit's cave, where by his fire
The hermit sits alone.
                        These beauteous forms,
Through a long absence, have not been to me
As is a landscape to a blind man's eye;
But oft, in lonely rooms, and 'mid the din   25
Of towns and cities, I have owed to them,
In hours of weariness, sensations sweet,
Felt in the blood, and felt along the heart,
And passing even into my purer mind,
With tranquil restorations—feelings, too,   30
Of unremembered pleasure: such, perhaps,
As have no slight or trivial influence
On that best portion of a good man's life,
His little, nameless, unremembered acts
Of kindness and of love. Nor less, I trust,   35
To them I may have owed another gift,
Of aspect more sublime: that blessèd mood
In which the burthen of the mystery,
In which the heavy and the weary weight
Of all this unintelligible world,   40
Is lightened—that serene and blessèd mood
In which the affections gently lead us on
Until, the breath of this corporeal frame
And even the motion of our human blood
Almost suspended, we are laid asleep   45
In body, and become a living soul,
While, with an eye made quiet by the power
Of harmony, and the deep power of joy,
We see into the life of things.
                                If this
Be but a vain belief, yet oh, how oft,   50
In darkness and amid the many shapes
Of joyless daylight, when the fretful stir
Unprofitable, and the fever of the world,

LINES . . . 14 *copses:* thickets.

298

Have hung upon the beatings of my heart,
How oft, in spirit, have I turned to thee, 55
O sylvan Wye! Thou wanderer through the woods,
How often has my spirit turned to thee!

And now, with gleams of half-extinguished thought,
With many recognitions dim and faint,
And somewhat of a sad perplexity, 60
The picture of the mind revives again:
While here I stand, not only with the sense
Of present pleasure, but with pleasing thoughts
That in this moment there is life and food
For future years. And so I dare to hope, 65
Though changed, no doubt, from what I was when first
I came among these hills, when like a roe
I bounded o'er the mountains, by the sides
Of the deep rivers and the lonely streams,
Wherever nature led; more like a man 70
Flying from something that he dreads than one
Who sought the thing he loved. For nature then
(The coarser pleasures of my boyish days,
And their glad animal movements, all gone by)
To me was all in all. —I cannot paint 75
What then I was. The sounding cataract
Haunted me like a passion; the tall rock,
The mountain, and the deep and gloomy wood,
Their colors and their forms, were then to me
An appetite, a feeling and a love, 80
That had no need of a remoter charm,
By thought supplied, nor any interest
Unborrowed from the eye. That time is past,
And all its aching joys are now no more,
And all its dizzy raptures. Not for this 85
Faint I, nor mourn, nor murmur. Other gifts
Have followed; for such loss, I would believe,
Abundant recompense. For I have learned
To look on nature, not as in the hour
Of thoughtless youth, but hearing oftentimes 90
The still, sad music of humanity,
Nor harsh nor grating, though of ample power
To chasten and subdue. And I have felt
A presence that disturbs me with the joy
Of elevated thoughts; a sense sublime 95
Of something far more deeply interfused,

299

Whose dwelling is the light of setting suns,
And the round ocean, and the living air,
And the blue sky, and in the mind of man:
A motion, and a spirit, that impels   100
All thinking things, all objects of all thought,
And rolls through all things. Therefore am I still
A lover of the meadows and the woods
And mountains, and of all that we behold
From this green earth; of all the mighty world   105
Of eye and ear—both what they half create,
And what perceive; well pleased to recognize
In nature and the language of the sense
The anchor of my purest thoughts, the nurse,
The guide, the guardian of my heart, and soul   110
Of all my moral being.
                            Nor, perchance,
If I were not thus taught, should I the more
Suffer my genial spirits to decay;
For thou art with me here upon the banks
Of this fair river—thou my dearest friend,   115
My dear, dear friend; and in thy voice I catch
The language of my former heart, and read
My former pleasures in the shooting lights
Of thy wild eyes. Oh, yet a little while
May I behold in thee what I was once,   120
My dear, dear sister! and this prayer I make,
Knowing that Nature never did betray
The heart that loved her; 'tis her privilege,
Through all the years of this our life, to lead
From joy to joy; for she can so inform   125
The mind that is within us, so impress
With quietness and beauty, and so feed
With lofty thoughts, that neither evil tongues,
Rash judgments, nor the sneers of selfish men,
Nor greetings where no kindness is, nor all   130
The dreary intercourse of daily life,
Shall ere prevail against us, or disturb
Our cheerful faith, that all which we behold
Is full of blessings. Therefore let the moon
Shine on thee in thy solitary walk;   135
And let the misty mountain winds be free
To blow against thee: and, in after years,

---

113 *genial:* native, inborn.   115 *friend:* his sister Dorothy.

When these wild ecstasies shall be matured
Into a sober pleasure; when thy mind
Shall be a mansion for all lovely forms,   140
Thy memory be as a dwelling-place
For all sweet sounds and harmonies: oh, then,
If solitude, or fear, or pain, or grief
Should be thy portion, with what healing thoughts
Of tender joy wilt thou remember me,   145
And these my exhortations! Nor, perchance—
If I should be where I no more can hear
Thy voice, nor catch from thy wild eyes these gleams
Of past existence—wilt thou then forget
That on the banks of this delightful stream   150
We stood together, and that I, so long
A worshiper of nature, hither came
Unwearied in that service; rather say
With warmer love—oh! with far deeper zeal
Of holier love. Nor wilt thou then forget   155
That after many wanderings, many years
Of absence, these steep woods and lofty cliffs,
And this green pastoral landscape, were to me
More dear, both for themselves and for thy sake!

                                        (1798)

EXPOSTULATION AND REPLY

"Why, William, on that old gray stone,
Thus for the length of half a day,
Why, William, sit you thus alone
And dream your time away?   4

"Where are your books? that light bequeathed
To beings else forlorn and blind?
Up, up! and drink the spirit breathed
From dead men to their kind.   8

"You look round on your Mother Earth
As if she for no purpose bore you;
As if you were her first-born birth,
And none had lived before you!"   12

                        301

One morning thus, by Esthwaite lake,
When life was sweet, I knew not why,
To me my good friend Matthew spake;
And thus I made reply: 16

"The eye—it cannot choose but see;
We cannot bid the ear be still.
Our bodies feel, where'er they be,
Against or with our will.   20

"Nor less I deem that there are powers
Which of themselves our minds impress;
That we can feed this mind of ours
In a wise passiveness.   24

"Think you, 'mid all this mighty sum
Of things forever speaking,
That nothing of itself will come,
But we must still be seeking?   28

"Then ask not wherefore here, alone,
Conversing as I may,
I sit upon this old gray stone
And dream my time away."   32

(1798)

THE TABLES TURNED:
AN EVENING SCENE ON THE SAME SUBJECT

Up, up, my friend, and quit your books,
Or surely you'll grow double.
Up, up, my friend, and clear your looks;
Why all this toil and trouble?   4

The sun, above the mountain's head,
A freshening luster mellow
Through all the long green fields has spread,
His first sweet evening yellow.   8

EXPOSTULATION AND REPLY. 13 *Esthwaite lake:* in Lancashire.   30 *Conversing:*
meditating.

302

Books! 'tis a dull and endless strife;
Come, hear the woodland linnet.
How sweet his music! On my life,
There's more of wisdom in it.   12

And hark, how blithe the throstle sings!
He too is no mean preacher.
Come forth into the light of things;
Let Nature be your teacher.   16

She has a world of ready wealth
Our minds and hearts to bless—
Spontaneous wisdom breathed by health,
Truth breathed by cheerfulness.   20

One impulse from a vernal wood
May teach you more of man,
Of moral evil and of good,
Than all the sages can.   24

Sweet is the lore which Nature brings;
Our meddling intellect
Misshapes the beauteous forms of things:
We murder to dissect.   28

Enough of Science and of Art!
Close up those barren leaves.
Come forth, and bring with you a heart
That watches and receives.   32

(1798)

STRANGE FITS OF PASSION HAVE I KNOWN

Strange fits of passion have I known;
And I will dare to tell,
But in the lover's ear alone,
What once to me befell.   4

When she I loved looked every day
Fresh as a rose in June,
I to her cottage bent my way
Beneath an evening moon.   8

STRANGE FITS . . . 1 *passion:* suffering.

303

Upon the moon I fixed my eye,
All over the wide lea.
With quickening pace my horse drew nigh
Those paths so dear to me. 12

And now we reached the orchard-plot;
And as we climbed the hill
The sinking moon to Lucy's cot
Came near, and nearer still. 16

In one of those sweet dreams I slept,
Kind nature's gentlest boon!
And all the while my eyes I kept
On the descending moon. 20

My horse moved on; hoof after hoof
He raised, and never stopped;
When down behind the cottage roof
At once the bright moon dropped. 24

What fond and wayward thoughts will slide
Into a lover's head!
"O mercy!" to myself I cried;
"If Lucy should be dead!" 28

(1800)

SHE DWELT AMONG THE UNTRODDEN WAYS

She dwelt among the untrodden ways
  Beside the springs of Dove:
A maid whom there were none to praise
  And very few to love; 4

A violet by a mossy stone
  Half hidden from the eye!
—Fair as a star, when only one
  Is shining in the sky. 8

She lived unknown, and few could know
  When Lucy ceased to be;
But she is in her grave, and oh,
  The difference to me! 12

(1800)

---

15 *cot:* cottage.

   She Dwelt . . . 2 *Dove:* uncertain; there are three River Doves (in Derbyshire, in Yorkshire, and in Westmoreland). Probably the last is meant.

A SLUMBER DID MY SPIRIT SEAL

A slumber did my spirit seal;
  I had no human fears.
She seemed a thing that could not feel
  The touch of earthly years.   4

No motion has she now, no force;
  She neither hears nor sees;
Rolled round in earth's diurnal course
  With rocks, and stones, and trees.   8

                      (1800)

COMPOSED UPON WESTMINSTER BRIDGE
SEPTEMBER 3, 1802

Earth has not anything to show more fair:
Dull would he be of soul who could pass by
A sight so touching in its majesty.
This City now doth, like a garment, wear   4
The beauty of the morning; silent, bare,
Ships, towers, domes, theaters, and temples lie
Open unto the fields and to the sky—
All bright and glittering in the smokeless air.   8
Never did sun more beautifully steep,
In his first splendor, valley, rock, or hill;
Ne'er saw I, never felt, a calm so deep!
The river glideth at his own sweet will.   12
Dear God! the very houses seem asleep,
And all that mighty heart is lying still!

                      (1807)

THE SOLITARY REAPER

Behold her, single in the field,
Yon solitary Highland lass!
Reaping and singing by herself:
Stop here, or gently pass!   4

Alone she cuts and binds the grain
And sings a melancholy strain.
O listen! for the vale profound
Is overflowing with the sound.   8

No nightingale did ever chant
More welcome notes to weary bands
Of travelers in some shady haunt
Among Arabian sands.   12
A voice so thrilling ne'er was heard
In springtime from the cuckoo-bird,
Breaking the silence of the seas
Among the farthest Hebrides.   16

Will no one tell me what she sings?
Perhaps the plaintive numbers flow
For old, unhappy, far-off things,
And battles long ago.   20
Or is it some more humble lay,
Familiar matter of today?
Some natural sorrow, loss, or pain
That has been, and may be again?   24

Whate'er the theme, the maiden sang
As if her song could have no ending.
I saw her singing at her work
And o'er the sickle bending;   28
I listened, motionless and still;
And, as I mounted up the hill,
The music in my heart I bore
Long after it was heard no more.   32

(1807)

THE WORLD IS TOO MUCH WITH US; LATE AND SOON

The world is too much with us; late and soon,
Getting and spending, we lay waste our powers.
Little we see in nature that is ours;
We have given our hearts away, a sordid boon!   4

THE SOLITARY REAPER. 16 *Hebrides:* islands west of Scotland. 17 *Will . . . sings:* the girl is singing in Gaelic, a language unknown to the poet. 18 *numbers:* meters, rhythms. 21 *lay:* song.

This sea that bares her bosom to the moon,
The winds that will be howling at all hours,
And are upgathered now like sleeping flowers:
For this, for everything, we are out of tune;   8
It moves us not. Great God! I'd rather be
A pagan suckled in a creed outworn,
So might I, standing on this pleasant lea,
Have glimpses that would make me less forlorn; 12
Have sight of Proteus rising from the sea,
Or hear old Triton blow his wreathèd horn.

(1807)

Samuel Taylor Coleridge (1772–1834)

THE EOLIAN HARP

My pensive Sara! Thy soft cheek reclined
Thus on mine arm, most soothing sweet it is
To sit beside our cot, our cot o'ergrown
With white-flower'd jasmine, and the broad-leaved myrtle
(Meet emblems they of innocence and love!),   5
And watch the clouds, that late were rich with light,
Slow saddening round, and mark the star of eve
Serenely brilliant (such should wisdom be)
Shine opposite! How exquisite the scents
Snatched from yon bean-field! and the world *so* hushed! 10
The stilly murmur of the distant sea
Tells us of silence.
            And that simplest lute,
Placed lengthways in the clasping casement, hark!

THE WORLD . . . 13 *Proteus:* a minor sea-god. 14 *Triton:* another sea-god who, as a messenger or herald, carried a conch-shell trumpet.

THE EOLIAN HARP: a rectangular soundbox across which were stretched gut strings, of different thicknesses, intended to be activated by the wind. The name comes from Æolus, god of the winds. 1 *Sara:* Sara Fricker, whom two months later Coleridge was to marry. 3 *cot:* cottage. 7 *star of eve:* Hesperus—a name given to Venus when it rises in the west.

How by the desultory breeze caressed,
Like some coy maid half yielding to her lover, 15
It pours such sweet upbraiding as must needs
Tempt to repeat the wrong! And now, its strings
Boldlier swept, the long sequacious notes
Over delicious surges sink and rise,
Such a soft floating witchery of sound 20
As twilight elfins make, when they at eve
Voyage on gentle gales from Fairy-Land,
Where melodies round honey-dropping flowers,
Footless and wild, like birds of Paradise,
Nor pause, nor perch, hovering on untamed wing! 25
Oh! the one life within us and abroad,
Which meets all motion and becomes its soul,
A light in sound, a sound-like power in light,
Rhythm in all thought, and joyance everywhere—
Methinks it should have been impossible 30
Not to love all things in a world so filled:
Where the breeze warbles, and the mute, still air
Is Music slumbering on her instrument.
    And thus, my love! as on the midway slope
Of yonder hill I stretch my limbs at noon, 35
Whilst through my half-closed eyelids I behold
The sunbeams dance, like diamonds, on the main,
And tranquil muse upon tranquillity,
Full many a thought uncalled and undetained,
And many idle flitting phantasies, 40
Traverse my indolent and passive brain,
As wild and various as the random gales
That swell and flutter on this subject lute!
    And what if all of animated nature
Be but organic harps diversely framed 45
That tremble into thought, as o'er them sweeps,
Plastic and vast, one intellectual breeze,
At once the soul of each, and God of all?
    But thy more serious eye a mild reproof
Darts, O belovèd woman! nor such thoughts, 50
Dim and unhallowed, dost thou not reject,
And biddest me walk humbly with my God.

14–25 *How by . . . untamed wing!:* the quality of the music produced by the
harp depends on the fact that the strings never vibrate as wholes but produce
only overtones of the fundamental notes. 25 *Nor . . . nor:* neither . . . nor.
37 *main:* sea.

Meek daughter in the family of Christ!
Well hast thou said, and holily dispraised
These shapings of the unregenerate mind: 55
Bubbles that glitter as they rise and break
On vain philosophy's aye-babbling spring.
For never guiltless may I speak of Him,
The Incomprehensible! save when with awe
I praise Him, and with faith that inly *feels;* 60
Who with His saving mercies healèd me,
A sinful and most miserable man,
Wildered and dark, and gave me to possess
Peace, and this cot, and thee, heart-honored maid!

(1796)

KUBLA KHAN

In Xanadu did Kubla Khan
A stately pleasure-dome decree;
Where Alph, the sacred river, ran
Through caverns measureless to man
    Down to a sunless sea. 5
So twice five miles of fertile ground
With walls and towers were girdled round;
And there were gardens bright with sinuous rills,
Where blossomed many an incense-bearing tree;
And here were forests ancient as the hills, 10
Enfolding sunny spots of greenery.
    But oh, that deep romantic chasm which slanted
Down the green hill athwart a cedarn cover!
A savage place! as holy and enchanted

KUBLA KHAN. According to Coleridge, this poem was composed during a dream induced by "an anodyne"—actually, opium. Just before falling asleep his eyes were upon the following lines in *Purchas His Pilgrimage* (1613): "In Xamdu did Cublai Can build a stately Palace, encompassing sixteene miles of plaine ground with a wall, wherein are fertile Meddowes, pleasant Springs, delightfull Streams, and all sorts of beasts of chase and game, and in the middest thereof a sumptuous house of pleasure" (Book IV, Chap. 13). Upon awakening, the poet, "taking his pen, ink, and paper, instantly and eagerly wrote down the lines that are here preserved." His writing was interrupted by "a person on business from Porlock" and could not afterwards be continued. Coleridge published the fragment as "a psychological curiosity." Xanadu, or Xamdu—perhaps near modern Peiping —was the seat of Kublai Khan (1216–1294), who founded the Mongol Empire. He was a grandson of Genghis Khan.

As e'er beneath a waning moon was haunted   15
By woman wailing for her demon-lover!
And from this chasm, with ceaseless turmoil seething,
As if this earth in fast, thick pants were breathing,
A mighty fountain momently was forced:
Amid whose swift, half-intermitted burst   20
Huge fragments vaulted like rebounding hail,
Or chaffy grain beneath the thresher's flail.
And 'mid these dancing rocks at once and ever
It flung up momently the sacred river.
Five miles meandering with a mazy motion   25
Through wood and dale the sacred river ran,
Then reached the caverns measureless to man,
And sank in tumult to a lifeless ocean.
And 'mid this tumult Kubla heard from far
Ancestral voices prophesying war!   30
   The shadow of the dome of pleasure
   Floated midway on the waves;
   Where was heard the mingled measure
   From the fountain and the caves.
It was a miracle of rare device,   35
A sunny pleasure-dome with caves of ice!

   A damsel with a dulcimer
   In a vision once I saw.
   It was an Abyssinian maid,
   And on her dulcimer she played,   40
   Singing of Mount Abora.
   Could I revive within me
   Her symphony and song,
   To such a deep delight 'twould win me,
That with music loud and long   45
I would build that dome in air,
That sunny dome! Those caves of ice!
And all who heard should see them there,
And all should cry, Beware! Beware!
His flashing eyes, his floating hair!   50
Weave a circle round him thrice,
And close your eyes with holy dread,
For he on honey-dew hath fed,
And drunk the milk of Paradise.

                  (1816)

---

41 *Mount Abora:* a made-up name? A reference to the Abor Hills in northwest
India seems unlikely.

From *ZAPOLYA: SONG*

A sunny shaft did I behold,
From sky to earth it slanted;
And poised therein a bird so bold—
Sweet bird, thou wert enchanted!   4

He sank, he rose, he twinkled, he trolled
Within that shaft of sunny mist;
His eyes of fire, his beak of gold,
All else of amethyst!   8

And thus he sang: "Adieu! adieu!
Love's dreams prove seldom true.
The blossoms they make no delay;
The sparkling dewdrops will not stay.   12
Sweet month of May,
We must away,
Far, far away!
Today! today!

(1817)

Thomas Moore *(1779–1852)*

LESBIA HATH A BEAMING EYE

Lesbia hath a beaming eye,
But no one knows for whom it beameth;
Right and left its arrows fly,
But what they aim at no one dreameth.
Sweeter 'tis to gaze upon   5
My Nora's lid that seldom rises:
Few its looks, but every one,
Like unexpected light, surprises!
Oh, my Nora Creina, dear,

LESBIA . . . 9 *Creina:* darling.

311

My gentle, bashful Nora Creina,　　　　　　　10
　　　　Beauty lies
　　　　In many eyes,
　But love in yours, my Nora Creina.

Lesbia wears a robe of gold,
　But all so close the nymph hath laced it,　　15
Not a charm of beauty's mold
　Presumes to stay where nature placed it.
Oh! my Nora's gown for me,
　That floats as wild as mountain breezes,
Leaving every beauty free　　　　　　　　20
　To sink or swell as Heaven pleases.
　　Yes, my Nora Creina, dear,
　My simple, graceful Nora Creina,
　　　　Nature's dress
　　　　Is loveliness—　　　　　　　　25
　The dress *you* wear, my Nora Creina.

Lesbia hath a wit refined,
　But, when its points are gleaming round us,
Who can tell if they're designed
　To dazzle merely, or to wound us?　　　30
Pillowed on my Nora's heart,
　In safer slumber love reposes—
Bed of peace! whose roughest part
　Is but the crumpling of the roses.
　　Oh, my Nora Creina, dear,　　　　　35
　My mild, my artless Nora Creina!
　　　　Wit, though bright,
　　　　Hath no such light
　As warms your eyes, my Nora Creina.

　　　　　　　　　　　　　　(1811)

312

Sir Walter Scott (1771–1832)

From ROKEBY

Allen-a-Dale

Allen-a-Dale has no fagot for burning,
Allen-a-Dale has no furrow for turning,
Allen-a-Dale has no fleece for the spinning,
Yet Allen-a-Dale has red gold for the winning.
Come, read me my riddle! Come, hearken my tale!
And tell me the craft of bold Allen-a-Dale.   6

The Baron of Ravensworth prances in pride,
And he views his domains upon Arkindale side;
The mere for his net, and the land for his game;
The chase for the wild, and the park for the tame.
Yet the fish of the lake, and the deer of the vale,
Are less free to Lord Dacre than Allen-a-Dale!   12

Allen-a-Dale was ne'er belted a knight,
Though his spur be as sharp and his blade be as bright;
Allen-a-Dale is no baron or lord,
Yet twenty tall yeomen will draw at his word;
And the best of our nobles his bonnet will vail,
Who at Rere-cross on Stanmore meets Allen-a-Dale.   18

Allen-a-Dale to his wooing is come;
The mother, she asked of his household and home:
"Though the castle of Richmond stand fair on the hill,
My hall," quoth bold Allen, "shows gallanter still.
'Tis the blue vault of heaven, with its crescent so pale,
And with all its bright spangles," said Allen-a-Dale.   24

The father was steel, and the mother was stone;
They lifted the latch, and they bade him be gone.
But loud, on the morrow, their wail and their cry:
He had laughed on the lass with his bonny black eye,
And she fled to the forest to hear a love-tale,
And the youth it was told by was Allen-a-Dale!   30

(1813)

ALLEN-A-DALE. 6 *craft:* trade. 9 *mere:* pond. 13 *ne'er belted a knight:* never earned, by winning knighthood, the right to wear a sword. 17 *vail:* doff.

From HEART OF MIDLOTHIAN

Proud Maisie

Proud Maisie is in the wood,
    Walking so early;
Sweet Robin sits on the bush,
    Singing so rarely.   4

"Tell me, thou bonny bird,
    When shall I marry me?"
"When six braw gentlemen
    Kirkward shall carry ye."   8

"Who makes the bridal bed,
    Birdie, say truly?"
"The grey-headed sexton
    That delves the grave duly.   12

"The glow-worm o'er grave and stone
    Shall light thee steady,
The owl from the steeple sing,
    'Welcome, proud lady.' "   16

                                        (1818)

George Noel Gordon, Lord Byron (1788–1824)

WHEN WE TWO PARTED

When we two parted
    In silence and tears,
Half broken-hearted,
    To sever for years,   4

PROUD MAISIE. 7 *braw:* brave, fine. 8 *Kirkward:* church-ward, toward the church.

Pale grew thy cheek and cold,
　Colder thy kiss:
Truly that hour foretold
　Sorrow to this. 8

The dew of the morning
　Sunk chill on my brow—
It felt like the warning
　Of what I feel now. 12
Thy vows are all broken,
　And light is thy fame;
I hear thy name spoken,
　And share in its shame. 16

They name thee before me,
　A knell to mine ear;
A shudder comes o'er me—
　Why wert thou so dear? 20
They know not I knew thee,
　Who knew thee too well.
Long, long shall I rue thee
　Too deeply to tell. 24

In secret we met—
　In silence I grieve
That thy heart could forget,
　Thy spirit deceive. 28
If I should meet thee
　After long years,
How should I greet thee?
　With silence and tears. 32

(1816)

From ENGLISH BARDS AND SCOTCH REVIEWERS

Next comes the dull disciple of thy school,
That mild apostate from poetic rule,
The simple Wordsworth, framer of a lay
As soft as evening in his favorite May,
Who warns his friend "to shake off toil and trouble, 5
And quit his books, for fear of growing double";

English Bards . . . Lines 235–64, 1053–70. 5–6 *"to shake . . . double"*: from
Wordsworth's "The Tables Turned," lines 1–4.

315

Who, both by precept and example, shows
That prose is verse, and verse is merely prose;
Convincing all, by demonstration plain,
Poetic souls delight in prose insane,   10
And Christmas stories tortured into rhyme
Contain the essence of the true sublime.
Thus, when he tells the tale of Betty Foy,
The idiot mother of "an idiot boy"—
A moon-struck, silly lad, who lost his way,   15
And, like his bard, confounded night with day—
So close on each pathetic part he dwells,
And each adventure so sublimely tells,
That all who view the "idiot in his glory"
Conceive the bard the hero of the story.   20
    Shall gentle Coleridge pass unnoticed here,
To turgid ode and tumid stanza dear?
Though themes of innocence amuse him best,
Yet still obscurity's a welcome guest.
If inspiration should her aid refuse   25
To him who takes a pixy for a muse,
Yet none in lofty numbers can surpass
The bard who soars to elegize an ass.
So well the subject suits his noble mind,
He brays the laureate of the long-eared kind.   30

                 *   *   *

The time hath been, when no harsh sound would fall
From lips that now may seem imbued with gall,
Nor fools nor follies tempt me to despise
The meanest thing that crawled beneath my eyes;
But now, so callous grown, so changed since youth,   35
I've learned to think, and sternly speak the truth;
Learned to deride the critic's starch decree,
And break him on the wheel he meant for me;
To spurn the rod a scribbler bids me kiss,
Nor care if courts and crowds applaud or hiss.   40
Nay, more: though all my rival rhymesters frown,
I too can hunt a poetaster down,
And, armed in proof, the gauntlet cast at once

---

13 *tale of Betty Foy:* in a poem called "The Idiot Boy."   26 *takes . . . muse:* an
early poem by Coleridge is called "Songs of the Pixies."   27 *numbers:* meters,
rhythms.   28 *soars . . . ass:* Byron is thinking of another early poem by Coleridge
called "To a Young Ass, Its Mother Being Tethered near It."   32 *lips:* the
present poet's.   33 *Nor . . . nor:* neither . . . nor.   43 *armed in proof:* wearing
tested armor.

316

To Scotch marauder, and to southern dunce.
Thus much I've dared; if my incondite lay 45
Hath wronged these righteous times, let others say;
This, let the world, which knows not how to spare,
Yet rarely blames unjustly, now declare.

(1822)

From DON JUAN

Canto II, Stanzas 199-201

Alas, the love of women! It is known
    To be a lovely and a fearful thing;
For all of theirs upon that die is thrown,
    And if 'tis lost, life hath no more to bring
To them but mockeries of the past alone,
    And their revenge is as the tiger's spring,
Deadly, and quick, and crushing; yet, as real
Torture is theirs; what they inflict, they feel. 8

They are right; for man, to man so oft unjust,
    Is always so to women; one sole bond
Awaits them—treachery is all their trust.
    Taught to conceal, their bursting hearts despond
Over their idol, till some wealthier lust
    Buys them in marriage—and what rests beyond?
A thankless husband, next a faithless lover,
Then dressing, nursing, praying, and all's over. 16

Some take a lover, some take drams or prayers;
    Some mind their household, others dissipation.
Some run away, and but exchange their cares,
    Losing the advantage of a virtuous station.
Few changes e'er can better their affairs,
    Theirs being an unnatural situation,
From the dull palace to the dirty hovel:
Some play the devil, and then write a novel. 24

(1822)

---

44 *Scotch marauder . . . southern dunce:* the Scottish reviewers and the English
bards. 45 *incondite:* confused, ill-constructed.

317

Percy Bysshe Shelley (1792–1822)

HYMN TO INTELLECTUAL BEAUTY

The awful shadow of some unseen power
  Floats though unseen among us, visiting
  This various world with as inconstant wing
As summer winds that creep from flower to flower.
Like moonbeams that behind some piny mountain shower,
    It visits with inconstant glance   6
    Each human heart and countenance:
Like hues and harmonies of evening—
    Like clouds in starlight widely spread—
    Like memory of music fled—
    Like aught that for its grace may be
Dear, and yet dearer for its mystery.   12

Spirit of Beauty, that dost consecrate
  With thine own hues all thou dost shine upon
  Of human thought or form, where art thou gone?
Why dost thou pass away and leave our state,
This dim vast vale of tears, vacant and desolate?
    Ask why the sunlight not forever   18
    Weaves rainbows o'er yon mountain river;
Why aught should fail and fade that once is shown;
    Why fear and dream and death and birth
    Cast on the daylight of this earth
    Such gloom; why man has such a scope
For love and hate, despondency and hope?   24

No voice from some sublimer world hath ever
  To sage or poet these responses given;
  Therefore the names of Demon, Ghost, and Heaven
Remain the records of their vain endeavor.
Frail spells! whose uttered charm might not avail to sever,
    From all we hear and all we see,   30
    Doubt, chance, and mutability.
Thy light alone—like mist o'er mountains driven,
    Or music by the night-wind sent
    Through strings of some still instrument,
    Or moonlight on a midnight stream—
Gives grace and truth to life's unquiet dream.   36

Love, hope, and self-esteem, like clouds depart
And come, for some uncertain moments lent.
Man were immortal and omnipotent,
Didst thou, unknown and awful as thou art,
Keep with thy glorious train firm state within his heart.
 Thou messenger of sympathies   42
 That wax and wane in lovers' eyes;
Thou that to human thought art nourishment,
 Like darkness to a dying flame:
 Depart not as thy shadow came;
 Depart not! lest the grave should be,
Like life and fear, a dark reality.   48

While yet a boy I sought for ghosts, and sped
 Through many a listening chamber, cave and ruin,
 And starlight wood, with fearful steps pursuing
Hopes of high talk with the departed dead.
I called on poisonous names with which our youth is fed—
 I was not heard; I saw them not.   54
 When, musing deeply on the lot
Of life, at that sweet time when winds are wooing
 All vital things that wake to bring
 News of birds and blossoming,
 Sudden, thy shadow fell on me;
I shrieked, and clasped my hands in ecstasy!   60

I vowed that I would dedicate my powers
 To thee and thine—have I not kept the vow?
 With beating heart and streaming eyes, even now
I call the phantoms of a thousand hours
Each from his voiceless grave; they have in visioned bowers
 Of studious zeal or love's delight   66
 Outwatched with me the envious night.
They know that never joy illumed my brow
 Unlinked with hope that thou wouldst free
 This world from its dark slavery;
That thou, O awful Loveliness,
Would'st give whate'er these words cannot express. 72

The day becomes more solemn and serene
 When noon is past; there is a harmony
 In autumn, and a luster in its sky,
Which through the summer is not heard or seen,
As if it could not be, as if it had not been.
 Thus let thy power, which like the truth   78
 Of nature on my passive youth

Descended, to my onward life supply
　　Its calm—to one who worships thee,
　　And every form containing thee;
　　Whom, Spirit fair, thy spells did bind
To fear himself, and love all human kind.　　84

　　　　　　　　　　　　　(1817)

OZYMANDIAS

　　I met a traveler from an antique land,
　　Who said: Two vast and trunkless legs of stone
　　Stand in the desert. Near them, on the sand,
　　Half sunk, a shattered visage lies, whose frown,　　4
　　And wrinkled lip, and sneer of cold command,
　　Tell that its sculptor well those passions read
　　Which yet survive, stamped on these lifeless things,
　　The hand that mocked them, and the heart that fed.　　8
　　And on the pedestal these words appear:
　　"My name is Ozymandias, king of kings;
　　Look on my works, ye mighty, and despair!"
　　Nothing beside remains. Round the decay　　12
　　Of that colossal wreck, boundless and bare
　　The lone and level sands stretch far away.

　　　　　　　　　　　　　(1818)

LOVE'S PHILOSOPHY

　　The fountains mingle with the river,
　　　　And the rivers with the ocean.
　　The winds of heaven mix forever
　　　　With a sweet emotion.　　4
　　Nothing in the world is single;
　　　　All things, by a law divine,
　　In one spirit meet and mingle.
　　　　Why not I with thine?　　8

　　See the mountains kiss high heaven,
　　　　And the waves clasp one another.
　　No sister-flower would be forgiven
　　　　If it disdained its brother.　　12

　　　　　　　320

And the sunlight clasps the earth,
 And the moonbeams kiss the sea:
What is all this sweet work worth,
 If thou kiss not me?   16

    (1819)

SONG TO THE MEN OF ENGLAND

Men of England, wherefore plow
For the lords who lay ye low?
Wherefore weave, with toil and care,
The rich robes your tyrants wear?   4

Wherefore feed, and clothe, and save,
From the cradle to the grave,
Those ungrateful drones who would
Drain your sweat, nay, drink your blood?   8

Wherefore, bees of England, forge
Many a weapon, chain, and scourge,
That these stingless drones may spoil
The forced produce of your toil?   12

Have ye leisure, comfort, calm,
Shelter, food, love's gentle balm?
Or what is it ye buy so dear
With your pain and with your fear?   16

The seed ye sow another reaps;
The wealth ye find another keeps;
The robes ye weave, another wears;
The arms ye forge, another bears.   20

Sow seed—but let no tyrant reap.
Find wealth—let no impostor heap.
Weave robes—let not the idle wear;
Forge arms—in your defense to bear.   24

Shrink to your cellars, holes, and cells;
In halls ye deck, another dwells.
Why shake the chains ye wrought? Ye see
The steel we tempered glance on ye.   28

With plow and spade, and hoe and loom,
Trace your grave, and build your tomb,
And weave your winding-sheet, till fair
England be your sepulcher.   32

    (1839)

321

John Keats *(1795–1821)*

ON FIRST LOOKING INTO CHAPMAN'S HOMER

Much have I traveled in the realms of gold,
   And many goodly states and kingdoms seen;
   Round many western islands have I been
Which bards in fealty to Apollo hold.   4
Oft of one wide expanse had I been told
   That deep-browed Homer ruled as his demesne;
   Yet did I never breathe its pure serene
Till I heard Chapman speak out loud and bold.   8
Then felt I like some watcher of the skies
   When a new planet swims into his ken;
Or like stout Cortez, when with eagle eyes
   He stared at the Pacific—and all his men   12
Looked at each other with a wild surmise,
   Silent, upon a peak in Darien.

                   (1816)

LA BELLE DAME SANS MERCI (REVISED VERSION)

O what can ail thee, knight-at-arms,
   Alone and palely loitering?
The sedge has withered from the lake,
   And no birds sing.   4

O what can ail thee, knight-at-arms,
   So haggard and so woe-begone?
The squirrel's granary is full,
   And the harvest's done.   8

ON FIRST LOOKING . . . 4 *Apollo:* god—among other things—of poetry. 6 *demesne:* domain, territory. 7 *serene:* a clear expanse of sky. 8 *Chapman:* George Chapman (1559?–1634), who translated Homer's *Iliad* into fourteen-syllable couplets in 1611 and his *Odyssey* in 1614–15. 10 *ken:* view. 11 *Cortez:* error for Balboa, who discovered the Pacific in 1513. 14 *Darien:* the isthmus of Panama.

LA BELLE DAME SANS MERCI: The beautiful lady without pity.

I see a lily on thy brow,
　　With anguish moist, and fever dew;
And on thy cheeks a fading rose
　　Fast withereth too.　　　　　　　12

"I met a lady in the meads,
　　Full beautiful—a faery's child.
Her hair was long, her foot was light,
　　And her eyes were wild.　　　　16

"I made a garland for her head,
　　And bracelets too, and fragrant zone;
She looked at me as she did love,
　　And made sweet moan.　　　　　20

"I set her on my pacing steed,
　　And nothing else saw all day long;'
For sidelong would she bend, and sing
　　A faery's song.　　　　　　　　24

"She found me roots of relish sweet,
　　And honey wild, and manna dew,
And sure in language strange she said,
　　'I love thee true.'　　　　　　　28

"She took me to her elfin grot,
　　And there she wept and sighed full sore,
And there I shut her wild, wild eyes
　　With kisses four.　　　　　　　　32

"And there she lullèd me asleep,
　　And there I dreamed—ah, woe betide!
The latest dream I ever dreamed
　　On the cold hill side.　　　　　36

"I saw pale kings, and princes too,
　　Pale warriors, death-pale were they all;
They cried, 'La Belle Dame sans Merci
　　Hath thee in thrall!'　　　　　　40

"I saw their starved lips in the gloam
　　With horrid warning gapèd wide,
And I woke and found me here,
　　On the cold hill's side.　　　　　44

---

18 *zone:* girdle, belt.　35 *latest:* last.

"And this is why I sojourn here
  Alone and palely loitering,
Though the sedge has withered from the lake,
  And no birds sing."   48

(1820)

ODE ON A GRECIAN URN

Thou still unravished bride of quietness,
  Thou foster-child of silence and slow time,
Sylvan historian, who canst thus express
  A flowery tale more sweetly than our rhyme:
What leaf-fringed legend haunts about thy shape   5
  Of deities or mortals, or of both,
    In Tempe or the dales of Arcady?
  What men or gods are these? What maidens loath?
What mad pursuit? What struggle to escape?
    What pipes and timbrels? What wild ecstasy?   10

Heard melodies are sweet, but those unheard
  Are sweeter; therefore, ye soft pipes, play on;
Not to the sensual ear, but, more endeared,
  Pipe to the spirit ditties of no tone.
Fair youth, beneath the trees, thou canst not leave   15
  Thy song, nor ever can those trees be bare;
    Bold lover, never, never canst thou kiss,
  Though winning near the goal—yet, do not grieve;
  She cannot fade, though thou hast not thy bliss.
    Forever wilt thou love, and she be fair!   20

Ah, happy, happy boughs! that cannot shed
  Your leaves, nor ever bid the spring adieu;
And, happy melodist, unwearièd,
  Forever piping songs forever new;
More happy love! more happy, happy love!   25
  Forever warm and still to be enjoyed,
    Forever panting, and forever young;
All breathing human passion far above,
  That leaves a heart high-sorrowful and cloyed,
    A burning forehead, and a parching tongue.   30

_____

ODE ON A GRECIAN URN. 7 *Tempe:* a valley near Mt. Olympus, in Greece.
Arcady: Arcadia, a mountainous area in the Peloponnesus of Greece, famed for
its pastoral simplicity. 10 *timbrels:* tambourines.

Who are these coming to the sacrifice?
　To what green altar, O mysterious priest,
Lead'st thou that heifer lowing at the skies,
　And all her silken flanks with garlands dressed?
What little town by river or seashore,　　　　　　　35
　　Or mountain-built with peaceful citadel,
　　　Is emptied of this folk, this pious morn?
And, little town, thy streets for evermore
　　Will silent be; and not a soul to tell
　　　Why thou art desolate, can e'er return.　　　40

O Attic shape! Fair attitude! with brede
　Of marble men and maidens overwrought,
With forest branches and the trodden weed:
　Thou, silent form, dost tease us out of thought
As doth eternity. Cold pastoral!　　　　　　　45
　　When old age shall this generation waste,
　　　Thou shalt remain, in midst of other woe
Than ours, a friend to man, to whom thou say'st,
　　"Beauty is truth, truth beauty"—that is all
　　　Ye know on earth, and all ye need to know.　　50

(1820)

TO AUTUMN

Season of mists and mellow fruitfulness,
　Close bosom-friend of the maturing sun;
Conspiring with him how to load and bless
　With fruit the vines that round the thatch-eves run;
To bend with apples the mossed cottage-trees,　　　5
　And fill all fruit with ripeness to the core;
　　To swell the gourd, and plump the hazel shells
　With a sweet kernel; to set budding more,
And still more, later flowers for the bees,
Until they think warm days will never cease,　　　10
　　For summer has o'er-brimmed their clammy cells.

---

41 *Attic:* pertaining to Attica, the region about ancient Athens. *brede:* embroidery, decoration. 42 *overwrought:* worked over, adorned. 49–50 *"Beauty ... know:* critics have recently disputed whether both these lines should be included within the quotation marks. The reference of "Ye," in line 50, is also controversial: is the word addressed to readers of the poem or to the vase?

325

Who hath not seen thee oft amid thy store?
　　Sometimes whoever seeks abroad may find
Thee sitting careless on a granary floor,
　　Thy hair soft-lifted by the winnowing wind;　　　15
Or on a half-reaped furrow sound asleep,
　　Drowsed with the fume of poppies, while thy hook
　　　Spares the next swath and all its twinèd flowers;
And sometimes like a gleaner thou dost keep
　　Steady thy laden head across a brook;　　　20
　　Or by a cider-press, with patient look,
　　　Thou watchest the last oozings hours by hours.

Where are the songs of spring? Aye, where are they?
　　Think not of them, thou hast thy music too—
While barrèd clouds bloom the soft-dying day,　　　25
　　And touch the stubble-plains with rosy hue.
Then in a wailful choir the small gnats mourn
　　Among the river sallows, borne aloft
　　　Or sinking as the light wind lives or dies;
And full-grown lambs loud bleat from hilly bourn;　　　30
　　Hedge-crickets sing; and now with treble soft
　　The red-breast whistles from a garden-croft,
　　　And gathering swallows twitter in the skies.

                                        (1820)

BRIGHT STAR, WOULD I WERE
STEADFAST AS THOU ART

Bright star, would I were steadfast as thou art—
　　Not in lone splendor hung aloft the night
And watching, with eternal lids apart,
　　Like nature's patient, sleepless eremite,　　　4
The moving waters at their priest-like task
　　Of pure ablution round earth's human shores,
Or gazing on the new, soft-fallen mask
　　Of snow upon the mountains and the moors:　　　8
No—yet still steadfast, still unchangeable,
　　Pillowed upon my fair love's ripening breast,

———

To Autumn. 28 *sallows:* willows. 30 *bourn:* domain, area. 32 *garden-croft:*
enclosed garden-patch.

Bright Star . . . 4 *eremite:* hermit.

326

To feel forever its soft fall and swell,
  Awake forever in a sweet unrest;
Still, still to hear her tender-taken breath,   12
  And so live ever—or else swoon to death.

              (1848)

Leigh Hunt *(1784–1859)*

RONDEAU: JENNY KISSED ME WHEN WE MET

Jenny kissed me when we met,
  Jumping from the chair she sat in.
Time, you thief, who love to get
  Sweets into your list, put that in: 4
Say I'm weary, say I'm sad,
  Say that health and wealth have missed me,
Say I'm growing old, but add,
  Jenny kissed me.   8

              (1838)

RONDEAU. A rondeau is properly a poem of fifteen lines with a complicated rhyme-scheme and a refrain selected from the opening line. Only the repetition of the first three words of the first line in the last makes this little poem resemble a rondeau.

Walter Savage Landor *(1775–1864)*

AH, WHAT AVAILS THE SCEPTERED RACE

Ah, what avails the sceptered race,
  Ah, what the form divine!
What every virtue, every grace!
  Rose Aylmer, all were thine.   4
Rose Aylmer, whom these wakeful eyes
  May weep, but never see,
A night of memories and of sighs
  I consecrate to thee.   8

(1806)

ON HIS SEVENTY-FIFTH BIRTHDAY

I strove with none, for none was worth my strife;
  Nature I loved, and next to nature, art;
I warmed both hands before the fire of life:
  It sinks, and I am ready to depart.   4

(1853)

Thomas Lovell Beddoes *(1803–1849)*

From DEATH'S JEST-BOOK

Song

Old Adam, the carrion crow,
  The old crow of Cairo;
He sat in the shower, and let it flow
  Under his tail and over his crest;   4
    And through every feather
    Leaked the wet weather;
  And the bough swung under his nest;
For his beak it was heavy with marrow.   8
  Is that the wind dying? Oh, no;
  It's only two devils, that blow
    Through a murderer's bones, to and fro,
    In the ghosts' moonshine.   12

Ho, Eve, my grey carrion wife!
  When we have supped on kings' marrow,
Where shall we drink and make merry our life?
  Our nest it is Queen Cleopatra's skull,   16
    'Tis cloven and cracked,
    And battered and hacked,
  But with tears of blue eyes it is full.
Let us drink then, my raven of Cairo.   20
  Is that the wind dying? Oh, no;
  It's only two devils, that blow
    Through a murderer's bones, to and fro,
    In the ghosts' moonshine.   24

          (1850)

Thomas Hood (1799–1845)

FAITHLESS NELLY GRAY: A PATHETIC BALLAD

Ben Battle was a soldier bold,
  And used to war's alarms;
But a cannon ball took off his legs,
  So he laid down his arms.   4

Now as they bore him off the field,
  Said he, "Let others shoot,
For here I leave my second leg,
  And the Forty-Second Foot."   8

The army surgeons made him limbs;
  Said he, "They're only pegs;
But there's as wooden members quite
  As represent my legs!"   12

Now Ben he loved a pretty maid,
  Her name was Nelly Gray;
So he went to pay her his devours
  When he'd devoured his pay.   16

But when he called on Nelly Gray,
  She made him quite a scoff;
And when she saw his wooden legs,
  Began to take them off.   20

"O Nelly Gray! O Nelly Gray!
  Is this your love so warm?
The love that loves a scarlet coat
  Should be more uniform!"   24

Said she, "I loved a soldier once,
  For he was blithe and brave;
But I will never have a man
  With both legs in the grave.   28

FAITHLESS NELLY . . . 11 *members:* that is, of Parliament. 15 *devours:* devoirs, respects. 20 *take them off:* apparently "find fault with them."

"Before you had those timber toes,
  Your love I did allow.
But then, you know, you stand upon
  Another footing now."   32

"Oh, Nelly Gray! Oh, Nelly Gray!
  For all your jeering speeches,
At duty's call, I left my legs
  In Badajos's breaches!"   36

"Why, then," said she, "you've lost the feet
  Of legs in war's alarms,
And now you cannot wear your shoes
  Upon your feats of arms."   40

"Oh, false and fickle Nelly Gray,
  I know why you refuse:
Though I've no feet, some other man
  Is standing in my shoes.   44

"I wish I ne'er had seen your face;
  But now, a long farewell!
For you will be my death—alas!
  You will not be my Nell!"   48

Now when he went from Nelly Gray,
  His heart so heavy got,
And life was such a burthen grown,
  It made him take a knot.   52

So round his melancholy neck
  A rope he did entwine,
And, for his second time in life,
  Enlisted in the Line.   56

One end he tied around a beam,
  And then removed his pegs;
And, as his legs were off, of course
  He soon was off his legs.   60

And there he hung, till he was dead
  As any nail in town;
For though distress had cut him up,
  It could not cut him down.   64

---

36 *Badajos's:* in May and June of 1811, during the Peninsular War, the British
besieged Badajoz, a fortress in western Spain. 51 *burthen:* burden.

331

A dozen men sat on his corpse
To find out why he died;
And they buried Ben in four crossroads,
With a stake in his inside.   68

(1826)

Alfred, Lord Tennyson (1809–1892)

MARIANA

"Mariana in the moated grange"
Measure for Measure

With blackest moss the flower plots
Were thickly crusted, one and all;
The rusted nails fell from the knots
That held the pear to the gable wall.   4
The broken sheds looked sad and strange:
Unlifted was the clinking latch;
Weeded and worn the ancient thatch
Upon the lonely moated grange.   8
She only said, "My life is dreary,
He cometh not," she said.
She said, "I am aweary, aweary—
I would that I were dead!"   12

Her tears fell with the dews at even;
Her tears fell ere the dews were dried.
She could not look on the sweet heaven
Either at morn or eventide.   16
After the flitting of the bats,
When thickest dark did trance the sky,
She drew her casement curtain by
And glanced athwart the glooming flats.   20

MARIANA. *Mariana . . . grange:* "There, at the moated grange, resides this dejected Mariana" (*Measure for Measure*, III, i). A grange is a farmhouse with its outlying buildings. 18 *trance:* entrance, bewitch.

She only said, "The night is dreary,
 He cometh not," she said,
She said, "I am aweary, aweary—
 I would that I were dead!"   24

Upon the middle of the night,
 Waking, she heard the night-fowl crow.
The cock sung out an hour ere light;
 From the dark fen the oxen's low   28
Came to her: without hope of change,
 In sleep she seemed to walk forlorn,
 Till cold winds woke the gray-eyed morn
About the lonely moated grange.   32
  She only said, "The day is dreary,
   He cometh not," she said.
  She said, "I am aweary, aweary—
   I would that I were dead!"   36

About a stone-cast from the wall
 A sluice with blackened waters slept,
And o'er it many, round and small,
 The clustered marish-mosses crept.   40
Hard by, a poplar shook alway,
 All silver-green with gnarlèd bark;
 For leagues no other tree did mark
The level waste, the rounding gray.   44
  She only said, "My life is dreary,
   He cometh not," she said.
  She said, "I am aweary, aweary—
   I would that I were dead!"   48

And ever when the moon was low
 And the shrill winds were up and away,
In the white curtain, to and fro,
 She saw the gusty shadow sway.   52
But when the moon was very low,
 And wild winds bound within their cell,
 The shadow of the poplar fell
Upon her bed, across her brow.   56
  She only said, "The night is dreary,
   He cometh not," she said.
  She said, "I am aweary, aweary—
   I would that I were dead!"   60

---

28 *fen:* marsh.   40 *marish-mosses:* marsh-mosses.

All day within the dreamy house
  The doors upon their hinges creaked.
The blue fly sung in the pane; the mouse
  Behind the mouldering wainscot shrieked,   64
Or from the crevice peered about.
  Old faces glimmered through the doors;
  Old footsteps trod the upper floors;
Old voices called her from without.   68
    She only said, "My life is dreary,
      He cometh not," she said.
    She said, "I am aweary, aweary—
      I would that I were dead!"   72

The sparrow's chirrup on the roof,
  The slow clock ticking, and the sound
Which to the wooing wind aloof
  The poplar made, did all confound   76
Her sense; but most she loathed the hour
  When the thick-moted sunbeam lay
  Athwart the chambers, and the day
Was sloping toward his western bower.   80
    Then, said she, "I am very dreary;
      He will not come," she said.
    She wept, "I am aweary, aweary—
      Oh, God, that I were dead!"   84

(1830)

ULYSSES

It little profits that an idle king,
By this still hearth, among these barren crags,
Matched with an agèd wife, I mete and dole
Unequal laws unto a savage race
That hoard, and sleep, and feed, and know not me.   5
I cannot rest from travel. I will drink
Life to the lees; all times I have enjoyed
Greatly, have suffered greatly, both with those
That loved me, and alone; on shore, and when
Through scudding drifts the rainy Hyades   10

ULYSSES. 10 *Hyades:* a group of stars in the constellation Taurus, supposed to
bring rain in May, when they rose with the sun.

Vexed the dim sea. I am become a name;
For, always roaming with a hungry heart,
Much have I seen and known—cities of men,
And manners, climates, councils, governments,
Myself not least, but honored of them all; 15
And drunk delight of battle with my peers,
Far on the ringing plains of windy Troy.
I am a part of all that I have met.
Yet all experience is an arch wherethrough
Gleams that untraveled world whose margin fades 20
Forever and forever when I move.
How dull it is to pause, to make an end,
To rust unburnished, not to shine in use!
As though to breathe were life. Life piled on life
Were all too little; and of one to me 25
Little remains; but every hour is saved
From that eternal silence, something more,
A bringer of new things; and vile it were
For some three suns to store and hoard myself,
And this gray spirit yearning in desire 30
To follow knowledge like a sinking star,
Beyond the utmost bound of human thought.
    This is my son, mine own Telemachus,
To whom I leave the scepter and the isle—
Well loved of me, discerning to fulfill 35
This labor, by slow prudence to make mild
A rugged people, and through soft degrees
Subdue them to the useful and the good.
Most blameless is he, centered in the sphere
Of common duties, decent not to fail 40
In offices of tenderness, and pay
Meet adoration to my household gods
When I am gone. He works his work, I mine.
    There lies the port; the vessel puffs her sail;
There gloom the dark broad seas. My mariners— 45
Souls that have toiled, and wrought, and thought with me,
That ever with a frolic welcome took
The thunder and the sunshine, and opposed
Free hearts, free foreheads—you and I are old.
Old age hath yet his honor and his toil; 50
Death closes all. But something ere the end,
Some work of noble note, may yet be done
Not unbecoming men that strove with Gods.
The lights begin to twinkle from the rocks;

335

The long day wanes; the slow moon climbs; the deep 55
Moans round with many voices. Come, my friends;
'Tis not too late to seek a newer world.
Push off, and sitting well in order smite
The sounding furrows; for my purpose holds
To sail beyond the sunset and the baths 60
Of all the western stars, until I die.
It may be that the gulfs will wash us down.
It may be we shall touch the Happy Isles,
And see the great Achilles, whom we knew.
Though much is taken, much abides; and though 65
We are not now that strength which in old days
Moved earth and heaven, that which we are, we are:
One equal temper of heroic hearts,
Made weak by time and fate, but strong in will
To strive, to seek, to find, and not to yield. 70

(1842)

From THE PRINCESS: A MEDLEY

Tear, Idle Tears, I Know Not What They Mean

Tears, idle tears, I know not what they mean.
Tears from the depth of some divine despair
Rise in the heart, and gather to the eyes
In looking on the happy autumn fields
And thinking of the days that are no more. 5

Fresh as the first beam glittering on a sail
That brings our friends up from the underworld;
Sad as the last which reddens over one
That sinks with all we love below the verge:
So sad, so fresh, the days that are no more. 10

---

63 *Happy Isles:* Elysium, the abode of the blest; thought to lie somewhere in the western sea.

THE PRINCESS: A MEDLEY (1847; some of the lyrics were added later) has to do with woman's place in society. The present lyric is sung to the harp by a maid who is herself moved to tears.

Ah, sad and strange as in dark summer dawns
The earliest pipe of half-awakened birds
To dying ears, when unto dying eyes
The casement slowly grows a glimmering square:
So sad, so strange, the days that are no more. 15

Dear as remembered kisses after death,
And sweet as those by hopeless fancy feigned
On lips that are for others; deep as love,
Deep as first love, and wild with all regret:
O death in life, the days that are no more. 20

(1850)

From IN MEMORIAM

LIV

Oh, yet we trust that somehow good
    Will be the final goal of ill,
    To pangs of nature, sins of will,
Defects of doubt, and taints of blood; 4

That nothing walks with aimless feet;
    That not one life shall be destroyed
    Or cast as rubbish to the void
When God hath made the pile complete; 8

That not a worm is cloven in vain;
    That not a moth with vain desire
    Is shriveled in a fruitless fire
Or but subserves another's gain. 12

Behold, we know not anything.
    I can but trust that good shall fall
    At last—far off—at last, to all,
And every winter change to spring. 16

So runs my dream; but what am I?
    An infant, crying in the night;
    An infant crying for the light,
And with no language but a cry. 20

IN MEMORIAM. A long elegy on Arthur Henry Hallam, a dear friend who died in 1833. The excerpt given here shows the skepticism against which Tennyson's religious faith had to battle.

337

LV

The wish, that of the living whole
  No life may fail beyond the grave,
  Derives it not from what we have
The likest God within the soul?   24

Are God and Nature then at strife,
  That Nature lends such evil dreams?
  So careful of the type she seems,
So careless of the single life,   28

That I, considering everywhere
  Her secret meaning in her deeds,
  And finding that of fifty seeds
She often brings but one to bear,   32

I falter where I firmly trod,
  And, falling with my weight of cares
  Upon the great world's altar-stairs
That slope through darkness up to God,   36

I stretch lame hands of faith, and grope,
  And gather dust and chaff, and call
  To what I feel is Lord of all,
And faintly trust the larger hope.   40

LVI

"So careful of the type?" But no—
  From scarpèd cliff and quarried stone
  She cries, "A thousand types are gone;
I care for nothing—all shall go.   44

"Thou makest thine appeal to me:
  I bring to life; I bring to death.
  The spirit does but mean the breath;
I know no more." And he, shall he,   48

Man, her last work, who seemed so fair,
  Such splendid purpose in his eyes,
  Who rolled the psalm to wintry skies,
Who built him fanes of fruitless prayer,   52

---

32 *to bear:* to germinate, bear fruit. 42 *scarpèd:* steeply sloping. 47 *The spirit
. . . breath:* the Latin word *spiritus* means, literally, "breath." 52 *fanes:* temples.

338

Who trusted God was love indeed,
  And love creation's final law—
  Though nature, red in tooth and claw
With ravine, shrieked against his creed—   56

Who loved, who suffered countless ills,
  Who battled for the True, the Just,
  Be blown about the desert dust,
Or sealed within the iron hills?   60

No more? A monster then, a dream,
  A discord. Dragons of the prime,
  That tare each other in their slime,
Were mellow music matched with him.   64

O life as futile, then, as frail!
  O for thy voice to soothe and bless!
  What hope of answer, or redress?
Behind the veil, behind the veil.   68

                    (1850)

From MAUD: A MONODRAMA

Part I, Section XXII

Come into the garden, Maud,
  For the black bat, night, has flown.
Come into the garden, Maud:
  I am here at the gate, alone.
And the woodbine spices are wafted abroad,
  And the musk of the rose is blown.   6

For a breeze of morning moves,
  And the planet of love is on high,
Beginning to faint in the light that she loves
  On a bed of daffodil sky;
To faint in the light of the sun she loves,
  To faint in his light, and to die.   12

---

62 *prime:* earliest days. 63 *tare:* tore. 66 *thy:* Hallam's.

MAUD is a long, quasi-dramatic poem about a passionate love affair. At this point the lover waits for his sweetheart in the garden after a ball to which he has not been invited. 8 *planet of love:* Venus, which rises before dawn in the east.

339

All night have the roses heard
The flute, violin, bassoon.
All night has the casement jessamine stirred
To the dancers dancing in tune;
Till a silence fell with the waking bird,
And a hush with the setting moon. 18

I said to the lily, "There is but one
With whom she has heart to be gay.
When will the dancers leave her alone?
She is weary of dance and play."
Now half to the setting moon are gone,
And half to the rising day.
Low on the sand, and loud on the stone,
The last wheel echoes away. 26

I said to the rose, "The brief night goes
In babble and revel and wine.
O young lord-lover, what sighs are those
For one that will never be thine?
But mine, but mine." So I sware to the rose,
"Forever and ever, mine." 32

And the soul of the rose went into my blood
As the music clashed in the hall;
And long by the garden lake I stood,
For I heard your rivulet fall
From the lake to the meadow and on to the wood—
Our wood, that is dearer than all; 38

From the meadow your walks have left so sweet
That whenever a March wind sighs
He sets the jewel-print of your feet
In violets blue as your eyes,
To the woody hollows in which we meet,
And the valleys of Paradise. 44

The slender acacia would not shake
One long milk-bloom on the tree;
The white lake-blossom fell into the lake
As the pimpernel dozed on the lea.
But the rose was awake all night for your sake,
Knowing your promise to me.
The lilies and roses were all awake;
They sighed for the dawn and thee. 52

340

Queen rose of the rosebud garden of girls,
  Come hither! the dances are done;
In gloss of satin and glimmer of pearls,
  Queen lily and rose in one.
Shine out, little head, sunning over with curls,
  To the flowers, and be their sun.   58

There has fallen a splendid tear
  From the passion-flower at the gate.
She is coming, my dove, my dear;
  She is coming, my life, my fate;
The red rose cries, "She is near, she is near!"
  And the white rose weeps, "She is late."
The larkspur listens, "I hear, I hear,"
  And the lily whispers, "I wait."   66

She is coming, my own, my sweet.
  Were it ever so airy a tread,
My heart would hear her and beat
  Were it earth in an earthy bed.
My dust would hear her and beat
  Had I lain for a century dead;
Would start and tremble under her feet,
  And blossom in purple and red.   72

(1855)

MILTON

Alcaics

O mighty-mouthed inventor of harmonies,
O skilled to sing of time or eternity,
  God-gifted organ-voice of England,
    Milton, a name to resound for ages;

MILTON. *Alcaics:* a meter used by the Greek lyric poet Alcaeus (ca. 600 B.C.) The pattern of the alcaic hendecasyllable was as follows: $\stackrel{\smile}{-} \smile - \stackrel{\smile}{-} - \smile \smile - \smile \stackrel{\smile}{-}$. The syllables marked with a macron are "long" (that is, prolonged in utterance), and those marked with a hook are "short" (pronounced quickly); those marked with both might be pronounced either way. Tennyson believed that in English, as in Greek and Latin, a syllable containing a short vowel became "long by position" if the vowel was followed by two or more consonants: for example, "the" in "the stately palm-woods." (He was most certainly wrong.) Accent or stress, which is the usual basis of English metrics, was irrelevant in the Greek system.

341

Whose Titan angels, Gabriel, Abdiel,   5
Starred from Jehovah's gorgeous armories,
    Tower, as the deep-domed empyrëan
    Rings to the roar of an angel onset—
Me rather all that bowery loneliness,
The brooks of Eden mazily murmuring,   10
    And bloom profuse and cedar arches,
    Charm, as a wanderer out in ocean,
Where some refulgent sunset of India
Streams o'er a rich ambrosial ocean isle,
    And crimson-hued the stately palm-woods   15
    Whisper in odorous heights of even.

(1863)

FRATER AVE ATQUE VALE

Row us out from Desenzano, to your Sirmione row!
So they rowed, and there we landed—"O venusta Sirmio!"
There to me through all the groves of olive in the summer glow,
There beneath the Roman ruin where the purple flowers grow,
Came that "Ave atque vale" of the Poet's hopeless woe—   5
Tenderest of Roman poets, nineteen hundred years ago;
"Frater ave atque vale," as we wandered to and fro,
Gazing at the Lydian laughter of the Garda Lake below:
Sweet Catullus's all-but-island, olive-silvery Sirmio!

(1883)

FRATER AVE ATQUE VALE: "Brother, hail and farewell!" From a Latin poem by Catullus (d. 54 B.C.) on his brother's death. 1 *Desenzano:* a town on Lake Garda, in Italy, near Sirmione, where Catullus had a villa. 2 *venusta Sirmio:* beautiful Sirmio. The phrase is from Catullus. 4 *purple flowers:* iris (Tennyson). 8 *Lydian laughter:* again a phrase from Catullus. The Etruscans, early inhabitants of this region, were thought to be descendants of the Lydians of Asia Minor. 9 *all-but-island:* the literal meaning of "peninsula" (*paene insula*).

Robert Browning (1812–1889)

PORPHYRIA'S LOVER

The rain set early in tonight,
  The sullen wind was soon awake,
It tore the elm-tops down for spite,
  And did its worst to vex the lake:
I listened with heart fit to break.   5
When glided in Porphyria; straight
  She shut the cold out and the storm,
And kneeled and made the cheerless grate
  Blaze up, and all the cottage warm;
Which done, she rose, and from her form   10
Withdrew the dripping cloak and shawl,
  And laid her soiled gloves by, untied
Her hat and let the damp hair fall,
  And, last, she sat down by my side
And called me. When no voice replied,   15
She put my arm about her waist,
  And made her smooth white shoulder bare,
And all her yellow hair displaced,
  And, stooping, made my cheek lie there,
And spread, o'er all, her yellow hair,   20
Murmuring how she loved me—she
  Too weak, for all her heart's endeavor,
To set its struggling passion free
  From pride, and vainer ties dissever,
And give herself to me forever.   25
But passion sometimes would prevail,
  Nor could tonight's gay feast restrain
A sudden thought of one so pale
  For love of her, and all in vain:
So, she was come through wind and rain.   30
Be sure I looked up at her eyes
  Happy and proud; at last I knew
Porphyria worshipped me; surprise
  Made my heart swell, and still it grew
While I debated what to do.   35

343

That moment she was mine, mine, fair,
   Perfectly pure and good: I found
A thing to do, and all her hair
   In one long yellow string I wound
Three times her little throat around,   40
And strangled her. No pain felt she;
   I am quite sure she felt no pain.
As a shut bud that holds a bee,
   I warily oped her lids: again
Laughed the blue eyes without a stain.   45
And I untightened next the tress
   About her neck; her cheek once more
Blushed bright beneath my burning kiss:
   I propped her head up as before,
Only, this time my shoulder bore   50
Her head, which droops upon it still:
   The smiling rosy little head,
So glad it has its utmost will,
   That all it scorned at once is fled,
And I, its love, am gained instead!   55
Porphyria's love: she guessed not how
   Her darling one wish would be heard.
And thus we sit together now,
   And all night long we have not stirred,
And yet God has not said a word!   60

(1836)

MY LAST DUCHESS

Ferrara

That's my last Duchess painted on the wall,
Looking as if she were alive. I call
That piece a wonder, now: Frà Pandolf's hands
Worked busily a day, and there she stands.
Will 't please you sit and look at her? I said   5
"Frà Pandolf" by design, for never read

My Last Duchess. The duke is Alphonso II of Ferrara, whose wife Lucrezia
died, while still young, in 1561. Later the Duke negotiated for marriage with
the Count of Tyrol's niece. 3 *Frà Pandolf:* "frà" means "brother," hence suggests a monk. No such painter is known.

344

Strangers like you that pictured countenance,
The depth and passion of its earnest glance,
But to myself they turned (since none puts by
The curtain I have drawn for you, but I)   10
And seemed as they would ask me, if they durst,
How such a glance came there; so, not the first
Are you to turn and ask thus. Sir 'twas not
Her husband's presence only called that spot
Of joy into the Duchess' cheek; perhaps   15
Frà Pandolf chanced to say, "Her mantle laps
Over my lady's wrist too much," or "Paint
Must never hope to reproduce the faint
Half-flush that dies along her throat." Such stuff
Was courtesy, she thought, and cause enough   20
For calling up that spot of joy. She had
A heart—how shall I say?—too soon made glad,
Too easily impressed; she liked whate'er
She looked on, and her looks went everywhere.
Sir, 'twas all one! My favor at her breast,   25
The dropping of the daylight in the west,
The bough of cherries some officious fool
Broke in the orchard for her, the white mule
She rode with round the terrace—all and each
Would draw from her alike the approving speech,   30
Or blush, at least. She thanked men—good! but thanked
Somehow—I know not how—as if she ranked
My gift of a nine-hundred-years' old name
With anybody's gift. Who'd stoop to blame
This sort of trifling? Even had you skill   35
In speech—which I have not—to make your will
Quite clear to such an one, and say, "Just this
Or that in you disgusts me; here you miss,
Or there exceed the mark"—and if she let
Herself be lessoned so, nor plainly set   40
Her wits to yours, forsooth, and made excuse—
E'en then would be some stooping; and I choose
Never to stoop. Oh, sir, she smiled, no doubt,
Whene'er I passed her; but who passed without
Much the same smile? This grew; I gave commands;   45
Then all smiles stopped together. There she stands
As if alive. Will 't please you rise? We'll meet
The company below, then. I repeat,
The Count your master's known munificence
Is ample warrant that no just pretense   50

345

Of mine for dowry will be disallowed;
Though his fair daughter's self, as I avowed
At starting, is my object. Nay, we'll go
Together down, sir. Notice Neptune, though,
Taming a sea horse, thought a rarity,   55
Which Claus of Innsbruck cast in bronze for me!

(1842)

THE BISHOP ORDERS HIS TOMB
AT ST. PRAXED'S CHURCH

Rome, 15—

Vanity, saith the preacher, vanity!
Draw round my bed: is Anselm keeping back?
Nephews—sons mine . . . ah, God, I know not! Well—
She, men would have to be your mother once,
Old Gandolf envied me, so fair she was!   5
What's done is done, and she is dead beside,
Dead long ago, and I am Bishop since.
And as she died, so must we die ourselves,
And thence ye may perceive the world's a dream.
Life, how and what is it? As here I lie   10
In this state-chamber, dying by degrees,
Hours and long hours in the dead night, I ask,
"Do I live, am I dead?" Peace, peace seems all.
St. Praxed's ever was the church for peace;
And so, about this tomb of mine. I fought   15
With tooth and nail to save my niche, ye know:
—Old Gandolf cozened me, despite my care;
Shrewd was that snatch from out the corner south
He graced his carrion with, God curse the same!
Yet still my niche is not so cramped but thence   20

---

56 *Claus of Innsbruck:* no such sculptor is known; but Innsbruck, in Austria, was at that time the Tyrolean capital.

THE BISHOP ORDERS HIS TOMB . . . 1 *the preacher:* the author of Ecclesiastes ("The Preacher"). 14 *St. Praxed:* St. Praxedes is said to have been the daughter of a Roman senator, Pudens, at whose house St. Paul stayed. The Roman church of St. Prassede, which is very ancient, was rebuilt in the ninth century and restored in the fifteenth century and later.

One sees the pulpit o' the epistle-side,
And somewhat of the choir, those silent seats,
And up into the aery dome where live
The angels, and a sunbeam's sure to lurk;
And I shall fill my slab of basalt there, 25
And 'neath my tabernacle take my rest,
With those nine columns round me, two and two,
The odd one at my feet where Anselm stands:
Peach-blossom marble all, the rare, the ripe
As fresh-poured red wine of a mighty pulse. 30
—Old Gandolf with his paltry onion-stone,
Put me where I may look at him! True peach,
Rosy and flawless: how I earned the prize!
Draw close: that conflagration of my church—
What then? So much was saved if aught were missed! 35
My sons, ye would not be my death? Go dig
The white-grape vineyard where the oil-press stood,
Drop water gently till the surface sink,
And if ye find . . . Ah, God, I know not, I!
Bedded in store of rotten fig-leaves soft, 40
And corded up in a tight olive-frail,
Some lump, ah, God, of *lapis lazuli,*
Big as a Jew's head cut off at the nape,
Blue as a vein o'er the Madonna's breast . . .
Sons, all have I bequeathed you, villas, all, 45
That brave Frascati villa with its bath;
So, let the blue lump poise between my knees,
Like God the Father's globe on both his hands
Ye worship in the Jesu Church so gay.
For Gandolf shall not choose but see and burst! 50
Swift as a weaver's shuttle fleet our years:
Man goeth to the grave, and where is he?
Did I say basalt for my slab, sons? Black—
'Twas ever antique-black I meant! How else
Shall ye contrast my frieze to come beneath? 55
The bas-relief in bronze ye promised me,
Those Pans and Nymphs ye wot of, and perchance

---

21 *epistle-side:* at Mass, the epistle is read from the south side of the altar and
the Gospel from the north side. 26 *tabernacle:* canopy. 30 *pulse:* strength.
31 *onion-stone:* a low-grade marble given to peeling. 37 *oil-press:* used for
crushing olives. 41 *frail:* a rush basket. 42 *lapis lazuli:* a bright blue stone.
46 *Frascati:* then a fashionable Roman suburb. 49 *Jesu Church:* Il Gesù, a
Jesuit church in Rome. 55 *frieze:* an ornamental border. 57 *wot:* know.

Some tripod, thyrsus, with a vase or so,
The Savior at his sermon on the mount,
Saint Praxed in a glory, and one Pan   60
Ready to twitch the Nymph's last garment off,
And Moses with the tables . . . but I know
Ye mark me not! What do they whisper thee,
Child of my bowels, Anselm? Ah, ye hope
To revel down my villas while I gasp   65
Bricked o'er with beggar's moldy travertine,
Which Gandolf from his tomb-top chuckles at!
Nay, boys, ye love me—all of jasper, then!
'Tis jasper ye stand pledged to, lest I grieve
My bath must needs be left behind, alas!   70
One block, pure green as a pistachio-nut;
There's plenty jasper somewhere in the world—
And have I not Saint Praxed's ear to pray
Horses for ye, and brown Greek manuscripts,
And mistresses with great smooth marbly limbs?   75
—That's if ye carve my epitaph aright,
Choice Latin, picked phrase, Tully's every word,
No gaudy ware like Gandolf's second line—
Tully, my masters? Ulpian serves his need!
And then how I shall lie through centuries,   80
And hear the blessed mutter of the Mass,
And see God made and eaten all day long,
And feel the steady candle-flame, and taste
Good, strong, thick, stupefying incense-smoke!
For as I lie here, hours of the dead night,   85
Dying in state and by such slow degrees,
I fold my arms as if they clasped a crook,
And stretch my feet forth straight as stone can point,
And let the bedclothes, for a mortcloth, drop
Into great laps and folds of sculptor's work;   90
And as yon tapers dwindle, and strange thoughts
Grow, with a certain humming in my ears,
About the life before I lived this life,
And this life too, popes, cardinals, and priests,

---

58 *tripod:* a three-legged support for a cauldron, much prized by the Greeks.
thyrsus: a staff borne by votaries of Bacchus.   60 *in a glory:* with a radiant halo.
62 *tables:* tablets (of the Ten Commandments).   66 *travertine:* a kind of lime-
stone.   77 *Tully:* Marcus Tullius Cicero.   79 *Ulpian:* a Late Latin writer (d. 228)
whose style was postclassical.   82 *see God made and eaten:* in the Mass, the wafer
and wine were thought to become the actual blood and body of Christ.
87 *crook:* the bishop's crozier.   89 *mortcloth:* funeral pall.

Saint Praxed at his sermon on the mount, 95
Your tall pale mother with her talking eyes,
And new-found agate urns as fresh as day,
And marble's language, Latin pure, discreet—
Aha, ELUCESCEBAT quoth our friend?
No Tully, said I, Ulpian at the best! 100
Evil and brief hath been my pilgrimage.
All *lapis,* all, sons! Else I give the Pope
My villas! Will ye ever eat my heart?
Ever your eyes were as a lizard's quick,
They glitter like your mother's for my soul, 105
Or ye would heighten my impoverished frieze,
Piece out its starved design, and fill my vase
With grapes, and add a visor and a Term,
And to the tripod ye would tie a lynx
That in his struggle throws the thyrsus down, 110
To comfort me on my entablature,
Whereon I am to lie till I must ask,
"Do I live, am I dead?" There, leave me, there!
For ye have stabbed me with ingratitude
To death—ye wish it—God, ye wish it—Stone— 115
Gritstone, a-crumble! Clammy squares which sweat
As if the corpse they keep were oozing through—
And no more *lapis* to delight the world!
Well, go! I bless ye. Fewer tapers there,
But in a row: and, going, turn your backs— 120
Aye, like departing altar-ministrants,
And leave me in my church, the church for peace,
That I may watch at leisure if he leers—
Old Gandolf—at me, from his onion-stone,
As still he envied me, so fair she was! 125

(1842)

---

99 ELUCESCEBAT: late form for *elucebat,* "shone forth." 108 *visor:* a mask.
Term: a post bearing a statue or bust, especially of Terminus, the Roman god
of boundaries. 109 *lynx:* a Christian symbol? 116 *gritstone:* a coarse stone
used for grinding.

349

DE GUSTIBUS—

Your ghost will walk, you lover of trees,
    (If our loves remain)
    In an English lane,
By a cornfield-side a-flutter with poppies.
Hark, those two in the hazel coppice—   5
A boy and a girl, if the good fates please,
    Making love, say—
    The happier they!
Draw yourself up from the light of the moon
And let them pass, as they will too soon,   10
    With the beanflowers' boon,
    And the blackbird's tune,
    And May, and June!

What I love best in all the world
Is a castle, precipice-encurled,   15
In a gash of the wind-grieved Apennine.
Or look for me, old fellow of mine
(If I get my head from out the mouth
O' the grave, and loose my spirit's bands,
And come again to the land of lands),   20
In a seaside house to the farther south,
Where the baked cicala dies of drouth,
And one sharp tree—'tis a cypress—stands,
By the many hundred years red-rusted,
Rough iron-spiked, ripe fruit-o'ercrusted,   25
My sentinel to guard the sands
To the water's edge. For, what expands
Before the house, but the great opaque
Blue breadth of sea without a break?
While, in the house, forever crumbles   30
Some fragment of the frescoed walls,
From blisters where a scorpion sprawls.
A girl barefooted brings, and tumbles
Down on the pavement, green-flesh melons,
And says there's news today—the king   35

DE GUSTIBUS: The first words of the adage, *De gustibus non est disputandum* (There is no arguing about tastes). 4 *cornfield:* field of grain. 5 *coppice:* grove or thicket. 16 *Apennine:* the Apennines are mountains in northern Italy. 22 *cicala:* cicada. 35 *the king:* Ferdinand II of the Two Sicilies.

Was shot at, touched in the liver-wing,
Goes with his Bourbon arm in a sling:
—She hopes they have not caught the felons.
Italy, my Italy!
Queen Mary's saying serves for me   40
    (When fortune's malice
    Lost her Calais):
Open my heart and you will see
Graved inside of it, "Italy."
Such lovers old are I and she—   45
So it always was, so shall ever be!

(1855)

Matthew Arnold (1822–1888)

IN HARMONY WITH NATURE

"In harmony with Nature"? Restless fool,
Who with such heat dost preach what were to thee,
When true, the last impossibility—
To be like Nature strong, like Nature cool!   4

Know, man hath all which Nature hath, but more,
And in that *more* lie all his hopes of good.
Nature is cruel, man is sick of blood;
Nature is stubborn, man would fain adore;   8

Nature is fickle, man hath need of rest;
Nature forgives no debt, and fears no grave;
Man would be mild, and with safe conscience blest.

Man must begin, know this, where Nature ends;   12
Nature and man can never be fast friends.
Fool, if thou canst not pass her, rest her slave!

(1849)

---

36 *liver-wing:* right arm. 40 *Queen Mary's saying:* that when she died "Calais" (lost in 1558) would be found written on her heart.

IN HARMONY WITH NATURE. Title, 1849: "To an Independent Preacher, who preached that we should be 'In Harmony with Nature.' " *Independent* means "not of the Established Church."

351

TO MARGUERITE—CONTINUED

Yes! in the sea of life enisled,
With echoing straits between us thrown,
Dotting the shoreless watery wild,
We mortal millions live *alone*.
The islands feel the enclasping flow,
And then their endless bounds they know.　　6

But when the moon their hollows lights,
And they are swept by balms of spring,
And in their glens, on starry nights,
The nightingales divinely sing,
And lovely notes, from shore to shore,
Across the sounds and channels pour—　　12

Oh! then a longing like despair
Is to their farthest caverns sent;
For surely once, they feel, we were
Parts of a single continent!
Now round us spreads the watery plain—
Oh, might our marges meet again!　　18

Who ordered, that their longing's fire
Should be, as soon as kindled, cooled?
Who renders vain their deep desire?
A God, a God their severance ruled!
And bade betwixt their shores to be
The unplumbed, salt, estranging sea.　　24

(1852)

DOVER BEACH

The sea is calm tonight.
The tide is full, the moon lies fair
Upon the straits; on the French coast the light
Gleams and is gone; the cliffs of England stand,
Glimmering and vast, out in the tranquil bay.　　5
Come to the window, sweet is the night air!

To Marguerite . . . 12 *sounds:* narrow channels of water or inlets of the sea.

Only, from the long line of spray
Where the sea meets the moon-blanched land,
Listen! you hear the grating roar
Of pebbles which the waves draw back, and fling,   10
At their return, up the high strand,
Begin, and cease, and then again begin,
With tremulous cadence slow, and bring
The eternal note of sadness in.

Sophocles long ago   15
Heard it on the Ægean, and it brought
Into his mind the turbid ebb and flow
Of human misery; we
Find also in the sound a thought,
Hearing it by this distant northern sea.   20

The Sea of Faith
Was once, too, at the full, and round earth's shore
Lay like the folds of a bright girdle furled.
But now I only hear
Its melancholy, long, withdrawing roar,   25
Retreating, to the breath
Of the night wind, down the vast edges drear
And naked shingles of the world.

Ah, love, let us be true
To one another! For the world, which seems   30
To lie before us like a land of dreams,
So various, so beautiful, so new,
Hath really neither joy, nor love, nor light,
Nor certitude, nor peace, nor help for pain;
And we are here as on a darkling plain   35
Swept with confused alarms of struggle and flight,
Where ignorant armies clash by night.

(1867)

DOVER BEACH. 15–18 *Sophocles . . . misery:* in *Antigone,* 583 ff., Sophocles
compares the coming of god-sent ills upon a household to the beating on the
shore of billows caused by the north wind. 28 *shingles:* beaches covered with
rounded stones or pebbles.

THE LAST WORD

Creep into thy narrow bed,
Creep, and let no more be said!
Vain thy onset! All stands fast.
Thou thyself must break at last.   4

Let the long contention cease!
Geese are swans, and swans are geese.
Let them have it how they will!
Thou art tired; best be still.   8

They out-talked thee, hissed thee, tore thee?
Better men fared thus before thee;
Fired their ringing shot and passed,
Hotly charged—and sank at last.   12

Charge once more, then, and be dumb!
Let the victors, when they come,
When the forts of folly fall,
Find thy body by the wall!   16

(1867)

Walt Whitman (1819–1892)

I HEAR AMERICA SINGING

I hear America singing, the varied carols I hear,
Those of mechanics, each one singing his as it should be blithe
    and strong,
The carpenter singing his as he measures his plank or beam,
The mason singing his as he makes ready for work, or leaves
    off work,
The boatman singing what belongs to him in his boat, the
    deck-hand singing on the steamboat deck,   5

354

The shoemaker singing as he sits on his bench, the hatter
  singing as he stands,
The woodcutter's song, the plowboy's on his way in the morn-
  ing, or at noon intermission or at sundown,
The delicious singing of the mother, or of the young wife at
  work, or of the girl sewing or washing,
Each singing what belongs to him or her and to none else,
The day what belongs to the day—at night the party of young
  fellows, robust, friendly, 10
Singing with open mouths their strong melodious songs.

(1860)

WHEN I HEARD THE LEARN'D ASTRONOMER

When I heard the learn'd astronomer,
When the proofs, the figures, were ranged in columns before
  me,
When I was shown the charts and diagrams, to add, divide, and
  measure them,
When I sitting heard the astronomer where he lectured with
  much applause in the lecture-room,
How soon unaccountable I became tired and sick, 5
Till rising and gliding out I wandered off by myself,
In the mystical moist night air, and from time to time,
Looked up in perfect silence at the stars.

(1865)

VIGIL STRANGE I KEPT
ON THE FIELD ONE NIGHT

Vigil strange I kept on the field one night;
When you my son and my comrade dropped at my side that
  day,
One look I but gave which your dear eyes returned with a
  look I shall never forget,
One touch of your hand to mine O boy, reached up as you
  lay on the ground,

355

Then onward I sped in the battle, the even-contested battle, 5
Till late in the night relieved to the place at last again I
made my way,
Found you in death so cold dear comrade, found your body
son of responding kisses (never again on earth responding),
Bared your face in the starlight, curious the scene, cool blew
the moderate night-wind,
Long there and then in vigil I stood, dimly around me the
battlefield spreading,
Vigil wondrous and vigil sweet there in the fragrant silent
night, 10
But not a tear fell, not even a long-drawn sigh, long, long I
gazed,
Then on the earth partially reclining sat by your side leaning
my chin in my hands,
Passing sweet hours, immortal and mystic hours with you
dearest comrade—not a tear, not a word,
Vigil of silence, love and death, vigil for you my son and my
soldier,
As onward silently stars aloft, eastward new ones upward
stole, 15
Vigil final for you brave boy (I could not save you, swift was
your death,
I faithfully loved you and cared for you living, I think we
shall surely meet again),
Till at latest lingering of the night, indeed just as the dawn
appeared,
My comrade I wrapped in his blanket, enveloped well his
form,
Folded the blanket well, tucking it carefully over head and
carefully under feet, 20
And there and then and bathed by the rising sun, my son in
his grave, in his rude-dug grave I deposited,
Ending my vigil strange with that, vigil of night and battlefield
dim,
Vigil for boy of responding kisses (never again on earth responding),
Vigil for comrade swiftly slain, vigil I never forget, how as
day brightened,
I rose from the chill ground and folded my soldier well in his
blanket, 25
And buried him where he fell.

(1865)

356

From WHEN LILACS LAST
IN THE DOORYARD BLOOMED

Come Lovely and Soothing Death

Come lovely and soothing death,
Undulate round the world, serenely arriving, arriving,
In the day, in the night, to all, to each,
Sooner or later delicate death. 4

Praised be the fathomless universe,
For life and joy, and for objects and knowledge curious,
And for love, sweet love—but praise! praise! praise!
For the sure-enwinding arms of cool-enfolding death. 8

Dark mother always gliding near with soft feet,
Have none chanted for thee a chant of fullest welcome?
Then I chant it for thee, I glorify thee above all,
I bring thee a song that when thou must indeed come, come
    unfalteringly. 12

Approach strong deliveress,
When it is so, when thou hast taken them I joyously sing the
    dead,
Lost in the loving floating ocean of thee,
Laved in the flood of thy bliss O death. 16

From me to thee glad serenades,
Dances for thee I propose saluting thee, adornments and feast-
    ings for thee,
And the sights of the open landscape and the high-spread sky
    are fitting,
And life and the fields, and the huge and thoughtful night. 20

The night in silence under many a star,
The ocean shore and the husky whispering wave whose voice
    I know,
And the soul turning to thee O vast and well-veiled death,
And the body gratefully nestling close to thee. 24

COME LOVELY AND SOOTHING DEATH. As the poet meditates on the death of
Abraham Lincoln, his song blends with that of a thrush which is singing in
the swamp.

357

Over the tree-tops I float thee a song,
Over the rising and sinking waves, over the myriad fields and
    the prairies wide,
Over the dense-packed cities all and the teeming wharves and
    ways,
I float this carol with joy, with joy to thee O death.   28

(1865–66)

Emily Dickinson *(1830–1886)*

241

I like a look of agony,
Because I know it's true.
Men do not sham convulsion,
Nor simulate a throe.   4

The eyes glaze once—and that is death.
Impossible to feign
The beads upon the forehead,
By homely anguish strung.   8

(1890)

328

A bird came down the walk;
He did not know I saw.
He bit an angleworm in halves
And ate the fellow, raw.   4

And then he drank a dew
From a convenient grass,
And then hopped sidewise to the wall
To let a beetle pass.   8

---

27 *ways:* no doubt in the nautical sense of structures of timbers from which
ships are launched.

He glanced with rapid eyes
That hurried all around—
They looked like frightened beads, I thought.
He stirred his velvet head 12

Like one in danger; cautious,
I offered him a crumb.
And he unrolled his feathers
And rowed him softer home 16

Than oars divide the ocean,
Too silver for a seam—
Or butterflies, off banks of noon,
Leap, plashless, as they swim. 20

(1891)

341

After great pain, a formal feeling comes.
The nerves sit ceremonious, like tombs;
The stiff heart questions, was it he that bore?
And yesterday, or centuries before? 4

The feet, mechanical, go round
A wooden way
Of ground, or air, or ought,
Regardless grown—
A quartz contentment, like a stone. 9

This is the hour of lead—
Remembered, if outlived,
As freezing persons recollect the snow:
First chill, then stupor, then the letting go. 13

(1929)

436

The wind tapped like a tired man,
And, like a host, "Come in!"
I boldly answered. Entered then
My residence within 4

---

328 13–14: ms., *Like one in danger, Cautious,/ I offered him a Crumb.* The mss. have been carefully edited by Thomas H. Johnson, *The Poems of Emily Dickinson* (Cambridge, Mass.: The Belknap Press of Harvard University Press, 1955).

341 3 *he:* ms., *He;* but Dickinson capitalized erratically.

A rapid, footless guest,
To offer whom a chair
Were as impossible as hand
A sofa to the air.   8

No bone had he to bind him;
His speech was like the push
Of numerous hummingbirds at once
From a superior bush.   12

His countenance, a billow;
His fingers, as he passed,
Let go a music, as of tunes
Blown tremulous in glass.   16

He visited, still flitting,
Then, like a timid man,
Again he tapped—'twas flurriedly—
And I became alone.   20

(1891)

520

I started early, took my dog,
And visited the sea.
The mermaids in the basement
Came out to look at me,   4

And frigates in the upper floor
Extended hempen hands,
Presuming me to be a mouse
Aground upon the sands.   8

But no man moved me till the tide
Went past my simple shoe—
And past my apron—and my belt—
And past my bodice too—   12

And made as he would eat me up
As wholly as a dew
Upon a dandelion's sleeve.
And then I started, too,   16

---

436 14 *as he passed:* Johnson has corrected *if he pass* (1891) from the ms.

360

And he—he followed close behind.
I felt his silver heel
Upon my ankle; then my shoes
Would overflow with pearl, 20

Until we met the solid town—
No one he seemed to know—
And, bowing, with a mighty look
At me, the sea withdrew. 24

(1891)

585

I like to see it lap the miles
And lick the valleys up,
And stop to feed itself at tanks,
And then, prodigious, step 4

Around a pile of mountains,
And, supercilious, peer
In shanties by the sides of roads,
And then a quarry pare 8

To fit its sides,
And crawl between
Complaining all the while
In horrid, hooting stanza—
Then chase itself downhill 13

And neigh like Boanerges;
Then, prompter than a star,
Stop, docile and omnipotent,
At its own stable door. 17

(1891)

712

Because I could not stop for Death,
He kindly stopped for me.
The carriage held but just ourselves
And Immortality. 4

520 22 *one:* from the ms., for *man* in the 1891 printing.

585 Johnson has corrected three 1891 readings from the ms.: 1, *see* for *hear;*
9, *sides* for *ribs;* 14, *And* for *And, or then.* 14 *Boanerges: Mark 3:17,* "sons of
thunder"—name given by Christ to the brothers James and John, two of the
Disciples.

We slowly drove; he knew no haste;
And I had put away
My labor, and my leisure too,
For his civility.   8

We passed the school where children strove
At recess, in the ring;
We passed the fields of gazing grain;
We passed the setting sun—   12

Or rather, he passed us.
The dews drew quivering and chill:
For only gossamer, my gown;
My tippet, only tulle.   16

We paused before a house that seemed
A swelling of the ground.
The roof was scarcely visible,
The cornice in the ground.   20

Since then 'tis centuries; but each
Feels shorter than the day
I first surmised the horses' heads
Were toward Eternity.   24

                                     (1890)

875

I stepped from plank to plank
A slow and cautious way;
The stars about my head I felt,
About my feet the sea.   4

I knew not but the next
Would be my final inch:
This gave me that precarious gait
Some call Experience.   8

                                     (1896)

---

712 Johnson has restored the following ms. readings: 9, *strove* for *played;*
10, *At recess, in the ring* for *Their lessons scarcely done;* 20, *in the ground* for
but a mound. Also, he has supplied the missing fourth stanza. I have retained
but each, in line 21, for *and yet* in the ms. 16 *tippet:* a kind of scarf.

875 2 *A slow and cautious way,* from the ms., for *So slow and cautiously* (1896).

362

974

The Soul's distinct connection
With immortality
Is best disclosed by Danger
Or quick Calamity—   4

As Lightning on a Landscape
Exhibits Sheets of Place—
Not yet suspected—but for Flash—
And Click—and Suddenness.   8

(1929)

986

A narrow fellow in the grass
Occasionally rides.
You may have met him—did you not?
His notice sudden is;   4

The grass divides as with a comb;
A spotted shaft is seen;
And then it closes at your feet
And opens further on.   8

He likes a boggy acre,
A floor too cool for corn.
Yet when a boy, and barefoot,
I more than once at noon   12
Have passed, I thought, a whiplash
Unbraiding in the sun,
When, stooping to secure it,
It wrinkled and was gone.   16

Several of nature's people
I know, and they know me.
I feel for them a transport
Of cordiality: 20

_974_ Printed from Johnson, who follows Miss Dickinson's ms. closely. Except
here and in _1129_, Miss Dickinson's spelling, punctuation, and capitalization have
been normalized.

363

But never met this fellow
Attended or alone
Without a tighter breathing
And zero at the bone.   24

(1891)

1078

The bustle in a house
The morning after death
Is solemnest of industries
Enacted upon earth: 4

The sweeping up the heart
And putting love away
We shall not want to use again
Until eternity.   8

(1890)

1129

Tell all the Truth but tell it slant—
Success in Circuit lies
Too bright for our infirm Delight
The Truth's superb surprise   4
As Lightning to the Children eased
With explanation kind
The Truth must dazzle gradually
Or every man be blind—

(1945)

1129 Printed from Johnson, who follows Miss Dickinson's ms. closely.

Gerard Manley Hopkins (1844–1889)

GOD'S GRANDEUR

The world is charged with the grandeur of God.
It will flame out, like shining from shook foil;
It gathers to a greatness, like the ooze of oil
Crushed. Why do men then now not reck his rod?   4
Generations have trod, have trod, have trod;
   And all is seared with trade; bleared, smeared with toil;
And wears man's smudge and shares man's smell: the soil
Is bare now, nor can foot feel, being shod.   8

And for all this, nature is never spent;
   There lives the dearest freshness deep down things;
And though the last lights off the black West went
   Oh, morning, at the brown brink eastward, springs—   12
Because the Holy Ghost over the bent
   World broods with warm breast and with ah! bright wings.

(1918)

THE STARLIGHT NIGHT

Look at the stars! look, look up at the skies!
O look at all the fire-folk sitting in the air!
The bright boroughs, the circle-citadels there!

GOD'S GRANDEUR. A note by Hopkins says that this poem is in "standard rhythm counterpointed." He meant that the basic iambic meter is accompanied by another rhythm which runs counter to it. The contrapuntal rhythm is produced chiefly by reversals (the substitution of trochees for iambs) in two successive feet, perhaps including "the sensitive second foot," where reversal is most unusual. The result is the creation of a second rhythm which is "mounted" upon the first, so that "two rhythms are in some manner running at once and we have something answerable to counterpoint in music, which is two or more strains of tune going on together." 2 *foil:* "I mean foil in the sense of leaf or tinsel. . . . Shaken goldfoil gives off broad glares like sheet lightning" (Hopkins). 3 *ooze of oil:* as from crushed olives. 4 *reck:* pay heed to. 9 *spent:* exhausted. 10 *things:* in things.

THE STARLIGHT NIGHT. "Standard rhythm open and counterpointed" (Hopkins). "Open" perhaps means that the rhythm takes no account of line-breaks: a foot may begin in one line and end in the next. 3 *boroughs:* cities.

Down in dim woods the diamond delves! the elves'-eyes! 4
The grey lawns cold where gold, where quickgold lies!
Wind-beat whitebeam! airy abeles set on a flare!
Flake-doves sent floating forth at a farmyard scare!
Ah well! it is all a purchase, all is a prize. 8

Buy then! bid then!—What?—Prayer, patience, alms, vows.
Look, look: a May-mess, like on orchard boughs!
    Look! March-bloom, like on mealed-with-yellow sallows!
These are indeed the barn; withindoors house 12
The shocks. This piece-bright paling shuts the spouse
Christ home, Christ and his mother and all his hallows.

(1918)

THE WINDHOVER: TO CHRIST OUR LORD

I cáught this mórning mórning's mínion, kíng-
    dom of dáylight's dáuphin, dapple-dáwn-drawn
        Fálcon, in his ríding
Of the rólling level úndernéath him steady áir, and stríding
Hígh there, how he rúng upon the réin of a wímpling wíng 4
In his ecstasy! then off, off forth on swing,
    As a skate's heel sweeps smooth on a bow-bend: the hurl and
        gliding
    Rebuffed the big wind. My heart in hiding
Stirred for a bird—the achieve of, the mastery of the thing! 8

---

4 *delves:* apparently used as a noun—"diggings" of diamonds. 5 *quickgold:*
probably "dew." The word may be formed by analogy with "quicksilver." 6
abeles: white poplars. The pronunciation is either *á-bles* or *a-béels.* 10 *May-
mess:* confusion or profusion of May. 11 *mealed-with-yellow sallows:* willows
of a mealy yellow color. 13 *shocks:* bundles of sheaves. 13–14 *the spouse/
Christ:* the Church is traditionally Christ's "bride." 14 *hallows:* holy ones, saints.
    The Windhover. "Falling paeonic rhythm, sprung and outriding." A *paeon*
is a four-syllable foot, of which one syllable (in Hopkins, always the first) is
stressed. Essentially, sprung rhythm requires only a given number of stresses in
the line and admits three, two, one, or no light syllables after each stress. "Out-
rides" are "one, two, or three slack syllables added to a foot and not counted
in the nominal scanning." Here there are five stresses in each line and a varying
number of light syllables. The stresses in the first four lines are marked to
suggest where Hopkins meant them to come. *Windhover:* a kind of falcon.
1 *minion:* darling. 2 *dauphin:* crown prince. 4 *rung:* in falconry, to "ring" is
to rise in a spiral. *wimpling:* undulating. 6 *bow-bend:* a shallow curve.

366

Brute beauty and valor and act, oh, air, pride, plume, here
   Buckle! AND the fire that breaks from thee then, a billion
Times told lovelier, more dangerous, O my chevalier!

No wonder of it: sheer plod makes plow down sillion   12
Shine, and blue-bleak embers, ah my dear,
   Fall, gall themselves, and gash gold-vermilion.

(1918)

FELIX RANDAL

Felix Randal the farrier, O is he dead then? my duty all ended,
Who have watched his mold of man, big-boned and hardy-
   handsome
Pining, pining, till time when reason rambled in it and some
Fatal four disorders, fleshed there, all contended?   4

Sickness broke him. Impatient he cursed at first, but mended
Being anointed and all; though a heavenlier heart began some
Months earlier, since I had our sweet reprieve and ransom
Tendered to him. Ah well, God rest him all road ever he
   offended!   8

This seeing the sick endears them to us, us too it endears.
My tongue had taught thee comfort, touch had quenched thy
   tears,
Thy tears that touched my heart, child, Felix, poor Felix
   Randal;

How far from then forethought of, all thy more boisterous
   years,   12
When thou at the random grim forge, powerful amidst peers,
Didst fettle for the great grey drayhorse his bright and batter-
   ing sandal!

(1918)

---

11 *told:* counted. *chevalier:* knight. 12 *sillion:* furrow.

  FELIX RANDAL: "Sonnet; sprung and outriding rhythm; six-foot lines" (Hopkins). 1 *farrier:* blacksmith. 6 *Being anointed:* with oil, in the Roman Catholic
rite of extreme unction. 7 *reprieve and ransom:* absolution following confession.
8 *all road ever:* in whatever way. 10 *touch:* by the finger, in placing oil on the
body. 12 *all:* during all. The omission of small words is common in Hopkins'
style. 13 *random:* built from random materials. 14 *fettle:* prepare.

SPRING AND FALL: TO A YOUNG CHILD

Márgarét, are you gríeving
Over Goldengrove unleaving?
Léaves, líke the things of man, you
With your fresh thoughts care for, can you?   4
Ah! ás the heart grows older
It will come to such sights colder
By and by, nor spare a sigh
Though worlds of wanwood leafmeal lie;   8
And yet you wíll weep and know why.
Now no matter, child, the name:
Sórrow's spríngs áre the same.
Nor mouth had, no nor mind, expressed   12
What heart heard of, ghost guessed:
It ís the blight man was born for,
It is Margaret you mourn for.

(1918)

Thomas Hardy (1840–1928)

THE SUBALTERNS

"Poor wanderer," said the leaden sky,
    "I fain would lighten thee,
But there are laws in force on high
    Which say it must not be."   4

—"I would not freeze thee, shorn one," cried
    The North, "knew I but how
To warm my breath, to slack my stride;
    But I am ruled as thou."   8

SPRING AND FALL . . . "Sprung rhythm" (Hopkins). The stresses are marked by
Hopkins but offer only partial guidance. 2 *unleaving:* dropping its leaves.
8 *wanwood:* decayed trees. *leafmeal:* leaves crumbled to a mealy texture, or
masses of separate (piecemeal) leaves. 13 *ghost:* spirit (as in "Holy Ghost").

THE SUBALTERNS: subordinates or (in the army) lieutenants.

368

—"Tomorrow I attack thee, wight,"
    Said Sickness. "Yet I swear
I bear thy little ark no spite,
    But am bid enter there." 12

—"Come hither, Son," I heard Death say;
    "I did not will a grave
Should end thy pilgrimage today,
    But I, too, am a slave!" 16

We smiled upon each other then,
    And life to me had less
Of that fell look it wore ere when
    They owned their passiveness. 20

(1901)

THE RUINED MAID

"O 'Melia, my dear, this does everything crown!
Who could have supposed I should meet you in Town?
And whence such fair garments, such prosperi-ty?"—
"O didn't you know I'd been ruined?" said she. 4

—"You left us in tatters, without shoes or socks,
Tired of digging potatoes, and spudding up docks;
And now you've gay bracelets and bright feathers three!"—
"Yes: that's how we dress when we're ruined," said she. 8

—"At home in the barton you said 'thee' and 'thou,'
And 'thik oon,' and 'theäs oon,' and 't'other'; but now
Your talking quite fits 'ee for high compa-ny!"—
"Some polish is gained with one's ruin," said she. 12

—"Your hands were like paws then, your face blue and bleak;
But now I'm bewitched by your delicate cheek,
And your little gloves fit as on any la-dy!"—
"We never do work when we're ruined," said she. 16

—"You used to call home-life a hag-ridden dream,
And you'd sigh, and you'd sock; but at present you seem
To know not of megrims or melancho-ly!"—
"True. One's pretty lively when ruined," said she. 20

THE RUINED MAID. 1 'Melia: Amelia. 6 spudding up docks: spading up weeds.
9 barton: farm. 10 thik oon: that one. theäs oon: this one. 11 'ee: ye. 18 sock:
sigh. 19 megrims: migraine headaches.

369

—"I wish I had feathers, a fine sweeping gown,
And a delicate face, and could strut about Town!"—
"My dear—a raw country girl, such as you be,
Cannot quite expect that. You ain't ruined," said she.   24

(1901)

LOVE THE MONOPOLIST

Young Lover's Reverie

The train draws forth from the station-yard,
 And with it carries me.
I rise, and stretch out, and regard
 The platform left, and see
An airy slim blue form there standing,
 And know that it is she.   6

While with strained vision I watch on,
 The figure turns round quite
To greet friends gaily; then is gone . . .
 The import may be slight,
But why remained she not hard gazing
 Till I was out of sight?   12

"O do not chat with others there,"
 I brood. "They are not I.
O strain your thoughts as if they were
 Gold bands between us; eye
All neighbor scenes as so much blankness
 Till I again am by!   18

"A troubled soughing in the breeze
 And the sky overhead
Let yourself feel; and shadeful trees,
 Ripe corn, and apples red,
Read as things barren and distasteful
 While we are separated!   24

LOVE THE MONOPOLIST. 19 *soughing:* rustling, murmuring. 22 *corn:* grain.

370

"When I come back uncloak your gloom
      And let in lovely day;
Then the long dark as of the tomb
      Can well be thrust away
With sweet things I shall have to practice,
      And you will have to say!"   30

                                        (1917)

                    NOBODY COMES

      Tree-leaves labor up and down,
            And through them the fainting light
            Succumbs to the crawl of night.
      Outside in the road the telegraph wire
            To the town from the darkening land
Intones to travelers like a spectral lyre
            Swept by a spectral hand.   7

      A car comes up, with lamps full-glare,
            That flash upon a tree:
            It has nothing to do with me,
      And whangs along in a world of its own,
            Leaving a blacker air;
And mute by the gate I stand again alone,
            And nobody pulls up there.   14

                                        (1925)

William Butler Yeats (1865–1939)

                    NO SECOND TROY

Why should I blame her that she filled my days
With misery, or that she would of late
Have taught to ignorant men most violent ways,
Or hurled the little streets upon the great,   4

No Second Troy. Yeats is thinking of Maud Gonne, a passionate Irish na-
tionalist whom he courted, unsuccessfully, for years.

                          371

Had they but courage equal to desire?
What could have made her peaceful with a mind
That nobleness made simple as a fire,
With beauty like a tightened bow, a kind   8
That is not natural in an age like this,
Being high and solitary and most stern?
Why, what could she have done, being what she is?
Was there another Troy for her to burn?   12

(1910)

THE MAGI

Now as at all times I can see in the mind's eye,
In their stiff, painted clothes, the pale unsatisfied ones
Appear and disappear in the blue depth of the sky
With all their ancient faces like rain-beaten stones,   4
And all their helms of silver hovering side by side,
And all their eyes still fixed, hoping to find once more,
Being by Calvary's turbulence unsatisfied,
The uncontrollable mystery on the bestial floor.   8

(1914)

THE SECOND COMING

Turning and turning in the widening gyre
The falcon cannot hear the falconer;
Things fall apart; the center cannot hold;
Mere anarchy is loosed upon the world,

THE MAGI. "I looked up one day into the blue of the sky, and suddenly
imagined, as if lost in the blue of the sky, stiff figures in procession" (Yeats).
The *Magi* are the three wise men who came from the east to worship the
infant Christ (*Matthew 2:1–12*). 8 *bestial floor:* the floor of the manger.

THE SECOND COMING. 1 *gyre:* a spiral (Yeats pronounced the *g* hard). Each
cycle of history was a "gyre" for Yeats: eventually it became so open that (line
3) it ceased to have any center. He believed that the birth of Christ marked
the end of a cycle which began with Babylonian culture about 2000 B.C. and
included Greco-Roman civilization.

The blood-dimmed tide is loosed, and everywhere 5
The ceremony of innocence is drowned;
The best lack all conviction, while the worst
Are full of passionate intensity.

Surely some revelation is at hand;
Surely the Second Coming is at hand. 10
The Second Coming! Hardly are those words out
When a vast image out of *Spiritus Mundi*
Troubles my sight: somewhere in sands of the desert
A shape with lion body and the head of a man,
A gaze blank and pitiless as the sun, 15
Is moving its slow thighs, while all about it
Reel shadows of the indignant desert birds.
The darkness drops again; but now I know
That twenty centuries of stony sleep
Were vexed to nightmare by a rocking cradle, 20
And what rough beast, its hour come round at last,
Slouches towards Bethlehem to be born?

(1921)

SAILING TO BYZANTIUM

That is no country for old men. The young
In one another's arms, birds in the trees
—Those dying generations—at their song,
The salmon-falls, the mackerel-crowded seas, 4
Fish, flesh, or fowl, commend all summer long
Whatever is begotten, born, and dies.
Caught in that sensual music all neglect
Monuments of unaging intellect. 8

6 *ceremony of innocence:* the ceremonial behavior characteristic of simple cultures. 7–8 *The best . . . intensity:* Yeats is thinking partly of the Russian Revolution, which was contemporary with the poem. 10 *Second Coming:* some new and perhaps violent change—not necessarily the return of Christ. 12 *Spiritus Mundi:* Spirit of the World, a kind of racial memory in which all human beings participated. Like Jung's "collective unconscious," it included significant images. 14 *shape . . . :* like that of the Great Sphinx. 19 *twenty centuries:* the Christian period.

SAILING TO BYZANTIUM. Byzantium was modern Istanbul, or Constantinople, after A.D. 476 the seat of the Eastern Roman—or Byzantine—Empire. At this period of his career, Yeats thought Byzantine art superior to Western European art because it was more abstract, less imitative of biological forms.

373

An aged man is but a paltry thing,
A tattered coat upon a stick, unless
Soul clap its hands and sing, and louder sing
For every tatter in its mortal dress, 12
Nor is there singing school but studying
Monuments of its own magnificence;
And therefore I have sailed the seas and come
To the holy city of Byzantium. 16

O sages standing in God's holy fire
As in the gold mosaic of a wall,
Come from the holy fire, perne in a gyre,
And be the singing-masters of my soul. 20
Consume my heart away; sick with desire
And fastened to a dying animal
It knows not what it is; and gather me
Into the artifice of eternity. 24

Once out of nature I shall never take
My bodily form from any natural thing,
But such a form as Grecian goldsmiths make
Of hammered gold and gold enameling 28
To keep a drowsy Emperor awake;
Or set upon a golden bough to sing
To lords and ladies of Byzantium
Of what is past, or passing, or to come. 32

(1928)

LEDA AND THE SWAN

A sudden blow: the great wings beating still
Above the staggering girl, her thighs caressed
By the dark webs, her nape caught in his bill,
He holds her helpless breast upon his breast. 4

13–14 *Nor is . . . magnificence:* the only schooling from which poets will benefit
is the study of excellent poetry. 17–18 *O sages standing . . . wall:* Yeats is
thinking of mosaic representations of haloed saints. 19 *perne:* whirl. The word
comes from *pern,* a spool or bobbin. For *gyre* see the note to line 1 of *The
Second Coming.* 27–30 *a form . . . to sing:* "I have read somewhere that in the
Emperor's palace at Byzantium was a tree made of gold and silver, and artificial
birds that sang" (Yeats).

LEDA AND THE SWAN. Zeus visited Leda in the form of a swan. As a result of
the union, Leda bore Helen, whose abduction by Paris caused the Trojan War
(line 10), and Clytemnestra, who killed her husband Agamemnon (line 11) upon
his return to Mycenae from Troy.

How can those terrified vague fingers push
The feathered glory from her loosening thighs?
And how can body, laid in that white rush,
But feel the strange heart beating where it lies? 8

A shudder in the loins engenders there
The broken wall, the burning roof and tower
And Agamemnon dead.
                    Being so caught up,
So mastered by the brute blood of the air, 12
Did she put on his knowledge with his power
Before the indifferent beak could let her drop?

(1928)

AMONG SCHOOL CHILDREN

I walk through the long schoolroom questioning;
A kind old nun in a white hood replies;
The children learn to cipher and to sing,
To study reading-books and history, 4
To cut and sew, be neat in everything
In the best modern way—the children's eyes
In momentary wonder stare upon
A sixty-year-old smiling public man. 8

I dream of a Ledaean body, bent
Above a sinking fire, a tale that she
Told of a harsh reproof, or trivial event
That changed some childish day to tragedy— 12
Told, and it seemed that our two natures blent
Into a sphere from youthful sympathy,
Or else, to alter Plato's parable,
Into the yolk and white of the one shell. 16

---

13 *put on his knowledge:* recognize who he was? acquire his knowledge of the future? Yeats thought of Zeus' visit to Leda as an "annunciation" of the Greek culture which was about to begin.

AMONG SCHOOL CHILDREN. 8 *public man:* Yeats was a senator. 9 *Ledaean:* like that of Leda (see *Leda and the Swan*). The poet is reminded of Maud Gonne (see note to *No Second Troy*) speaking of herself as a young girl. 15 *Plato's parable:* in the *Symposium,* Plato says, in a parable, that at first male and female were joined in a spherical body which had two faces, four hands and feet, and so forth. Later the spheres were split, with the result that ever since the halves have sought to reunite. 16 *yolk:* the sphere suggests the egg from which the children of Leda (mentioned in line 9) were born; but the metaphor is of close union.

375

And thinking of that fit of grief or rage
I look upon one child or t' other there
And wonder if she stood so at that age—
For even daughters of the swan can share
Something of every paddler's heritage—   20
And had that color upon cheek or hair,
And thereupon my heart is driven wild:
She stands before me as a living child.   24

Her present image floats into the mind—
Did Quattrocento finger fashion it
Hollow of cheek as though it drank the wind
And took a mess of shadows for its meat?
And I though never of Ledaean kind   28
Had pretty plumage once—enough of that,
Better to smile on all that smile, and show
There is a comfortable kind of old scarecrow.   32

What youthful mother, a shape upon her lap
Honey of generation had betrayed,
And that must sleep, shriek, struggle to escape
As recollection or the drug decide,   36
Would think her son, did she but see that shape
With sixty or more winters on its head,
A compensation for the pang of his birth,
Or the uncertainty of his setting forth?   40

Plato thought nature but a spume that plays
Upon a ghostly paradigm of things;
Solider Aristotle played the taws
Upon the bottom of a king of kings;   44

---

26 *Quattrocento finger:* the finger of a fifteenth-century (Italian) artist. How the
poet conceived of Quattrocento art is suggested by the next two lines. 34 *honey
of generation:* the male's semen, or, more abstractly, the attractiveness of the
sex act. Yeats says that the phrase was borrowed from *The Cave of the Nymphs,*
by Porphyry (233–ca. 304); but the idea that the honey is a "drug" which destroys the memory of prenatal freedom was his own. The infant "sleeps" or
struggles to escape mortal existence (line 35) as the drug works strongly or not.
41 *spume:* foam or froth, as of waves. 42 *paradigm:* strictly, a grammatical
example of inflectional forms; more broadly, a pattern. The allusion is to
Plato's belief that natural forms are less "real" than concepts of forms; for example, an actual bed is transitory, the idea of a bed permanent. 43–44 *Solider
Aristotle . . . king of kings:* Aristotle, a "solider" philosopher than Plato because he was less scornful of matter, sometimes flogged his pupil Alexander the
Great with a strap ("taws").

World-famous golden-thighed Pythagoras
Fingered upon a fiddle-stick or strings
What a star sang and careless Muses heard:
Old clothes upon old sticks to scare a bird.   48

Both nuns and mothers worship images,
But those the candles light are not as those
That animate a mother's reveries,
But keep a marble or a bronze repose.   52
And yet they too break hearts—O Presences
That passion, piety or affection knows,
And that all heavenly glory symbolize—
O self-born mockers of man's enterprise;   56

Labor is blossoming or dancing where
The body is not bruised to pleasure soul,
Nor beauty born out of its own despair,
Nor blear-eyed wisdom out of midnight oil.   60
O chestnut-tree, great-rooted blossomer,
Are you the leaf, the blossom or the bole?
O body swayed to music, O brightening glance,
How can we know the dancer from the dance?   64

                        (1928)

CRAZY JANE TALKS WITH THE BISHOP

I met the Bishop on the road
And much said he and I.
"Those breasts are flat and fallen now,
Those veins must soon be dry;
Live in a heavenly mansion,
Not in some foul sty."   6

"Fair and foul are near of kin,
And fair needs foul," I cried.
"My friends are gone, but that's a truth

---

45 *golden-thighed Pythagoras:* Pythagoras, a Greek philosopher who flourished about 532 B.C., was said to have been seen when undressed to have a thigh of gold. He was a mathematician who developed a theory of musical harmony based on numbers. This was later applied to the heavenly bodies, which were thought to produce music by revolving in appropriately spaced orbits.

Nor grave nor bed denied,
Learned in bodily lowliness
And in the heart's pride. 12

"A woman can be proud and stiff
When on love intent;
But Love has pitched his mansion in
The place of excrement;
For nothing can be sole or whole
That has not been rent." 18

(1932)

Edwin Arlington Robinson (1869–1935)

RICHARD CORY

Whenever Richard Cory went down town,
We people on the pavement looked at him:
He was a gentleman from sole to crown,
Clean favored, and imperially slim. 4

And he was always quietly arrayed,
And he was always human when he talked;
But still he fluttered pulses when he said,
"Good-morning," and he glittered when he walked. 8

And he was rich—yes, richer than a king—
And admirably schooled in every grace:
In fine, we thought that he was everything
To make us wish that we were in his place. 12

So on we worked, and waited for the light,
And went without the meat, and cursed the bread;
And Richard Cory, one calm summer night,
Went home and put a bullet through his head. 16

(1897)

CRAZY JANE . . . 10 *Nor . . . nor:* neither . . . nor.
RICHARD CORY. 11 *in fine:* finally, in short.

FOR A DEAD LADY

No more with overflowing light
Shall fill the eyes that now are faded,
Nor shall another's fringe with night
Their woman-hidden world as they did.   4
No more shall quiver down the days
The flowing wonder of her ways,
Whereof no language may require
The shifting and the many-shaded.   8

The grace, divine, definitive,
Clings only as a faint forestalling;
The laugh that love could not forgive
Is hushed, and answers to no calling;   12
The forehead and the little ears
Have gone where Saturn keeps the years;
The breast where roses could not live
Has done with rising and with falling.   16

The beauty, shattered by the laws
That have creation in their keeping,
No longer trembles at applause,
Or over children that are sleeping;   20
And we who delve in beauty's lore
Know all that we have known before
Of what inexorable cause
Makes Time so vicious in his reaping.   24

(1910)

THE MILL

The miller's wife had waited long,
   The tea was cold, the fire was dead;
And there might yet be nothing wrong
   In how he went and what he said: 4

FOR A DEAD LADY. 14 *where Saturn keeps the years:* Saturn, or Cronus, ruled the universe during a Golden Age, when men suffered no illness, old age, or death.

379

"There are no millers any more,"
  Was all that she had heard him say;
And he had lingered at the door
  So long that it seemed yesterday. 8

Sick with a fear that had no form
  She knew that she was there at last;
And in the mill there was a warm
  And mealy fragrance of the past. 12
What else there was would only seem
  To say again what he had meant;
And what was hanging from a beam
  Would not have heeded where she went. 16

And if she thought it followed her,
  She may have reasoned in the dark
That one way of the few there were
  Would hide her and would leave no mark: 20
Black water, smooth above the weir
  Like starry velvet in the night,
Though ruffled once, would soon appear
  The same as ever to the sight. 24

(1920)

NEW ENGLAND

Here where the wind is always north-north-east
And children learn to walk on frozen toes,
Wonder begets an envy of all those
Who boil elsewhere with such a lyric yeast 4
Of love that you will hear them at a feast
Where demons would appeal for some repose,
Still clamoring where the chalice overflows
And crying wildest who have drunk the least. 8

Passion is here a soilure of the wits,
We're told, and Love a cross for them to bear;
Joy shivers in the corner where she knits
And Conscience always has the rocking-chair, 12
Cheerful as when she tortured into fits
The first cat that was ever killed by Care.

(1925)

Edgar Lee Masters (1869–1950)

From SPOON RIVER ANTHOLOGY

Daisy Fraser

Did you ever hear of Editor Whedon
Giving to the public treasury any of the money he received
For supporting candidates for office?
Or for writing up the canning factory
To get people to invest?   5
Or for suppressing the facts about the bank,
When it was rotten and ready to break?
Did you ever hear of the Circuit Judge
Helping anyone except the "Q" railroad,
Or the bankers? Or did Rev. Peet or Rev. Sibley   10
Give any part of their salary, earned by keeping still,
Or speaking out as the leaders wished them to do,
To the building of the water works?
But I—Daisy Fraser who always passed
Along the streets through rows of nods and smiles   15
And coughs and words such as "there she goes,"
Never was taken before Justice Arnett
Without contributing ten dollars and costs
To the school fund of Spoon River!

                                                       (1915)

Lucinda Matlock

I went to the dances at Chandlerville,
And played snap-out at Winchester.
One time we changed partners,
Driving home in the moonlight of middle June,
And then I found Davis.   5
We were married and lived together for seventy years,

SPOON RIVER ANTHOLOGY: A collection of imaginary epitaphs on the tombstones of a cemetery.

LUCINDA MATLOCK. 2 *snap-out:* a variety of "snap (or crack) the whip" in which anyone who lets go is eliminated?

Enjoying, working, raising the twelve children,
Eight of whom we lost
Ere I had reached the age of sixty.
I spun, I wove, I kept the house, I nursed the sick,   10
I made the garden, and for holiday
Rambled over the fields where sang the larks,
And by Spoon River gathering many a shell,
And many a flower and medicinal weed—
Shouting to the wooded hills, singing to the green valleys.   15
At ninety-six I had lived enough, that is all,
And passed to a sweet repose.
What is this I hear of sorrow and weariness,
Anger, discontent and drooping hopes?
Degenerate sons and daughters,   20
Life is too strong for you—
It takes life to love life.

(1916)

Robert Frost (1875–1963)

THE TUFT OF FLOWERS

I went to turn the grass once after one
Who mowed it in the dew before the sun.

The dew was gone that made his blade so keen
Before I came to view the leveled scene.   4

I looked for him behind an isle of trees;
I listened for his whetstone on the breeze.

But he had gone his way, the grass all mown,
And I must be, as he had been—alone.   8

"As all must be," I said within my heart,
"Whether they work together or apart."

But as I said it, swift there passed me by
On noiseless wing a bewildered butterfly,   12

Seeking with memories grown dim o'er night
Some resting flower of yesterday's delight.

And once I marked his flight go round and round,
As where some flower lay withering on the ground. 16

And then he flew as far as eye could see,
And then on tremulous wing came back to me.

I thought of questions that have no reply,
And would have turned to toss the grass to dry; 20

But he turned first, and led my eye to look
At a tall tuft of flowers beside a brook,

A leaping tongue of bloom the scythe had spared
Beside a reedy brook the scythe had bared. 24

The mower in the dew had loved them thus,
By leaving them to flourish, not for us,

Nor yet to draw one thought of ours to him,
But from sheer morning gladness at the brim. 28

The butterfly and I had lit upon,
Nevertheless, a message from the dawn,

That made me hear the wakening birds around,
And hear his long scythe whispering to the ground, 32

And feel a spirit kindred to my own;
So that henceforth I worked no more alone;

But glad with him, I worked as with his aid,
And weary, sought at noon with him the shade; 36

And dreaming, as it were, held brotherly speech
With one whose thought I had not hoped to reach.

"Men work together," I told him from the heart,
"Whether they work together or apart." 40

(1913)

383

FIRE AND ICE

Some say the world will end in fire,
Some say in ice.
From what I've tasted of desire
I hold with those who favor fire.
But if it had to perish twice,   5
I think I know enough of hate
To say that for destruction ice
Is also great
And would suffice.

(1923)

STOPPING BY WOODS ON A SNOWY EVENING

Whose woods these are I think I know.
His house is in the village though;
He will not see me stopping here
To watch his woods fill up with snow.   4

My little horse must think it queer
To stop without a farmhouse near
Between the woods and frozen lake
The darkest evening of the year.   8

He gives his harness bells a shake
To ask if there is some mistake.
The only other sound's the sweep
Of easy wind and downy flake.   12

The woods are lovely, dark and deep,
But I have promises to keep,
And miles to go before I sleep,
And miles to go before I sleep.   16

(1923)

384

ACQUAINTED WITH THE NIGHT

I have been one acquainted with the night.
I have walked out in rain—and back in rain.
I have outwalked the furthest city light.

I have looked down the saddest city lane.
I have passed by the watchman on his beat
And dropped my eyes, unwilling to explain.   6

I have stood still and stopped the sound of feet
When far away an interrupted cry
Came over houses from another street,

But not to call me back or say good-by;
And further still at an unearthly height,
One luminary clock against the sky   12

Proclaimed the time was neither wrong nor right.
I have been one acquainted with the night.

(1928)

DESERT PLACES

Snow falling and night falling fast, oh, fast
In a field I looked into going past,
And the ground almost covered smooth in snow,
But a few weeds and stubble showing last.   4

The woods around it have it—it is theirs.
All animals are smothered in their lairs.
I am too absent-spirited to count;
The loneliness includes me unawares.   8

And lonely as it is that loneliness
Will be more lonely ere it will be less—
A blanker whiteness of benighted snow
With no expression, nothing to express.   12

They cannot scare me with their empty spaces
Between stars—on stars where no human race is.
I have it in me so much nearer home
To scare myself with my own desert places.   16

(1936)

385

Vachel Lindsay *(1879–1931)*

From THE BOOKER WASHINGTON TRILOGY

I Simon Legree—A Negro Sermon
(To be read in your own variety of Negro dialect.)

Legree's big house was white and green.
His cotton-fields were the best to be seen.
He had strong horses and opulent cattle,
And bloodhounds bold, with chains that would rattle.
His garret was full of curious things: 5
Books of magic, bags of gold,
And rabbits' feet on long twine strings.
But he went down to the Devil.

Legree he sported a brass-buttoned coat,
A snake-skin necktie, a blood-red shirt.   10
Legree he had a beard like a goat,
And a thick hairy neck, and eyes like dirt.
His puffed-out cheeks were fish-belly white,
He had great long teeth, and an appetite.
He ate raw meat, 'most every meal,   15
And rolled his eyes till the cat would squeal.

His fist was an enormous size
To mash poor niggers that told him lies:
He was surely a witch-man in disguise.
But he went down to the Devil.   20

He wore hip-boots, and would wade all day
To capture his slaves that had fled away.
But he went down to the Devil.

He beat poor Uncle Tom to death
Who prayed for Legree with his last breath.   25
Then Uncle Tom to Eva flew,

SIMON LEGREE: a harsh Southern planter who buys Uncle Tom as a slave in
Harriet Beecher Stowe's *Uncle Tom's Cabin* (1852). 26 *Eva:* a saintly but delicate child of St. Clare, who for a time owns Uncle Tom in New Orleans. She
dies young.

To the high sanctoriums bright and new;
And Simon Legree stared up beneath,
And cracked his heels, and ground his teeth:
And went down to the Devil. 30

He crossed the yard in the storm and gloom;
He went into his grand front room.
He said, "I killed him, and I don't care."
He kicked a hound, he gave a swear;
He tightened his belt, he took a lamp, 35
Went down cellar to the webs and damp.
There in the middle of the moldy floor
He heaved up a slab, he found a door—
And went down to the Devil.

His lamp blew out, but his eyes burned bright. 40
Simon Legree stepped down all night—
Down, down to the Devil.
Simon Legree he reached the place,
He saw one half of the human race,
He saw the Devil on a wide green throne, 45
Gnawing the meat from a big ham-bone,
And he said to Mister Devil:

    "I see that you have much to eat—
    A red ham-bone is surely sweet.
    I see that you have lion's feet; 50
    I see your frame is fat and fine,
    I see you drink your poison wine—
    Blood and burning turpentine."

And the Devil said to Simon Legree:
    "I like your style, so wicked and free. 55
    Come sit and share my throne with me,
    And let us bark and revel."
And there they sit and gnash their teeth,
And each one wears a hop-vine wreath.
They are matching pennies and shooting craps, 60
They are playing poker and taking naps.
And old Legree is fat and fine:
He eats the fire, he drinks the wine—
Blood and burning turpentine— 65
    Down, down with the Devil;
      Down, down with the Devil;
        Down, down with the Devil.

(1917)

387

Wallace Stevens (1879–1955)

THE EMPEROR OF ICE-CREAM

Call the roller of big cigars,
The muscular one, and bid him whip
In kitchen cups concupiscent curds.
Let the wenches dawdle in such dress   4
As they are used to wear, and let the boys
Bring flowers in last month's newspapers.
Let be be finale of seem.
The only emperor is the emperor of ice-cream.   8

Take from the dresser of deal,
Lacking the three glass knobs, that sheet
On which she embroidered fantails once
And spread it so as to cover her face.   12
If her horny feet protrude, they come
To show how cold she is, and dumb.
Let the lamp affix its beam.
The only emperor is the emperor of ice-cream.   16

(1923)

PETER QUINCE AT THE CLAVIER

I

Just as my fingers on these keys
Make music, so the selfsame sounds
On my spirit make a music, too.

THE EMPEROR OF ICE-CREAM. 3 *concupiscent curds:* presumably "enticing ice cream," although "concupiscent" properly means not "desirable" but "eagerly desirous" or even "lustful." 9 *deal:* a cheap wood, usually pine or fir. 11 *fantails:* birds with fan-like tails.

PETER QUINCE . . . Peter Quince is the carpenter who acts as stage manager of the rustics' play about Pyramus and Thisbe in Shakespeare's *A Midsummer Night's Dream.* The story of Susanna and the Elders, which occupies much of the poem, comes from *The History of Susanna* and is accessible in any copy of

Music is feeling, then, not sound;
And thus it is that what I feel,   5
Here in this room, desiring you,

Thinking of your blue-shadowed silk,
Is music. It is like the strain
Waked in the elders by Susanna.

Of a green evening, clear and warm,   10
She bathed in her still garden, while
The red-eyed elders watching, felt

The basses of their beings throb
In witching chords, and their thin blood
Pulse pizzicati of Hosanna.   15

II

In the green water, clear and warm,
Susanna lay.
She searched
The touch of springs,
And found   20
Concealed imaginings.
She sighed,
For so much melody.

Upon the bank, she stood
In the cool   25
Of spent emotions.
She felt, among the leaves,
The dew
Of old devotions.

---

the Bible that contains the apocrypha. Susanna, "a very delicate woman, and
beauteous," was the wife of Joacim, a rich Jew whose house was often visited
by two "ancients of the people," or elders. They became enamored of her,
caught her alone in a garden as she prepared to bathe, and threatened to report
having seen her commit adultery with a young man if she did not lie with them.
She refused, was brought to trial, and was about to be put to death when the
prophet Daniel—then still a youth—obtained conflicting answers from the elders
to the question, "Under what tree sawest thou them accompanying together?"
Their falsity thus revealed, the elders were executed instead of Susanna.
15 *pizzicati:* notes played by plucking musical strings instead of bowing them.
Hosanna: Hebrew cry of praise.

She walked upon the grass,   30
Still quavering.
The winds were like her maids,
On timid feet,
Fetching her woven scarves,
Yet wavering.   35

A breath upon her hand
Muted the night.
She turned—
A cymbal crashed,
And roaring horns.   40

III

Soon, with a noise like tambourines,
Came her attendant Byzantines.

They wondered why Susanna cried
Against the elders by her side;

And as they whispered, the refrain   45
Was like a willow swept by rain.

Anon, their lamps' uplifted flame
Revealed Susanna and her shame.

And then, the simpering Byzantines
Fled, with a noise like tambourines.   50

IV

Beauty is momentary in the mind—
The fitful tracing of a portal;
But in the flesh it is immortal.

The body dies; the body's beauty lives.
So evenings die, in their green going,   55
A wave, interminably flowing.
So gardens die, their meek breath scenting
The cowl of winter, done repenting.
So maidens die, to the auroral

---

49 *Byzantines:* Stevens appears to think of the maids as simpering and chattering like Eastern slaves.

Celebration of a maiden's choral. 60
Susanna's music touched the bawdy strings
Of those white elders; but, escaping,
Left only Death's ironic scraping.
Now, in its immortality, it plays
On the clear viol of her memory, 65
And makes a constant sacrament of praise.

(1923)

THE IDEA OF ORDER AT KEY WEST

She sang beyond the genius of the sea.
The water never formed to mind or voice,
Like a body wholly body, fluttering
Its empty sleeves; and yet its mimic motion
Made constant cry, caused constantly a cry, 5
That was not ours although we understood,
Inhuman, of the veritable ocean.

The sea was not a mask. No more was she.
The song and water were not medleyed sound
Even if what she sang was what she heard, 10
Since what she sang was uttered word by word.
It may be that in all her phrases stirred
The grinding water and the gasping wind;
But it was she and not the sea we heard.

For she was the maker of the song she sang. 15
The ever-hooded, tragic-gestured sea
Was merely a place by which she walked to sing.
Whose spirit is this? we said, because we knew
It was the spirit that we sought and knew
That we should ask this often as she sang. 20

If it was only the dark voice of the sea
That rose, or even colored by many waves;
If it was only the outer voice of sky
And cloud, of the sunken coral water-walled,
However clear, it would have been deep air, 25
The heaving speech of air, a summer sound
Repeated in a summer without end
And sound alone. But it was more than that,
More even than her voice, and ours, among

391

The meaningless plungings of water and the wind, 30
Theatrical distances, bronze shadows heaped
On high horizons, mountainous atmospheres
Of sky and sea.
           It was her voice that made
The sky acutest at its vanishing.
She measured to the hour its solitude. 35
She was the single artificer of the world
In which she sang. And when she sang, the sea,
Whatever self it had, became the self
That was her song, for she was the maker. Then we,
As we beheld her striding there alone, 40
Knew that there never was a world for her
Except the one she sang and, singing, made.

Ramon Fernandez, tell me, if you know,
Why, when the singing ended and we turned
Toward the town, tell why the glassy lights, 45
The lights in the fishing boats at anchor there,
As the night descended, tilting in the air,
Mastered the night and portioned out the sea,
Fixing emblazoned zones and fiery poles,
Arranging, deepening, enchanting night. 50

Oh! Blessed rage for order, pale Ramon,
The maker's rage to order words of the sea,
Words of the fragrant portals, dimly-starred,
And of ourselves and of our origins,
In ghostlier demarcations, keener sounds. 55

                           (1936)

THE IDEA . . . 52 *maker:* an old meaning of "maker" is "poet."

392

Ezra Loomis Pound (1885–   )

PORTRAIT D'UNE FEMME

Your mind and you are our Sargasso Sea,
London has swept about you this score years
And bright ships left you this or that in fee:
Ideas, old gossip, oddments of all things,
Strange spars of knowledge and dimmed wares of price.   5
Great minds have sought you—lacking someone else.
You have been second always. Tragical?
No. You preferred it to the usual thing:
One dull man, dulling and uxorious,
One average mind—with one thought less, each year.   10
Oh, you are patient, I have seen you sit
Hours, where something might have floated up.
And now you pay one. Yes, you richly pay.
You are a person of some interest, one comes to you
And takes strange gain away: 15
Trophies fished up; some curious suggestion;
Fact that leads nowhere; and a tale or two,
Pregnant with mandrakes, or with something else
That might prove useful and yet never proves,
That never fits a corner or shows use,   20
Or finds its hour upon the loom of days:
The tarnished, gaudy, wonderful old work;
Idols and ambergris and rare inlays,
These are your riches, your great store; and yet
For all this sea-hoard of deciduous things,   25
Strange woods half sodden, and new brighter stuff:
In the slow float of differing light and deep,
No! there is nothing! In the whole and all,
Nothing that's quite your own.
                    Yet this is you.   30

                    (1912)

PORTRAIT D'UNE FEMME: Portrait of a Lady. 1 *Sargasso Sea:* a calm area of
the Atlantic near the West Indies where weeds and other floating debris accumulate. 3 *in fee:* in possession. 18 *mandrakes:* herbs long thought, because the
forked root suggested the human figure, to have magical properties.

THE STUDY IN AESTHETICS

The very small children in patched clothing,
Being smitten with an unusual wisdom,
Stopped in their play as she passed them
And cried up from their cobbles:

>   Guarda! Ahi, guarda! ch' è be'a!   5

But three years after this
I heard the young Dante, whose last name I do not know—
For there are, in Sirmione, twenty-eight young Dantes and
    thirty-four Catulli;
And there had been a great catch of sardines,
And his elders   10
Were packing them in the great wooden boxes
For the market in Brescia, and he
Leapt about, snatching at the bright fish
And getting in both of their ways;
And in vain they commanded him to *sta fermo!*   15
And when they would not let him arrange
The fish in the boxes
He stroked those which were already arranged,
Murmuring for his own satisfaction
This identical phrase: 20
>   Ch' è be'a.
And at this I was mildly abashed.

>   (1916)

The Study in Aesthetics. 4 *cobbles:* presumably loose cobblestones. 5 *Guarda! Ahi, guarda! ch' è be'a!* Look, oh, look—how beautiful! *Be'a* is dialectal for *bella.* 8 *Sirmione:* a peninsula on Lake Garda, in northern Italy. The Roman lyric poet Catullus (84?–54 B.C.) had a villa here. *Catulli:* the Latin plural of *Catullus.* 12 *Brescia:* a city in Lombardy. 15 *sta fermo:* stand still!

E. P. ODE POUR L'ÉLECTION
DE SON SÉPULCHRE

I

For three years, out of key with his time,
He strove to resuscitate the dead art
Of poetry; to maintain "the sublime"
In the old sense. Wrong from the start—   4

No, hardly, but seeing he had been born
In a half savage country, out of date;
Bent resolutely on wringing lilies from the acorn;
Capaneus; trout for factitious bait;   8

Ἴδμεν γάρ τοι πάνθ’, ὅς’ ἐνὶ Τροίῃ
Caught in the unstopped ear;
Giving the rocks small lee-way
The chopped seas held him, therefore, that year.   12

His true Penelope was Flaubert,
He fished by obstinate isles;
Observed the elegance of Circe's hair
Rather than the mottoes on sun-dials.   16

Unaffected by "the march of events,"
He passed from men's memory in *l'an trentiesme*
De son eage; the case presents
No adjunct to the Muses' diadem.   20

E. P. ODE POUR L'ÉLECTION . . . Ezra Pound's Ode for the Choice of His Tomb. The title is from a French poem by Pierre de Ronsard (1524–1585), who, however, actually wrote about *choosing* a tomb. 3 *"the sublime"*: the title of a famous critical treatise, usually attributed to Longinus, of the third century A.D. 8 *Capaneus:* one of the Seven against Thebes, and the first of the Seven to die. He rushed against the walls shouting that even Zeus could not stop him, but was killed by a thunderbolt. *factitious:* artificial, contrived; the phrase apparently means "victim of false allurements," but it would appear to characterize the public rather than the poet. 9: "For we know all those things which in Troy"—*Odyssey XII,* 189. A Romanized transliteration would run as follows: *Idmen gar toi panth', hos' eni Troi-e.* 13 *Penelope:* the faithful wife to whom Odysseus struggled to return after the Trojan War. *Flaubert:* Gustave Flaubert (1821–1880), French novelist who strove to attain perfection of form and style. 15 *Circe:* an enchantress in the *Odyssey.* 16 *mottoes on sun-dials:* the antithesis of good poetry. 18–19 *l'an . . . eage:* the thirtieth year of his age. (The *s* in *trentiesme* is silent.) The phrase is borrowed from the fifteenth-century French poet François Villon.

II

The age demanded an image
Of its accelerated grimace,
Something for the modern stage,
Not, at any rate, an Attic grace; 24

Not, not certainly, the obscure reveries
Of the inward gaze;
Better mendacities
Than the classics in paraphrase! 28

The "age demanded" chiefly a mould in plaster,
Made with no loss of time,
A prose kinema, not, not assuredly, alabaster
Or the "sculpture" of rhyme. 32

III

The tea-rose tea-gown, etc.
Supplants the mousseline of Cos,
The pianola "replaces"
Sappho's barbitos. 36

Christ follows Dionysus,
Phallic and ambrosial
Made way for macerations;
Caliban casts out Ariel. 40

All things are a flowing,
Sage Heracleitus says;
But a tawdry cheapness
Shall outlast our days. 44

---

24 *Attic:* pertaining to Attica, of which Athens was the center. 31 *kinema:*
German for *cinema.* 34 *mousseline of Cos:* muslin from the Greek island of Cos,
famed for its cloth. 35 *pianola:* player-piano. 36 *barbitos:* Greek for an instrument like the lyre. 37 *Dionysus:* the Greek equivalent of Bacchus, worshipped
with orgiastic rites. 39 *macerations:* emaciations. Pound is thinking of the
austerities of hermits and saints. 40 *Caliban . . . Ariel:* respectively, a brutish
slave and an airy spirit in Shakespeare's *The Tempest.* 42 *Heracleitus:* Greek
philosopher (fl. 500 B.C.) who taught that everything is constantly undergoing
change.

Even the Christian beauty
Defects—after Samothrace;
We see τὸ καλόν
Decreed in the market place. 48

Faun's flesh is not to us,
Nor the saint's vision.
We have the press for wafer;
Franchise for circumcision. 52

All men, in law, are equals.
Free of Pisistratus,
We choose a knave or an eunuch
To rule over us. 56

O bright Apollo,
τίν' ἄνδρα, τίν' ἥρωα, τίνα θεόν,
What god, man, or hero
Shall I place a tin wreath upon! 60

IV

These fought in any case,
and some believing,
    pro domo, in any case . . .

Some quick to arm. 64
some for adventure,
some from fear of weakness,
some from fear of censure,
some for love of slaughter, in imagination, 68
learning later . . .
some in fear, learning love of slaughter;

Died some, pro patria,
    non "dulce" non "et decor" . . . 72
walked eye-deep in hell

---

46 *Samothrace:* Greek island on which the statue of the Winged Victory, now in the Louvre, was found. 47 τὸ καλόν: the beautiful. 51 *wafer:* the "bread" sanctified in the Mass. It has a cross pressed on it by the mold. 54 *Pisistratus:* Athenian tyrant of the fifth century B.C. 58: translated in the next line. In Roman characters, *tin' andra, tin' heroa, tina theon. Tin'* means "what." The phrase is varied from Pindar's *Second Olympian Ode,* line 2. 63 *pro domo:* for home. 71-72 *pro . . . decor:* for the fatherland, but neither "sweet" nor "fitting." The line is quoted, with the addition of negatives, from Horace (*Odes,* III, ii, 13): "It is sweet and fitting to die for the fatherland."

believing in old men's lies, then unbelieving
came home, home to a lie,
home to many deceits,
home to old lies and new infamy; 76
usury age-old and age-thick
and liars in public places.

Daring as never before, wastage as never before. 80
Young blood and high blood,
fair cheeks, and fine bodies;

fortitude as never before

frankness as never before, 84
disillusions as never told in the old days,
hysterias, trench confessions,
laughter out of dead bellies.

V

There died a myriad, 88
And of the best, among them,
For an old bitch gone in the teeth,
For a botched civilization.

Charm, smiling at the good mouth, 92
Quick eyes gone under earth's lid,

For two gross of broken statues,
For a few thousand battered books.

(1920)

Thomas Stearns Eliot (1888–   )

THE LOVE SONG OF J. ALFRED PRUFROCK

S' io credessi che mia risposta fosse
a persona che mai tornasse al mondo,
questa fiamma staria senza più scosse;

ma per ciò che giammai di questo fondo
non tornò vivo alcun, s' i' odo il vero,
senza tema d' infamia ti rispondo.

Let us go then, you and I,
When the evening is spread out against the sky
Like a patient etherized upon a table;
Let us go, through certain half-deserted streets,
The muttering retreats   5
Of restless nights in one-night cheap hotels
And sawdust restaurants with oyster-shells:
Streets that follow like a tedious argument
Of insidious intent
To lead you to an overwhelming question . . .   10
Oh, do not ask, "What is it?"
Let us go and make our visit.

In the room the women come and go
Talking of Michelangelo.

The yellow fog that rubs its back upon the window-panes,   15
The yellow smoke that rubs its muzzle on the window-panes
Licked its tongue into the corners of the evening,
Lingered upon the pools that stand in drains,
Let fall upon its back the soot that falls from chimneys,
Slipped by the terrace, made a sudden leap,   20
And seeing that it was a soft October night,
Curled once about the house, and fell asleep.

LOVE SONG . . . *S' io credessi* . . . "If I believed that my reply would be to
someone who might return to the world, this flame would stand still without
shaking longer; but because no one ever returned alive from this depth, if I
hear the truth, I reply without fear of infamy." (Dante, *Inferno*, XXVII, 61–66.)
The speaker is Guido da Montefeltro, now in the eighth circle of Hell, where
each spirit lives within fire; the instrument of speech is a tongue of flame. Dante
has just asked the spirit who he is.

And indeed there will be time
For the yellow smoke that slides along the street,
Rubbing its back upon the window-panes;
There will be time, there will be time
To prepare a face to meet the faces that you meet;
There will be time to murder and create,
And time for all the works and days of hands
That lift and drop a question on your plate;
Time for you and time for me,
And time yet for a hundred indecisions,
And for a hundred visions and revisions,
Before the taking of a toast and tea.

In the room the women come and go
Talking of Michelangelo.

And indeed there will be time
To wonder, "Do I dare?" and, "Do I dare?"
Time to turn back and descend the stair,
With a bald spot in the middle of my hair—
(They will say: "How his hair is growing thin!")
My morning coat, my collar mounting firmly to the chin,
My necktie rich and modest, but asserted by a simple pin—
(They will say: "But how his arms and legs are thin!")
Do I dare
Disturb the universe?
In a minute there is time
For decisions and revisions which a minute will reverse.

For I have known them all already, known them all:—
Have known the evenings, mornings, afternoons,
I have measured out my life with coffee spoons;
I know the voices dying with a dying fall
Beneath the music from a farther room.
So how should I presume?

And I have known the eyes already, known them all—
The eyes that fix you in a formulated phrase,
And when I am formulated, sprawling on a pin,
When I am pinned and wriggling on the wall,
Then how should I begin
To spit out all the butt-ends of my days and ways?
And how should I presume?

25

30

35

40

45

50

55

60

---

29 *works and days:* the title of a Greek poem by Hesiod, eighth century B.C.

400

And I have known the arms already, known them all—
Arms that are braceleted and white and bare
(But in the lamplight, downed with light brown hair!)
Is it perfume from a dress   65
That makes me so digress?
Arms that lie along a table, or wrap about a shawl.
    And should I then presume?
    And how should I begin?

Shall I say, I have gone at dusk through narrow streets   70
And watched the smoke that rises from the pipes
Of lonely men in shirt-sleeves, leaning out of windows? . . .

    I should have been a pair of ragged claws
Scuttling across the floors of silent seas.

And the afternoon, the evening, sleeps so peacefully!   75
Smoothed by long fingers,
Asleep . . . tired . . . or it malingers,
Stretched on the floor, here beside you and me.
Should I, after tea and cakes and ices,
Have the strength to force the moment to its crisis?   80
But though I have wept and fasted, wept and prayed,
Though I have seen my head [grown slightly bald] brought
        in upon a platter,
I am no prophet—and here's no great matter;
I have seen the moment of my greatness flicker,
And I have seen the eternal Footman hold my coat, and
        snicker,   85
And in short, I was afraid.

    And would it have been worth it, after all,
After the cups, the marmalade, the tea,
Among the porcelain, among some talk of you and me,
Would it have been worth while,   90
To have bitten off the matter with a smile,
To have squeezed the universe into a ball
To roll it toward some overwhelming question,
To say: "I am Lazarus, come from the dead,
Come back to tell you all, I shall tell you all"—   95
If one, settling a pillow by her head,
    Should say: "That is not what I meant at all.
    That is not it, at all."

82–83 *head . . . prophet:* that is, no John the Baptist, whose head was brought
to Salome upon a "charger." See Matthew *14:1–11.* 94 *Lazarus:* raised from
death by Jesus; see *John 11:1–44.*

401

And would it have been worth it, after all,
Would it have been worth while, 100
After the sunsets and the dooryards and the sprinkled streets,
After the novels, after the teacups, after the skirts that trail
    along the floor—
And this, and so much more?—
It is impossible to say just what I mean!
But as if a magic lantern threw the nerves in patterns on a
    screen: 105
Would it have been worth while
If one, settling a pillow or throwing off a shawl,
And turning toward the window, should say:
    "That is not it at all,
    That is not what I meant, at all." 110

No! I am not Prince Hamlet, nor was meant to be;
Am an attendant lord, one that will do
To swell a progress, start a scene or two,
Advise the prince; no doubt, an easy tool,
Deferential, glad to be of use, 115
Politic, cautious, and meticulous;
Full of high sentence, but a bit obtuse;
At times, indeed, almost ridiculous—
Almost, at times, the Fool.

I grow old . . . I grow old . . . 120
I shall wear the bottoms of my trousers rolled.

Shall I part my hair behind? Do I dare to eat a peach?
I shall wear white flannel trousers, and walk upon the beach.
I have heard the mermaids singing, each to each.

I do not think that they will sing to me. 125

I have seen them riding seaward on the waves
Combing the white hair of the waves blown back
When the wind blows the water white and black.

We have lingered in the chambers of the sea
By sea-girls wreathed with seaweed red and brown 130
Till human voices wake us, and we drown.

(1917)

---

105 *magic lantern:* an instrument akin to the modern slide-projector. 113
progress: a state procession. 117 *sentence:* sententious utterance. 121 *rolled:*
probably "with cuffs"—an unmodish style.

GERONTION

Thou hast nor youth nor age
But as it were an after dinner sleep
Dreaming of both.

Here I am, an old man in a dry month,
Being read to by a boy, waiting for rain.
I was neither at the hot gates
Nor fought in the warm rain
Nor knee deep in the salt marsh, heaving a cutlass,   5
Bitten by flies, fought.
My house is a decayed house,
And the jew squats on the window sill, the owner,
Spawned in some estaminet of Antwerp,
Blistered in Brussels, patched and peeled in London.   10
The goat coughs at night in the field overhead;
Rocks, moss, stonecrop, iron, merds.
The woman keeps the kitchen, makes tea,
Sneezes at evening, poking the peevish gutter.
            I an old man,   15
A dull head among windy spaces.

Signs are taken for wonders. "We would see a sign!"
The word within a word, unable to speak a word,
Swaddled with darkness. In the juvescence of the year
Came Christ the tiger   20

In depraved May, dogwood and chestnut, flowering judas,
To be eaten, to be divided, to be drunk
Among whispers; by Mr. Silvero
With caressing hands, at Limoges
Who walked all night in the next room;   25

GERONTION. From Greek *gerōn, -ontos,* "old man." *Epigraph:* from Shakespeare's *Measure for Measure,* III, i. The Duke is attempting to reconcile Claudio to death. 3 *hot gates:* the literal meaning of *Thermopylae,* where the Spartans defeated the Persians in 480 B.C. 9 *estaminet:* coffee and smoking house. 12 *stonecrop:* a mosslike plant which grows among rocks. *merds:* dung, feces. 18 *word within . . . speak a word:* Christ, the *logos* or Word, is "in" such a word as "Christ." *Verbum Infans,* "the Infant Word" (used in a sermon by Lancelot Andrewes, 1555–1626), means, literally, "the unspeaking Word." 19 *juvescence:* youth. 21 *judas:* a tree named after the traitorous disciple. 22 *eaten . . . drunk:* cf. the institution of the Last Supper, *Matthew 26:26–28.* 23–28: *Silvero, Hakagawa, Tornquist, von Kulp:* the names suggest various races and cultures—Italian, Japanese, Swedish, German.

By Hakagawa, bowing among the Titians;
By Madame de Tornquist, in the dark room
Shifting the candles; Fräulein von Kulp
Who turned in the hall, one hand on the door.
 Vacant shuttles   30
Weave the wind. I have no ghosts,
An old man in a draughty house
Under a windy knob.

 After such knowledge, what forgiveness? Think now
History has many cunning passages, contrived corridors   35
And issues, deceives with whispering ambitions,
Guides us by vanities. Think now
She gives when our attention is distracted
And what she gives, gives with such supple confusions
That the giving famishes the craving. Gives too late   40
What's not believed in, or if still believed,
In memory only, reconsidered passion. Gives too soon
Into weak hands, what's thought can be dispensed with
Till the refusal propagates a fear. Think
Neither fear nor courage saves us. Unnatural vices   45
Are fathered by our heroism. Virtues
Are forced upon us by our impudent crimes.
These tears are shaken from the wrath-bearing tree.

 The tiger springs in the new year. Us he devours. Think at
  last
We have not reached conclusion, when I   50
Stiffen in a rented house. Think at last
I have not made this show purposelessly
And it is not by any concitation
Of the backward devils.
I would meet you upon this honestly.   55
I that was near your heart was removed therefrom
To lose beauty in terror, terror in inquisition.
I have lost my passion: why should I need to keep it
Since what is kept must be adulterated?
I have lost my sight, smell, hearing, taste and touch: 60
How should I use them for your closer contact?

30–31 *Vacant . . . wind:* cf. *Job 7:6–7:* "My days are swifter than a weaver's shuttle . . . my life is wind."   33 *knob:* a rounded hill.   48 *tree:* the Tree of the Knowledge of Good and Evil, from which Adam and Eve ate.   49 *tiger . . . year:* an allusion to the Last Judgment?   53 *concitation:* rousing, inciting. 57 *inquisition:* questioning.

These with a thousand small deliberations
Protract the profit of their chilled delirium,
Excite the membrane, when the sense has cooled,
With pungent sauces, multiply variety   65
In a wilderness of mirrors. What will the spider do,
Suspend its operations, will the weevil
Delay? De Bailhache, Fresca, Mrs. Cammel, whirled
Beyond the circuit of the shuddering Bear
In fractured atoms. Gull against the wind, in the windy
    straits   70
Of Belle Isle, or running on the Horn,
White feathers in the snow, the Gulf claims,
And an old man driven by the Trades
To a sleepy corner.
                        Tenants of the house,   75
Thoughts of a dry brain in a dry season.

                                                    (1920)

JOURNEY OF THE MAGI

"A cold coming we had of it,
Just the worst time of the year
For a journey, and such a long journey:
The ways deep and the weather sharp,
The very dead of winter."   5
And the camels galled, sore-footed, refractory,
Lying down in the melting snow.
There were times we regretted
The summer palaces on slopes, the terraces,
And the silken girls bringing sherbet.   10
Then the camel men cursing and grumbling
And running away, and wanting their liquor and women,

---

68 *De Bailhache, Fresca, Mrs. Cammel:* again, apparently, not real names.
69 *circuit . . . Bear:* the circle described in the sky by the Big Dipper (*Ursa
Major,* "Great Bear"). 70–71 *straits . . . Isle:* between Labrador and Newfound-
land. *Horn:* Cape Horn, at the southern tip of South America. 73 *Trades:* trade
winds.

JOURNEY OF THE MAGI. The Magi were the three wise men who came from
the East to worship the infant Christ. 1–5 *"A cold . . . winter":* phrases in the
quoted passage are drawn verbatim from the 1622 "Nativity Sermon" of Lancelot Andrewes. 10 *sherbet:* a cooled fruit drink.

405

And the night-fires going out, and the lack of shelters,
And the cities hostile and the towns unfriendly
And the villages dirty and charging high prices: 15
A hard time we had of it.
At the end we preferred to travel all night,
Sleeping in snatches,
With the voices singing in our ears, saying
That this was all folly. 20

Then at dawn we came down to a temperate valley,
Wet, below the snow line, smelling of vegetation;
With a running stream and a water-mill beating the darkness,
And three trees on the low sky,
And an old white horse galloped away in the meadow. 25
Then we came to a tavern with vine-leaves over the lintel,
Six hands at an open door dicing for pieces of silver,
And feet kicking the empty wine-skins.
But there was no information, and so we continued
And arrived at evening, not a moment too soon 30
Finding the place; it was (you may say) satisfactory.

All this was a long time ago, I remember,
And I would do it again, but set down
This set down
This: were we led all that way for 35
Birth or Death? There was a Birth, certainly,
We had evidence and no doubt. I had seen birth and death,
But had thought they were different; this Birth was
Hard and bitter agony for us, like Death, our death.
We returned to our places, these Kingdoms, 40
But no longer at ease here, in the old dispensation,
With an alien people clutching their gods.
I should be glad of another death.

(1927)

---

41 *old dispensation:* that of the Old Law, abrogated by the coming of Christ.

406

John Crowe Ransom (1888–   )

BELLS FOR JOHN WHITESIDE'S DAUGHTER

There was such speed in her little body,
And such lightness in her footfall,
It is no wonder that her brown study
Astonishes us all.   4

Her wars were bruited in our high window.
We looked among orchard trees and beyond,
Where she took arms against her shadow,
Or harried unto the pond   8

The lazy geese, like a snow cloud
Dripping their snow on the green grass,
Tricking and stopping, sleepy and proud,
Who cried in goose, Alas,   12

For the tireless heart within the little
Lady with rod that made them rise
From their noon apple dreams, and scuttle
Goose-fashion under the skies!   16

But now go the bells, and we are ready;
In one house we are sternly stopped
To say we are vexed at her brown study,
Lying so primly propped.   20

(1924)

407

Archibald MacLeish (1892–)

THE END OF THE WORLD

Quite unexpectedly as Vasserot
The armless ambidextrian was lighting
A match between his great and second toe
And Ralph the lion was engaged in biting   4
The neck of Madame Sossman while the drum
Pointed, and Teeny was about to cough
In waltz-time swinging Jocko by the thumb—
Quite unexpectedly the top blew off: 8

And there, there overhead, there, there, hung over
Those thousands of white faces, those dazed eyes,
There in the starless dark the poise, the hover,
There with vast wings across the canceled skies,   12
There in the sudden blackness the black pall
Of nothing, nothing, nothing—nothing at all.

(1926)

MEMORY GREEN

Yes and when the warm unseasonable weather
Comes at the year's end of the next late year
And the southwest wind that smells of rain and summer
Strips the huge branches of their dying leaves,   4

And you at dusk along the Friedrichstrasse
Or you in Paris on the windy quay
Shuffle the shallow fallen leaves before you
Thinking the thoughts that like the grey clouds change,   8

You will not understand why suddenly sweetness
Fills in your heart nor the tears come to your eyes:
You will stand in the June-warm wind and the leaves falling:
When was it so before, you will say, With whom?   12

MEMORY GREEN. 5 *Friedrichstrasse:* an important street in Berlin.

You will not remember this at all: you will stand there
Feeling the wind on your throat, the wind in your sleeves,
You will smell the dead leaves in the grass of a garden:
You will close your eyes: With whom, you will say,

Ah where?   16

(1930)

Wystan Hugh Auden (1907–   )

O WHERE ARE YOU GOING?

"O where are you going?" said reader to rider,
"That valley is fatal when furnaces burn,
Yonder's the midden whose odors will madden,
That gap is the grave where the tall return."   4

"O do you imagine," said fearer to farer,
"That dusk will delay on your path to the pass,
Your diligent looking discover the lacking
Your footsteps feel from granite to grass?"   8

"O what was that bird," said horror to hearer,
"Did you see that shape in the twisted trees?
Behind you swiftly the figure comes softly,
The spot on your skin is a shocking disease?"   12

"Out of this house"—said rider to reader,
"Yours never will"—said farer to fearer,
"They're looking for you"—said hearer to horror,
As he left them there, as he left them there.   16

(1932)

O WHERE ARE YOU GOING? 3 *midden:* dunghill, trash heap.

WHO'S WHO

A shilling life will give you all the facts:
How Father beat him, how he ran away,
What were the struggles of his youth, what acts
Made him the greatest figure of his day: 4
Of how he fought, fished, hunted, worked all night,
Though giddy, climbed new mountains; named a sea:
Some of the last researchers even write
Love made him weep his pints like you and me.   8

With all his honors on, he sighed for one
Who, say astonished critics, lived at home;
Did little jobs about the house with skill
And nothing else; could whistle; would sit still   12
Or potter round the garden; answered some
Of his long marvelous letters but kept none.

(1936)

THE CLIMBERS

Fleeing the short-haired mad executives,
The sad and useless faces round my home,
Upon the mountains of my fear I climb;
Above, the breakneck scorching rock, the caves,   4
No col, no water; with excuse concocted,
Soon on a lower alp I fall and pant,
Cooling my face there in the faults that flaunt
The life which they have stolen and perfected.   8

Climbing with you was easy as a vow:
We reached the top not hungry in the least,
But it was eyes we looked at, not the view,
Saw nothing but ourselves, left-handed, lost;   12
Returned to shore, the rich interior still
Unknown. Love gave the power, but took the will.

(1936)

THE CLIMBERS. 5 *col:* a pass or saddle between mountain ridges. 7 *faults:* in
the geological sense, the line of a break in rock strata.

MUSÉE DES BEAUX ARTS

About suffering they were never wrong,
The Old Masters: how well they understood
Its human position; how it takes place
While someone else is eating or opening a window or just
    walking dully along;
How, when the aged are reverently, passionately waiting   5
For the miraculous birth, there always must be
Children who did not specially want it to happen, skating
On a pond at the edge of the wood:
They never forgot
That even the dreadful martyrdom must run its course   10
Anyhow in a corner, some untidy spot
Where the dogs go on with their doggy life and the torturer's
    horse
Scratches its innocent behind on a tree.

In Brueghel's Icarus, for instance: how everything turns away
Quite leisurely from the disaster; the plowman may   15
Have heard the splash, the forsaken cry,
But for him it was not an important failure; the sun shone
As it had to on the white legs disappearing into the green
Water; and the expensive delicate ship that must have seen
Something amazing, a boy falling out of the sky,   20
Had somewhere to get to and sailed calmly on.

(1940)

THE UNKNOWN CITIZEN

To JS/07/M/378—
This Marble Monument
Is Erected by the State

He was found by the Bureau of Statistics to be
One against whom there was no official complaint,
And all the reports on his conduct agree

MUSÉE DES BEAUX ARTS: Museum of Fine Arts. 14 *Icarus:* Icarus fell into the
sea when, with wings made for him by his father Daedalus, he flew too near
the sun and the wax used as a cement melted. The painting is by Pieter
Brueghel (1525?–1569).

411

That, in the modern sense of an old-fashioned word, he was
    a saint,
For in everything he did he served the Greater Community.   5
Except for the War till the day he retired
He worked in a factory and never got fired,
But satisfied his employers, Fudge Motors Inc.
Yet he wasn't a scab or odd in his views,
For his Union reports that he paid his dues   10
(Our report on his Union shows it was sound),
And our Social Psychology workers found
That he was popular with his mates and liked a drink.
The Press are convinced that he bought a paper every day
And that his reactions to advertisements were normal in every
    way.   15
Policies taken out in his name prove that he was fully insured,
And his Health-card shows he was once in hospital but left it
    cured.
Both Producers Research and High-Grade Living declare
He was fully sensible to the advantages of the Installment
    Plan
And had everything necessary to the Modern Man,   20
A phonograph, a radio, a car, and a frigidaire.
Our researchers into Public Opinion are content
That he held the proper opinions for the time of year;
When there was peace, he was for peace; when there was war,
    he went.
He was married and added five children to the population,   25
Which our Eugenist says was the right number for a parent of
    his generation,
And our teachers report that he never interfered with their
    education.
Was he free? Was he happy? The question is absurd:
Had anything been wrong, we should certainly have heard.

                                    (1940)

THE UNKNOWN CITIZEN. 9 *scab:* a strikebreaker or nonunion worker. 26
Eugenist: an expert in eugenics, the science of improving the breed by controlling
heredity.

APPENDIX:

SUGGESTIONS

TO THE TEACHER

Like all the other teaching aids offered in the present text, what follows is meant to be helpful but not dictatorial. Seasoned teachers sometimes like to experiment, and teachers who are not satisfied with their current methods may appreciate hints. In any event, the chronological order in which the poems are printed in the anthology is less well suited to a course entitled "Introduction to Poetry" (or some equivalent) than to a historical survey. The order was adopted because of a wish to avoid prescription. It is less arbitrary than, for example, a merely alphabetical arrangement by poets, and yet it is obviously not programmatic, so that every instructor is encouraged to make his own day-by-day assignments. The plan which follows, however, is recommended as one tested way of helping students overcome obstacles to the understanding and enjoyment of poetry. It will be understood that the allotments of time and the poems to be assigned may be modified at will.

Stage One: Poetic Indirection (Four Days)

The first step is to create an awareness that poetry is a special mode of discourse. This is most economically done by assigning immediately poems which are clearly, even strikingly, unlike ordinary prose—poems which are, so to speak, quintessentially poetic, not poems which offer minimal difficulty. It is better (I think) to give the student an initial shock than to lull him for a time into the misconception that poetry is simply more "beautiful" or more "songlike" than prose. Presentation of difficult works at the outset not only prepares him to develop new habits of perception but also—by stimulating class argument—gets the course off to a lively start. The rule that instruction ought to begin with the simple and move toward the complex can still be honored, in a fashion, if the early assignments consist of poems which are not made adventitiously difficult by archaic diction, recondite allusions, dependence upon unknown conventions, and the like.

Browning's "My Last Duchess" is one of many possible first choices. The central problem here, for the beginner, is not "Can you tell why this is poetry?" or "Do you admire the skill with which the poet has handled his materials?" but quite simply, "Do you *get* it? Do you understand what has happened and is happening now?" Many members of the class will not have understood the speaker's implications, and, by failing to do so, will have mistaken the poem's total gist. The demonstration that the meanings fall together into one (and only one) basic pattern will give some of the students a gratifying sense of perceptiveness and will engage the intelligence of the rest by forcing them to explain their misinterpretations. The reaction will hardly be boredom. On the contrary, there is likely to be vigorous, even heated, discussion. As the students leave the room, they will not be oppressed by a dismal sense that the teacher will expect them, throughout the semester, to gush about their "reactions" or to identify metaphors and similes. Technical devices, structural fitnesses, literary history, and the students' emotional responses can wait—these are far less important than seeing what is actually in the poem. Already they will have begun to develop a special way of reading poetry as a result of discovering that it may be necessary to infer what is not directly stated.

The anthology contains many poems which are either "got" or "not got"—for instance, Dickinson's "I like to see it lap the miles" and "A narrow fellow in the grass." The student who does not correctly identify what is being described has again simply failed the assignment. Although these poems are relatively easy—indeed, "My Last Duchess" is not really hard—they make a similar point: that instead of explaining his subject the poet often *presents* it. Hopkins' "Spring and Fall: To a Young Child" permits the same discrimination between "right" and "wrong" readings. What is "the blight man was born for"? Why does Margaret grieve when she sees the leaves fall? Even Ransom's "Bells for John Whiteside's Daughter" fits well in this group. The reader must grasp, first, what the occasion of the poem is, and, secondly, what startles and moves the poet. The tendency for poetry to be indirect which is illustrated by such poems (although, from another point of view, the indirectness is really a directness unparalleled in expository prose) is itself the subject of Dickinson's "Tell all the truth, but tell it slant." Other poems which must also first be "got," whatever else is to be done with them, are the following: E. A. Robinson, "The Mill"; Wyatt, "They flee from me"; Browning, "De Gustibus—"; Stevens, "The Emperor of Ice-Cream"; Eliot, "The Love Song of J. Alfred Prufrock"; and perhaps even Blake, "Ah, Sunflower!" Not all poetry avoids the direct statement of meaning; but the student cannot be apprised too early that he must be sensitive to implications, and an understanding that one reading is preferable to others if it clears the meaning more effectively cannot be acquired too early. The greater part of the class hours can, in fact, be given over to showing that the "right" interpretations are those which cause all the poetic details to snap cleanly into place. Nothing tends more fatally to reduce poetry to triviality than the common student belief that there can be no appeal from the assertion, "This is what the poem means *to me.*" Concurrently, Chapters I–IV can be assigned as outside reading and will alert the students to certain elementary pitfalls.

Stage Two: Imagery, Especially Visual Imagery (Four Days)

A second step may be to invite attention to images in the hope of stimulating students to see more vividly and accurately. (Chapters V and VI are relevant here.) It will already have become evident that presentation, as opposed to explication, involves the setting up of objects for the reader's contemplation; if he is unable to perceive them, or if he loads his perceptions with what I. A. Richards has called "mnemonic irrelevancies," he will fail to draw proper inferences. Almost any poetry which is richly visual is appropriate for assignment at this point. My own preference would be to begin with poems which have little or no figurative value: for example, Keats' "To Autumn" and "Ode on a Grecian Urn," Tennyson's "Mariana," Marlowe's "Hero and Leander," Coleridge's "Kubla Khan," Collins' "Ode to Evening," Shakespeare's "When icicles hang by the wall," Dickinson's "A bird came down the walk" and "The wind tapped like a tired man." Later the focus could shift to vividly descriptive poems in which the objects imply meanings: the excerpt from Milton's *Paradise Regained,* Auden's "Musée des Beaux Arts," Hardy's "Nobody Comes," Wordsworth's "Composed Upon Westminster Bridge," Eliot's "Journey of the Magi," Hopkins' "The Starlight Night."

Stage Three: Figurative Language (Six Days)

In this stage metaphors and symbols, insinuated into the immediately preceding assignments, would come directly into focus. Students must be made to realize rather early that they are badly disoriented to poetry if they are not at home with analogical resemblances. Because analogies are of widely varying kinds, the approach might well be from the more familiar kinds of resemblances to the more surprising and abstruse. Shakespeare's "Sonnet XVIII" and Arnold's "To Marguerite—Continued" should cause little trouble; nor, indeed, should any of a dozen other sonnets (Wyatt's "Whoso list to hunt, I know where is an hind," Spenser's "Sonnet XVIII" from *Amoretti,* Surrey's "Love, that doth reign and live," and even, as a protest against too easy comparisons, Shakespeare's "Sonnet CXXX"). The emphasis should be on points of contact—and perhaps, occasionally, also on divergences—between the vehicle and the tenor. Suckling's " 'Tis now, since I sat down" develops a metaphor of siege at length. From this beginning it will be possible to move toward the greater difficulty of Herbert's "Humility," "Peace," and "Artillery," and from them to Vaughan's "The Shower" and "The World," and then to three interesting pieces by Dickinson: "I stepped from plank to plank," "The soul's distinct connection," and "After great pain a formal feeling comes." Donne's "The Canonization" rejects certain metaphors and asserts others. Quarles' "Emblem" is an exercise in the reading of symbols. Pound's "The Study of Aesthetics" implicitly defines beauty in terms of a child's reactions to two apparently dissimilar objects. It is useful, and perhaps kind, for the teacher now and then to assign a poem by which he himself is puzzled; some students come alive only when the discussion seems to have reached an impasse. For me, though perhaps not for others, Stevens' "Peter Quince at the Clavier" is such a poem. Obviously the intention is to say something about beauty, but I myself cannot tell what. Chapters VII and VIII are relevant to this stage.

Stage Four (Two Days)

The subject of ambiguity and ambivalence may conveniently be introduced next; the students may be asked to read Chapter IX at the same time. My own view is that it should not be dwelt upon, for there is serious danger that the students will become more adept at pulling poems apart than at perceiving their unity. Hopkins' "The Windhover" and Donne's "Hymn to God My God, in My Sickness," which are referred to in the chapter, may be assigned as readings along with the exercise on Donne's "Love's Alchemy." Eliot's "Gerontion" is full of ambiguous details, however clear its total purport; conversely, Auden's "O where are you going?" may be found to have ambiguous purport. (Of course such specific judgments will not be shared by all teachers.) The students should be encouraged to read each word and phrase in depth, as it were, but should not be praised for discovering interpretative possibilities which are denied by the immediate context or the poem's whole drift.

Stage Five: Tonality and the Implied Speaker (Six Days)

The opportunities here are very rich. Chapters X and XI contain explications of the basic principles; for the rest, almost any poem in the anthology can serve as the basis of a class exercise. Even an apparently trivial poem like Hardy's "The Ruined Maid" raises interesting problems. What is the character of the main speaker? Does the tonality imply condemnation of conventional morality and social institutions? Other exercises can be based on Shakespeare's "Sonnet XCIV," Rochester's "The Maimed Debauchee," Edgar Lee Masters' "Daisy Fraser," Auden's "The Unknown Citizen," Hardy's "The Subalterns," the excerpt from Smart's *Rejoice in the Lamb*. Donne's "The Ecstasy" provokes the perennially intriguing question whether the poem intends a serious exploration of the relation of body and soul in love or is a witty attempt at seduction. The examination can usefully be focused on tone. The many satires in the text fit well in this section: for instance, Dryden's "Mac Flecknoe," Jonson's "On Something that Walks Somewhere," Oldham's "A Satire Addressed to a Friend," Ralegh's "The Nymph's Reply to the Shepherd," Swift's "Phyllis, or The Progress of Love," Pope's "The Rape of the Lock" (of which there was space only for Canto III), Gay's "The Toilette," the excerpts from Crabbe's "The Village" and Byron's *Don Juan*.

Stage Six: Prosody (Three Days)

The discussion in Chapter XII will serve as an introduction, and the exercises which follow it may constitute a preliminary assignment. Thereafter the following poems, or parts of them, can appropriately be analyzed: Herrick, "The Argument of His Book"; Milton, *Paradise Lost* or *Paradise Regained* (any dozen lines of the excerpts printed); Prior, "A Lover's Anger"; Scott, "Proud Maisie"; Tennyson, "Ulysses" and "Tears, Idle Tears"; parts of Shakespeare's songs; Burns, "To a Mouse"; Pope, "Timon's Villa"; Campion, "When to her lute Corinna sings." Because the largest body of English poetry is in iambic pentameter, an effort should be made to illustrate the wide variety of effect obtainable within that measure. Some attention should also be paid, however, to stanzaic patterns. The melodic aspect of poetry should be stressed throughout this unit, for the historical relation of poetry to song is important.

Stage Seven: Form (Six Days)

Chapter XIII will provide a frame of reference. The emphasis should probably fall first on schematic structures like those illustrated in the chapter and afterwards on more subtle forms and the contributions made by form to total meaning. Frost's "Fire and Ice" is an especially perspicuous short poem; Donne's "Holy Sonnet VII" absorbs schematic elements into something more complex; many other sonnets, because of their restricted scope, can be assigned early. The attention may next shift to organic forms; and here, more than elsewhere, the giving of advice is dangerous. Those poems should be chosen for really searching analysis into which the teacher himself has the deepest and clearest insights. Some of my own choices might be Yeats' "Among School Children," Stevens' "The Idea of Order at Key West," Marvell's "The Garden," Whitman's "Come lovely and soothing death," Blake's "The Echoing Green," Hopkins' "Felix Randal," Auden's "Oh Where Are You Going?" and perhaps Pound's "E. P. Ode pour L'Élection de son Sépulchre" (which might or might not prove to stand up under the test). The effort should be not merely to discover how the parts coalesce into a whole but also to perceive how the form itself limits and defines the meaning. The unit as a whole is likely to be especially taxing for both teacher and student, but it can also be especially rewarding.

Stage Eight: Historical Backgrounds (Six Days)

A final or semifinal stage can be the relating of older poetry to its historical context. Chapter XIV offers a summary discussion of principles. The best poems to be assigned at this step are those which are most deeply rooted in history or convention: such relatively long pieces as Spenser's *The Shepherd's Calendar (October)*, the same author's "Prothalamion," Donne's "Satire III," Carew's "An Elegy Upon . . . Dr. Donne," Quarles' "Emblem" (if it has not previously been discussed), and Milton's "Lycidas." Dryden's "Mac Flecknoe" might well be reserved for this section instead of being assigned at Stage Five. Most of these poems will require at least one day for adequate exploration, and some will require several days; also, the instructor will perhaps now and then offer brief lectures on knowledge or attitudes which poets in different epochs expect their readers to possess. Briefer poems can also be assigned. Jonson's "Come, my Celia, let us prove" is a crib from Catullus; some of his short pieces are modeled on Martial; Johnson's *The*

Vanity of Human Wishes is Juvenalian satire; Wyatt and Surrey derive from Petrarch. This phase of the course may serve as an introduction to the survey course in English Literature which some of the students may elect in a later term.

Stage Nine: Evaluation (Three Days)

In my opinion evaluation should take up class time only briefly, if at all. The judgment of art, aside from the favorable evaluation which is implied by feeling interest and taking pains to understand, ought ideally to be preceded by a wider acquaintance with art works than that which can be acquired in a semester; practically, it should at least depend upon sensitive and responsible apprehension of the object at hand. Some of the fundamental problems are described in Chapter XV. If only one or two poems are to be evaluated, I would suggest works whose aesthetic status is equivocal—Pope's *Essay on Criticism,* which has a firm place in literary history despite objections that it is merely versified prose, or Crashaw's "The Flaming Heart," which may be thought either wonderfully ecstatic or a monument to execrable taste. But the instructor may choose instead poems which he thinks to be indisputably "good" and require the student to give reasons why they deserve admiration.

Summary

The above schedule, if followed to the letter, would fill forty class hours—enough, together with midterm examinations and required papers, to constitute a semester's program. If instruction is based on quarters instead of semesters, the materials will have to be reduced either by shortening the stages or by omitting some of them. If the instructional period is longer than forty-four or forty-five days—as it may be at institutions where the registration and final examination periods are short—the final weeks can be used to review techniques which have caused special trouble; or each student can be required to read a small volume of poems written by an author to whom he feels especially drawn.

Two suggestions about assignments can be added. The first is that at the beginning of the semester the assignments should be relatively short so that the students will not be irked by having to read attentively. The second is that relatively easy poems should often be assigned along with hard ones, in the hope that reading poetry will not always seem to be a chore. The anthology contains many short lyrics and humorous poems which yield enjoyment readily.

Finally, it may be said once more that the purpose of the foregoing suggestions has not been to dictate. What serves one teacher beautifully will seldom suit another perfectly, and we must all find teaching methods which will work for us.

INDEX
OF FIRST LINES

INDEX OF FIRST LINES

Whole poems printed in the Introduction *and both whole poems and excerpts printed in the* Anthology *are listed here. Excerpts—often very brief—which have been quoted in the* Introduction *are not listed.*

INDEX OF TOPICS

INDEX OF TOPICS

This index is limited to the Introduction, *pp. 3-123. Since the focus in the* Introduction *was on principles of interpretation and critical concepts, the names of poets are excluded, but other proper names—mostly those of critics—are registered. Poetic excerpts and whole poems quoted in the* Introduction *are listed in the* Index of Authors, Titles, Excerpts, Textual References.

433

INDEX

OF AUTHORS, TITLES,

EXCERPTS, TEXTUAL REFERENCES

INDEX OF AUTHORS, TITLES, EXCERPTS, TEXTUAL REFERENCES

All the complete poems contained in the Introduction *and the* Anthology *are entered here by author and title (if there is a title—if not, the poem can be located in the* Index of First Lines*); also, poetic excerpts printed in the* Introduction *are entered by page number, as are references to poets and to a few prose writers. Where numbers are separated by a semicolon, those which precede the semicolon refer to complete poems, those which follow it refer to poetic excerpts— many of them discussed—and to incidental allusions to the author. Names of authors are capitalized, titles of poems italicized.*